Philosophy for AS and A Level

Philosophy for AS and A Level is an accessible textbook for the new 2017 AQA Philosophy syllabus. Structured closely around the AQA specification this textbook covers the two units shared by the AS and A Level, Epistemology and Moral Philosophy, in an engaging and student-friendly way. With chapters on 'How to do philosophy', exam preparation providing students with the philosophical skills they need to succeed, and an extensive glossary to support understanding, this book is ideal for students studying philosophy.

Each chapter includes:

- argument maps that help to develop students' analytical and critical skills
- comprehension questions to test understanding
- discussion questions to generate evaluative argument
- explanation of and commentary on the AQA set texts
- 'Thinking harder' sections
- cross-references to help students make connections
- bullet-point summaries of each topic.

The companion website hosts a wealth of further resources, including PowerPoint slides, flashcards, further reading, weblinks and handouts, all structured to accompany the textbook. It can be found at www.routledge.com/cw/alevelphilosophy.

Michael Lacewing is a teacher of philosophy and theology at Christ's Hospital school, and a former Reader in Philosophy and Vice-Principal Academic at Heythrop College, University of London. He is founder of the company A Level Philosophy (www.alevelphilosophy.co.uk), and advises the British Philosophical Association on matters related to philosophy in schools.

Philosophy for AS and A Level

Epistemology and Moral Philosophy

Michael Lacewing

Routledge
Taylor & Francis Group

LONDON AND NEW YORK

First published 2017
by Routledge
2 Park Square, Milton Park, Abingdon, Oxon OX14 4RN

and by Routledge
711 Third Avenue, New York, NY 10017

Routledge is an imprint of the Taylor & Francis Group, an informa business

British Library Cataloguing-in-Publication Data
A catalogue record for this book is available from the British Library

Library of Congress Cataloging-in-Publication Data
Names: Lacewing, Michael, 1971- author.
Title: Philosophy for AS and A level : epistemology and moral philosophy / Michael
Lacewing.
Description: New York : Routledge, 2017. | Includes index.
Identifiers: LCCN 2016057926 | ISBN 9781138690394 (pbk. : alk. paper)
Subjects: LCSH: Knowledge, Theory of--Textbooks. | Ethics--Textbooks.
Classification: LCC BD161 .L26 2017 | DDC 121.076--dc23
LC record available at https://lccn.loc.gov/2016057926

ISBN: 978-1-138-69039-4 (pbk)
ISBN: 978-1-315-17186-9 (ebk)

Typeset in Frutiger
by Saxon Graphics Ltd, Derby

Visit the companion website: www.routledge.com/cw/alevelphilosophy

Printed and bound in Great Britain by
TJ International Ltd, Padstow, Cornwall

Contents

Illustrations

Figures

Argument maps

Table

CHRIST'S HOSPITAL

A SCHOOL LIKE NO OTHER

Christ's Hospital is an independent co-educational boarding and day school for boys and girls aged 11–18 with 870 pupils. It is unique for a UK independent boarding school in that it educates a proportion of its pupils for free, and many at a reduced rate. This stems from its founding charter as a charitable school. It was established in 1552 by King Edward VI to care for poor and homeless children of the City of London, and the generosity of donors has built up an endowment that enables Christ's Hospital to maintain its charitable tradition. School fees are paid on a means-tested basis, with substantial subsidies paid by the school, so that pupils from a wide range of social and cultural backgrounds are able to have a high quality, independent boarding school education.

The school, set in 1,200 acres of rolling Sussex countryside, has an impressive history of high academic achievement with an average of 12% of pupils each year taking up places at Oxford or Cambridge, and 98% of leavers going on to top Universities in the UK and abroad. Offering a choice of A levels, Pre-U, and International Baccalaureate (IB) courses, it provides a healthy, stimulating and comfortable environment in which pupils learn to be independent, making the most of their abilities, whether in academia, sports, music or fine arts. The pupils grow up with a strong sense of responsibility towards each other, the school and the world around them.

Introduction

The AQA A Level and AS Level Philosophy courses aim to introduce you, as a student, to some key concepts and methods in philosophy, studied as an academic discipline. The AS level raises two big philosophical questions: 'What, and how, do we know?' and 'What is morally right and good?' The A level covers these two questions and adds two more: 'Does God exist?' and 'What is the mind?' They both introduce you to philosophy by considering some of the very best attempts to answer these questions, the arguments of some of the very best philosophers in history as well as recent discussions. In this textbook, we look at the first two issues, which the AS and A level share. In an accompanying textbook for A level only, we look at the issues of God and the mind.

One aim of this textbook is, of course, to cover the ideas and arguments that are on the syllabus. But it aims at more than that. First, it aims to show you *how* to do philosophy – not just to tell you, but to show you, what philosophical thinking and philosophical writing is like. This is important because the AS level and A levels aim to introduce the methods of philosophy, as well as the ideas. Second, it aims to get you *engaging* in the argument. The discussion is provocative and leaves many lines of thought hanging. So, for instance, you might come up with new objections or replies that haven't yet been discussed, or argue that a particular point is convincing or implausible. That's the idea. This textbook doesn't try to tell you what *should* be said, only (some of) what *could* be said. (That leads to one important difference between this book and your essays. The book tries to be evenhanded, and doesn't often draw firm conclusions. In your essays, you'll be expected to defend a particular point of view.)

How to use this book

How to do philosophy

If you haven't done any philosophy before, you'll soon find that it involves reading and thinking in ways that can be quite different from how you normally read and think. In Chapter 1, I talk about what is involved in doing philosophy – how to reason, read, and write philosophically. Philosophy is all about reasoning and argument. So it is probably worth at least skimming the section on PHILOSOPHICAL ARGUMENT (p. 6) before going on to study Chapter 2 or Chapter 3. And it is worth having a look at the section on ENGAGING WITH THE TEXT (p. 17) to help you read this textbook. But Chapter 1 is intended as a resource to which you can return again and again, as and when you need to.

Each paragraph of Chapters 2 and 3 is intended to be taken as a thought to be considered, reread, and reflected on. *Philosophy needs to be read slowly, and more than once, to be understood.* You will probably find, in addition, that you are not able to completely understand a particular theory until you also understand rival theories that oppose it. And so, at the end of each major section (e.g. 'Perception as a source of knowledge'), you may feel that you need to return to earlier discussions in that section, to think about them again in the light of what you learned later.

Following the syllabus

Epistemology is covered in Chapter 2 and Moral Philosophy in Chapter 3. Each chapter opens with a brief synopsis of what the chapter covers and what you should be able to do by the end of it. This is followed by the AQA syllabus, which I have structured by topic and subtopic. The bullet points from the syllabus are used to structure the discussion, with each section further divided by the main ideas, arguments and objections. The table of contents, with its many headings and subheadings, shows how each part relates to the others. There is also an INDEX BY SYLLABUS CONTENT on p. 437, which provides the page numbers on which each bullet point of the syllabus is discussed.

Additional features

Alongside the text, there are a number of features in the margin. Most commonly, there are questions that test your understanding and cross-references to other relevant discussions and ideas. To get the most out of the book, stop and answer the questions – in your own words – as you go along. The questions are the kinds that you'll find on the exam, so it is good practice for that. It is also worth following up cross-references, especially when you have read, but forgotten, the sections referred to. (Cross-references marked by a book icon ☐ refer to the companion textbook, *Philosophy for A Level: Metaphysics of God and Metaphysics of Mind*.) Understanding philosophy is often about being able to make connections. Also in the margin are occasional illustrations, definitions of technical terms, and references to philosophical texts where the argument being discussed can be found.

You'll frequently come across sections called 'Thinking harder'. These discuss more difficult ideas or take the arguments deeper – so you'll need to think harder. They will extend and develop your knowledge, helping you to understand more about the issue being discussed.

Throughout the book, you'll find figures that provide illustrations and examples to support your understanding and connect the issues to real life situations. You'll also find 'argument maps', visual representations of arguments and their logical structure. I explain these further in UNDERSTANDING ARGUMENTS AND ARGUMENT MAPS (p. 10).

At the end of each main section covering a theory or debate, there is a list of 'Key points', summarising clearly the main issues the section has covered. And at the end of each topic, there is a 'Summary' in the form of a list of questions, to show what issues have been addressed. Both the Key points and the Summary should help with exam revision and testing your knowledge.

Set texts

The syllabus includes a list of 'set texts'. Many of the arguments identified in the syllabus content come from these texts. You aren't expected to read the texts (though it would be good to try to read some of them), but you are expected to understand and be able to evaluate the arguments they discuss. To help with this, you'll find these texts and the arguments they present discussed in gray-shaded boxes. All the texts listed in the syllabus are discussed at some point, and they are included in the INDEX BY SYLLABUS CONTENT (p. 437), so you can look up the discussion of any text in order of author.

Glossary

The glossary provides brief definitions for an extensive list of terms. I have included terms that have a technical philosophical use, that identify an important philosophical concept, or that name a theory, argument or objection. While such terms are explained in the text, if you can't understand or remember the explanation, use the glossary to help you. It should also prove a useful resource for revision.

Companion website and further resources

You can find further resources supporting the study of AQA Philosophy on the Routledge companion website, www.routledge.com/cw/alevelphilosophy. The resources include:

1. handouts based on this text, including material on philosophical skills, revision and exam technique
2. PowerPoint presentations
3. extension material, covering a number philosophical ideas or arguments that are not on the syllabus but are directly relevant to it
4. further reading lists
5. helpful weblinks
6. flashcards, for revising and testing your knowledge of philosophical terms and the names of theories and objections
7. the AQA list of texts with links where provided, and
8. a commentary on Descartes' *Meditations*.

Acknowledgements

Thanks to Rebecca Shillabeer and Anna Callander at Routledge for their work on developing this textbook, to Jim Thomas for his insightful and patient copyediting, and to my colleagues at Heythrop College for supporting my work with A level philosophy. Thanks also to the AQA subject team for answering a number of queries on the interpretation of the syllabus. And a special thanks goes to Joanne Lovesey for her stellar work on compiling the glossary.

Chapter 1

How to do philosophy

Philosophy is thinking in slow motion.

John Campbell

This chapter introduces you to a way of thinking about philosophy – as argument – which is also a way of thinking philosophically. It also covers three skills that you need to do philosophy well: reasoning (or argument), reading and writing.

It is worth skimming through at the least the first section on argument before beginning Chapters 2 or 3, as well as reading the section ENGAGING WITH THE TEXT (p. 17), which may help you with reading this textbook. But without actually *doing* some philosophy, this chapter may be a little too abstract to understand completely. So perhaps come back to it when you need to. The importance of arguments and how to understand them will become clearer when you've thought about and discussed some arguments in philosophy.

Philosophical argument

At the heart of philosophy is philosophical argument. Arguments are different from assertions. Assertions are simply stated; arguments always involve giving reasons. An argument is a reasoned inference from one set of claims – the premises – to another claim, the conclusion. The premises provide reasons to believe that the conclusion is true. If the premises are true, the conclusion is more likely to be true. Arguments seek to 'preserve truth' – true premises will lead to a true conclusion. Philosophers distinguish between two types of argument – deductive and inductive.

Deductive argument

Successful deductive arguments are *valid* – if the premises are true, then the conclusion *must* be true. In this case, we say that the conclusion is *entailed* by the premises. Here is a famous example:

Premise 1: Socrates is a man.
Premise 2: All men are mortal.
Conclusion: Socrates is mortal.

A valid deductive argument with true premises, like this example, is called *sound*.

But a valid deductive argument doesn't have to have true premises. Here is an example (abbreviating 'Premise' to 'P' and 'Conclusion' to 'C'):

P1. There are gnomes in my house.
P2. My house is in Oxford.
C. Therefore, there are gnomes in Oxford.

In this example, if the premises are true, then the conclusion must be true, so the argument is valid. But the first premise is false, because there aren't any gnomes in my house (not even garden gnomes).

It is important to recognise that truth and validity are *different* properties. We've just seen that a valid argument can have false premises. Here's an example of an invalid argument with true premises (and even a true conclusion):

P1. This book was written on a computer.
P2. Computers were invented by people.
C. Therefore, eagles are birds.

Give an example of a) an invalid argument; b) a valid argument with false premises; and c) a sound argument.

As these examples show, there are two ways that a deductive argument can fail. First, it could be *invalid*: even if the premises are true, it is possible that the conclusion might be false (the truth of the premises doesn't mean that the conclusion must be true). Second, it could have false premises, even if the conclusion is entailed by the premises. (As a variant of this: it may be that we don't or cannot *know* whether the premises are true or not.) If a deductive argument is either invalid or it has at least one false premise, it is *unsound*.

Inductive argument

Explain and illustrate the difference between inductive and deductive arguments.

A successful inductive argument is an argument whose conclusion is supported by its premises. If the premises are true, the conclusion is *more likely* to be true; the truth of the premises increases the probability that the conclusion is true. But it is still possible that the conclusion is false. So inductive arguments are not described as 'valid' or 'sound'. Instead, an inductive argument with true premises that provide strong support for the conclusion is sometimes called 'cogent'.

But they can also go wrong in just two ways. First, the premises might not make the conclusion more probable (or, at least, not by much). Second, one or more of the premises may be false. In either case, the premises don't offer good reasons for believing the conclusion is true.

One type of induction is induction through enumeration, as in this famous example:

P1. This swan is white.
P2. This other swan is white.
P3. That third swan is white.
…
P500. That swan is white as well.
C. All swans are white.

The example shows that an inductive argument can be a good argument, but the conclusion can still be false!

There are other types of inductive argument apart from enumerative induction. We shall look at hypothetical reasoning next.

HYPOTHETICAL REASONING

In hypothetical reasoning, we try to work out the best hypothesis that would explain or account for some experience or fact.

> A hypothesis is a proposal that needs to be confirmed or rejected by reasoning or experience.

Medical diagnosis provides an example – what would explain exactly *this* set of symptoms? This isn't a matter of comparing this case with other cases which all have exactly the same symptoms. There may only be some overlap or the case might involve some complication, such as more than one disease being involved. We use hypothetical reasoning – if such-and-such were true (e.g. the patient has disease *x*), would that explain the evidence we have? The evidence supplies the premises of the argument, and the conclusion is that some hypothesis is true because it accounts for the evidence.

When we are using hypothetical reasoning, it is not usually enough to find some hypothesis that *can* explain the evidence. We want to find the *best* hypothesis. To do this, we first need to know what makes for a *good* hypothesis. Philosophers have argued for several criteria.

1. Simplicity: the best-known is probably Ockham's razor, which says 'Don't multiply entities beyond necessity.' Don't put forward a hypothesis that says many different things exist when a simpler explanation will do as well. A simpler explanation is a better explanation, as long as it is just as successful. For example, the explanation that plants flower in the spring in response to an increase in light and temperature is a better explanation than saying that they flower in the spring because that's when the fairies wake them up. The second explanation is committed to the existence of fairies – and we shouldn't think that fairies exist unless there is something we cannot explain without thinking they exist.
2. Accuracy: a good hypothesis fits the evidence that we are trying to explain.
3. Plausibility: a good hypothesis fits with what else we already know.
4. Scope: a good hypothesis explains a wide range of evidence.
5. Coherence: a good hypothesis draws and explains connections between different parts of the evidence.

The best hypothesis will be the hypothesis that demonstrates all these virtues to a higher degree than alternative hypotheses. A lot of philosophy involves arguing about which theory provides the best hypothesis to account for our experience.

> What makes for a good hypothesis?

Understanding arguments and argument maps

Understanding arguments is central to doing philosophy well. That is why throughout this book, you will be asked to outline and explain arguments. You'll be asked to do so in the exam as well.

Understanding an argument involves identifying the conclusion, identifying the premises, and understanding how the premises are supposed to provide reasons for believing the conclusion. Use linguistic clues, like 'since', 'because', 'if …, then …' and many others, to help you do this. It is also important to distinguish between what someone supposes for the purposes of argument, and what they actually want to assert as reasons for believing the conclusion.

Many arguments involve quite a complex structure, with some premises establishing an initial conclusion, which is then used as a premise to establish a second conclusion. In coming to understand an argument, it can be very helpful to create an *argument map*. This is a visual diagram of how the argument works – its 'logical structure'. Psychologists have shown that using argument maps greatly improves one's ability to think critically.

Here is a simplified version of the first map in Chapter 3:

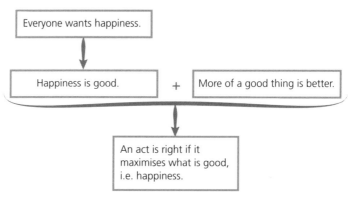

Map 1.1 An argument map

You can find out more about argument maps online at https://en. wikipedia.org/wiki/ Argument_map.

There are argument maps throughout this book, and you will also be asked to construct your own argument maps. To understand the maps and make your own, there are several things you need to know about argument mapping.

1. A simple argument is made up of one conclusion and one reason. The reason may be given in a single premise, but you may need to combine two or more 'co-premises' to make up the reason. Thus

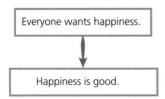

   is a simple argument with a single premise, while

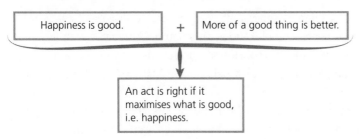

   is a simple argument with two co-premises that must be combined to support the conclusion. This is shown by the '+' between the boxes and the line that runs below both of them.

2. A complex argument is an argument that links several simple arguments. Map 1.1 is an example.

3. Each box in an argument map should have just one claim inside it, written as a full sentence. And it should contain no reasoning. Thus, 'Happiness is good because everyone wants happiness' should not be entered in a box, but must be broken down as shown.

4. A line ending in an arrow indicates a relation of support. The line leads from the reason and points to the claim supported.

5. A line ending in '-|' indicates an objection. Here is our argument again, but with an objection added. (In this example, the objection is marked against the conclusion, and notes a way that even if the premises are true, the conclusion may be false.)

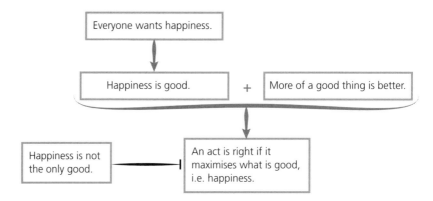

6. Our examples show that you can create argument maps for simple arguments, complex arguments and even debates with arguments for and against the conclusion, objections, responses and so on. (For examples of maps of a debate, see Map 2.14, p. 136, and Map 3.18, p. 395.)

7. Argument maps can be more or less complete. According to some guides, argument maps must all be deductive, with every premise stated. On this approach, our first simple argument should be:

However, there are two difficulties with insisting on deductive completeness. First, if you are trying to map how people actually argue, then it is a mistake to turn every argument into a deduction. For example, hypothetical reasoning is misrepresented if you try to turn it into a deduction. To argue that happiness is good, someone may not want to claim that it is *always* true that what people want is good; they may simply be assuming that if everyone wants something, that is *good evidence* that it is good.

Second, while it can be worthwhile trying to construct a complete argument map, complete maps can become very complicated. A partial one can be sufficient to help one understand the main moves and logical structure of an argument.

In this book, many of the argument maps are *neither complete nor deductive*, but I trust they will be useful in helping you to understand the arguments being discussed.

Evaluating arguments

When you evaluate an argument, you are yourself *making* an argument. You are arguing that the argument evaluated is either a good or bad argument. In other words, the conclusion of your evaluation is that the argument evaluated is a good/bad argument, and you have to provide reasons to support this claim. There are three types of reason you can give, three different ways of evaluating arguments:

1. As already stated above, you can argue that one or more of the premises is false (or unknown). If you are right, then the argument does not give you a reason to believe the conclusion, because it rests on a false (or unknown) premise.

2. As also already stated above, you can argue that the conclusion does not follow from the premises. If you are evaluating a deductive argument, you are claiming that the argument is not valid. If you are evaluating an inductive argument, you are claiming that the argument is not cogent, i.e. the premises do not provide a (good or strong) reason to believe the conclusion. For example, with inferring the best hypothesis, you could argue that the conclusion is not the best explanation for the premises, e.g. that it isn't plausible or simple, or at least that the argument doesn't show that it is, e.g. there may be other explanations that haven't been considered.

3. You can also evaluate the formal features of an argument. Without worrying about whether it is true, you can ask whether it is clear, whether the premises are relevant to the conclusion, whether the support offered by the premises has been demonstrated, and so on. You may want to offer an improvement on the argument, e.g. rephrasing it to be clearer, supplying missing premises, identifying assumptions, and so on.

Evaluating claims

In addition to evaluating arguments, you can evaluate claims on their own. In evaluating a claim, you provide an argument for thinking that it is true or false.

For any claim C (e.g. 'God exists'), we need to distinguish arguments for and against the claim from arguments about these arguments, as shown in this diagram:

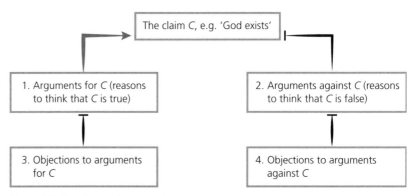

Figure 1.1 Four types of argument

An argument for or against a claim is an argument that the claim is true or false. An argument for or against an argument is an argument that the argument is successful or fails. This means that objections to an argument are not the same as arguments for the opposite claim.

Suppose I provide an argument with the conclusion that God exists (Box 1). You respond by making an objection to my argument, e.g. that one of the premises is false (Box 3). In doing this, you argue that I haven't shown that God exists; you haven't argued that God doesn't exist. At the end of my argument and your objection, we should conclude that we don't yet know whether God exists or not, but we don't have reason to conclude that God doesn't exist. (For that conclusion, we need an argument in Box 2.)

When you are arguing for or against a claim, don't overstate your case. Your claim is only as strong as the reasons that you can provide for it.

In essay questions on the exam, you are typically asked to evaluate a claim. You need to break this down into a series of arguments and their evaluation (discussed below in WRITING PHILOSOPHY, p. 19). After you've explained the claim, for each section of the answer, you should consider an argument for or against the claim, objections to that argument, and possible responses. If you use inductive arguments, e.g. hypothetical reasoning, you'll also need to indicate how *strong* or cogent you think the argument is. If you have one argument for a conclusion and another argument against the conclusion, you'll need to consider which argument is stronger, e.g. by using the criteria for a good argument set out in HYPOTHETICAL REASONING (p. 9). You will also need to think about which arguments, and which objections, are the *most important and critical* ones to discuss, given the conclusion you want to reach.

An aside: why reason?

Why, you may wonder, should we place so much importance on reasoning in this way? Is it worth it? Here are four quick reasons in favour of reasoning:

1. To discover the truth
2. To uncover poor reasoning, e.g. fallacies (see below) and sophistry
3. To recognise when, where and how a dialogue ceases to be reasonable or instructive
4. To probe both sides of a controversial issue in a sensitive and intelligent way.

Can I justify these claims? If I present an argument in favour of reasoning, then I'm using reasoning to justify reasoning, which is circular. Then again, if you object to reasoning for this reason, you are using reasoning to make your objection! An alternative justification of reason is to check the results of reasoning by a different method. Science does this all the time by hypothesis and observation. In many cases, we can confirm, by observation, that the conclusion of a piece of reasoning is correct. Some people are sceptical about reasoning or claim, for example, that all beliefs are equally 'reasonable'. For an excellent discussion dismantling this view, see Stephen Law's *Believing Bullshit*, Ch. 4.

To criticise an argument or claim is not necessarily to reject it. You can be concerned to reject bad reasons because you want to find stronger ones! To show respect to someone does not require that you agree with them. Taking someone else's thought seriously – so seriously that you test it rigorously in your mind – is to pay them a compliment.

It is important to remember that the *point* of philosophical argument is not personal victory.

Fallacies

See 'Fallacies', at www.nizkor.org/features/fallacies/; 'Fallacies: alphabetic list (unique)', at http://changing minds.org/ disciplines/ argument/fallacies/ fallacies_unique. htm; and 'List of fallacies', at http:// en.wikipedia.org/ wiki/List_of_fallacies

A fallacy, as philosophers use the word, is not a mistake of fact or truth. A fallacy is an error in reasoning. More exactly, it is an argument in which the premises do not offer rational support to the conclusion. If the argument is deductive, then it is fallacious if it is not valid. If the argument is inductive, it is fallacious if the argument is not cogent, i.e. the premises do not make it (much) more likely that the conclusion is true.

There are many types of fallacy; the *Nizkor Project* lists 42, *Changing Minds* 53, and *Wikipedia* over 100. It's good to become familiar with some of the main types. If you do, it is really important to understand *why* the fallacy is a fallacy.

Spotting fallacies has two purposes: 1) evaluating the strength of an argument and 2) improving it. When learning how to spot fallacies, try to develop the skill of how you would reformulate the argument to avoid committing a fallacy. It is not always clear-cut whether a fallacy is being committed or not, and the answer depends on just how the premises are being deployed or further assumptions being made. The question is always ultimately about the strength of support the premises offer.

To learn how to avoid fallacies in your own work, it can be helpful to learn first how to spot them! Fallacies are always easier to spot in someone else's work, so start with people you don't know, then look at the work of other students, then try to spot them in your own work.

Reading philosophy

The syllabus includes a list of books and articles to read and think about. If you read these texts, you may find it challenging, especially if you haven't read any philosophy before. You may not know much about the background of the text – when was it written and why? The form of the text is difficult – there can be long and complicated arguments, unfamiliar words, an unusual style of language, and abstract ideas. It is unclear just how the text should be interpreted, and commentaries on the texts often disagree. This section provides some guidance that may help. But the first thing to remember is that it is *normal* to feel confused and challenged.

Approaching the text

For these first three points, you'll need to use a commentary on the text, or an introduction:

1. Contextualise: it can help to set the scene, but this shouldn't be restricted to a historical understanding. An awareness of central ideas is useful.
2. Identify what philosophical *problems* the text addresses.
3. Get an overview: look at the title, introductory and concluding paragraphs, and the chapter and section headings. Knowing the conclusion does not ruin the text (it isn't a detective story). Understanding the structure can help fit different arguments and claims together.

These next three points are about how to interact with the text:

4. For long texts, don't feel the need to start at the beginning. Start with what will best get you into the thinking of the author, e.g. connections to previous topics, points of interest, etc.
5. Don't get bogged down in details: reading the text more than once is helpful and often necessary. Read it quickly first, noting the main points, skimming what is most unclear; then read it again more closely.
6. Distinguish the text from secondary interpretation: for example, knowing what other people said Descartes said is not knowing what Descartes said.

Engaging with the text

The following points relate to reading any philosophy, including this textbook:

1. Read slowly and actively: philosophy should not be read like fiction or even most non-fiction. *Philosophy needs to be read slowly, and often more than once, to be understood*. Take notes and constantly question

not only whether you've understood what the author is trying to say, but also whether what s/he says is true, and whether the arguments support the conclusions.

2. Look for signposts: sentences that indicate what the text is about, what has been, is being, or will be argued.

3. Ask what the passage of text offers: a new concept, a framework for understanding an issue, an argument for a conclusion?

4. Argument mapping: find the arguments. Identify premises, inferences and conclusions. Break arguments down into steps (there can be many interim conclusions).

5. Don't be afraid to challenge: try to find inconsistencies in the text, but also try to find ways to interpret the text to remove the inconsistencies.

6. Ask what interpretation best fits the purpose of the author. Does an interpretation presuppose ideas that were not available to the author?

7. Know the point of any example used: examples can seize the imagination and memory, but knowing its purpose and what it is supposed to show is central to understanding the text.

8. Look up key words in a dictionary of philosophy: don't be lazy, and don't use a normal dictionary (for philosophical words) as they won't capture or explain the relevant sense.

Beyond the text

1. Visualise: if you put the text, or the arguments within it, into some other visual form, that can help generate understanding.

2. Use secondary sources carefully: always question the authority of secondary sources, and always go back to the text.

3. Find different ways to think about and interact with the text. These will help you understand more than if you simply read it. For example, you might want to
   a. practise précis (either rewrite a passage more briefly in your own words or, if you have the text electronically, try deleting words while retaining the argument);
   b. rewrite a passage of the text in a different genre (e.g. a detective story);
   c. select quotations that make important points (good for revision);
   d. mark up the text for premises, conclusions, linguistic clues, etc.;
   e. do some argument mapping.

Writing philosophy

What you need to know

Different types of knowledge are needed to do well in philosophy. Each is tested by different types of question on the exam. You can be asked to define a term, explain a claim or an argument, compare two positions in a debate, explain a position and present an objection, or, finally, to evaluate a claim. Here are five types of knowledge that are relevant to doing all this well:

See UNDERSTANDING THE QUESTION, p. 407.

1. *Understanding what the question is asking*: For each type of question, you need to understand what the question is asking you to *do*. So you need to know the difference between a definition, an explanation, and what is needed for an evaluative essay.
2. *Knowledge of the issue*: You need to understand the relevant concept, argument or claim. Evaluating claims is most complex. You'll need to know what the options are, the key arguments defending and attacking the claim, the theories that philosophers have defended that pull different arguments and claims together into a coherent whole.
3. *Structure of arguments*: Knowing how an argument works (or doesn't) is more than knowing the conclusion and the premises used; it is understanding *how* the premises are supposed to connect together to support the conclusion. With your own arguments, you equally need to understand how they work, and you should present them with a clear structure.
4. *Relevance*: A good part of philosophical skill is a matter of selecting ideas, concepts, examples and arguments that you encountered in the material you studied that are relevant to the question. Knowing what is relevant is a special kind of knowledge, which involves thinking carefully about what you know about arguments and theories in relation to the question asked.
5. *Critical discussion*: When you evaluate a claim, it is important to know that *presenting* ideas is distinct from *critically discussing* those ideas. You need to understand whether an argument succeeds or fails and why, and be able to present and compare arguments, objections and counter-arguments to argue towards the most plausible position. You will usually need to draw on more than one source or author, and above all *think*.

Planning an essay

When you are answering a short-answer question, what you need to do is straightforward. You don't need to make any choices about *what* concepts or arguments to talk about, since that is specified by the question. You should still organise your thoughts before writing. But essays – both coursework essays and in the exam – need to be planned in more detail.

1. Take time to understand the question in detail. Most weak essays are weak because they fail to answer the actual question.
2. Keep the question in mind throughout writing, to ensure that your thought and planning stay relevant. Someone should be able to tell from the essay itself what question it is answering.
3. If it is appropriate, think about challenging the question. Does it make assumptions that can be questioned?
4. Brainstorm to generate ideas of what you might discuss. (In an exam, recall the relevant revision plan.) One way is through 'successive elaboration' – take a single-sentence statement of a position, and then make it more detailed, e.g. by providing some premises, then think what would be necessary to establish the premises, etc. Another is 'conceptual note-taking', simply writing what comes to mind: even starting from 'I don't know anything about *x*' suggests and leads to others, such as 'I don't know what *x* means' and 'So and so defines *x* as …'. Half-formed thoughts are better developed when out on the page.
5. If you are researching the essay, start by making the relevant ideas familiar, but make decisions on what to concentrate on, and narrow your research to achieve depth in a few central areas.
6. An essay needs shape, it is always directed towards a conclusion, so you'll need to decide what to include and what to leave out.
7. Don't aim to cover too much; three main arguments is usually enough. Even fewer can be fine if you go into real depth.
8. Plan an essay that argues for a particular position. You will often want to argue for or against a specific claim (as in a debate). But you don't have to. For example, you can argue that we can't know either way. Whatever your conclusion (the claim you want to make), you'll need to defend it, even the claim that we can't know something. Have it in mind

throughout the plan and writing. The essay should read like one long argument (taking in various smaller arguments, objections and replies) for your conclusion.

9. The evaluative discussion is the most important part of the essay, so only introduce and explain material that you will use in discussion. You can think of this as two halves: the arguments in favour of your conclusion; and the objections to your arguments, or separate arguments against your conclusion, and replies to them. Make sure you consider the objections and counter-arguments. Even if you are defending your point of view strongly (which is fine), you need to consider fairly what can be said against it.

10. In light of all of the above points, write a plan which includes key points (definitions, arguments, objections, etc.) and the paragraph structure.

11. Each paragraph presents an idea. Paragraphs should not be divided on *length*, but as 'units of thought'. If you made a one-sentence summary of each paragraph, would the resulting account of the essay read logically?

Writing an essay

Once again, I'll just provide some advice on the most difficult writing task, the essay:

1. Plan the essay. It is very rare that good philosophical essays are written 'off the cuff', taking each thought as it occurs to you in turn. An essay is not (just) a test of memory, but of intelligence, which includes organisation and clarity.

2. However, new ideas will probably occur as you write. It is fine to deviate from the plan, but think through new ideas before incorporating them to make sure they are good, and to structure them.

3. The usual starting point for constructing an argument is explaining other people's ideas. The idea here is to be *accurate* and *sympathetic*. An argument works best when the ideas are presented *as strongly as possible* – otherwise the opponent can simply rephrase the idea, and your counter-argument falls apart.

4. In general, aim to be concise. Present the kernel of the idea clearly and relevantly. Stick to what you need to present in order to properly discuss

the question. This can involve surrounding detail, since you need to show an awareness of the situation of the topic in the subject. But be selective and relevant.

5. Never just *report* or *allude to* the arguments you have read – *make* the argument. To use a metaphor from war, you are not a reporter at the front line, but a combatant engaged for one side or the other.

6. Use the three-part structure: make a point, back it up, show its relevance.

7. In critical discussion, reflect on what a particular argument actually demonstrates, and whether there are counter-arguments that are better. You should be able to argue both for and against a particular view. Relate these arguments to each other, evaluating which is stronger and why. You need to work at shaping the material and 'generating a discussion'.

8. Alternatively, you may want to relate a particular argument to a broader context, e.g. a philosopher's overall theory, other philosophers' ideas on the same issue, etc. – in general, work to understand the relation between the parts and the whole.

9. Understand and be careful about the strength of your assertions. It is important to know whether your arguments indicate that 'all … (e.g. lies are wrong)', 'some …', 'most …', or 'typically …'. It is also important to distinguish between whether this *is* so, or *must* be so, or simply *may be* so.

10. Never introduce new material in the concluding paragraph of the essay. The essay's conclusion should reflect the argument of the essay. Don't feel you have to personally agree with your conclusion! Essays are not confessions of belief.

11. In an exam setting, you also need to keep note of the time, and leave time to review and correct what you've written.

A standard essay structure

1. Introduction: how you understand the question, what you'll argue for (and perhaps some indication of how you will discuss the question)

2. An explanation of the claim to be evaluated, perhaps including some of the relevant background theory, and either including or followed by …

3. The arguments in favour of the claim (give the arguments, and if you think they work, argue that the reasoning is valid and the premises are true)
4. Objections to these arguments and replies to the objections
5. Arguments against the claim
6. Objections to these arguments
7. Conclusion: a clear statement showing how the claim is supported/ defeated by the arguments discussed. This will require you to make some points, either as you go along or in the conclusion, about which arguments or objections are strongest and why.

> Alternatively, you may consider objections to each argument (in (3)) in turn as you consider the argument.

> There may not be time or space for (5) and (6) in every case, and you can still write a very good essay without them.

General advice

When doing coursework essays:

1. Do not wait until you have finished your research to start writing the essay. If you find, as your research continues, that someone else has written what you've written, then reference it; if you find an objection, then explain it and explain why it is wrong, or, if the objection persuades you, rewrite what you've written as 'one might think …' and use the objection to show why it is wrong.
2. Rewrite the essay – almost no one does themselves justice in one draft.
3. Quotations do not substitute for understanding. Use them when you want to illustrate the precise wording of an idea or back up an interpretation.
4. Don't plagiarise.

In both coursework and exam essays:

5. Be precise, especially with words that have a philosophical meaning, like 'valid', 'assume', 'infer'.
6. Be clear. Being vague gives the reader the sense that you don't really know what you are talking about. Don't hide behind long words – it rarely impresses people who understand them. Use technical terms in context, and make sure that the philosophical meaning of ordinary words is clear – if not, provide a quick definition.

7. Don't use long and involved sentences. Use active, not passive, constructions, e.g. 'Plato argued ...' not 'It was argued by Plato ...'.

8. Include signposts. Generally speaking, the first sentence of a paragraph should give some indication to a reader as to where you are in the argument (e.g. 'A second criticism of the argument that ...').

9. While it is acceptable to use the first person ('I'), this should not be to say 'I feel ...' or 'I think ...' or 'In my opinion ...' as though such an assertion adds any weight to the plausibility of the conclusion. The whole essay is what you think, however it is phrased.

Chapter 2

Epistemology

Knowledge is central to life. Without any knowledge at all, we would die, very quickly. At the most basic level, as physical creatures, we want to know where to find food and shelter. We develop technology to help meet these needs and others, so we need to understand how things happen in the world and how we can affect it. As social creatures, we want to live with other people and make arrangements with them. We want to know what people expect, how they feel, or just where to meet on Saturday night. We need to communicate, so we need to know a language. As curious creatures, we simply want to know – how did I come to exist, what am I, how did the universe begin, what is right and wrong, does God exist? In these and countless other ways, knowledge matters to us.

But what is knowledge and how can we gain it? What can we know and what is beyond us? And how do we know what we know? These questions are also questions about human nature, about what it is to be human. How are human beings 'hooked up' to the world? What 'faculties' do we have that enable us to gain knowledge? These questions are central to the branch of philosophy called epistemology.

In this chapter, we will look at some of these questions and discuss some answers to them in depth. There are many topics and theories in epistemology that we won't study. But rather than look at lots of ideas briefly, conducting a survey, we can often get a better sense of philosophy and how it works by looking more closely at a few debates in detail. When we take this approach, though, it is easy to get lost in the details of theories and arguments. If that happens, it is worth recalling the big questions, the

Please see the ADDITIONAL FEATURES (p. 3) for an explanation of the different kinds of marginal boxes and what they mean. Please see CHAPTER 1 HOW TO DO PHILOSOPHY (p. 6) for explanations of philosophical argument and how to understand argument maps.

Quotations from and pages references for works by Descartes, Locke, Berkeley, Leibniz and Hume are taken from the electronic translations and editions available at www.earlymodern texts.com.

Epistemology is the study (-*ology*) of knowledge (*episteme*) and related concepts, including belief, justification and certainty. It looks at the nature, possibility and sources of knowledge.

real motivation and interest, that lie behind philosophical debates. We can understand more about ourselves and our relation to the world if we can understand more about knowledge, what it is, how we have it, and what limitations there may be on what we can know. We can also understand more about philosophy generally, how it works and what kinds of answers it might be able to offer to some of the questions – on right and wrong, on God, on the nature of the mind – that we asked above.

So, in this chapter, we will discuss just four questions. The first is the question of what knowledge is. Unless we understand what we are talking about in talking about 'knowledge', we won't get far in answering the questions about how and what we can know. We will look at a famous definition of knowledge that was widely accepted from almost the beginnings of philosophy in Plato until 1963, when Edmund Gettier published a paper that showed that the definition was wrong. We will discuss four responses and developments following Gettier's argument.

The second issue is how perception gives us knowledge. That we gain knowledge from our senses seems uncontroversial, and a quick, common-sense answer to the question of how we are 'hooked up' to the world is this: the world is made up of physical objects that exist outside, and independently of, our minds. We discover this physical world and gain knowledge about it through our senses (vision, hearing, touch, etc.). In other words, we perceive it. But is this right? What is the best account of perception? Does perception, in fact, give us knowledge of a physical world that exists independent of our minds? We will see that the common-sense picture gets complicated very quickly.

In the third part of this chapter, we ask whether we can have knowledge that doesn't come from the senses, but from 'reason'. If we understand 'reason' as that part of the mind we use to think with, then there are two quite different ways in which knowledge might come from reason. First, knowledge could be 'built into' our minds from the beginning, that is, we may have knowledge that is innate. Second, there may be knowledge we can gain just by rational thought; perhaps mathematics is an example.

The fourth topic is philosophical scepticism and the limits of our knowledge. Scepticism challenges us on whether we know what we think we know. We will use a number of the theories we will have studied in earlier parts of the chapter to see how far this challenge can be met.

By the end of the chapter, you should be able to analyse, explain, and evaluate a number of arguments for and objections to theories about what knowledge is, whether and how we perceive physical objects, whether we have any innate knowledge or knowledge gained through pure reasoning, and what the limits of our knowledge are.

Syllabus checklist ✓

The AQA AS and A level syllabus for this topic is:

I. What is knowledge?

✓ The distinction between acquaintance knowledge, ability knowledge and propositional knowledge

✓ The nature of definition (including Linda Zagzebski) and how propositional knowledge may be analysed/defined

The tripartite view

✓ Propositional knowledge is defined as justified true belief: *S* knows that *p* if and only if:

1   *S* is justified in believing that *p*,

2   *p* is true, and

3   *S* believes that *p* (individually necessary and jointly sufficient conditions)

Issues with the tripartite view including:

✓ The conditions are not individually necessary

✓ The conditions are not sufficient – cases of lucky true beliefs (including Edmund Gettier's original two counterexamples)

- Responses: alternative post-Gettier analyses/definitions of knowledge including:
    - Strengthen the justification condition (i.e. infallibilism)
    - Add a 'no false lemmas' condition (J+T+B+N)
    - Replace 'justified' with 'reliably formed' (R+T+B) (i.e. reliabilism)
    - Replace 'justified' with an account of epistemic virtue (V+T+B)

II. Perception as a source of knowledge

A. Direct realism

✓ The immediate objects of perception are mind-independent objects and their properties

Issues including:
✓ The argument from illusion
✓ The argument from perceptual variation
✓ The argument from hallucination
✓ The time-lag argument

and responses to these issues

B. Indirect realism

✓ The immediate objects of perception are mind-dependent objects (sense-data) that are caused by and represent mind-independent objects
  • John Locke's primary/secondary quality distinction

Issues including:
✓ The argument that it leads to scepticism about the existence of mind-independent objects
  • Responses including:
    ○ Locke's argument from the involuntary nature of our experience
    ○ The argument from the coherence of the various kinds of experience, as developed by Locke and Catharine Trotter Cockburn (attributed)
    ○ Bertrand Russell's response that the external world is the 'best hypothesis'
✓ The argument from George Berkeley that we cannot know the nature of mind-independent objects because mind-dependent ideas cannot be like mind-independent objects

C. Berkeley's idealism

✓ The immediate objects of perception (i.e. ordinary objects such as tables, chairs, etc.) are mind-dependent objects
✓ Arguments for idealism including
  • Berkeley's attack on the primary/secondary property distinction
  • Berkeley's 'master' argument

Issues including:
✓ Arguments from illusion and hallucination
✓ Idealism leads to solipsism
✓ Problems with the role played by God in Berkeley's idealism (including how can Berkeley claim that our ideas exist within God's mind given that he believes that God cannot feel pain or have sensations?)

and responses to these issues

III. Reason as a source of knowledge

A. Innatism

✓ Arguments from
  • Plato (i.e. the 'slave boy' argument) and
  • Gottfried Leibniz (i.e. his argument based on necessary truths)

Empiricist responses including:
✓ Locke's arguments against innatism
✓ The mind as a *tabula rasa* (the nature of impressions and ideas, simple and complex concepts)

and issues with these responses

B. The intuition and deduction thesis

✓ The meaning of 'intuition' and 'deduction' and the distinction between them
✓ René Descartes' notion of 'clear and distinct ideas'
✓ His *cogito* as an example of an a priori intuition

✓   His arguments for the existence of God and his proof of the external world as examples of a priori deductions

Empiricist responses including:
✓   Responses to Descartes' *cogito*
✓   Responses to Descartes' arguments for the existence of God and his proof of the external world (including how Hume's fork might be applied to these arguments)

and issues with these responses

IV. The limits of knowledge

✓   Particular nature of philosophical scepticism and the distinction between philosophical scepticism and normal incredulity
✓   The role/function of philosophical scepticism within epistemology
✓   The distinction between local and global scepticism and the (possible) global application of philosophical scepticism
✓   Descartes' sceptical arguments (the three 'waves of doubt')
✓   Responses to scepticism: the application of the following as responses to the challenge of scepticism:
    ●   Descartes' own response
    ●   Empiricist responses (Locke, Berkeley and Russell)
    ●   Reliabilism

I. What is knowledge?

A. Knowledge and its definition

Our first task is to understand what knowledge is. To do this, we will first distinguish between different types of knowledge, before focusing on just one type, 'propositional knowledge'. We will look at a famous analysis of propositional knowledge known as the tripartite view, objections to it, and four theories that respond to these objections in different ways.

One issue to keep in mind throughout the discussion is what an analysis of knowledge is or could be and why we want one.

By the end of the section, you should be able to demonstrate a good understanding of the debate regarding the definition of knowledge and be able to evaluate a range of arguments and positions in that debate.

Types of knowledge

To understand what 'knowledge' is, we first need to think about what *kind* of knowledge we are trying to understand. Importantly, we can distinguish the kind of knowledge involved in skills and abilities from knowledge about the world. The first kind, 'ability knowledge', is knowing *how* to do something. For example, I know how to ride a bike. The second kind of knowledge involves being 'in cognitive contact with reality', as Zagzebski puts it.

> Zagzebski, 'What is knowledge?', §1

We can subdivide this second kind of knowledge into two further kinds. The first is 'acquaintance knowledge'. This is knowledge that involves direct contact with something in experience, e.g. a person, a place or one's own thoughts and feelings. For example, I know Oxford, I know my wife, and I know what I'm thinking. In acquaintance knowledge, the word 'know' is (normally) followed by a noun (or pronoun) – 'Oxford', 'my wife', 'what I'm thinking'.

The second kind of 'cognitive contact with reality' is 'propositional knowledge'. Propositional knowledge is knowledge *about* some part of reality, which I may or may not have experienced myself. It is knowledge *that* some claim – a proposition – is true or false. A proposition is a declarative statement, or more accurately, what is expressed by a declarative statement, e.g. 'eagles are birds'. Propositions can go after the phrases 'I believe that …' and 'I know that …'. I know that eagles are birds, that 2 + 2 = 4, and that Oxford is a city in England.

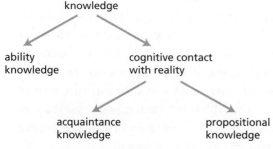

> Explain and illustrate the three types of knowledge.

Figure 2.1 Types of knowledge

Ability knowledge and acquaintance knowledge will be important for a debate on the Metaphysics of Mind. See RESPONSES TO THE KNOWLEDGE ARGUMENT, p. 295.

PROPOSITIONAL KNOWLEDGE

Our interest lies just with propositional knowledge, so we won't talk any more about ability knowledge or acquaintance knowledge here. One reason that philosophers have written more about propositional knowledge is that it is the form of knowledge that we can pass on to each other. By contrast, to know a person, you need to 'get to know' them by meeting them, talking with them, and so on. You can't know them just from other people's reports. Indeed, it's hard for us to say (to each other) just what we 'know' when we know someone.

From now on, our question is 'What is propositional knowledge?' When I talk of 'knowledge', I mean 'propositional knowledge'.

Propositions can be true or false. But only true propositions describe how reality is. Knowledge is a relation between a subject and some part of reality. So to be in contact with reality, what we know must be a true proposition, not a false one. But what more can we say about knowledge?

The definition of knowledge

Is the question 'What is knowledge?' one that we can answer? If so, is the answer a definition of knowledge? And what kind of definition?

ZAGZEBSKI, 'WHAT IS KNOWLEDGE?', §2

The purpose and nature of definition

In everyday life, we have different purposes for enquiring into what something is. For example, we might seek to define knowledge in order to recognise instances of knowledge and learn more about how to get knowledge. This is a practical purpose. We might be satisfied by some rough and ready guidance, such as 'to know something, you can't just believe it – you have to have a reason to believe it'. Alternatively, we may want to understand the concept KNOWLEDGE and how it relates to other, related concepts, such as TRUTH, EVIDENCE and so on. This is a theoretical purpose. The aim in this case is to find a more precise definition that tells us exactly what knowledge is, rather than help us achieve it.

When a word refers to a concept, I put it in capital letters.

We also offer each other different sorts of definition. In one kind, we concentrate on breaking down the concept defined into other concepts, e.g. 'a bachelor is an unmarried man'. In another kind, we try to say something about the *nature* of what we are defining, e.g. 'water is H_2O'. For this second kind of definition – called 'real definition' – to be possible, the thing we are defining has to *have* a 'nature', something that makes it what it is independently of how we think about it. Water is like this, but many of our concepts don't pick out things with a 'nature'. They refer instead to something that we have created, e.g. CUP-HOLDER, or unified with language, e.g. TREE. Does knowledge have a 'nature', something we need to discover about what knowledge really is to reach the correct answer?

Necessary and sufficient conditions

Ever since Plato, many philosophers have tried to provide definitions of some concept, *C*, by identifying 'necessary and sufficient conditions' for *C*. Conditions are related to conditional statements, which take the form 'if *x*, then *y*'. Conditional statements relate the truth of two propositions, e.g. 'it is raining' and 'I am getting wet', e.g. 'If it is raining, then I am getting wet.' The conditional asserts that if the first statement (known as the antecedent) is true, then the second statement (the consequent) is also true. Suppose I am standing outside with no protection against the weather. Then the conditional is true: *if* it is raining, then I am getting wet. It follows that if the antecedent is true (it is raining), then the consequent is true (I'm getting wet). It also follows that if the consequent is false (I am not getting wet), then the antecedent is false (it is not raining).

How do conditional statements help with definition? Suppose our antecedent is 'Mr A is a bachelor'. What consequent in 'If Mr A is a bachelor, then ...' will make this conditional always true (whoever Mr A is)? Well, 'If Mr A is a bachelor, then Mr A is unmarried' is always true. Being unmarried is a *necessary* condition for being a bachelor; if Mr A were married, then it would be impossible for Mr A to be a bachelor. But is being unmarried enough for being a bachelor? No: Ms B is unmarried, but she isn't a bachelor. So being unmarried isn't a *sufficient* condition for being a bachelor. There is another necessary condition for being bachelor: being a man. So 'If Mr A is a bachelor, then Mr A is unmarried and Mr A is a man' is always true. Each of these two conditions is necessary. But are these two conditions, taken together, sufficient, or are we missing something else? To test for sufficient conditions, swap the conditional around and see if it remains true: 'If Mr A is unmarried and Mr A is a man, then Mr A is a bachelor.' That's always true, so our two necessary conditions are, taken together, sufficient.

This has an important consequence: whenever the statement 'Mr A is a bachelor' is true, the statement 'Mr A is an unmarried man' is true, and vice versa. This allows us to provide a definition of 'bachelor' in terms of 'unmarried man'.

We find the same result with water, where we are seeking a real definition not a conceptual definition. 'If some stuff x is water, then x is H_2O' and 'If some stuff x is H_2O, then x is water' are both true (if we take 'water' to cover ice and steam as well).

So finding necessary and sufficient conditions is a method for providing a definition. We can apply this to knowledge. Suppose our antecedent is that someone, S, knows some proposition, p. If S knows that p, what follows? What can we say that will always be true of someone who has propositional knowledge? We said above that knowledge involves 'cognitive contact with reality' so that we can only know what is true. So we can say, 'If S knows that p, then p is true.' If I know that eagles are birds, then 'eagles are birds' is true. This can become part of our definition of what knowledge is: knowledge is always knowledge of true propositions.

That 'p is true' is one condition for knowledge of p. It is a *necessary* condition – we can't have knowledge of p if p is false. But is that *all we need* for knowledge? Is it a *sufficient* condition for knowledge? Certainly not. There are many true propositions that I do not know. For example, there is some true proposition that states how many people there are alive in Europe in 2017. But I don't know that proposition. What other conditions are necessary for knowledge?

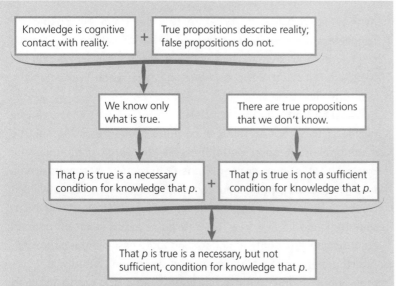

Map 2.1 Why truth is a necessary but not sufficient condition of knowledge

If we can find the necessary and sufficient conditions for knowledge, then we can offer a definition of knowledge in these terms. In the next section, we look at the 'tripartite view', the claim that knowledge has three conditions: that *p* is true, that *S* believes that *p*, and that *S*'s belief that *p* is justified.

Explain the method of finding necessary and sufficient conditions to define a concept.

Testing definitions

Suppose someone claims 'If *A* is unmarried, then *A* is a bachelor.' This is a general claim, made without exceptions or qualifications (such as 'except when …', 'unless …', 'on the whole …', 'normally, …'). We could show that such a general claim is false by finding a *counterexample*, an instance that it rules out. In this case, we can offer the example of a spinster – an unmarried woman.

Not every definition aspires to be a general claim, true without exception. For instance, those definitions that are offered for some practical purpose aren't concerned with counterexamples. In such cases, we are only seeking to understand the concept roughly or how it applies 'normally' or something similar. However, if a theory or a definition offers necessary and sufficient conditions, it makes a

Explain why a single counterexample shows that a general claim is false.

general claim. We can therefore test the claim by looking for counterexamples, trying to show either that one of the conditions is not necessary or that all the conditions taken together are still not sufficient. This is the approach we will take when evaluating the tripartite view below.

A definition, whether it offers a general claim or not, can be better or worse. For example, 'A bachelor is a bachelor' – while true – is hopeless. A good definition will not be circular, using the concept that is being defined in the definition. 'A bachelor is not a swan' is also unhelpful. A good definition will not be negative if it can be positive. A good definition will be informative – it will tell us something we don't know. It will help explain the concept defined by using concepts that we understand more easily in the definition. And there are other marks of a good definition. When we discuss the various definitions of knowledge below, it is worth thinking about whether the definitions are good definitions.

Can propositional knowledge be defined?

Can knowledge be defined in terms of necessary and sufficient conditions? If so, will we have a real definition that tells us the true nature of knowledge? The theories and philosophers we will discuss aim at such a definition. We might doubt its success in advance. For example, different societies have meant different things by KNOWLEDGE. Or again, sometimes we are quite generous with the word, e.g. I know that Descartes wrote the *Meditations*, but other times, we make more stringent demands, e.g. do I really *know* that my experience isn't illusory, that I'm not in *The Matrix* or *The Truman Show* (and if I don't know that, do I really know that Descartes wrote the *Meditations*)? Or again, the kind of knowledge we gain by, say, seeing something in front of us may be quite different from the kind of knowledge we gain by abstract reasoning, e.g. a young child can have the first kind of knowledge but not the second. And so on. Could there really be an abstract characterisation of what knowledge is that holds true in all these cases?

Zagzebski suggests that we should adopt the aim of providing a real definition of knowledge at least until we can show that we have failed to find one. The only way we will know that we cannot give necessary and sufficient conditions for knowledge is by trying and failing to succeed.

Key points: knowledge and its definition

- There are different types of knowledge: acquaintance, ability, and propositional knowledge. Theories of knowledge discussed here are about propositional knowledge.
- If knowledge involves 'cognitive contact with reality', and only true propositions describe reality, then we can know only true propositions, not false ones.
- Definitions explain a concept in terms of other concepts. But in real definitions, we also try to describe the nature of what we define.
- We can sometimes provide a definition using necessary and sufficient conditions. If the definition is right, then when something meets the necessary and sufficient conditions, it is an example of what we are defining, e.g. we can define 'bachelor' as 'an unmarried man' because if *A* is an unmarried man, *A* is a bachelor and vice versa.
- If we can find necessary and sufficient conditions for knowledge, we can provide a definition of knowledge. We can test proposed definitions by looking for counterexamples.

B. The tripartite view

The tripartite definition of knowledge

In this section, we discuss the claim, deriving from Plato's dialogue *Theaetetus*, that knowledge is a belief that is both true and justified. This claim was widely accepted until 1963, when Edmund Gettier published a very strong objection.

The tripartite definition of knowledge claims that knowledge is justified true belief. It claims that you know some proposition, *p*, if and only if

1. the proposition *p* is true,
2. you believe that *p*, and
3. your belief that *p* is justified.

The tripartite definition aims to provide a complete analysis of the concept and nature of propositional knowledge. Its three conditions, taken together, are intended to be equivalent to knowledge, to be the same thing as knowledge. So, first, if you fulfil those conditions, then you know the proposition. *If* all the three conditions it lists are satisfied – if you have a justified true belief that *p* – then you know that *p*. You don't need anything else for knowledge; the three conditions, together, are *sufficient*. Second, if you know some proposition, you fulfil exactly those three conditions. *If* you know that *p*, then you have a justified true belief that *p*. There is no other way to know that *p*, no other analysis of knowledge. So, it claims, each of the three conditions is *necessary*. If *p* is false, or you don't believe that *p*, or your belief that *p* is not justified, then you don't know that *p*. The conditions are necessary and sufficient conditions for knowledge that *p*.

The definition puts forward *two* conditionals: if all three conditions are satisfied, then you know that *p*; and if you know that *p*, then all three conditions are satisfied. This is what is meant by the phrase 'if and only if' – that the conditions that follow are both necessary and sufficient. We may thus conclude that knowledge and justified true belief *are the same thing*. Justified true belief is necessary for knowledge (you can't have knowledge without it), but it is also sufficient for knowledge (you don't need anything else).

WHY JUSTIFIED TRUE BELIEF?

Why accept the tripartite view and adopt these three conditions for knowledge? We noted earlier (p. 31) that Zagzebski describes knowledge as a form of cognitive contact with reality. Reality is described or comprised by what is true, not what is false; what is false is precisely what reality *isn't*. As a result, we can only know what is true. This is a reason to adopt the first condition, that *p* is true.

The idea of 'cognitive contact' also motivates the second condition. Propositional knowledge is a relation between the person who has knowledge and the proposition that is known. The relation involves the person taking some proposition to be true. Taking a proposition to be true is to believe it. If I take 'eagles are birds' to be true, if I assent to it, then I believe it.

But what is it for a belief to be 'justified' and why think knowledge must involve justified belief? One's 'justification' for a belief is what one offers as a reason or evidence to accept it. To understand the importance of justification, we first need to understand that a belief can be true and yet not justified. For example, someone on a jury might think that the person on trial is guilty just from the way they dress. Their belief, that the person is guilty, might be true; but how someone dresses isn't evidence for whether they are a criminal! True beliefs can be formed or held on irrational grounds, for no good reason. Or again true beliefs can just be *lucky*. For example, there is a lot of evidence that astrology does not make accurate predictions, and my horoscope has often been wrong. Suppose on one occasion, I read my horoscope and believe a prediction, although I know there is evidence against thinking it is right. And then this prediction turns out true!

Zagzebski notes that we think knowledge is *good*; it is desirable and perhaps it is praiseworthy in some sense. Knowledge is undoubtedly good for helping us satisfy our needs and desires (from knowing where the closest supermarket is to finding a cure for cancer); many people have thought that it is also good in itself, irrespective of whether we can use knowledge (e.g. knowing about the origin of the universe). Whatever the reason why knowledge is good, we seek out knowledge for ourselves and support others who do so. We understand that knowledge can be difficult to acquire, requiring motivation or special skills, and we value these.

'What is knowledge?', p. 94

The examples show that lucky or irrational true beliefs are not good in the way knowledge is. They certainly aren't praiseworthy. The tripartite theory explains this in terms of justification. Justification is what someone takes as their reason or evidence (or other basis) for their belief. In both examples, it is counter-intuitive to say that the belief counts as knowledge, because the person has no reason, no evidence, no justification, for their belief. We ought not to form our beliefs in this way, even if they sometimes turn out true. When we form a belief, we should do so rationally, on the basis of reasons and evidence. If we do, then our belief will be justified. And this belief, if it is also true, says the tripartite theory, will amount to knowledge.

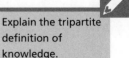

Explain the tripartite definition of knowledge.

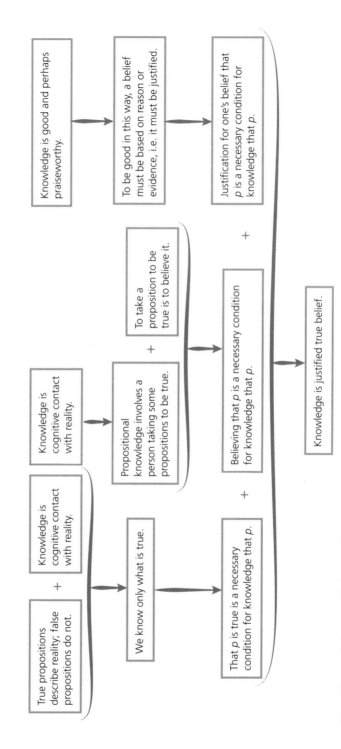

Map 2.2 Knowledge is justified true belief

The following text appears within the map:

Knowledge is good and perhaps praiseworthy.

To be good in this way, a belief must be based on reason or evidence, i.e. it must be justified.

Justification for one's belief that *p* is a necessary condition for knowledge that *p*.

Knowledge is cognitive contact with reality.

Propositional knowledge involves a person taking some propositions to be true.

To take a proposition to be true is to believe it.

Believing that *p* is a necessary condition for knowledge that *p*.

Knowledge is justified true belief.

True propositions describe reality; false propositions do not.

Knowledge is cognitive contact with reality.

We know only what is true.

That *p* is true is a necessary condition for knowledge that *p*.

Thinking harder: a note on certainty

Some philosophers have thought that another difference between knowledge and belief is certainty. Knowledge must be certain; beliefs don't have to be. If a belief isn't certain, then it can't count as knowledge. We can only really *know* something if we can be certain of it.

But how 'certain' does certainty have to be? We will see in DESCARTES' SCEPTICAL ARGUMENTS (p. 189) that Descartes searches for knowledge by ruling out everything that it is *possible* to doubt (including the existence of anything beyond his own mind). The difficulty with defining knowledge as believing a true proposition that it is impossible to doubt is that we end up with very little knowledge indeed. Since we tend to think that we do know all sorts of things that it is *possible* to doubt, this is clearly not how we usually think about knowledge.

The tripartite theory does not claim that a belief must be certain to be knowledge. To say a belief is justified is not to say that it is certain. We have good reasons to believe many things that it remains possible to doubt.

Of course, some of these beliefs may be false. We are *fallible*. It is possible to have a false justified belief – many scientific theories that we have now discarded are false, but the evidence available at the time was strong. For example, before Galileo invented the telescope, there was good reason to think that the planets circled the Earth and little evidence that they didn't. But this is why, according to the tripartite view, we must say that knowledge is justified *true* belief, and not simply justified belief. If some belief that we take to be true turns out to be false, then it is not knowledge. If we discover that it is false, e.g. by uncovering new evidence, then we should give up the claim to know it.

See INFALLIBILISM, p. 53, and THE PARTICULAR NATURE OF PHILOSOPHICAL SCEPTICISM, p. 185.

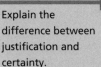

Explain the difference between justification and certainty.

Are the conditions individually necessary?

We can raise two kinds of objection to the tripartite definition of knowledge by searching for counterexamples. First, it may be that one of the conditions is not necessary for knowledge – can we have knowledge without justified true belief? Second, it may be that all of the conditions together are still not sufficient for knowledge – can we have justified true belief without knowledge? We will discuss the first question in this section, and the second question in the next section.

JUSTIFICATION IS NOT A NECESSARY CONDITION OF KNOWLEDGE

Is justification necessary for knowledge, or could knowledge be simply 'true belief'? We can object that sometimes we use the word 'know' just to mean 'believe truly', without worrying about justification. If I ask, 'Do you know who wrote the *Meditations*?', I'm only interested in whether you have the true belief that it was Descartes.

We can understand this in terms of the practical purpose of knowledge. If you can reliably inform me in answer to my query, perhaps that's enough for practical purposes to talk of knowledge. But this won't do as a definition for theoretical purposes. In particular, as we saw above, it fails to capture what is good about knowledge, since true belief can be formed and held in both good ways and bad. If you don't have a good reason for believing that Descartes wrote the *Meditations*, then the mere fact that your belief is true doesn't make it knowledge.

However, even if true belief is not sufficient for knowledge, that doesn't mean that *justification* is a necessary condition. There may be some *other* condition that turns true belief into knowledge. We will return to this challenge to justification in RELIABILISM, p. 55.

> **Does true belief on its own ever amount to knowledge?**

TRUTH IS NOT A NECESSARY CONDITION OF KNOWLEDGE

The issue of truth is, strictly speaking, an issue in metaphysics, rather than epistemology. We connected the idea that knowledge involves truth to Zagzebski's claim that knowledge is cognitive contact with reality. What 'reality' is, is an issue in metaphysics. And the question of what we should mean by 'truth' can become quite a challenging one. Nevertheless, we can make some important points on whether a definition of knowledge should include mention of truth, whatever truth turns out to be.

Could knowledge be simply justified belief? In an everyday sense, it is difficult to see how. Justified beliefs can be true or false. People can believe propositions that aren't true. For example, someone may claim that flamingos are grey, and *think* that they know this. They could even be justified, e.g. their science teacher told them, and they saw a grey picture of a flamingo in a textbook. But they are mistaken: flamingos are not grey, but pink. Of course, they *believe* that flamingos are grey, they may even be *certain* that

> Metaphysics is the branch of philosophy that asks questions about the fundamental nature of reality. *Meta-* means above, beyond or after; physics enquires into the physical structure of reality – but there may be more to understanding reality than what physics can explain.

flamingos are grey. But given the idea that knowledge involves cognitive contact with reality, a false belief is not knowledge. You can't know something false, or so it seems.

Thinking harder: relativism about truth

What if many people, perhaps a whole society, share a particular false belief and have good reasons for doing so? For instance, almost everybody used to believe that the Earth is flat. It does, after all, look that way. Should we say that people used to know that the Earth is flat? Or should we say that they didn't know it, they only believed it, because their belief was false?

One response to this line of thought is to adopt some form of *relativism*. We reject talking about 'truth' without qualification, and talk instead about what is 'true for' someone or some society. Knowledge could still be justified true belief, but because what is 'true' is relative to someone or some society, knowledge is also relative.

Let us assume that the belief that the Earth is flat was justified. Is there any sense in which we can say that this belief was 'true for' people in the past? To say it was 'true for them' must be to say more than simply that they believed it. We all agree they believed it, but to believe that some proposition is true is not the same as the proposition being true. If all it takes to make something true is to believe, then the best cure for cancer is simply to believe that one doesn't have cancer! If there is no difference between a belief and a true belief, then how does anyone get less than 100% on any exam? To make sense of our lives, we must allow that beliefs can be true or false. So for a belief to be 'true for' someone, this can't simply mean that they believe it. So what does it mean?

A second difficulty arises with the idea of 'true for': if we say that it was true, for people in the past, that Earth is flat, and it is true for us now that the Earth is a sphere, the question arises how both of these claims about the Earth can be true. Did the Earth miraculously change from being flat to being a sphere? Did a change in people's beliefs change the shape of the Earth? No one believes that.

What, if anything, does it mean to say that a claim is 'true for' someone?

Perhaps we can defend relativism by giving up all talk of truth (and perhaps all talk of 'reality'), and restrict ourselves to talking about what people believe. Knowledge is simply justified belief. We cannot ask 'what shape is the Earth (truly)?', we can only ask 'what shape is the Earth ('for us')?' There is no 'objective truth' about the shape of the Earth.

However, it seems hard to resist the claim that the modern view of the shape of the Earth is closer to the truth than the ancient theory. For instance, we have more evidence, e.g. photos from space, than they did. To make the claim that our beliefs are true while those of some other culture are false is not to say that their beliefs were unjustified or irrational or unintelligent. We are discussing truth, not justification, and the evidence available to people changes over time. Nor is it to say that our beliefs are *certain* or *infallible*.

The response that *no one knows* the shape of the Earth because we could be mistaken is irrelevant – it retreats from relativism to scepticism, a completely different view. To allow that we could be mistaken assumes that there is some non-relative truth! To claim that 'there is a truth that we don't know' is very different from claiming that 'there is no objective truth and what we know is relative to society'.

We discuss relativism further in extension material available on the companion website.

See THE PARTICULAR NATURE OF PHILOSOPHICAL SCEPTICISM, p. 185.

Is truth a necessary condition for knowledge?

BELIEF IS NOT A NECESSARY CONDITION OF KNOWLEDGE

There are two strengths of the objection that belief is not necessary for knowledge. The weak objection is that sometimes it is possible to know something without believing it. The strong objection is that knowledge is never a form of belief.

The weak objection: suppose John is sitting an exam, but he's very nervous and has no confidence in his answers. Suppose when answering 'Which philosopher wrote the *Meditations*?', he writes 'Descartes'. He's right, and the answer isn't a lucky guess – he has remembered what he learned. So it is plausible to say that John knows the answer, he knows more than he thinks – he's just unconfident. But because he's unconfident, we should say that John doesn't *believe* that the answer is Descartes. So he knows the answer without believing it.

We can defend the tripartite definition by replying in one of two ways. We could say that John doesn't know the answer. Although there is a sense in which he remembers the answer, because he doesn't 'commit' to the answer that occurs to him, he doesn't believe what he remembers. Alternatively, we could say that John does know that the answer is 'Descartes', because he believes this, although this belief is *unconscious* or 'tacit'. This unconscious belief amounts to knowledge.

Plato presents arguments for the claim that knowledge is never belief. What is a matter of belief is not known, and what is a matter of knowledge is not believed. Instead, belief and knowledge involve different 'faculties' and take different 'objects'. He appeals to the connection between knowledge, truth and reality to make the case. First, knowledge is infallible, because you cannot know what is false. But beliefs, however, can be mistaken. Belief and knowledge have different powers. So belief cannot be knowledge. Second, knowledge is only of what is real. We cannot have knowledge of what is not real or does not exist. Knowledge is 'about' what is real. By contrast, ignorance relates to what is not real, what does not exist, i.e. 'nothing'. If you are completely ignorant of something, you don't think of it at all; if you don't understand it, you can't form an opinion about its reality. If there is something between what is real and what is not real (e.g. what is constantly changing from one thing to another), then there must be something between knowledge and ignorance. This is belief – neither knowledge nor ignorance. Belief and knowledge have different objects.

The Republic, 477a–478e, 509d–511e

Plato argues that we may divide reality into the realm of the 'sensible' – what we detect through our senses – and the realm of the 'intelligible', what we discover using the intellect. Belief relates to the former, knowledge to the latter. So we form beliefs about the changeable, natural world; but we gain knowledge – using reasoning in mathematics and philosophy – of abstract things, like numbers and concepts.

As Zagzebski notes (p. 93), almost everyone now agrees that Plato is wrong to distinguish belief and knowledge as he does. First, knowledge and belief need not be different faculties even if knowledge is always true and belief is not. This difference isn't a result of different 'powers', but because knowledge is always true and justified belief whereas belief in general can be true or false, justified or unjustified.

Second, belief and knowledge do not need to be about different things. Because what is known is always true, you cannot know something that goes from true to false. Plato seems to try to explain this by saying that we

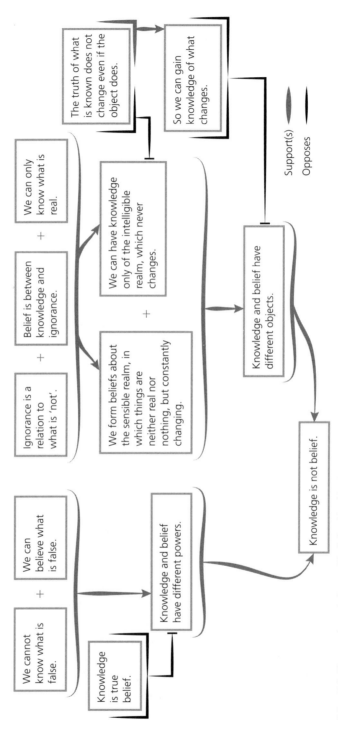

Map 2.3 Plato on knowledge and belief, with objections

The truth of what is known does not change even if the object does.

So we can gain knowledge of what changes.

We can only know what is real.

Belief is between knowledge and ignorance.

We can have knowledge only of the intelligible realm, which never changes.

Ignorance is a relation to what is 'not'.

We form beliefs about the sensible realm, in which things are neither real nor nothing, but constantly changing.

Knowledge and belief have different objects.

Knowledge is not belief.

We cannot know what is false.

We can believe what is false.

Knowledge is true belief.

Knowledge and belief have different powers.

Support(s)

Opposes

can only know about things that cannot change. But a different explanation is to separate the truth that is known from the object by talking about truth at a time or in a context. For example, I can know that a particular object of sense experience – this book – has a particular property, e.g. it is a certain size. Yet its size can change, for example if you burn it. What I know is that the book is this size *now* (at a specific moment in time), and this truth won't change even if the size of the book changes. Plato seems to have confused a property of knowledge (the truth of the proposition known doesn't change) with a property of the object of knowledge (it doesn't change).

Explain one argument for the claim that belief is not a necessary condition of knowledge and one reply to that argument.

Gettier's objection: are the conditions jointly sufficient?

Edmund Gettier famously presented cases in which we want to say that someone has justified true belief but *not* knowledge. They show that the three conditions of the tripartite definition are not sufficient for knowledge.

GETTIER, 'IS JUSTIFIED TRUE BELIEF KNOWLEDGE?'

Gettier starts by claiming, uncontroversially, that DEDUCTIVE ARGUMENT (p. 7) preserves justification. Suppose you are justified in believing that *p* (say, that Socrates is a man and that all men are mortal), and *p* entails another proposition, *q* (that Socrates is mortal). If you deduce *q* from *p*, you are also justified in believing that *q*. Your reasons for believing the premises are also reasons for believing the conclusion, because if the premises are true, the conclusion must be true.

He then gives two counterexamples to the tripartite definition. In the first, Smith and Jones are applying for the same job. Smith has excellent reason to believe that Jones will get the job, e.g. Smith has been told this by the employer. Smith also has excellent reason to believe that Jones has ten coins in his pocket, e.g. Smith has just counted them. Therefore, both of these beliefs are justified. Smith then puts the two beliefs together and deduces that the man who will get the job has ten coins in his pocket. This belief is *justified*, because it is inferred deductively from justified beliefs. However, it turns out that Jones doesn't get the job, Smith does. It also so happens that, unknown to him, Smith also has ten coins in his pocket. So Smith's belief that the man who will get the job has ten coins in his pocket happens to be *true*.

Smith's belief is both true and justified, but we shouldn't say that Smith *knows* that the man who will get the job has ten coins in his pocket. Smith inferred his belief from a *false* belief, namely that Jones would get the job. So the *reason* Smith has for his belief is false. What makes his belief true (Smith, who has ten coins in his pocket, gets the job) has come apart from what justifies his belief (the evidence that Jones, who has ten coins in his pocket, will get the job). There is no connection between what justifies his belief and his belief's being true. We might say that it is only by *luck* that his belief is true.

In the second counterexample, Smith believes that Jones owns a Ford. Smith remembers that for as long as he has known him, Jones has always had a Ford, and Jones has just offered Smith a lift while driving a Ford. So Smith's belief is justified. Smith then thinks about another acquaintance of his, Brown, and wonders where he is. He has no idea, and chooses a place name at random, Barcelona, say. He then deduces the belief (quite oddly, but don't worry about that) that either Jones owns a Ford or Brown is in Barcelona.

An either/or claim is called a 'disjunction'. A disjunction is true if either (or both) of the two 'disjuncts' are true. So 'Either Jones owns a Ford or Brown is in Barcelona' is true if

1.   Jones owns a Ford, or
2.   Brown is in Barcelona, or
3.   Both (1) and (2) are true.

Now, from 'Jones owns a Ford', Smith can deduce that 'Either Jones owns a Ford or Brown is in Barcelona', because it is impossible for the premise 'Jones owns a Ford' to be true and the conclusion 'Either Jones owns a Ford or Brown is in Barcelona' to be false. His belief that either Jones owns a Ford or Brown is in Barcelona is also justified, because he has deduced it from his justified belief that Jones owns a Ford. However, unknown to Smith, Jones has just sold his Ford and is currently driving a rented Ford, so he *doesn't* own a

Ford. But by complete coincidence, and unknown to Smith, Brown *is* in Barcelona. So the proposition 'Either Jones owns a Ford or Brown is in Barcelona' is true – not because of (1), Jones owns a Ford, but because of (2), Brown is in Barcelona.

So Smith's belief is both true and justified, but we shouldn't say that Smith *knows* that either Jones owns a Ford or Brown is in Barcelona. Once again, Smith inferred his belief from a *false* belief, namely that Jones owns a Ford. So the *reason* Smith has for his belief is false. What makes his belief true (that Brown is in Barcelona) has come apart from what justifies his belief (that Jones owns a Ford). There is, again, no connection between what justifies his belief and his belief's being true.

Thought experiments are a philosophical method designed to test a hypothesis or philosophical claim through imagining a hypothetical situation and coming to a judgement. We can use thought experiments, like the examples Gettier gives, to test definitions of knowledge. Examples of justified true belief without knowledge became known as 'Gettier cases'. They all describe situations in which we have justified true belief, but not knowledge, because the belief is only true *by chance*, given the evidence that justifies it. So justified true belief is not *sufficient* for knowledge.

Explain Gettier's objection to the tripartite theory of knowledge, first in prose, then by drawing an argument map (using one example).

This shows that justified true belief is not the *same* as knowledge. If *A* is the same thing as *B*, then you cannot have *A* without *B* or *B* without *A*. *A* and *B* are just one thing – you have it or you don't. For example, you can't have water without H_2O. If you could, that would show that water is not the same thing as H_2O. So if knowledge isn't justified true belief in Gettier cases, then knowledge and justified true belief can come apart. That shows that they are not the same thing, and so the definition of knowledge as justified true belief is false.

Is knowledge justified true belief?

Key points: the tripartite view

- The tripartite view of knowledge claims to give necessary and sufficient conditions for knowledge. If you have a justified true belief that *p*, you know that *p*; the conditions are sufficient for knowledge. And if you know that *p*, you have a justified true belief that *p*; the conditions are necessary for knowledge.

- If justified true belief is both necessary and sufficient for knowledge, it is the same thing as knowledge.
- 'Cognitive contact with reality' means assenting to what is true. So knowledge involves true belief. And knowledge is good, while forming beliefs without good reason is not good. So knowledge involves justified beliefs.
- The tripartite view allows for a distinction between justification and certainty. If knowledge need not be certain, we can be fallible about what we know.
- Although we sometimes use the word 'know' to mean 'believe truly', knowledge is not true belief. True beliefs may or may not be justified. To be knowledge, a true belief must be justified.
- Relativism about truth rejects talk of 'objectively' true belief. Truth is relative. However, because we understand a 'true' proposition to describe reality, it can be hard to make sense of the idea of relative truth. Not all beliefs are true beliefs.
- Someone may know something without consciously believing it, e.g. if they are unconfident. But we can respond that their knowledge is an unconscious justified true belief.
- Plato argues that because knowledge is always true, while belief is not, knowledge and belief are different faculties and are about different objects. We can respond that knowledge is simply true belief, and that the truth of what we know doesn't change even if the object does, because what we know is true at a particular time.
- Gettier uses counterexamples to argue that it is possible to have justified true belief without knowledge. And so justified true belief is not knowledge. A Gettier case is one in which what makes a person's belief true is not related to what justifies it.

C. Responses

Gettier's argument poses a serious challenge to the tripartite definition of knowledge. In the resulting debate over what knowledge is, most attention has focused on the claim about justification. One response is to *strengthen* what we mean by justification in the case of knowledge. Another is to say that we need to *replace* the justification condition with something else. But we start with a simpler idea.

Add a 'no false lemmas' condition (J+T+B+N)

Smith doesn't know that the man who will get the job has ten coins in his pocket, we said, because he inferred this belief from a false belief, namely that Jones will get the job. Similarly, he inferred his belief that either Jones owns a Ford or Brown is in Barcelona from his belief that Jones owns a Ford. To deal with these two cases, all we need to do is to add an extra condition to the definition of knowledge. You know that *p* if and only if

1. *p* is true,
2. you believe that *p*,
3. your belief that *p* is justified, and
4. you did not infer that *p* from a false belief.

Condition (4) is called the 'no false lemmas' condition. A lemma is a claim part way through an argument. For example, Smith concluded that Jones will get the job from being told by the employer; and he then used that information to conclude that the man with ten coins in his pocket will get the job. So 'Jones will get the job' is a lemma.

Condition (4) certainly deals with Gettier's two examples. But it doesn't deal with the underlying worry about truth and justification 'coming apart'. There are Gettier cases that satisfy condition (4) without the person having knowledge.

Zagzebski describes such a case based on induction. Dr Jones has very good evidence that her patient, Smith, is suffering from virus *X*, e.g. the symptoms and the lab tests are all consistent with Smith having this virus and no other known virus produces these results. Jones therefore believes that Smith has virus *X*, and this belief is justified. However, Smith's symptoms and lab results are caused by Smith having the unknown virus *Y*. But, by chance, Smith has *just* caught virus *X*, so recently that it has not caused any symptoms nor does it show up in lab tests. So Dr Jones' belief that Smith has virus *X* is true. So her belief is both true and justified. But she does not know that Smith has virus *X* because the evidence from which she infers her belief has nothing to do with the fact that Smith has virus *X* as it is all caused by virus *Y*.

'What is knowledge?', p. 101

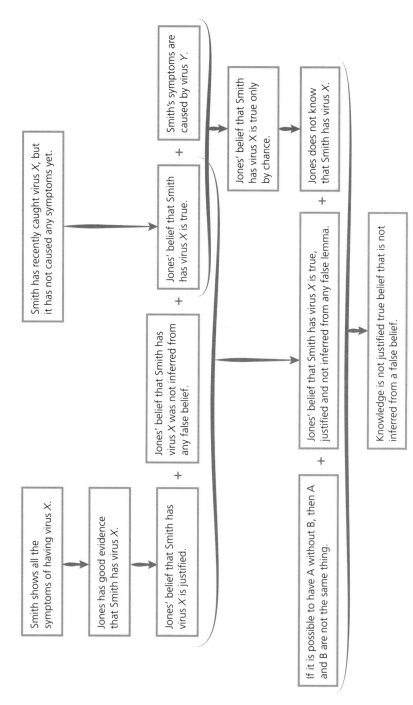

Map 2.4 Zagzebski's objection to the 'no false lemmas' definition of knowledge

This example satisfied condition (4). All the evidence is *true* – Smith does manifest the symptoms he does and the lab reports are accurate. Only the diagnosis is false. So Dr Jones did not infer her true and justified belief that Smith has virus *X* from any false belief, yet it is still not knowledge.

Does the 'no false lemmas' response to Gettier succeed? If so, how? If not, why not?

Infallibilism

Gettier has assumed that Smith's beliefs – that Jones will get the job, that he has ten coins in his pocket, that Jones owns a Ford – are justified. Because they are justified, his deductions, that the man who will get the job has ten coins in his pocket and that either Jones owns a Ford or Brown is in Barcelona, are justified. But we can challenge Gettier's assumption. While Smith has good reasons for the beliefs from which he starts, perhaps these reasons aren't enough for justification. If so, then his conclusions will not be justified either.

The tripartite definition of knowledge does not tell us what it is for a belief to be justified, although we noted (p. 41) that it does not usually require certainty. Infallibilism argues that knowledge is *certain*. One way of combining this with the tripartite view is to say that justification requires certainty. We can say that if a belief is not certain, then it is not justified, or at least, it is not sufficiently justified to count as knowledge. The implication that we should draw from Gettier cases is not that knowledge is not justified true belief, but that our beliefs are rarely sufficiently justified to count as knowledge.

Zagzebski notes (p. 101) that Gettier cases arise because of the gap between truth and justification. The challenge to the tripartite theory is how to bridge that gap. The suggestion of infallibilism is to make justification so strong that it is impossible for a justified belief to be false. Justification as certainty somehow guarantees the truth of the belief, so truth and justification can't come apart, and Gettier cases become impossible.

What kind of certainty is relevant to knowledge? The *feeling* of certainty won't help. That could vary from one person to another, e.g. you might *feel certain* that God exists or that your friends will never betray you. This kind of certainty is subjective and psychological, a feeling of conviction. But we can all make mistakes, and be certain of something even though what we are certain of is not true. So a feeling of certainty can't guarantee truth. Instead, the kind of certainty involved must relate to the belief being *infallible* in some way. For whatever reason, it is impossible that we could be making a mistake.

Descartes adopts a view of this kind. See DESCARTES' SCEPTICAL ARGUMENTS, p. 189. Similarly, Locke says that we only have knowledge of how the physical world is at the time we experience it. Anything else is merely belief with a high degree of probability (*An Essay Concerning Human Understanding*, Bk 4, Ch. 9, §9).

For more on this idea, see Descartes on CLEAR AND DISTINCT IDEAS, p. 156.

With this in mind, here is an argument for infallibilism, the view that we only know a proposition if our belief is infallible:

P1. No one can know what is false.
C1. Therefore, if I know that *p*, then I can't be mistaken about *p*.
C2. Therefore, for justification to secure knowledge, justification must guarantee truth.
C3. Therefore, if I am justified in believing that *p*, I *can't possibly* be mistaken.
C4. Therefore, if it is possible that I am mistaken, then I can't be justified in believing that *p*.
C5. Therefore, infallibilism is true.

What is infallibilism?

Infallibilism defends the tripartite view of knowledge and rules out Gettier cases, because in these cases I do not have *justified* true belief.

But is this a good definition of knowledge? It is rare that the justification of our beliefs rules out the *possibility* of error. Infallibilism entails that we have very little knowledge (even if we still have many beliefs that are very probably true). It also identifies what is *good* or praiseworthy or desirable about knowledge as its infallibility. But is that right? Perhaps it would be better to find a definition of knowledge that allows us more of it and recognises something good about knowledge without seeking immunity to error.

Is infallibilism a good definition of knowledge?

Thinking harder: rejecting the argument for infallibilism

The argument for infallibilism rests on a logical error. (C1) 'If I know that *p*, then I can't be mistaken about *p*', has more than one meaning, depending on how one understands 'can't':

C1a.   It can't be the case that if I know that *p*, I *am* mistaken that *p*.

We should agree with this, because of (P1) 'No one can know what is false.'

C1b.   If I know that *p*, I *can't possibly* be mistaken that *p*.

This is what infallibilism assumes in moving from (C1) through (C2) to (C3). It is a much stronger claim than (C1a), because it says that not only am I *not* mistaken, but I *can't possibly be* mistaken that *p*. Obviously, there are many cases of perception or memory in which I *could* be mistaken that *p*, but in fact I am not, and my true belief rests on evidence, so there are good reasons why I am not mistaken.

The argument for infallibilism slips from (C1a), inferred from (P1), to (C1b), used to support (C3). But this is a mistake, confusing one claim for another.

The two claims are distinct, since one is a claim about whether I *am* mistaken, and the other is a claim about whether I *could be* mistaken. So the argument fails. To accept infallibilism, we need some other, independent reason to believe (C1b).

> This is called the fallacy of equivocation.

> Explain the difference between the claims 'If I know that *p*, I am not mistaken' and 'If I know that *p*, I cannot be mistaken.'

Reliabilism (R+T+B)

If we allow justification to amount to less than certainty, then a gap remains between truth and justification. This makes it possible to construct Gettier cases in which truth and justification come apart, creating cases in which justified true belief is not knowledge. But if we strengthen justification so that it is certainty, as infallibilism argues, then it looks like we end up with scepticism, or at least, much less knowledge than we normally take ourselves to have. So perhaps the solution is to reject the idea that knowledge requires justification.

Reliabilism claims that you know that *p* if and only if

1. *p* is true,
2. you believe that *p*, and
3. your belief is produced by a reliable cognitive process.

A reliable cognitive process is just one that produces a high percentage of true beliefs. Examples include perception, memory and testimony. True beliefs caused by such processes count as knowledge. (Of course, if these processes cause a false belief – if you misperceive or misremember or someone lies to you – then your belief isn't knowledge, but that's because it is *false*.)

Figure 2.2 Animals use their knowledge to solve problems

One advantage of reliabilism is that it allows young children and animals to have knowledge. It is odd to say, of many animals, that they have reasons or evidence for their beliefs – they don't have that kind of sophisticated psychology. But they get around the world very well indeed, so it is also odd to deny that they have knowledge. Reliabilism explains both points. Children and animals have knowledge because their true beliefs are caused by reliable processes; whether they have a justification for their beliefs is irrelevant.

Zagzebski notes (p. 95) that reliabilism understands knowledge as a 'natural' good, like strength or beauty. It isn't something that is praiseworthy, e.g. we don't deserve credit for having good eyesight, but it is something desirable. Perhaps, in particular, having reliably true beliefs confers a significant benefit on a creature, e.g. it can act in a way that satisfies its desires. This contrasts with the justified true belief theory: believing something only on good evidence or with good reason is something that we do, something that we can be praised for doing, while believing irrationally or without evidence is something that we can be criticised for doing.

However, reliabilism doesn't solve Gettier's challenge. Here's another Gettier case. Henry is driving through the countryside. He doesn't know it, but in this part of the country – call it 'Barn County' – there are lots of fake barns, mere barn facades. But they have been built so that they look just like real barns when seen from the road. As he drives along, Henry often thinks

What is reliabilism?

Alvin Goldman, 'Discrimination and perceptual knowledge'

'There's a barn', or 'Hey, there's another barn.' These beliefs don't count as knowledge because they are false. But just once, Henry thinks 'There's a barn' when he is looking at the one and only real barn in the area. This belief is true. And it is produced by a very reliable process, namely vision. But it is not knowledge, because – as in other Gettier cases – it is only a matter of *luck* that Henry's belief is true in this one instance. But reliabilism has to say Henry *does* know there's a barn. His belief is true and produced by a reliable process. The problem is that in Barn County, this reliable process has produced a true belief in circumstances in which the belief still seems only accidentally true.

Zagzebski's example of Dr Jones and the virus (p. 51) provides another counterexample. Diagnosing whether someone suffers from virus *X* by looking at their symptoms and the results of their lab tests is a reliable process (the diagnosis is correct in a high percentage of cases). But in this one case where the patient suffers from unknown virus *Y* and has only just contracted virus *X*, the process produces a true belief that is nevertheless not knowledge.

Just as people who hold the tripartite view made amendments to the original definition by adding or strengthening conditions, reliabilists can try to avoid Gettier cases the same way. But Zagzebski argues that this whole approach simply won't work.

TRUTH AND THE THIRD CONDITION

Both the tripartite view and reliabilism share a common approach to the analysis of knowledge. They claim that knowledge is true belief + some third condition that is closely connected to truth but independent from it – justification or being the product of reliable cognitive processes. As Gettier cases show, the independence of this third condition allows the possibility that it comes apart from truth – that the truth of the belief is lucky, not the result of the third condition.

ZAGZEBSKI, 'WHAT IS KNOWLEDGE?', §3, PP. 101–4

Zagzebski argues that as long as the third condition is independent of truth like this, no matter how we add to the conditions for knowledge, we will always be able to construct Gettier cases that show that the proposed definition of knowledge is incorrect.

Why does she think this? Because there is a 'recipe' for making up such cases, no matter what the additional conditions are – as long as the additional conditions are independent of truth. Let's call the additional conditions *Q* (justification, justification + no false lemmas, reliable cognitive processes, etc.), so the proposed definition is that knowledge = true belief that is *Q*.

1. Start with a belief that is *Q* but false as a result of 'bad luck', e.g. Henry believes, of a facade in Barn County, that it is a barn.
2. Now add some 'good luck' so that the belief is true after all, e.g. Henry happens to be looking at the one real barn in Barn County.
3. This true belief will be *Q*, since it is exactly like the false belief that is *Q*, but happens, by luck, to be true. But it will not be knowledge, because it is true by luck.
4. So for any theory where *Q* is independent of truth, knowledge is not true belief + *Q*.

What if we say knowledge is true belief that is not accidentally true? First, as a definition, this is terrible – it is vague, negative and no help. What is it for a belief to be 'non-accidentally true'? Second, the third condition – that the belief is non-accidentally true – is not independent of truth, so it is no objection to Zagzebski's argument.

The force of her argument is that we need a definition of knowledge that demonstrates both how and why truth and the third condition are *connected*, and not merely *added* together. As with justification and reliability, this connection will have something to do with why knowledge is good in a way that mere true belief is not (see p. 39). This leads us to an account of 'epistemic virtue'.

Explain Zagzebski's argument that no analysis of knowledge that merely adds conditions to true belief can escape Gettier cases.

Virtue epistemology (V+T+B)

There are different versions of virtue epistemology, with different understandings of 'virtue' and different analyses of knowledge in terms of virtue. However, they all agree that in some sense, you know that *p* if and only if

1. *p* is true,
2. you believe that *p*, and
3. your belief is a result of you exercising your 'epistemic' or 'intellectual' virtues.

The thought behind (3) is that knowledge is a form of achievement for which you deserve credit. Rather than analysing knowledge in terms of a *process*, as reliabilism does, virtue epistemology focuses on the *person* and what they *do* in forming their beliefs.

This mirrors the emphasis on the person in ARISTOTELIAN VIRTUE ETHICS (p. 268).

However, if this third condition is understood independently of truth, then the analysis will be open to objection from Zagzebski's argument above. So we will focus on Zagzebski's own analysis of knowledge that seeks to avoid this problem.

ZAGZEBSKI'S ANALYSIS OF KNOWLEDGE

ZAGZEBSKI, 'WHAT IS KNOWLEDGE?', §§4, 5

Zagzebski's definition of propositional knowledge is 'belief arising out of acts of intellectual virtue' (p. 109). In other words, you know that *p* if and only if

1. you believe that *p*,
2. your belief that *p* arises from an act (or acts) of intellectual virtue.

We associate virtues more with ethics, but here we are concerned with epistemic or intellectual virtues. Zagzebski develops her account of an intellectual virtue from Aristotle's theory of virtues.

See ARISTOTLE'S ACCOUNT OF VIRTUES, p. 279.

A virtue is a state of a person that is good by way of helping the person achieve some good purpose or goal. Moral virtues, such as generosity or kindness, aim at moral goods, such as well-being. Intellectual virtues aim at intellectual goods, especially truth. Zagzebski defines a virtue as having two components.

1. A virtue motivates us to pursue what is good; in the case of intellectual virtues, we are motivated to discover the truth – so we care about believing what is true, not false.

2. A virtue involves a component that enables us to be successful – it gives us the ability to be reliable in forming true beliefs.

For example, being open-minded is an intellectual virtue that disposes us to care about carefully considering views that conflict with our own and it enables us to do this successfully.

Now, someone who has an intellectual virtue will reliably believe what is true, *but not always*. Everyone makes mistakes. So while a belief that is the product of a person's exercising their virtues is epistemically good, it is still not completely good if it is false. On the other hand, as we have noted repeatedly, a belief that is true is good, but it is not completely good if it is only accidentally true. The same is true in ethics. Helping someone is good – but if one does so accidentally, then the act is not completely good. Aiming to help someone is good – but if one fails, then again the act is not completely good. And aiming to help, messing it up, but through sheer good luck, ending up helping after all is still not completely good!

The morally best action will be one that aims to help, succeeds, and succeeds *as a result* of acting in the way a virtuous person would act. Call this an 'act of virtue'. People with the relevant virtue, e.g. kindness, will be disposed to help and will reliably succeed, so they will reliably perform acts of kindness. However, Zagzebski notes that someone could perform such an action without having the *virtue* of kindness (the disposition to help reliably on many occasions) as long as they act in the way a virtuous person would act on *this* occasion.

See also THE ROLE OF EDUCATION IN THE DEVELOPMENT OF A MORAL CHARACTER, p. 285.

Similarly, someone may form a belief on the basis of an *act* of intellectual virtue, e.g. by being open-minded on this occasion, without being open-minded generally. As long as, on this occasion, the person is motivated to find the truth (as a virtuous person would be) and does what a virtuous person would typically do (e.g. carefully considering a view that conflicts with their own), and the person succeeds in forming a true belief as a result, then the person performs an act of intellectual virtue.

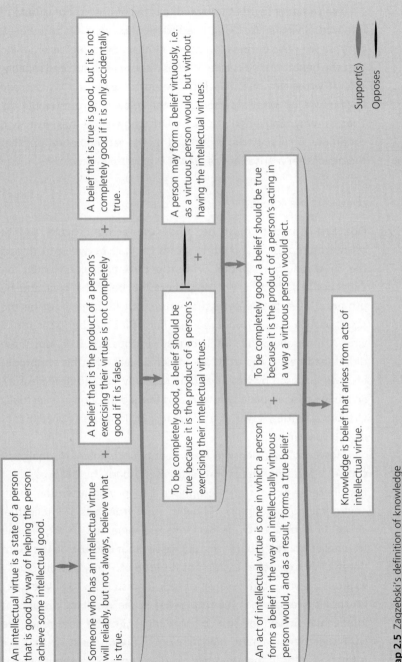

An intellectual virtue is a state of a person that is good by way of helping the person achieve some intellectual good.

Someone who has an intellectual virtue will reliably, but not always, believe what is true.

A belief that is the product of a person's exercising their virtues is not completely good if it is false.

A belief that is true is good, but it is not completely good if it is only accidentally true.

To be completely good, a belief should be true because it is the product of a person's exercising their intellectual virtues.

A person may form a belief virtuously, i.e. as a virtuous person would, but without having the intellectual virtues.

To be completely good, a belief should be true because it is the product of a person's acting in a way a virtuous person would act.

An act of intellectual virtue is one in which a person forms a belief in the way an intellectually virtuous person would, and as a result, forms a true belief.

Knowledge is belief that arises from acts of intellectual virtue.

Support(s)

Opposes

Map 2.5 Zagzebski's definition of knowledge

We can now say that knowledge is belief arising out of acts of intellectual virtue. We don't need to mention that it is *true* belief, because we have defined 'an act of intellectual virtue' as entailing that the belief formed is true. Virtues dispose us to succeed reliably, acts of virtue are ones in which we do succeed, and we succeed because we do what a person with the relevant virtues would do. That is why Zagzebski's analysis of knowledge has just two conditions: that *p* is true is entailed by the second condition, that the belief that *p* arises out of acts of intellectual virtue.

Explain Zagzebski's epistemic virtue theory of knowledge.

EVALUATING THE ACCOUNT

Our first question must be, does the account avoid Gettier counterexamples? It should: it avoids the gap between truth and the 'third condition' that allows Gettier cases to be constructed. On Zagzebski's definition, not only must the belief be true and be produced by acts of intellectual virtue, but its truth must be *the result* of such acts. Dr Jones reached her belief that her patient had virus *X* through various intellectually virtuous activities, but these didn't lead her to the truth about her patient (that his symptoms, etc., were caused by virus *Y* and he had only just acquired virus *X*). So while Dr Jones' belief was true and formed through intellectually virtuous activities, it wasn't true *because* Dr Jones performed acts of intellectual virtue.

However, take Henry in Barn County once again. Normally, of course, when Henry sees and recognises a barn, he believes it is a barn because he sees and recognises it by paying attention to his environment. So normally, his belief arises from acts of intellectual virtue. In Barn County, he performs the same acts to acquire the true belief 'there's a barn'. Should we say that because he is in Barn County, his true belief is true not *because* of Henry's intellectually virtuous activities but because of luck (and so it isn't knowledge)? Or should we say that his true belief is the result of his acts of intellectual virtue (and so it is knowledge) since he does reach the truth that there is a barn, even if he doesn't reach the truth that this is the *only* barn in the area? We need to know more about what it is for a belief to be true *because* it arises from acts of intellectual virtue before we can reach a verdict in cases like this. As it stands, the analysis is too vague.

A second issue is this. In WHY JUSTIFIED TRUE BELIEF (p. 38), we noted that knowledge is good – certainly desirable and perhaps also praiseworthy. The tripartite view explains the goodness of knowledge in terms of justification – we should form our beliefs on the basis of reasons and evidence. If we don't, we can be blamed. This also restricts knowledge to adult human beings, it seems. Reliabilism explains the goodness of knowledge in terms of the benefits it confers on us. It is a desirable natural good. This also allows that animals and children have knowledge.

Zagzebski's theory explains the goodness of knowledge in terms of intellectual virtues. Does this restrict knowledge to adult human beings? Or can children and animals perform 'acts of intellectual virtue'? If we define 'virtue' broadly enough, Zagzebski says, acts of intellectual virtue can include not only intellectually demanding actions, such as engaging in complex reasoning, but also relatively automatic, unconscious ones, such as looking or remembering. In these latter cases, the motivation to 'find the truth' doesn't need to be obvious – one simply wants to know what is in one's environment or what happened yesterday. And the relevant virtues, e.g. being attentive, need not demand much – an attentive person need only pay as much attention as needed to reach the truth. So young children, at least, can have knowledge just as soon as they can tell the difference between truth and falsehood and are motivated to find the truth.

A third issue concerns the place of virtue in knowledge. There are two objections here:

1. Suppose someone generally believes whatever they read on the internet. They don't exercise caution or check other sources of evidence. So they don't have some important intellectual virtues. Now suppose that on one occasion, they come across some strange and interesting claim and really want to know if it is true, so they do spend enough time finding other evidence,

and so reach the truth. They have performed an act of intellectual virtue. But this is completely out of character. Do we really want to say that this person has knowledge, given that for lots of relevantly similar claims, they simply can't be bothered to find out what is true? Isn't their true belief still only 'accidentally' true even though it arose from acts of intellectual virtue? Should we grant knowledge only to people who *have* intellectual virtues at least to some significant degree?

2. Why does someone's *motive* make a difference to whether they have knowledge or not? Take animals: they simply acquire true beliefs in a very reliable way. Do their motives really matter? We can extend the case to people as well. As long as one discovers the truth reliably, and on this occasion one's belief is true because of one's ability to discover the truth reliably, what should motives matter? So do we need *virtues*, rather than reliable processes, in the analysis of knowledge?

Is knowledge belief that arises from acts of intellectual virtue?

Key points: responses

- The 'no false lemmas' amendment to the tripartite definition of knowledge adds the fourth condition that you don't infer your belief from anything false. While this deals with Gettier's own examples, there are other counterexamples in which someone arrives at a justified true belief without relying on a false inference, but the resulting belief still isn't knowledge.
- Infallibilism strengthens the justification condition, claiming that to be knowledge, a belief must be certain. We can object that that leads to scepticism, because most beliefs are not certain.
- Infallibilism argues that if I cannot know what is false, then when I know that *p*, I *can't be* mistaken. Justification therefore requires certainty. But this argument is wrong. If I know that *p*, it can't be that I *am* mistaken. But it can happen that I am not mistaken even though I *could* be.
- Reliabilism claims that knowledge is true belief caused by a reliable process. It understands knowledge as a natural good. But there are

Gettier cases, such as Barn County, that are counterexamples to reliabilism.

- Zagzebski argues that any definition of knowledge that merely adds conditions to true belief will always face Gettier cases that exploit the independence of the third condition from truth.
- Zagzebski defines knowledge as belief that arises from an act (or acts) of intellectual virtue. Virtues both motivate us and enable us to succeed in pursuing some good, e.g. truth. An act of intellectual virtue is one in which a person succeeds in achieving true belief as a result of doing what a virtuous person would do.
- We may object that it is unclear when a belief is true 'as a result' of exercising intellectual virtues and whether children and animals can perform acts of intellectual virtue and so have knowledge.

Summary: what is knowledge?

In this section on knowledge, we considered what a definition of knowledge might be before looking at the claim that knowledge is justified true belief, Gettier's objection, and four responses to Gettier. In our discussion and evaluation of these theories, we have looked at the following issues:

1. There are different types of knowledge. Our concern is only with propositional knowledge.
2. How might we define propositional knowledge and how do necessary and sufficient conditions help?
3. Could there be knowledge that is not justified?
4. Could there be knowledge without objective truth, e.g. is truth only ever 'relative'?
5. Is knowledge a form of belief or a different faculty?
6. Does justified true belief amount to knowledge in all cases?
7. Is justified true belief sufficient for knowledge if it hasn't been inferred from anything false?
8. Does knowledge require certainty? Can I know that p if it is possible that I am wrong about p?
9. Is knowledge true belief that is caused by a reliable cognitive process?
10. Is knowledge belief that arises from acts of intellectual virtue?
11. Why is knowledge good? Is it praiseworthy as well as desirable?

II. Perception as a source of knowledge

In the previous section, we discussed what knowledge is. But how do we gain knowledge? If knowledge involves being in 'cognitive contact' with reality, what means of being in contact with reality do we have? The first that probably comes to mind is sense perception, which is our awareness of physical objects through our senses. But there may be other ways we have of gaining knowledge. Perhaps some knowledge is 'innate', already 'built into' our minds in some way. Yet other knowledge we may gain by reasoning. We shall discuss perception in this section, and look at these other two suggestions in REASON AS A SOURCE OF KNOWLEDGE (p. 114).

There may be other sources of knowledge as well, but we won't look beyond perception and reason in this chapter. For instance, we are not asking how we can know what is *inside* our minds. How do you know that you are thinking what you are thinking? How do you know that you are feeling pain when you are? These are interesting questions, but the answers, whatever they are, are not our concern here.

So, the most obvious and immediate answer to the question 'how do we gain knowledge of what is outside our minds?' is 'sense experience'. Sense experiences are those experiences given to us by our senses – sight, hearing, smell, taste and touch, as well as bodily sensations. We can use our senses to perceive the world outside our minds. But *how* does perception by sense experience tell us about the world, and *what* do we learn about the nature of the world using perception? To answer these questions, we will need to think carefully about what sense perception involves.

Philosophers of perception divide into realists and idealists. Realists claim that what we perceive are physical objects, which exist independent of our minds and of our perceptions. Idealists argue that physical objects are not, in fact, independent of our minds. What they are, and so what we perceive, are mental things – ideas of some kind. Because it denies that physical objects exist independent of our minds, idealism is also sometimes called an 'anti-realist' theory of perception.

The question of whether physical objects exist is actually a question in metaphysics, not epistemology. One question in metaphysics is 'what exists?' So the debate between realist and idealist theories of perception deals with both epistemology (how do we know?) and some metaphysics (what exists?).

Knowledge of our own minds is discussed in the Metaphysics of Mind. See EPIPHENOMENALIST DUALISM, p. 200, and THE ASYMMETRY BETWEEN SELF-KNOWLEDGE AND KNOWLEDGE OF OTHER PEOPLE'S MENTAL STATES, p. 259.

What does realism about perception claim?

The study of what exists is called ontology (the study (-*ology*) of what exists or 'being' (*ont*-)).

In this section, we will look at three theories of perception: direct realism, indirect realism, and idealism. There are many other philosophical theories of perception, but we will discuss just these three. By the end of the section, you should be able to demonstrate not just knowledge, but a good understanding, of each of the three theories, and be able to analyse, explain, and evaluate several arguments for and against each one.

A. Direct realism

It is common sense to say that we perceive physical objects, and these exist independently of our minds. 'Physical objects' include tables, books, our own bodies, plants, mountains…. Cosmology and the theory of evolution suggest that physical objects, such as stars and planets, existed for billions of years before minds existed to experience them. And it is part of our idea of physical objects that they continue to exist when we don't perceive them. When I leave my study, all the physical objects – the desk, the chairs, the books and so on – remain just as they are. Physical objects exist objectively in space and time.

> We could also call them 'material' objects. But physics shows that matter and energy are interchangeable. So 'physical objects' is better, because physics is the science that studies what such things are, ultimately, made of.

Direct realism is the natural starting point for thinking about perception. According to direct realism, what we perceive through our senses are just these very things, physical objects, together with their various properties. When I perceive my desk, for example, I perceive its size, shape, colour, smell and texture (I've never experienced its taste, but I could, I suppose!). So, direct realism claims that what we perceive are mind-independent physical objects and their properties. Another way of putting this is to say that the 'immediate object' of perception is the physical object itself. There isn't something else, e.g. a mental image, that we perceive in perceiving physical objects.

> **?**
>
> What is direct realism?

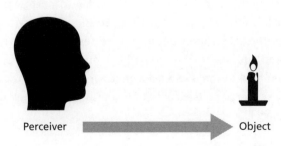

Perceiver ⟶ Object

Figure 2.3 Direct realism

Direct realists explain that we can gain knowledge through perception because perception is a form of 'openness' to the world. What perception gives us is a direct awareness of mind-independent objects. Importantly, our awareness of these objects is sensitive to how the objects are – differences in the properties of the objects we perceive will be detected by differences in our perceptual experience of them.

The argument from perceptual variation

RUSSELL, *THE PROBLEMS OF PHILOSOPHY*, CH. 1

A little reflection suggests that what we perceive isn't quite the same as what is 'out there'. Bertrand Russell gives an example of looking at a shiny, brown table. We say it is brown, but it doesn't actually look an even brown colour all over: depending how the light falls, some parts are lighter than others, and some are even white from the shininess. So Russell objects that saying the table is brown means no more than that it looks brown 'to a normal spectator from an ordinary point of view under usual conditions of light' – but why think that this colour is more real, more a property of the table, than any of the other colours that you experience? Just what colour any part of the table looks to you depends on where you stand. If you and someone else look at the table together, you will see different patterns of colour. Suppose a shiny spot on the table looks light brown to you but white to the other person. The table can't *be* both brown and white in the same spot at one time.

Russell then runs the same argument, appealing to variations in our perceptual experience, for the properties of texture and shape. The table might be smooth to touch, but at a microscopic level, there are all kinds of bumps and dips – so should we say that when we touch the table, the smoothness we feel is a property of the table? And the shape that something appears to have, like its colour, varies with the angle from which you view it. A rectangular table, from every angle except 90 degrees, does not look perfectly rectangular.

Locke makes a similar point, and explains why we don't normally notice this, in *An Essay Concerning Human Understanding*, Bk 2, Ch. 9, §§8, 9.

Figure 2.4 Is the table the same colour all over?

These examples draw our attention to a distinction between appearance and reality. Obviously, much of the time, we talk as though things are just as they seem. But, clearly, we also distinguish between appearance and reality – and Russell remarks that having any skill as a painter requires that one does.

All this perceptual variation causes a real problem for the direct realist. The direct realist says I perceive physical objects and their properties, in this case the table, 'directly', as they are. The argument from perceptual variation runs like this:

P1. There are variations in perception.
P2. Our perception varies without corresponding changes in the physical object we perceive. (For instance, the table remains rectangular, even as the way it looks to me changes as I look at it from different angles.)
C1. Therefore, the properties physical objects have and the properties they appear to have are not identical.
C2. Therefore, what we are immediately aware of in perception is not exactly the same as what exists independently of our minds.
C3. Therefore, we do not perceive physical objects directly.

We now need a name for talking about what we are immediately aware of in perception, e.g. the colour and shape of the table as I see it now. Russell calls these 'sense-data' (singular: 'sense-datum').

1) Give your own example that supports the view that what we 'see' is not what is 'out there'. 2) Present the argument from perceptual variation as an argument map.

For further discussion, see WHAT ARE SENSE-DATA?, p. 79.

Explain the argument from perceptual variation as an objection to direct realism.

When I look at the table, I have a (visual) sensation – I am immediately aware of something. The 'content' of my sensation – what I am immediately aware of – is sense-data (on Russell's view). We can also think of sense-data as appearances (how things appear to us to be).

Sense-data are distinct from the table. The table exists independently of my perception of it, while sense-data are defined as what it is that I perceive – so they depend on my perception. If I close my eyes, the colour and shape of the table as seen by me, cease to exist. And the colour and shape of the table as seen by me varies from where I look at it, while we don't want to say that the table itself varies in this way. We can summarise the argument so far by saying that perceptual variation shows that what we directly perceive are not physical objects, but sense-data.

RESPONSES

For further discussion, see LOCKE'S DISTINCTION BETWEEN PRIMARY AND SECONDARY QUALITIES, p. 80.

We can challenge Russell's claim that there is no good reason to say that one of the colours we experience the table as having is more real than the others. As he notes, what we *mean* by the colour of an object is the colour that it appears to have when seen by normal observers under normal conditions. That we don't *always* see this colour – that our perception of its colour varies – doesn't show that direct realism is false: we can still say that we see the table, and its colour, under normal conditions. After all, we do all see it as some shade of *brown* (shading to white), rather than some of us seeing it as brown, others as red, others as blue. So, in seeing its colour (as some variant of brown), we see the table and its properties.

With shape, we have an even better reason to privilege the claim that the table is rectangular, rather than obtuse – we can use its shape to perform various actions, like getting it through a narrow doorway, which will only succeed if it *is* rectangular and not obtuse.

But the argument from perceptual variation does show that direct realism needs a more sophisticated account of what it is to see the table and its properties. To develop this, we need to introduce the idea of a 'relational property'. A relational property is a property that something has only in relation to something else (and, in some cases, only in some circumstances). For example, 'being to the north of' is a relational property; Manchester is to the north of London. Another example is 'being in love with'; Jack is in love with Joan. Notice that in these examples, it is Manchester and Jack that have the properties; but we can only say what properties these are by mentioning other things – London and Joan.

What is a relational property?

In perception, we can be aware of a range of properties, some of which the object has independent of our minds, and some of which it has in relation to being perceived. For instance, a rectangular table has the property of 'looking obtuse'. The property of 'looking obtuse' is a distinct property from 'being obtuse' – so a table can *be* rectangular and *look* obtuse. The property of 'looking obtuse' is a relational property, in this case, a property the table has in relation to being *seen*. 'Looking obtuse' is a property *the table* has, claims direct realism, not the property of a sense-datum. And we can even explain why the table has the property of looking obtuse (to us) in terms of its being rectangular plus facts about light and vision.

Direct realism can claim that in perceiving physical objects, some of the properties we perceive are relational properties while others are not. It doesn't have to claim that *all* the properties of physical objects, as we perceive them, are mind-independent as long as there is a clear sense in which we are directly aware of physical objects themselves. This response challenges the inference from (C2) to (C3) on p. 69.

The argument from illusion

Figure 2.5 A pencil in water

We have seen that the appearance/reality distinction challenges direct realism. We can appeal to illusions to press the case. If you look at a pencil half-submerged in water, it looks crooked; but it isn't. We see a crooked pencil, but the pencil isn't crooked. However, *just* from what you experience, you can't tell whether you are seeing an illusion or not. Someone who doesn't know about the illusion thinks they are seeing a crooked pencil. It *looks* just like a crooked pencil. The point applies generally to illusions. From *just* what we see in an illusion, without other background knowledge, we cannot tell whether what we are seeing is an illusion or not. Illusions can be 'subjectively indistinguishable' from veridical perception. This provides an argument against direct realism.

An experience is veridical if it represents the world as it actually is.

P1. We perceive something having some property *F* (e.g. a pencil that is crooked).
P2. When we perceive something as having some property *F*, then there is something that is *F*. (*Something* we see is *F*.)
P3. In an illusion, the physical object does not have the property *F* (the pencil is not crooked).
C1. Therefore, in illusions, what has the property *F* is something mental, a sense-datum.
C2. Therefore, in illusions, we see sense-data, and not physical objects, immediately.
P4. Illusions can be 'subjectively indistinguishable' from veridical perception.
C3. Therefore, we see the same thing, namely sense-data, in both illusions and veridical perception.
C4. Therefore, in all cases, we see sense-data, and not physical objects, immediately.
C5. Therefore, direct realism is false.

Explain the argument from illusion.

Explain direct realism's response to the arguments from perceptual variation and illusion.

Direct realism can give the same reply as before. When the pencil in water looks crooked, there is nothing that *is* crooked; (P2) is wrong. Instead, the pencil has the property of *looking crooked* when half-submerged in water. There is a difference between the property 'being crooked' and the (relational) property 'looking crooked'. Usually, of course, something looks crooked when it is crooked. But the two properties can come apart, and something can look crooked when it is straight. So, in illusions, we perceive the 'looks' properties of physical objects, and these 'looks' properties don't match the 'is' properties of the object. But we still directly perceive physical objects and their properties.

Thinking harder: the argument from hallucination

We have seen that direct realism can explain the difference between how things are and how they appear to us, in cases of perceptual variation and illusion, by appealing to the 'looks' properties of physical objects. But how can direct realism respond to the challenge of hallucinations? We can experience perceptual hallucinations – not just visual ones, but auditory and olfactory hallucinations as well. As with illusions, hallucinations can be subjectively indistinguishable from veridical perception. But here we can't say that what is seen is how some physical object looks, because no physical object is seen at all! So direct realism's reply to the previous arguments won't work here.

P1. In a hallucination, we perceive something having some property *F*.
P2. When we perceive something as having some property *F*, then there is something that is *F*.
P3. In a hallucination, we don't perceive a physical object at all.
C1. Therefore, what we perceive must be mental – sense-data.
P4. Hallucinations can be experiences that are 'subjectively indistinguishable' from veridical perceptions.
C2. Therefore, we see the same thing, namely sense-data, in both hallucinations and veridical perception.
C3. Therefore, in all cases, we see sense-data, and not physical objects, immediately.
C4. Therefore, direct realism is false.

Outline the argument from hallucination.

The disjunctive theory of perception

There is another way that direct realism can challenge (P2). If something looks a certain way, then one of *two quite different things* is going on: *either* I directly perceive a mind-independent physical object that is *F* or (as in the case of hallucination) it appears to me just *as if* there is something that is *F*, but there is nothing that *is F*. According to the disjunctive theory of perception, hallucinations and veridical perception are two completely different kinds of mental state, because in hallucination, the person isn't

An either/or claim is called a disjunction.

connected up to the world. They can *seem* exactly the same, but that doesn't prove that they *are* the same. The fact that hallucinations are subjectively indistinguishable from veridical perception tells us nothing significant about what *perception* is. In hallucination, we don't *perceive* anything, we *imagine* it. To imagine something is not to perceive something mental, such as sense-data, but not to perceive anything at all. Perception is a relation of the subject to the world, a form of 'cognitive contact'. Hallucination is not.

We can use this to challenge (C2). And so the argument from hallucination doesn't show that in veridical perception, we perceive sense-data instead of physical objects.

Explain the disjunctive theory of perception.

The time-lag argument

It takes time for light waves, or sound waves, or smells, to get from physical objects to our sense organs. For example, it takes 8 minutes for light from the sun to reach the Earth. If you looked at the sun (not a good idea!), you would actually be seeing it as it was 8 minutes ago. If it blew up, you would see it normally for 8 minutes after it had blown up – it wouldn't even exist anymore, and you'd still see it! Therefore, we could argue, you aren't seeing it directly.

However, it would be a mistake to think that this shows that what you perceive is a sense-datum of the sun. The 'image' you see is not mental but *physical*, carried in light waves. The light waves exist during those 8 minutes. So *if* you see the sun indirectly, then it is because you see light waves directly. But then what we perceive immediately is not the sun, but the light from the sun. We can generalise: what we perceive is the physical medium by which we detect physical objects (light waves, sound waves, chemicals for smell and taste). So, we don't perceive (ordinary) physical objects directly.

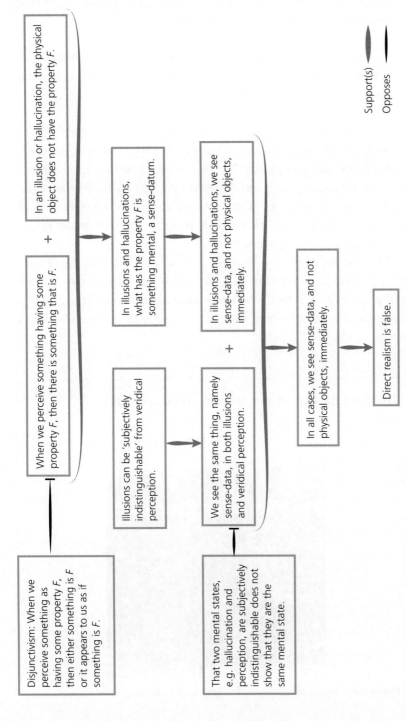

Disjunctivism: When we perceive something as having some property F, then either something is F or it appears to us as if something is F.

When we perceive something having some property, F, then there is something that is F.

+

In an illusion or hallucination, the physical object does not have the property F.

In illusions and hallucinations, what has the property F is something mental, a sense-datum.

Illusions can be 'subjectively indistinguishable' from veridical perception.

We see the same thing, namely sense-data, in both illusions and veridical perception.

That two mental states, e.g. hallucination and perception, are subjectively indistinguishable does not show that they are the same mental state.

In illusions and hallucinations, we see sense-data, and not physical objects, immediately.

+

In all cases, we see sense-data, and not physical objects, immediately.

Direct realism is false.

Support(s)

Opposes

Map 2.6 The arguments from illusion and hallucination combined, with the direct realist's objections

Direct realism can reply that this is a confusion between *how* we perceive and *what* we perceive. Compare these two pairs of questions:

1. 'Can you see the lake?' and 'Can you see the light reflecting off the lake?'
2. 'Can you see the paper?' and 'Can you see the light reflecting from the paper?'

In (1), we can turn our attention from the lake to the light reflecting off it. So we can talk, literally, about seeing the light. But in (2) there is no difference in *what* one is supposed to see. To 'see' the light that the paper reflects is just to see the paper. In fact, you cannot *see* the light itself – only the paper. So, direct realism can argue, except in special conditions, we don't perceive light waves directly and physical objects indirectly. Light waves are part of the story of how we see physical objects.

The time lag involved in how we perceive means we see the physical object as it was a moment before, not as it is now. This means that we literally see (into) the past. We always experience the world as it was a moment ago, or in astronomy, when we look at distant stars and galaxies, we look into the distant past.

Explain the time-lag argument. Does it succeed as an objection to direct realism?

Thinking harder: direct realism and openness

Figure 2.6 Can you describe this scene without referring to physical objects?

We said that direct realism understands perception as 'openness' to the world (p. 68), a direct awareness of mind-independent objects. We can get a fuller sense of this by trying to describe what we see. We would usually do so by referring to physical objects: 'I see a desk, covered with pens and paper, and a plant.' If we perceive the world via sense-data, the immediate 'content' of what we perceive is mental. So try to describe your experience in terms of sense-data, without referring to any physical objects. You could talk about 'coloured patches' standing in spatial relations (above, below, left, right, etc.) to each other. But this is very awkward, and it is virtually impossible for any normal scene. What shape is that green patch on the left? – well, 'plant-shaped'! But 'plant' refers to a physical object. So our way of describing sense-data is dependent on concepts of physical objects. We can't give an account of what we experience without referring to physical objects, even if we try.

What this shows is that our perceptual experience presents what we perceive *as* mind-independent objects. That doesn't *prove* that we perceive mind-independent objects, but it does make such a claim highly intuitive. Only direct realism holds onto this basic intuition of 'openness'. It is very counter-intuitive to think, then, that what we perceive are sense-data. Any theory that claims that we perceive sense-data has to say that perception is not what it seems to be. It has to say that it *seems* that we immediately perceive mind-independent objects, but we don't. We need very strong reasons to accept that perception is misleading in this way.

Do we perceive physical objects directly?

Key points: direct realism

- Direct realism claims that physical objects exist independently of our minds and of our perceptions of them.
- Direct realism claims that perception is a form of 'openness' to the world, giving us direct awareness of physical objects that is sensitive to their properties.
- The argument from perceptual variation notes that different people may perceive the same physical object differently. Therefore, what each person perceives is how the object appears to them. This appearance is mind-dependent sense-data. Physical objects are therefore not perceived directly.

- The arguments from illusion and hallucination claim that in illusions and hallucinations, we see something, but we do not see the physical world as it is. What we see are sense-data. The arguments depend on the assumption that when we have a perception of something having some quality *F*, then there must be something that is *F*.
- Direct realism rejects this assumption. To the arguments from perceptual variation and illusion, direct realism can reply that the physical object has the relational property of *looking* a certain way. What you perceive is how the physical object looks.
- Disjunctivists argue that hallucinations are a completely different type of mental state to perception. So we cannot generalise from cases of hallucination to claim that in perception, we see sense-data.
- The time-lag argument points out that what you see is not how the physical world is, because light and sound take time to travel from the physical object to your senses.
- Direct realists reply that this only shows that, when we reflect on *how* we perceive physical objects, we should conclude that we perceive them in the past.
- Direct realists note that when we describe what we perceive, we use physical object concepts. This shows that perception presents us with (what seem to be) mind-independent objects. To deny this is therefore very counter-intuitive.

B. Indirect realism

Figure 2.7 Indirect realism

Indirect realism claims that we perceive physical objects which are mind-independent, but we do so via, or in virtue of, perceiving mind-dependent sense-data that are caused by and represent physical objects. We perceive sense-data immediately, and physical objects indirectly, mediated by our perception of sense-data.

What are sense-data?

When we first introduced the term 'sense-data' (p. 69), we used Russell's definition of them as the 'content' of my perceptual experience. The arguments from PERCEPTUAL VARIATION (p. 68), ILLUSION (p. 71) and HALLUCINATION (p.73) show that, whatever sense-data are, they cannot be physical objects. Sense-data (if they exist at all) exist as part of the mind.

Assuming realism about physical objects, we can draw the following contrasts:

1. Sense-data are mental things which are the way we perceive them to be. They are appearances, and so are exactly as they seem. There is no further reality to an appearance than how it appears. By contrast, physical objects can appear differently from how they really are.
2. Sense-data only exist while they are being experienced. An experience must be experienced by someone to exist at all. Physical objects can exist when no one experiences them.
3. Sense-data are 'private'. No one else can experience *your* sense-data. They are the particular sense-data they are, by definition, as part of your consciousness. Physical objects are 'public'. One and the same object can be experienced by different people.

> When Russell was writing, in the early twentieth century, some philosophers thought that sense-data were mind-independent. But this understanding quickly gave way to other theories that treated sense-data as mind-dependent, and this is how we shall understand them.

> What are sense-data?

Why indirect realism?

Arguments in favour of indirect realism often begin as objections to direct realism, discussed above. We can combine these to form the following general argument supporting indirect realism:

P1. There are many perceptual experiences in which what we experience are not the properties of physical objects.

P2. When we perceive something as having some property *F*, then there is something that is *F*.

C1. In such cases, given that what we perceive is not the way the world is, what we perceive are sense-data.

P3. Such cases are subjectively indistinguishable from veridical perception.

See HYPOTHETICAL
REASONING, p. 9.

P4. When two perceptual experiences are subjectively indistinguishable, they are perceptual experiences of the same thing. (This claim is the best hypothesis, given (P3).)

C2. Therefore, we *always* perceive sense-data (not just in cases in which what we perceive is not the way the world is).

P5. Nevertheless, except in hallucinations, it still makes sense to say we perceive *the world*. In cases of both veridical perception and illusion, the sense-data we perceive are caused by and represent physical objects. This representation can be accurate or inaccurate in certain ways – physical objects may be as they appear to us, or they may differ in certain ways.

C3. Therefore, we perceive physical objects indirectly, via sense-data.

Indirect realists, of course, are unpersuaded by the replies given by direct realists to the arguments from perceptual variation, illusion and hallucination. (P4) records this: direct realism does not satisfactorily explain what two subjectively indistinguishable perceptual experiences have in common. A better explanation is to accept that we perceive sense-data in all cases. (P5) states the commitment to realism, and introduces two new ideas about the relation between sense-data and physical objects, namely that sense-data are caused by physical objects and that they represent them. We shall look at each of these claims in turn, asking whether indirect realism can defend them, in SCEPTICISM ABOUT THE EXISTENCE OF MIND-INDEPENDENT OBJECTS (p. 83) and REPRESENTATION, RESEMBLANCE AND THE NATURE OF PHYSICAL OBJECTS (p. 90). Before that, we develop indirect realism further by looking at an important distinction in the qualities that we perceive physical objects to have.

Explain the argument from non-veridical perception to indirect realism, first in prose, then as an argument map.

Locke's distinction between primary and secondary qualities

John Locke defended a form of indirect realism. As part of his theory, he argued that we can distinguish the qualities that we perceive – such things as shape, size, colour, warmth and so on – into two kinds. He uses the distinction to provide an additional argument for rejecting direct realism in favour of indirect realism.

While the distinction between 'primary' and 'secondary' qualities is most famously associated with Locke, many other philosophers and scientists working at the same time (the seventeenth century) also made the distinction in some form.

See DESCARTES' PROOF OF THE EXTERNAL WORLD (p. 174) for another account of the distinction.

LOCKE, *AN ESSAY CONCERNING HUMAN UNDERSTANDING*, BK 2, CH. 8

Locke's argument begins in Bk 2, Ch. 8, §8. A 'quality' is a 'power' that a physical object has 'to produce an idea in our mind'. So a snowball has the powers – the qualities – to produce in us the ideas of 'white', 'cold' and 'round'.

Locke then argues that qualities are of two different kinds. Primary qualities are qualities that are 'utterly inseparable' from the object whatever changes it goes through, e.g. even if it is divided into smaller and smaller pieces. The object has these properties 'in and of itself'. The primary qualities are extension (Locke also talks of size), shape, motion, number and solidity. Secondary qualities are qualities that physical objects have that are 'nothing but powers to produce various sensations in us'. Locke lists 'colours, sounds, tastes, and so on', later adding smells and temperature.

The important phrase here is 'nothing but'. Primary qualities, of course, also produce sensations in us – both the roundness (primary quality) and the whiteness (secondary quality) of the snowball cause sensations in us. But shape is a quality that the snowball has irrespective of whether we perceive it or not. Colour, by contrast, has to be understood in terms of how the snowball affects us. By definition, colour is something that is experienced in vision. So it is a quality that an object can have only in relation to its being seen by someone. And similarly for sound, taste and the other secondary qualities. By contrast, primary qualities are those properties of an object that are not related by definition to perceivers.

The distinction between primary and secondary qualities is a distinction between qualities that physical objects have 'in themselves', and qualities they have that are related to how they are perceived.

Explain and illustrate the difference between primary and secondary qualities.

Locke on primary qualities

Why does Locke pick out extension, shape, motion, number and solidity as primary qualities? He says that these qualities cannot be separated from a physical object. For example, physical objects must always have some size and shape, they must always be at rest or in motion of some kind, they can be counted. By contrast, physical objects don't have to have the secondary qualities of colour or smell, e.g. odourless, clear glass.

Is Locke's list right? He believed that when you break up physical objects, you get smaller objects which also have all the primary qualities. But physics has moved on, and subatomic particles aren't like physical objects that we know in lots of ways. Many of them have some form of electrical charge and many of them can behave as much like packets of energy as like small bits of matter. We may want to change Locke's definition of primary qualities to those qualities that *physics* tells us physical objects have 'in and of themselves'.

In Bk 2, Ch. 4, Locke explains what he means by 'solidity'. He does *not* mean to contrast being 'solid' with being liquid or gas. Rather, solidity is the quality of a physical object whereby it takes up space and excludes other physical objects from occupying exactly the same space. This is just as true of liquids and gases; if I fill an empty glass with water, the liquid drives the air out. If I add air to a balloon, the balloon inflates, pushing air outside the balloon away from the space now filled by the balloon (and the air inside it). Just as anything physical has to have some size and shape, thinks Locke, it must also take up space.

Explain why, for Locke, solidity is a primary quality.

Qualities and resemblance

In Bk 2, Ch. 8, §15, Locke argues that our perceptual experiences of primary qualities 'resemble' the primary qualities of the object. Physical objects have shape, extension and so on just as we perceive them. By contrast, our perceptual experiences of secondary qualities don't resemble the object as it is in itself at all. Secondary qualities are the result of the primary qualities of the object's 'imperceptible parts' (§15) – or as we would now put it, its atomic and molecular structure. Light, by which we perceive colour, can be explained in terms of the effects and activity of subatomic particles, smell in terms of chemical compounds, and so on. Physics and chemistry deal only with primary qualities – the size, shape, motion and so on of tiny bits of matter. So secondary qualities as we perceive them are nothing like what they are in the object, namely macroscopic effects of the primary properties of atoms and molecules.

Locke uses the distinction to argue for indirect realism. The world as we experience it through our senses and the world as it is 'in itself', as science describes it, are quite different. We experience all the wonderful secondary properties of the senses; the world as described by science is 'particles in motion' and empty space. It must be, then, that we don't perceive physical objects directly.

Explain and illustrate what Locke means by 'resemblance'.

We discuss secondary qualities and the argument for indirect realism further in extension material.

Scepticism about the existence of mind-independent objects

RUSSELL, *THE PROBLEMS OF PHILOSOPHY*, CH. 2

Russell ends his argument in favour of sense-data in Ch. 1 with a puzzle. If what we perceive directly are sense-data, then all we *know* about are sense-data. We believe that 'behind' the sense-data there are real physical objects, that physical objects cause our sense-data. But how can we know this? To know that physical objects cause sense-data, we first have to know that physical objects *exist*. But the only access we have to physical objects is through our sense-data.

Although Russell doesn't comment on this, his line of thought forms an objection to indirect realism. Because we directly perceive sense-data, we cannot know that a world of physical objects – a world external to and independent of our minds – exists. Scepticism is the view that we cannot know a particular claim, in this case the claim that physical objects exist. Indirect realism leads to scepticism about the existence of mind-independent objects. And if we can't know that physical objects exist, we can't know that sense data are

On scepticism, see THE PARTICULAR NATURE OF PHILOSOPHICAL SCEPTICISM, p. 185.

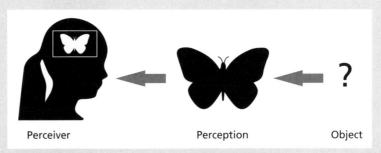

Perceiver   Perception   Object

Figure 2.8 Scepticism about mind-independent objects

Outline the argument that indirect realism leads to scepticism about the existence of mind-independent objects.

caused by physical objects. But this is a claim that indirect realism itself makes! So if indirect realism is true, we can't know that it is true.

The existence of the external world is the best hypothesis

Russell offers two responses, both appealing to how we should *explain* what we do know. The first is this:

P1. The fact that sense-data are private means that no two people actually ever perceive the same thing, unless we can say that there are physical objects that they both perceive (indirectly).
P2. People have very similar sense-data if they are at the same place and time.
P3. The best explanation of this is that there are physical objects causing their sense-data: they both perceive the same physical object.
C1. So physical objects exist.

Russell rejects this argument because it assumes something that we can't know: that there are other people, that they have sense-data, and that their sense-data are similar to mine. To assume that there are other people is to assume that there are physical objects, since people are physical objects. But the question was how, from my sense-data, do I know that there are physical objects? In answering that question, I can't *assume* that there are physical objects (such as other people) – that's begging the question!

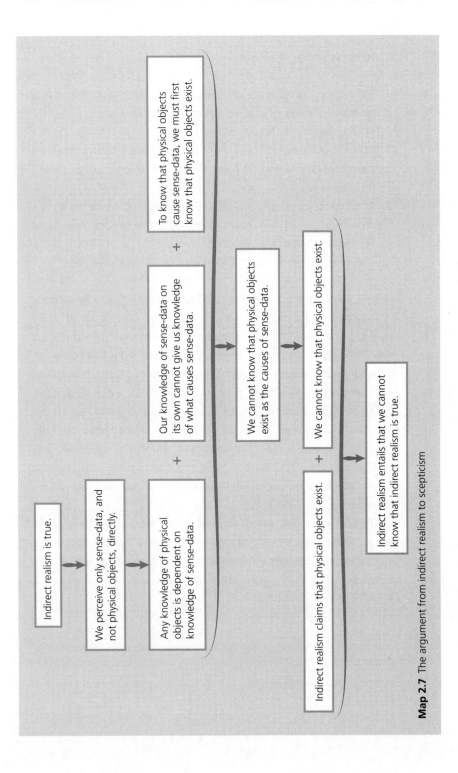

Map 2.7 The argument from indirect realism to scepticism

On this type of argument, see HYPOTHETICAL REASONING, p. 9. For a deductive argument for the existence of physical objects, see DESCARTES' PROOF OF THE EXTERNAL WORLD, p. 174.

Explain the argument that the best explanation of sense-data is that sense-data are caused by mind-independent physical objects.

This issue is discussed further in the Metaphysics of Mind, THE PROBLEM OF OTHER MINDS I, p. 199.

So Russell offers a second argument.

P1. Either physical objects exist and cause my sense-data or physical objects do not exist and do not cause my sense-data.
P2. I can't *prove* either claim is true or false.
C1. Therefore, I have to treat them as hypotheses. (A hypothesis is a proposal that needs to be confirmed or rejected by reasoning or experience.)
P3. The hypothesis that physical objects exist and cause my sense-data is better. (This is essentially (P5) in the general argument for indirect realism (p. 79–80).)
C2. Therefore, physical objects exist and cause my sense-data.

What is Russell's argument for (P3)? One way to test a hypothesis is to see whether it explains why my experience is the way it is. If I see a cat first in a corner of the room and then later on the sofa, then if the cat is a physical object, it travelled from the corner to the sofa when I wasn't looking. If there is no cat apart from what I see in my sense-data, then the cat does not exist when I don't see it. It springs into existence first in the corner, and then later on the sofa. Nothing connects my two perceptions. But that's incredibly puzzling – indeed, it is *no explanation at all* of why my sense-data are the way they are! So the hypothesis that there is a physical object, the cat, that causes what I see is the best explanation of my sense-data.

(Russell runs the same argument for supposing that other people have minds. When I perceive how people behave, e.g. when talking to me, the best explanation of my experience is that it is caused by what they say (a physical event) and what they say is caused by their thoughts.)

TWO SUPPORTING ARGUMENTS

LOCKE, *AN ESSAY CONCERNING HUMAN UNDERSTANDING*, BK 4, CH. 11; TROTTER COCKBURN (ATTRIBUTED), 'A LETTER FROM AN ANONYMOUS WRITER TO THE AUTHOR OF THE MINUTE PHILOSOPHER'

The syllabus mentions two further responses to scepticism about the existence of mind-independent objects from Locke and in a letter written to George Berkeley attributed to Catherine Trotter Cockburn.

Trotter Cockburn was objecting to BERKELEY'S IDEALISM (p. 96), the third theory of perception we will discuss.

Locke's argument from the involuntary nature of our experience

Locke notes that in perception, I cannot avoid having certain sense-data 'produced' in my mind. By contrast, if I turn from perception to memory or imagination, e.g. by shutting my eyes, I find that I can choose what I experience. Perceptual experiences – which 'I have whether I want them or not – must be produced in my mind by some exterior cause' (§5), namely physical objects.

The argument from the coherence of the various kinds of experience

Locke and Trotter Cockburn both present arguments from comparing perceptual experiences from different senses. Locke notes that our different senses 'confirm' the information that each supplies. If I see a fire and doubt whether it is real, I can confirm its reality by touching it (§7). Trotter Cockburn notes that one and the same object causes perceptual experiences through different senses. The experiences themselves are very different, e.g. seeing an object and hearing the sound it makes. But we learn which visual experiences go with which auditory experiences, e.g. seeing a dog and hearing a dog's bark. With the association made, we can accurately infer from one experience to the other; just from seeing a dog, we know what sound it will make. And if we experience a change in vision, e.g. a train moving from near to far, we can infer the change in sound, e.g. its horn becoming quieter. Why would we be able either to confirm our experiences using a different sense, or be able to predict them, unless there is something which both senses perceive but that is independent of being perceived by any particular sense?

An example

Locke brings the two responses together in an extended example. I know from experience that I can change how a piece of paper looks by writing on it. (This connects sight and proprioception – my sense of my hand moving.) I can plan what to write, and I know in advance what the paper will look like. But I cannot bring about the sense-data of seeing the paper with words on it just by imagination; I have to actually write. And once I have written something, I can't change the words I see. This shows that sense-data aren't 'merely playthings of my imagination'. Finally, if someone else reads those words aloud, what I hear corresponds to what I intended to write. And this 'leaves little reason for doubt' that the words as written on the paper exist independent of my mind.

Outline two reasons why we should think that physical objects exist.

Discussion

Locke claims to have *shown* that mind-independent objects exist, that there 'must' be some external cause of sense-data. But this is overstating the case, and Trotter Cockburn is more accurate in talking of inferring such a cause. Both are presenting the same argument as Russell, strengthening it by adding further features of our experience that need explaining. If physical objects don't exist, we can't explain

1. why sense-data aren't under our control but imagination and memory are;
2. why we should get the same information from different senses;
3. why we can infer from perceptual experiences of one sense, e.g. vision, what perceptual experiences we would have in another sense, e.g. audition;
4. the very complex interaction between our actions and our perceptions.

So we have very good reason to claim that physical objects exist and cause our sense data.

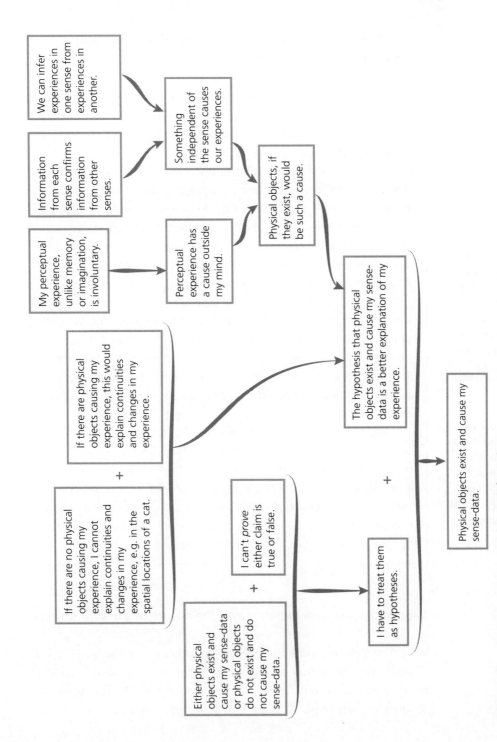

Map 2.8 Physical objects as the best explanation of experience

Thinking harder: the existence of mind-independent objects is not a hypothesis

If indirect realism is correct, then it seems the existence of physical objects remains a *hypothesis*, something we have to *infer*. Direct realism can argue that this is a significant weakness. First, perhaps some other hypothesis that explains our sense-data is just as good, but we just don't know it. (Berkeley develops this point to argue for idealism in IDEALISM AND GOD, p. 104.) Second, it is very counter-intuitive to think that perception doesn't put us in direct touch with physical objects. If we have to infer the existence of physical objects, then we aren't 'open' (p. 76) to the world in perception.

Indirect realism can respond to these objections by rejecting the theories of Russell, Locke and Trotter Cockburn. They write as if sense-data 'come between' us and the world, with physical objects merely being the cause of sense-data, so that in perceiving sense-data, we *aren't* also perceiving physical objects. But instead, we should say that we perceive physical objects via sense-data. Sense-data don't get in the way of perceiving physical objects. They are *how* we perceive physical objects. They don't block our access to the external world, they mediate it. The existence of the external world is *not a hypothesis*. It is something that we experience in perception.

But what of the fact that sense-data differ from the physical objects they represent, e.g. in perceptual variation and illusions? Doesn't this show that sense-data come between us and the world? No, this is all explicable in terms of physical objects and their effects on us, and *only* in these terms. The best explanation of illusions and perceptual variation needs *both* sense-data and physical objects. We can develop this thought by appealing to how sense-data represent physical objects (next).

> Compare: we describe the world using words. But words don't get in the way of describing the world. We couldn't describe the world without them!

> If indirect realism is true, can we know that there are mind-independent physical objects that cause our sense-data?

Representation, resemblance and the nature of physical objects

Indirect realism maintains that sense-data are not only caused by mind-independent objects, they also *represent* them. One way of understanding this is to say that mind-independent physical objects are like our experiences of them in many respects. Locke says that physical objects 'resemble' our sense-data (p. 82). For example, physical objects have shape and size, and so resemble my experience of their shape and size. At the very least, we can say that there are *systematic correlations* between what we experience and the nature of the world. My experience of the shape and size of an object is (at the very least) systematically correlated with what shape and how large the physical object is. Perception is the source of our knowledge of not only the existence of mind-independent objects, but also something of their nature.

This then raises the question, what are physical objects really like? Of all the properties I experience physical objects having, which ones do they have? How should we draw the distinction between the appearance of physical objects and their reality? Locke answers this question by talking about the primary and secondary qualities of physical objects. Secondary qualities as we experience them are nothing like how physical objects are in themselves. However, our experience shows us that physical objects 'in themselves' have primary qualities which we then experience.

> LOCKE'S DISTINCTION BETWEEN PRIMARY AND SECONDARY QUALITIES, p. 80.

But how do we know that physical objects have primary qualities that resemble our experience of them? One difficulty is that, in general, we can't tell what a cause is like just from its effects. Consider: if all you knew was smoke, would you be able to work out that its cause was fire? Fire is very different from smoke. Experience shows that the world is full of surprising causal relationships. So, if all we experience are sense-data, how can we know whether the world is similar to how it appears to us in sense-data, say in having the primary qualities we experience, or whether it is very different? Can we rule out the claim that physical objects cause our experiences of primary and secondary qualities, but don't resemble these experiences at all?

> Explain the difference between scepticism about the existence of mind-independent objects and scepticism about the nature of such objects.

BERKELEY'S ARGUMENT THAT MIND-DEPENDENT IDEAS CANNOT BE LIKE MIND-INDEPENDENT OBJECTS

Locke claims that primary qualities in the object resemble our experience of them. For example, the squareness of a physical object resembles the squareness we see. Berkeley questioned whether this makes sense.

BERKELEY, *THREE DIALOGUES BETWEEN HYLAS AND PHILONOUS*, FIRST DIALOGUE, P. 25

As THE ARGUMENT FROM PERCEPTUAL VARIATION (p. 68) notes, our sense-data change depending on the conditions of perception but the physical object does not. This applies just as much to primary qualities as secondary qualities. For instance, a rectangular table remains rectangular, even as the way it looks to me changes as I look at it from different angles. This is true of the size and shape of almost all the physical objects we commonly perceive. Furthermore, we constantly flit our eyes from one thing to another, so what we experience at any moment changes. Again, we don't take these changes in our sense-data to be the result of changes in the physical objects we are looking at.

This forms the basis of an objection: how can our sense-data, which are 'perpetually fleeting and variable', be 'like' or 'resemble' a physical object that is 'fixed and constant'? For instance, how can circular sense-data and oval sense-data both resemble something that has just one shape? If you want to say that one of these appearances resembles the object, while all the others do not, then how do we distinguish which is the 'true copy' – the true size or shape?

Figure 2.9 A plate viewed from above and from an angle

Second, physical objects are themselves not something we experience (directly) – we only experience the sense-data that they cause. But how can something that we don't experience (a mind-independent physical object) be like something that is experienced (mind-dependent sense-data)? What can we mean when we say that the shape of the table 'resembles' the shape we see? How can squareness (as it is in the object) resemble the idea of squareness? Our ideas of size, shape, motion and so on derive from our perceptual experience. The *only* idea of shape we have is the one we see (or feel). We can only make sense of the table's squareness in terms of our experience of squareness. There is nothing like a perceptual experience except another perceptual experience. So we can't meaningfully say that our sense-data are like or resemble physical objects. But in that case, Berkeley concludes, if indirect realism is true, then we can't know the nature of mind-independent objects.

Explain Berkeley's two arguments that indirect realism leads to scepticism about the nature of physical objects.

Discussion

Indirect realists have generally agreed that Locke's idea of 'resemblance' between sense-data and physical objects is problematic. But, they say, we can still argue that sense-data *represent* physical objects (just not by resembling them). The pattern of causal relations between the external world and our sense-data is very *detailed* and *systematic*. We can explain how sense-data represent physical objects in terms of this complex causation.

But does this answer the objection? Because causes and effects can be very different, if we understand representation just in terms of detailed and systematic causal relation, it seems that we still won't know what mind-independent objects are like in themselves.

Can indirect realism avoid scepticism about the nature of mind-independent objects?

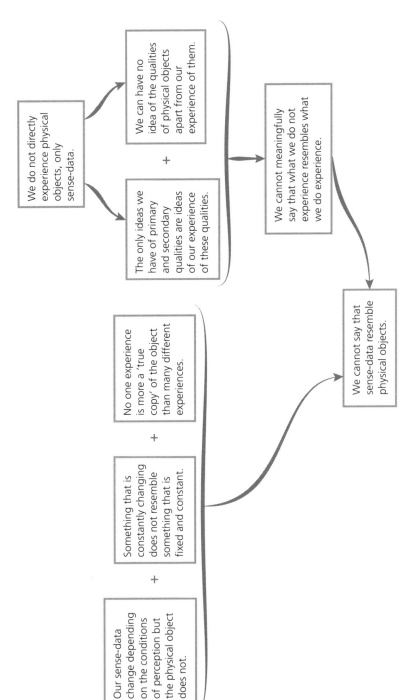

Map 2.9 Berkeley's argument against resemblance

Key points: indirect realism

- Indirect realism claims that we perceive mind-independent physical objects via, or in virtue of, perceiving mind-dependent sense-data that are caused by and represent physical objects.
- Sense-data are private (by definition belonging to someone's consciousness); they only exist while they are being experienced; and they are exactly as they seem. Physical objects are public, exist when not being perceived, and can be different from how they appear.
- Indirect realism claims that when we perceive something having some property F, then there is something that is F. If it is not the physical object, it must be something mental – sense-data – that we perceive.
- However, we can't tell the difference between non-veridical and veridical perception. Therefore, in each case, we are perceiving the same thing. Since we are perceiving sense-data in cases of non-veridical perception, we should infer that we always perceive sense-data.
- Locke distinguishes between primary and secondary qualities. Locke's primary qualities are extension (or size), shape, motion, number and solidity. Secondary qualities are colours, sounds, tastes, smells and temperature.
- Indirect realism faces an objection that if all we experience are sense-data, how do we know what causes them? How do we know physical objects exist at all?
- Russell argues that we cannot prove that physical objects exist, but that this claim is the best explanation for our experience.
- Locke argues that we can infer that physical objects exist from the fact that our perceptual experiences are involuntary. The existence of physical objects is also the best explanation for the fact that information from one sense coheres with information from another (Locke) and that we can infer perceptual experiences in one sense from those in another (Trotter Cockburn).
- We can object that indirect realism entails that our belief in physical objects remains a hypothesis, which is counter-intuitive since it denies that perception involves an 'openness' to the world.
- An alternative interpretation of indirect realism claims that we perceive physical objects via sense-data, and so the existence of physical objects is not a hypothesis.

- Indirect realism claims that sense-data are not only caused by mind-independent objects, they also represent them. Locke says our perceptual experiences resemble physical objects in their primary qualities.
- Berkeley objects that it makes no sense to say that sense-data resemble mind-independent physical objects.
- Indirect realists can reply that sense-data represent physical objects not by resembling them, but by a very detailed and systematic causal relation.

C. Berkeley's idealism

Berkeley rejects our usual understanding of physical objects as *mind-independent*. He claims that reality is dependent on minds. The ordinary objects of perception – tables, chairs, trees and other physical objects – must be perceived in order to exist at all. The only things that exist are minds (that perceive) and what minds perceive. The claim that nothing exists that is independent of mind is idealism. Does it make sense, and why does Berkeley argue for it?

> *Esse est percipi (aut percipere)* – to be is to be perceived (or to perceive).

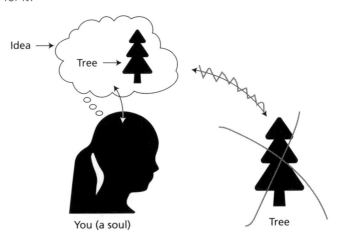

Figure 2.10 Berkeley's idealism

Berkeley on primary and secondary qualities

Berkeley begins his *Three Dialogues between Hylas and Philonous* by arguing, like Locke, that secondary qualities are mind-dependent. This is an attack on direct realism. But he then uses similar arguments to show that *primary* qualities are also mind-dependent, and so indirect realism is also unsatisfactory.

BERKELEY, *THREE DIALOGUES BETWEEN HYLAS AND PHILONOUS*, FIRST DIALOGUE, PP. 1–15

Berkeley on secondary qualities (pp. 1–12)

Berkeley, in the character of Philonous, begins by arguing that 'sensible things', i.e. things perceived by the senses, must be perceived *immediately* by the senses. The causes of our perceptions – the reality behind appearances – if they are not immediately perceived, we must infer. Whatever is inferred is not perceived: because what we perceive is immediately apparent to us, if we need to infer something then we aren't perceiving it. So if we need to infer the causes of our perceptions, we should not say that such causes are themselves perceived.

Philonous then argues that what we immediately perceive are the qualities of things, and nothing more. Through vision, we perceive colours, shapes, size, etc.; through hearing, sounds; through smell, odours – and so on. Each sense perceives particular types of qualities. There is nothing we perceive in addition to these qualities.

Do these qualities exist independently of being perceived? The character Hylas, who plays the role of the realist, starts off as a very simple direct realist. He claims that whatever we perceive exists independently of our minds, and in the form in which we perceive it. Thus heat, as we feel it, exists in the object.

Philonous points out that intense heat, or indeed intense cold, light, sound, pressure, can all be experienced as pain, but pain obviously doesn't exist 'in' physical objects. If we say these secondary qualities are in the object, then we have to say that at some point, it also has the quality of pain. Hylas responds that the heat (light, etc.) isn't itself pain, but *causes* pain. Philonous objects that we feel just one unified sensation of painful heat (painful light, etc.). In fact, *all* our perceptions of secondary qualities are accompanied by some form of pleasure or pain.

Since this is an empirical argument, we can challenge it on empirical grounds. Is Berkeley right to say that we can't distinguish between the sensation of heat and that of pain? If he is right for some sensations, is he right for all sensations? Can we not, for

'Empirical' means relating to or deriving from experience, especially sense experience, but also including experimental scientific investigation.

Explain Berkeley's argument that secondary qualities are mind-dependent because all sensations of secondary qualities are accompanied by pleasure or pain.

How would a direct realist respond to Berkeley's argument here?

instance, distinguish between the sensation of sweetness and the sensation of pleasure we associate with it?

Berkeley's second argument for thinking secondary qualities are mind-dependent is THE ARGUMENT FROM PERCEPTUAL VARIATION (p. 68). He repeats an example from Locke of placing a hot and a cold hand in a bowl of tepid water. The water feels hot to the cold hand and cold to the hot hand, but the water cannot *be* both hot and cold. He later develops the argument in relation to colours:

P1. A cloud from a distance looks pink, but up close, it loses its colour (or appears grey).
P2. A solid physical object, viewed through a microscope, appears to have different colours than those it has when viewed normally.
P3. Different animals perceive the colours of objects differently.
P4. If colours really existed in physical objects, then to change the colour, it would be necessary to change the object itself. But, of course, different kinds of light – daylight, candlelight, etc. – change the colour of an object without changing the object.
C1. Therefore, all colours are appearances, not properties of physical objects.

Suppose we insist that secondary qualities 'really' exist in the object as physical particles in motion (light waves, sound waves, the chemicals of smell and taste). Berkeley points out that if we say that sound is a vibration of the air, then we can't hear sound, since vibrations are something perceived by sight or touch. If we say that colour is tiny particles of matter in motion (photons with a particular energy, perhaps), then we can't see 'real' colour, since we cannot see these tiny particles moving. And that is very counter-intuitive.

Berkeley's attack on the primary/secondary quality distinction (pp. 13–15)

Having persuaded Hylas to agree that secondary qualities are mind-dependent, Philonous (Berkeley) argues that the argument from perceptual variation applies equally well to primary qualities.

P1. What looks small to me may look huge to a small animal.

P2. What looks small from a distance looks large when viewed close up.

P3. What looks smooth to the naked eye appears craggy and uneven under a microscope.

P4. If you look at a circle straight on, it looks circular. But if I'm looking at it from an angle, it looks elliptical. We see it differently, but it doesn't change.

P5. Even motion isn't constant. We measure the speed of motion by how quickly our minds work – to a creature that responds much faster than us, e.g. a housefly, our fastest movements appear leisurely.

P6. In the case of colour, when an object appears to have many colours, depending on how it is perceived, we can't say that it has one real colour which is independent of how we perceive it.

C1. Therefore, (P1)–(P5) show that we can't say that an object has one real shape or size or motion, independent of how it is perceived.

C2. Therefore, the primary qualities of objects are just as mind-dependent as secondary qualities.

The argument from perceptual variation begins by supporting indirect realism, but turns into an objection to it: primary qualities vary just as much as secondary qualities, and so we have no reason to attribute either kind of property to something that exists independent of our perceptual experiences.

Explain Berkeley's attack on the distinction between primary and secondary qualities, first in prose, then as an argument map.

The immediate objects of perception are mind-dependent objects

We have seen that Berkeley argues that both primary and secondary qualities are mind-dependent. He has also argued that when we perceive physical objects, we don't perceive anything *in addition* to its primary and secondary qualities. This gives us the following simple argument:

P1. Everything we perceive is either a primary or a secondary quality.

P2. Both primary and secondary qualities are mind-dependent.

C1. Therefore, nothing that we perceive exists independently of the mind: the objects of perception are entirely mind-dependent.

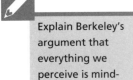

Explain Berkeley's argument that everything we perceive is mind-dependent.

This doesn't show that there aren't any mind-independent physical objects, because they could exist *unperceived*. But as we shall see, Berkeley goes on to argue that the idea of a physical object as something that exists independently of our perception of it is an idea so problematic that we should reject it entirely.

Once we grant Berkeley's claim that all we perceive are primary and secondary qualities, it becomes more difficult to reject his later arguments for idealism. One way to challenge his idealism, therefore, is to argue that we can be said to perceive physical objects themselves, and not just their qualities. This is what direct realism claims with its idea of perception as 'openness' (p. 76); it rejects (P1).

BERKELEY, *THREE DIALOGUES BETWEEN HYLAS AND PHILONOUS*, FIRST DIALOGUE, PP. 19–23

Three arguments against mind-independent objects

1. 'A material substratum'

Suppose we perceive only primary and secondary qualities. If there were no mind-independent objects, what would 'have' the qualities we experience? On p. 19, Hylas argues that we need the idea of 'a material substratum' – the stuff or substance that possesses primary and secondary qualities and holds them together to make one thing, one physical object. This 'material substratum' can exist unperceived.

Berkeley responds that this idea is, in fact, incoherent. The 'material substratum' is *never* perceived, since it is distinct from its primary and secondary qualities, and we have said that all we perceive are primary and secondary qualities. So what can we say about it? Once you list all the qualities of a table, what is left of the table? For instance, size is a quality – if the matter of the table is distinct from its qualities, then in itself, it has no size! If substance exists unperceived, it exists without any qualities at all.

Figure 2.11 Table as perceived

Figure 2.12 Table without solidity

Look at this table. Think of the difference between looking at it in black and white, and how it would look in colour. Now try to picture it without its solidity. Now try to picture it without its shape.

Figure 2.13 Table without size or shape

Locke saw the point, and accepted that the idea of substance was the idea of something unknown. A realist view of physical objects involves a mystery. Worse, Berkeley argues, physical substance is quite literally inconceivable – we can say nothing about how it exists at all.

Locke, *An Essay Concerning Human Understanding*, Bk 2, Ch. 23

Is the concept of 'physical substance' coherent?

2. 'We perceive physical objects'

Don't we just see that physical objects exist? On p. 21, Berkeley argues that neither our senses nor reason supports such a claim.

P1. As argued previously, all we perceive are primary and secondary qualities, not mind-independent physical objects.
C1. Therefore, our experience cannot verify the hypothesis that there is a mind-independent physical world.
P2. Worse still, the hypothesis of 'physical substance' is not one that is even *suggested* by experience.

Outline Berkeley's argument from experience to idealism.

C2. So close attention to experience supports the claim that all there is (all we can say there is) is what we can experience.
P3. What we experience are ideas.
C3. Therefore, our experience supports idealism, not realism.

3. Scepticism

Berkeley's next argument is captured in the last remarks of the First Dialogue: supposing that the objects of perception can and do exist independently of being perceived leads to scepticism (see Scepticism about the existence of mind-independent objects, p. 83, and Representation, resemblance and the nature of physical objects, p. 90). How can we connect up our experiences to something 'beyond' them – which, following the objection just made, we can't even describe or understand? How can we know that ideas really do represent (and represent accurately) something that exists completely independently of them? If there were mind-independent physical objects, we can know nothing about them. By contrast, if there is no mind-independent reality, then what we perceive is what there is, namely ideas, and so perception can give us knowledge of what there is.

Compare and contrast Berkeley's three arguments. Which do you think is the strongest and why?

Berkeley's 'master' argument

On p. 21, Berkeley provides another argument against the possibility of the objects of perception being mind-independent. It has come to be known as his 'master' argument, since he appears to set great weight upon it. Thus, Philonous says, 'I am willing to let our whole debate be settled as follows: If you can conceive it to be possible for any mixture or combination of qualities, or any sensible object whatever, to exist outside the mind, then I will grant it actually to be so.' Hylas responds that he is thinking of a tree existing unperceived by anyone. Philonous objects that what Hylas is thinking depends on his mind. He isn't actually thinking of a tree that exists independently of any mind; he is imagining a tree standing 'in some solitary place' where no one perceives it. But all the time, he is *thinking* of such a tree. We cannot think of a tree that is neither perceived nor conceived of. We can think of the idea of a tree, but not of a tree that exists independently of the mind.

Outline Berkeley's 'master' argument.

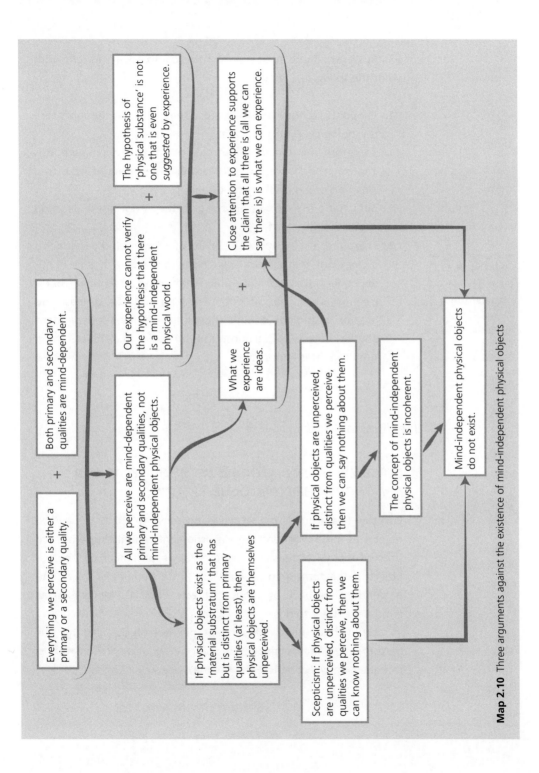

Map 2.10 Three arguments against the existence of mind-independent physical objects

However, Berkeley seems to have confused a *thought* with what the thought is *about*.

P1. Thoughts cannot exist outside the mind – thoughts are psychological events or states.

C1. Therefore, my *thinking* of a tree is not mind-independent. It is impossible (inconceivable) that there is a thought of a tree when no one is thinking of a tree.

P2. But what a thought is *about*, e.g. a tree, is not the same thing as the thought itself.

C2. Therefore, just because my thinking of a tree is mind-dependent, it does not follow that *what I am thinking of* is also mind-dependent. It is not impossible (inconceivable) to think that a tree may exist when no one is thinking of it. (Or, at least, the 'master' argument doesn't show this – if mind-independent physical objects are inconceivable for some *other* reason, then this thought is impossible.)

> **?**
>
> Does Berkeley show that there is no reason to think that mind-independent physical objects exist?

Idealism and God

BERKELEY, *THREE DIALOGUES BETWEEN HYLAS AND PHILONOUS*, THIRD DIALOGUE, PP. 41–2

Berkeley has argued that it makes no sense to think of physical objects as mind-independent. His arguments entail that what we think of as physical objects – indeed, what we must mean by 'physical object' if the term is to be coherent – are *bundles of ideas*, the perceptions we have of physical objects. Physical objects exist as mind-dependent things.

But without mind-independent physical objects causing our perceptions, what explains why we perceive what we do? Answering this question will complete the outline of Berkeley's idealist theory.

P1. As (the ideas that comprise) physical objects are mind-dependent, there are three possible causes of my perceptions: ideas, my mind, and another mind.

P2. Ideas (including the ideas that comprise physical objects) don't cause anything.

P3. If (the ideas that comprise) physical objects depended on *my* mind, then I would be able to control what I perceive.

P4. But I can't. Perception is quite different to imagining; in perception, we are more passive – the sensations just occur to us, and we can't control them. Imagination is voluntary, but perception is involuntary.

C1. Therefore, (the ideas that comprise) physical objects don't depend on my mind.

C2. Therefore, (the ideas that comprise) physical objects must exist in another mind, which then wills that I perceive them.

C3. Given the complexity and systematicity of our perceptions, that mind must be God.

Explain the difference between perception and imagination.

For a different account of the relation between perception, physical objects and God, see DESCARTES' PROOF OF THE EXTERNAL WORLD, p. 174.

Explain Berkeley's argument for the claim that our perceptions are caused by God.

Thinking harder: idealism and the cause of our perceptions

Why does Berkeley claim (P2), that ideas can't be causes? At pp. 32ff., Berkeley spells this out. Think about the functioning of the mind. Should we say that thoughts think themselves, or that the mind thinks thoughts? Should we say that our perceptions cause our experience of them or that the mind perceives? Berkeley thinks the latter option is clearly better. Ideas themselves are *passive*; we *do* things with ideas in thought or we receive them in perception. How could an *idea* 'make' you think it or perceive it? It is the mind, and only the mind, that can cause, that is active – the mind that perceives, thinks, wills and so on.

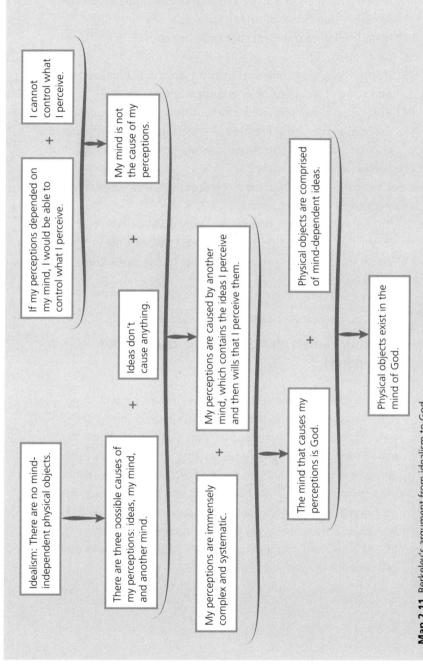

Map 2.11 Berkeley's argument from idealism to God

I cannot control what I perceive.

+

If my perceptions depended on my mind, I would be able to control what I perceive.

My mind is not the cause of my perceptions.

+

Idealism: There are no mind-independent physical objects.

There are three possible causes of my perceptions: ideas, my mind, and another mind.

+

Ideas don't cause anything.

My perceptions are caused by another mind, which contains the ideas I perceive and then wills that I perceive them.

+

Physical objects are comprised of mind-dependent ideas.

My perceptions are immensely complex and systematic.

+

The mind that causes my perceptions is God.

+

Physical objects exist in the mind of God.

Berkeley uses this thought not only to support idealism in the argument above. He also gives two arguments for the claim that 'matter' can't be the cause of our perception. Hylas suggests that 'matter' is simply *whatever* is the cause of our perceptions. Berkeley responds:

P1. Matter in the normal sense of the word, i.e. as mind-independent and possessing primary qualities, cannot exist (as argued previously).
C1. Therefore, to talk any sense about matter, we must think of it as our perceptions of it.
P2. What we perceive – primary and secondary qualities – are ideas.
C2. Given that ideas are passive, whatever causes our perceptions must be a mind, not 'matter'.

In a second argument, Berkeley points to our ignorance of how mind and matter can interact (pp. 27 and 36). Realism requires that our minds are causally affected by mind-independent physical objects. Suppose physical objects causally affect our sense organs, which then affect our brains. Philosophers and scientists have struggled with the next step – how does what happens in our brains causally affect our conscious perception? How can something physical and mind-independent possibly cause an idea in a mind? How could nerve signals in the brain produce sensations of sound and colour? Three hundred years after Berkeley made the objection, the puzzle still remains unsolved.

Compare and contrast Berkeley's idealism and indirect realism.

Berkeley is aware that his idealism is counter-intuitive. But, he argues, it follows from his previous arguments, and there is nothing impossible about his conclusion. We know from our own experience that minds can give rise to thoughts. At the end of the Third Dialogue, Berkeley adds that many metaphysical puzzles can be solved by adopting idealism: for example, we can establish the existence of God and dissolve problems about the ultimate nature of matter, how matter can cause ideas in a mind, and how matter could ever produce mind. The rest of his defence of idealism amounts to answering possible objections and correcting misunderstandings.

Issues with Berkeley's idealism

We discuss two further objections, concerning the objective reality of physical objects and scientific investigation, in extension material.

We have seen how idealism can emerge from objections to realism. But it is no improvement if it faces equally powerful objections of its own. In this section, we discuss three objections and Berkeley's responses. The objections relate to illusions, solipsism and the role of God. Since we just reached Berkeley's conclusion that our perceptions are caused by God, we start with this issue.

BERKELEY, *THREE DIALOGUES BETWEEN HYLAS AND PHILONOUS*, THIRD DIALOGUE

Problems with the role played by God in Berkeley's idealism

However persuasive one finds Berkeley's arguments regarding perception, one may object to his appeal to God. It is important to note, however, that Berkeley does not *assume* that God exists, and then wheel him in to resolve philosophical difficulties in his theory. Rather, the existence of God is an inference, supported by the arguments. The cause of our perceptions is a mind, because we can only conceive of minds being active: 'I have no notion of any action other than volition, and I can't conceive of volition as being anywhere but in a spirit' (p. 48). The 'variety, order, and manner' of what I perceive shows that the mind that produces these ideas is 'wise, powerful, and good, beyond anything I can comprehend' (Second Dialogue, p. 31). I derive the idea of God from my knowledge of my own mind, 'heightening its powers and removing its imperfections' (p. 43).

But the exact relationship between (the mind of) God and what we perceive is puzzling. Berkeley infers that our perceptions are caused by God. Physical objects don't depend on my mind; but as ideas, they depend on some other mind. So, Berkeley says that they *exist in* the mind of God (Second Dialogue, p. 31). But does this make sense? There are three reasons to think that ideas we are caused to have, whether perceptions or sensations, can't be part of God's mind:

P1. My perceptions and sensations are part of my mind. What I perceive and feel is in my mind, not God's mind.
P2. God can't have the sorts of perceptual experiences I have – God doesn't perceive as I do, and does not undergo sensations, such as pain (p. 49).
P3. The ordinary objects of my perception change and go out of existence, but God's mind is said to be unchanging and eternal.
C1. Therefore, what I perceive and feel can't be part of God's mind.

Berkeley clarifies his theory by responding:

1. What I perceive is a *copy* of the idea in God's mind.
2. The ideas of physical objects exist in God's mind not as perceptions, but as part of God's *understanding*. The same is true of sensations. So while God doesn't *perceive* the colour red or *feel* pain, he knows what it is for us to undergo these experiences.
3. What I perceive, which changes, is what God *wills* me to perceive. The whole of creation exists in God's understanding, eternally; 'things … may properly be said to begin their existence … when God decreed they should become perceptible to intelligent creatures'.

We will see that understanding the role of God in Berkeley's idealism enables us to understand his responses to the other objections that can be raised.

Explain the relationship, according to Berkeley, between ideas in the mind of God and what we perceive.

Arguments from illusion and hallucination

On p. 47, Hylas asks how idealism can explain illusions. Since we perceive ideas, there must be an idea that corresponds to the illusion. But we don't want to say that the physical object is as it looks in the illusion. If we see a pencil half-submerged in water, it looks crooked, but it isn't. But the pencil is just what we see; and what we see is crooked, not straight.

See THE ARGUMENT FROM ILLUSION, p. 71.

Berkeley's response is that we aren't misperceiving – what we perceive in the case of the half-submerged pencil *is* crooked. However, this is misleading if we infer that the pencil would feel crooked if we touched it or would look crooked when pulled out of the water. So illusions mislead us regarding the ideas we might *associate* with what we perceive.

This entails that the pencil *is* crooked when half-submerged. Because Berkeley argues that reality is the ideas we perceive; there is no appearance–reality distinction. But to say the pencil is crooked is very odd indeed – it just sounds false!

In *Three Dialogues*, Berkeley doesn't consider or respond to this objection. Elsewhere in his writings, however, he replies that the problem here is with language. He agrees that we shouldn't *say* 'The pencil is crooked', since what we understand that to mean is that it would look crooked under normal conditions. And this is false. So to avoid this implication, we should say 'The pencil looks crooked' – and this is correct.

Compare and contrast the idealist and the direct realist explanations of illusions (p. 71).

What about hallucinations? Berkeley discusses these, in the form of dreams, on p. 45. Hallucinations are products of imagination. Normally, imagination is voluntary and perception is not (see IDEALISM AND GOD, p. 104). But hallucinations are *involuntary*, like perceptions, so Berkeley provides two other criteria that mark off hallucinations from perception. First, they are 'dim, irregular, and confused'. Second, even if they were as 'vivid and clear' as perceptions, they are not coherently connected with the rest of our perceptual experience.

To this, we might object that these criteria mark a difference of *degree* – perceptual experiences can be more or less clear or dim, more or less coherently connected with other experiences. But surely the difference between hallucination and perception is a difference in *kind*. In perception, you experience something that exists outside your mind; in hallucination, you don't. In response, perhaps Berkeley could agree – the ideas you perceive originate in God, but in hallucination they don't. His criteria are only supposed to indicate *how we can tell*.

Explain Berkeley's accounts of illusions and of hallucinations.

Idealism leads to solipsism

Solipsism is the view that only oneself, one's mind, exists. There are no mind-independent physical objects and there are no other minds either. We can object that Berkeley's THREE ARGUMENTS AGAINST MIND-INDEPENDENT OBJECTS (p. 100) – starting from the claim that everything I perceive is mind-dependent – lead to the conclusion that all that exists is my own experience. Or at least, experience gives me no reason to believe that anything apart from my experience exists (or can exist). If all I perceive are ideas, what reason do I have to think that other minds exist? For that matter, what reason do I have to think that minds (including God) exist? After all, I do not perceive minds.

Berkeley doesn't discuss this objection from solipsism explicitly, though Hylas expresses a version of it on p. 43, and Berkeley makes a number of remarks we can draw upon. He accepts that 'strictly speaking', I have no idea of a mind. But because I am a mind – a 'thinking substance' – I know I exist.

P1. The mind is that which (actively) perceives, thinks and wills, while ideas are passive.
P2. I am aware of myself as capable of this activity.
C1. Therefore, I am not my ideas, but a mind.
P3. Being a mind myself, I have a 'notion' of what a mind is.
C2. Therefore, it is possible that other minds exist.
P4. My perceptions don't originate in my mind.
C3. Therefore, they are caused by some other mind.
C4. The complexity, regularity, etc., of my experience indicates that this mind is God.

See IDEALISM AND GOD, p. 104.

Set out this argument as an argument map.

Explain and then respond to the objection that idealism leads to solipsism.

Is Berkeley's idealism true?

> As for other finite minds – other people – Berkeley doesn't spend much time on the matter, but indicates that there is evidence in my experience that they exist. Their existence, as Russell also argues (THE EXISTENCE OF THE EXTERNAL WORLD IS THE BEST HYPOTHESIS, p. 84), is a matter of inference.

Key points: Berkeley's idealism

- Idealism claims that all that exists are minds and ideas. What we think of as physical objects are, in fact, bundles of ideas.
- Berkeley argues that everything we perceive is either a primary or a secondary quality. We don't perceive anything in addition to these.
- He claims the argument from perceptual variation shows that secondary qualities are mind-dependent. He then argues that the argument applies as much to primary qualities. Therefore, primary qualities are mind-dependent as well.
- Since both primary and secondary qualities are mind-dependent, and we perceive nothing in addition to primary and secondary qualities, everything we perceive is mind-dependent.
- The idea of mind-independent objects doesn't make sense: if we argue that we need a 'material substratum' in which qualities exist, we have no conception of this independent of its qualities.
- Idealism solves the objection to indirect realism that we cannot know how the world is. In experiencing ideas, we are experiencing the world.
- Berkeley's 'master argument' claims that we cannot conceive of anything existing independent of all minds. When we think of such a thing, our thinking of it makes it not mind-independent. We can object that Berkeley confused thought with what a thought is about.
- If physical objects are no more than their primary and secondary qualities, and these are ideas, then we cannot say that physical objects cause our perceptions, because ideas are passive. Therefore, what causes our perceptions must be a mind, not matter.
- Because I do not cause my perceptions, what I perceive must originate in another mind. Given the complexity of what I perceive, that mind must be God.

- We cannot claim that 'matter' causes our perceptions. 'Matter' cannot exist, so we must talk of our perceptions of it, and ideas cannot be causes. Nor do we have any idea how 'matter' can cause ideas.
- How can what I perceive exist in God's mind? Berkeley explains that I perceive copies of ideas that exist eternally in God's understanding when God wills me to do so.
- Illusions are misleading not because we misperceive, but because we make false inferences about what we would perceive. To mark the fact that the perception is not 'normal', we say that what we see 'looks' a certain way rather than 'is' a certain way.
- Idealism can mark off hallucinations from perception as less clear and not connected coherently with the rest of our perceptual experience.
- We can object that I don't know that any other minds exist (solipsism). Berkeley argues that we can reason that the ideas I perceive originate in the mind of God, and that my experience contains evidence that there are also other minds like mine.

Summary: perception as a source of knowledge

In this section on perception as a source of knowledge, we have considered three theories:

1. Direct realism: we directly perceive physical objects, which exist independently of the mind.
2. Indirect realism: via sense-data, we indirectly perceive physical objects, which exist independently of the mind.
3. Idealism: we directly perceive 'physical objects', but these do not exist independently of the mind – they are collections of ideas.

In our discussion and evaluation of these theories, we have looked at the following issues:

1. How do we explain variations between what people perceive?
2. What do we perceive in an illusion or hallucination?
3. Are hallucinations the same kind of mental state as perceptions or a completely different kind which merely seems the same?

4. Does perception involve being 'open' to physical objects?
5. Do the arguments from illusion, secondary qualities, or perceptual variation support the existence of sense-data?
6. What are primary and secondary qualities? Is there a valid distinction between them?
7. If we perceive only sense-data directly, can we know whether physical objects exist?
8. If there are mind-independent physical objects, can we know that sense-data accurately represent them?
9. Can we form a coherent idea of physical objects existing independently of the mind? Do we have any experience that supports this claim?
10. Does what we perceive exist in the mind of God, who wills our perceptual experiences?
11. Can idealism satisfactorily distinguish between perceptions of physical objects and illusions or hallucinations?

III. Reason as a source of knowledge

Rationalism, empiricism and innatism

Does all our knowledge, directly or indirectly, come from perception? Or does *reason* provide us with an independent source of knowledge? This question goes to the very heart of epistemology in reflecting on how human beings are 'hooked up' to the world (see p. 25). It makes a central contribution to our understanding of the nature and possibilities of human thought. The debate over the origin (and nature) of our knowledge coincided with the scientific revolution in Europe. The debate led to the first proposals about how modern science works and the type of knowledge it can give us. And because philosophy is a form of thinking that relies (more) on reasoning than on an empirical investigation of the world, this debate also has implications for the nature and scope of philosophy itself.

To help us think about the question, we need to make a number of distinctions, the first between two types of knowledge, and the second and third between ways in which propositions can be true. With those distinctions in place, we will be able to describe three positions on the origin of our knowledge. We will look at more precise definitions later on, but for now very roughly, empiricism claims that all our knowledge comes from sense experience, rationalism claims that we can gain further knowledge by pure reasoning, while innatism claims that our minds are innately predisposed to know certain truths. By the end of this section, you should be able to demonstrate a good understanding of these three positions and be able to evaluate a range of arguments for and against each position.

A PRIORI/A POSTERIORI KNOWLEDGE

We may draw a distinction between two *types of knowledge*, based on how we know whether a proposition is true:

On propositions, see Types of knowledge, p. 31.

A priori: We have *a priori* knowledge of a proposition if we do not require sense experience to know it to be true. An example is 'Bachelors are unmarried'. If you understand what the proposition means, then you can see straightaway that it must be true. You don't need to find bachelors and ask them if they are married or not. Another example is '537 + 654 = 1191'. You can figure out whether this is true just by thinking about it.

A posteriori: Propositions that can only be established through sense experience are known *a posteriori*. An example is 'There are more than 6 billion people on the Earth'.

The a priori/a posteriori distinction rests on how we check or establish knowledge of a proposition. How we come to *understand* the proposition is irrelevant. To learn what a proposition means, to acquire the concepts or words involved, we may well always need sense experience. For instance, to understand 'Bachelors are unmarried', we will first need to learn English, and that requires sense experience. But how we learn to understand a proposition is a different issue from how, once we understand it, we check if it is true.

Explain and illustrate the distinction between a priori and a posteriori knowledge.

(Philosophers sometimes also talk about a priori and a posteriori concepts. An a posteriori concept is one that is derived from experience. An a priori concept is one that cannot be derived from experience. We will discuss some examples in Issues with the empiricist theory of concepts (p. 141).)

ANALYTIC/SYNTHETIC PROPOSITIONS

The contrast between 'analytic' and 'synthetic' is a contrast between *types of proposition*:

Analytic: A proposition is *analytic* if it is true or false just in virtue of the meanings of the words. Many analytic truths, such as 'squares have four sides', are obvious, but some are not, e.g. 'In five days' time, it will have been a week since the day which was tomorrow three days ago' (think about it!).

Synthetic: A proposition is *synthetic* if it is not analytic, i.e. it is true or false not just in virtue of the meanings of the words, but in virtue of the way the world is, e.g. 'ripe tomatoes are red'.

1) Explain the analytic/synthetic distinction. 2) Come up with three different examples of analytic propositions and three of synthetic propositions.

You may have already noticed a similarity between the examples for a priori knowledge and analytic propositions. 'Bachelors are unmarried' – an example of a priori knowledge – is also an analytic proposition. 'Squares have four sides' – an example of an analytic proposition – is also an example of a priori knowledge. So is all a priori knowledge just knowledge of analytic propositions? It is a question we return to below. But first, the third distinction.

NECESSARY/CONTINGENT TRUTH

The distinction between 'necessary' and 'contingent' draws a different contrast in *how propositions can be true*:

A similar distinction is made in Metaphysics of God between necessary and contingent existence. See ONTOLOGICAL ARGUMENTS, p. 56, AQUINAS' THIRD WAY, p. 114, and LEIBNIZ'S ARGUMENT FROM CONTINGENCY, p. 116.

Contingent: A proposition is contingently true (or false) if it is possible that it *could* be true or false. Of course, it will *be* either true or false, but the world could have been different. It is true that you are reading this book; but you could have been doing something else – it could have been false. So it is contingently true. It is contingently true that there are more types of insect than there are of any other animal. This wasn't always true, and one day it might be false again.

Necessary: A proposition is necessarily true if it *must* be true (or necessarily false if it *must* be false). Mathematical propositions are necessarily true (or false): 2 + 2 must equal 4; it is not possible (logically or perhaps mathematically possible) for 2 + 2 to equal any other number. Likewise, analytic truths are necessary: if a proposition is true by definition, then it *must* be true. If a square is, by definition, a closed two-dimensional figure with four sides, it is impossible for there to be a square with three sides. It simply wouldn't be a square.

Explain and illustrate the distinction between necessary and contingent truth.

(Of course, it is possible that the figure '2' could have been *used to mean* the number 3 or the word 'square' used to mean triangle. But then '2 + 2' wouldn't mean 2 + 2; it would mean 3 + 3. To test whether a proposition is true or false, in all cases, you have to *keep the meanings of the words the same*. If '2' means 2, and '4' means 4, then 2 + 2 must equal 4.)

DEFINING RATIONALISM, EMPIRICISM AND INNATISM

We can now return to our question of whether reason provides us with knowledge. A posteriori knowledge is knowledge from sense experience, so if reason is a source of knowledge at all, then it provides us with a priori knowledge (of either analytic or synthetic propositions). But how would 'reason' provide such knowledge? In fact, philosophers have proposed two *distinct* theories. The first, INNATISM (p. 120), is that such knowledge is 'innate', built into that part of the mind with which we think about and understand the world. The second theory is that we can gain knowledge using rational insight and reasoning (see THE INTUITION AND DEDUCTION THESIS, p. 150).

Historically, philosophers who defended the claim that reason is a source of knowledge, such as Plato, Descartes and Leibniz, connected these two theories and defended both of them, while philosophers who rejected the claim, such as Locke and Hume, rejected both theories. The first group of philosophers were called 'rationalists', because they defended reason as a source of knowledge; the second group were called 'empiricists', because they argued that all our knowledge derives from sense experience. The two groups also disagreed on how we acquire concepts, and so produced 'rationalist' and 'empiricist' theories of this as well (see THE MIND AS A '*TABULA RASA*', p. 137, and ISSUES WITH THE EMPIRICIST THEORY OF CONCEPTS, p. 141). To mark their historical nature, let's call these two families of theories 'classical rationalism' and 'classical empiricism'.

We should now note that the claim that we have innate knowledge can be separated from the claim that we have knowledge through rational intuition and reasoning, and one could be true without the other. It is more useful, therefore, to split the classical debate into two separate debates. In particular, let us split 'classical rationalism' into the following two claims, and re-use 'rationalism' for just one of these claims:

Innatism: Innatism (about knowledge) claims that we have some innate knowledge.

Rationalism: Rationalism claims that we have some a priori knowledge from rational insight and reasoning.

For now, we can keep 'empiricism' to mean:

Empiricism: Empiricism (about knowledge) claims that all our knowledge comes from experience, and so there is no a priori knowledge which is either innate or gained from rational insight and reasoning.

Once we get into the debate, we will be able to refine our definitions of rationalism and empiricism further (see EMPIRICIST ALTERNATIVES, p. 151). But we should clarify immediately that we are excluding knowledge of our own minds from the debate. We can each know such truths as 'I feel sad' or 'I am thinking about unicorns'. How? Not, obviously, through sense experience, nor reason (and certainly not innately). We don't need to worry about this. The argument is about knowledge of things other than our own minds.

We can develop our understanding of the debates between classical rationalism and empiricism using the distinctions we drew earlier. We noticed in passing that the a priori/a posteriori and analytic/synthetic distinctions might line up. This would mean that our knowledge of true analytic propositions is always a priori; and our knowledge of true synthetic propositions is always a posteriori. Is this right?

1. Everyone agrees that analytic propositions are known a priori. However, what is the source of this knowledge? Is such knowledge innate? Is it gained by reasoning? Or is it, as empiricists argue, something else again, e.g. a form of conceptual knowledge?
2. Are all synthetic propositions known a posteriori? Empiricists argue that they are. But could we know some synthetic propositions a priori, either innately or through reasoning?

These are questions we shall discuss. How do they connect to the third distinction above, between necessary and contingent truth? Historically, philosophers agreed that knowledge of propositions that are necessarily true is a priori knowledge while knowledge of propositions that are contingently true is a posteriori. Why? Because a posteriori knowledge is knowledge of how the world is, gained through our senses, and surely the world as we experience it could always have been a different way – so all propositions about the world *could* have been true or false. But it is hard to see how necessary truths could be established a posteriori. Take the claim that '2 + 2 = 4' or 'Squares have four sides'. Leibniz points out that our sense experience

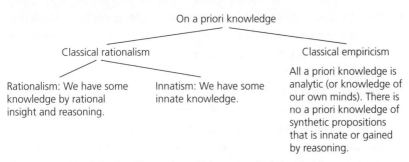

On a priori knowledge

Classical rationalism

Rationalism: We have some
knowledge by rational
insight and reasoning.

Innatism: We have some
innate knowledge.

Classical empiricism

All a priori knowledge is
analytic (or knowledge of
our own minds). There is
no a priori knowledge of
synthetic propositions
that is innate or gained
by reasoning.

Figure 2.14 Classical rationalism and empiricism on a priori knowledge

only provides us with information about particular instances – that *these* two apples and these two apples make four apples, that *this* square has four sides, and so on. But 'however many instances confirm a general truth, they aren't enough to establish its universal necessity'. Our experience tells us how things *are*, but not how things *must be*. If we reject this, and argue that '2 + 2 = 4' is just a generalisation of our experience so far, then we are saying that it is possible, one day, that 2 + 2 will equal some other number. But this is inconceivable.

Leibniz, *New Essays on Human Understanding*, p. 2

All necessary truths tell us how things must be. Because experience doesn't tell us how things must be, it seems that all knowledge of necessary truths must be a priori. If our knowledge of necessary truths is innate or gained through rational insight and reasoning, then this will show that empiricism is false.

In what follows, we will look first at arguments that we have innate knowledge (and empiricist objections) and then at Descartes' arguments that we have knowledge through insight and reasoning (and empiricist objections). After looking at the debate over knowledge, we discuss something that knowledge presupposes, namely concepts. Do these also all derive from experience, or are some concepts innate?

Key points: rationalism, empiricism and innatism

- We can draw a distinction between a priori and a posteriori knowledge. We know a proposition a priori if such knowledge is not established on the basis of sense experience. Propositions that can only be established through sense experience are known a posteriori.

- We can draw a distinction between analytic and synthetic propositions. A proposition is analytic if it is true or false just in virtue of the meanings of the words. A proposition is synthetic if it is not analytic, but true or false in virtue of the way the world is.
- We can draw a distinction between necessary and contingent truth. A proposition is contingently true if it is possible that it could be either true or false. A proposition is necessarily true if it must be true.
- Innatism (about knowledge) claims that we have some innate knowledge. Because knowledge depends on concepts, if we have innate knowledge, we have innate concepts as well.
- Rationalism claims that we have some a priori knowledge from rational insight and reasoning. We will refine this definition later.
- 'Classical rationalists', such as Descartes and Leibniz, defended both rationalism and innatism.
- Empiricism (about knowledge) claims that there is no a priori knowledge which is either innate or gained from rational insight and reasoning. We will refine this definition later. Classical empiricists also argued that there are no innate concepts.
- While everyone agrees that analytic propositions are known a priori, not everyone agrees that all synthetic propositions are known a posteriori. Empiricists argue that they are; rationalists and innatists deny this.
- Leibniz argues that knowledge of necessary truths is a priori, because experience can only tell us how things are, not how they must be.

A. Innatism

Innatism about knowledge argues that there is at least some innate knowledge. Exactly what 'innate' means in this context is disputed. But the claim is that some knowledge is part of the mind, already 'in' the mind from birth, rather than gained from experience. If there is any innate knowledge, it cannot be a posteriori, but must be a priori. If we want to say that 'reason' is the source of this knowledge, then we can say that the knowledge is built into the 'faculty' of reason, that part of the mind with which we think about and understand the world.

The debate between innatism and classical empiricism is about whether there is any innate *propositional* knowledge. Everyone can agree that there is innate *ability* knowledge. Of course babies are born knowing how to breathe, how to see (and apparently, how to hold their breath under water!). We can also agree that they have certain psychological abilities, such as memory and the disposition to learn a language. But is there any innate propositional knowledge?

What is innate knowledge?

If there is, then there must also be innate *concepts*. A proposition is structured by concepts, e.g. 'All squares have four sides' uses the concepts SQUARE and FOUR. So the debate over innatism also concerns whether there are innate concepts.

A reminder: when a word refers to a concept, I put it in capital letters.

Two arguments for innate knowledge

PLATO'S SLAVE BOY ARGUMENT

Plato's dialogue *Meno* is mostly about virtue. But it includes an extended example and discussion of innate knowledge.

> ## PLATO, *MENO* (81E FF.)
>
> Our interest begins with Socrates saying 'You argue that man cannot enquire either about that which he knows, or about that which he does not know; for if he knows, he has no need to enquire; and if not, he cannot; for he does not know the very subject about which he is to enquire.' This is 'Meno's Paradox'. Put another way, it says that it is impossible to learn anything because, for anything you might learn, either you already know about it or you don't know about it. If you already know about it, learning is unnecessary; if you don't know about it, you won't know how to go about learning it.
>
> Plato's solution to this puzzle is to say that learning is a form of *remembering*. He demonstrates this by Socrates asking Meno's slave boy a series of questions about a theorem in geometry.
>
> Socrates draws a square in the ground that is 2 feet × 2 feet. Its total area is therefore 4 square feet. How long are the sides of a square with a total area of 8 square feet? The slave boy has not been taught geometry, and yet is able to work out the right answer in response to Socrates *only asking questions*. The boy first guesses that the sides will each be 4 feet long, but when asked what 4 feet × 4 feet is, he realises that the area of this square is 16 square feet,

not 8 square feet. The answer must be between 2 feet and 4 feet – he guesses 3 feet. But again, when asked what 3 feet × 3 feet is, he realises this square would be 9 square feet, not 8 square feet.

Socrates then draws three more squares of 2 feet × 2 feet, arranging them with touching sides to make one big square of 4 feet × 4 feet. He then draws a diagonal line across each small square, dividing them into triangles. The four diagonals are arranged to form a (square) diamond in the middle of the big square. Through questioning, he gets the slave boy to agree that each triangle is half of 4 square feet, i.e. 2 square feet. There are four such triangles making up the diamond, which is therefore 8 square feet. The sides of the diamond are the diagonals of the original 2 foot × 2 foot squares. So a square with an area of 8 square feet has sides the length of the diagonal of a square that is 4 square feet.

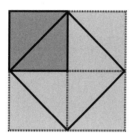

Figure 2.15 Meno square

The boy wasn't taught any geometry, yet he correctly answers each stage of the proof (or realises his mistake). How? He didn't gain the knowledge from experience, so he must have recovered the answers from within his mind, i.e. the knowledge must be innate. *The argument for innate knowledge is that we have knowledge that we can't have gained from experience.* Plato's example is supposed to show that all we need to recover our innate knowledge is the right 'prompts' from experience (in this case, Socrates' questions).

(Socrates goes on to argue that the mind must exist from before birth to have gained this knowledge in a previous form of existence. Socrates' questions triggered the knowledge he had from before birth, but had forgotten – just as memories can be triggered by some event or question. However, we don't have to draw *this* conclusion about the pre-existence of the mind. Other explanations of innate knowledge are possible.)

Explain Plato's argument for innate knowledge.

LEIBNIZ ON KNOWLEDGE OF NECESSARY TRUTHS

LEIBNIZ, *NEW ESSAYS ON HUMAN UNDERSTANDING*, PREFACE, P. 2; BK 1, CH. 1, P. 19

We noted above (p. 119) that Leibniz argues that knowledge of necessary truths is not derived from experience. Experience only teaches us how things are on any occasion; it cannot teach us how things must be. And so knowledge of necessary truths is a priori.

On p. 19, Leibniz then argues that we should regard such a priori knowledge of necessary truths as innate. We discover their truth in a priori reasoning by 'attending carefully and methodically to what is already in our minds'. This is what Plato's example of the slave boy shows. (In fact, in a broad sense of 'innate', all the knowledge we gain by a priori reasoning from 'basic' innate knowledge can also be called innate. Here Leibniz links innate knowledge to a priori knowledge that is gained by rational intuition and deductive reasoning.) An example of such innate, a priori knowledge is 'It is impossible for the same thing to be and not to be'. We can know the general truth of this claim by reflecting on it; but sense experience can't teach us this, for the reasons already given above.

Importantly, saying that this knowledge is innate doesn't mean that we can discover our innate knowledge without *any* sense experience. We need sense experience in order to form abstract thoughts; we rely on words, letters, sounds, which we learn from experience. That makes sense experience *necessary* but not *sufficient* for our knowledge of necessary truths. If sense experience isn't sufficient, then the knowledge must already be part of our minds.

Explain Leibniz's argument that knowledge of necessary truths must be innate.

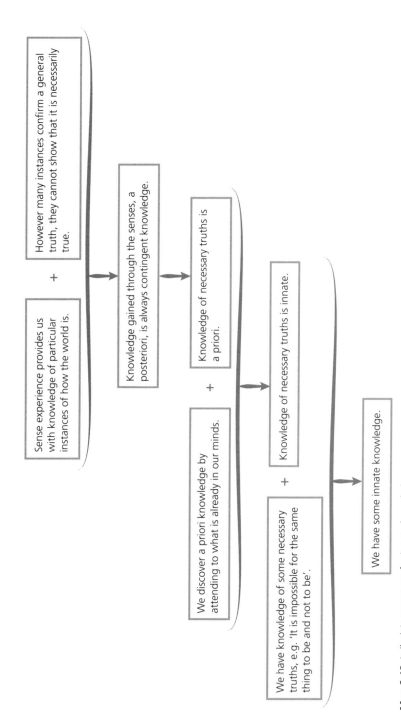

Map 2.12 Leibniz's argument for innate knowledge

Sense experience provides us with knowledge of particular instances of how the world is.

+

However many instances confirm a general truth, they cannot show that it is necessarily true.

Knowledge gained through the senses, a posteriori, is always contingent knowledge.

Knowledge of necessary truths is a priori.

We discover a priori knowledge by attending to what is already in our minds.

+

Knowledge of necessary truths is innate.

We have knowledge of some necessary truths, e.g. 'It is impossible for the same thing to be and not to be'.

We have some innate knowledge.

Locke's arguments against innate knowledge

The claim that there is innate knowledge raises a number of issues. One is whether Plato and Leibniz are right that the only explanation of our knowledge of geometry or other a priori necessary truths is that it is innate. Even if we accept that we cannot learn this knowledge from experience, perhaps there is another explanation of it. We will return to this in ALTERNATIVE EMPIRICIST ACCOUNTS (p. 132). A second is whether we can really make sense of the idea of innate knowledge. What are we really saying when we say that knowledge is 'innate'? If we get clear on that, does any knowledge qualify? This is the line of argument with which John Locke begins his attack on innatism.

LOCKE, *AN ESSAY CONCERNING HUMAN UNDERSTANDING*, BK 1, CH. 2

Locke argues that we have no innate knowledge. He begins by asking how we acquire our ideas. By 'idea', he means 'whatever it is that the mind can be employed about in thinking' (Bk 1, Ch. 1, §8). Or again, an 'idea' is any 'immediate object of perception, thought, or understanding' (Bk 2, Ch. 8, §8). So he uses the word to cover a very wide range of mental phenomena. An idea can be

See also HUME ON IMPRESSIONS AND IDEAS, p. 137.

1. a complete thought, taking the form of a proposition, e.g. 'bananas are yellow';
2. a sensation or sensory experience, e.g. a visual sensation of yellow; or
3. a concept, e.g. YELLOW.

What, according to Locke, is an idea?

Our focus here is on propositions, as these are what we can know or not know.

Locke understands innate ideas as 'thoughts printed on to the soul at the point of existence, which it brings into the world with it' (Bk 1, Ch. 2, §1). As examples of potential innate knowledge, taken from the debate at the time, he offers 'Whatever is, is' and 'It is impossible for the same thing to be and not to be.' He assumes that innate knowledge must be universal – every human being has it (§3).

However, the converse is not true: just because some claim is universally accepted, that doesn't mean it is innate – it may be that we could explain in some other way why everyone agrees.

Locke then argues:

P1. If there is innate knowledge, it is universal (§3).
P2. For an idea to be part of the mind, the mind (the person) must know or be conscious of it: 'it seems to me nearly a contradiction to say that there are truths imprinted on the soul that it doesn't perceive or understand. No proposition can be said to be in the mind which it has never known or been conscious of' (§5).
C1. Therefore, innate knowledge is knowledge that every human being is or has been conscious of.
P3. Children and 'idiots' do not know theorems in geometry or 'It is impossible for the same thing to be and not to be' (§4). (They do not know these claims, because they do not understand them.)
C2. Therefore, these claims are not innate.
P4. There are *no* claims that are universally accepted, including by children and 'idiots'.
C3. Therefore, there is no innate knowledge.

By 'idiots', Locke means people with severe learning disabilities (not a term of abuse).

Applying this line of thought to Plato's example of the slave boy, Locke can say that his knowledge of geometry can't be innate, as not everyone has the knowledge that he 'remembers' under Socrates' questioning. Whatever the explanation of how he knows what he knows, it isn't that the knowledge is innate. The same applies to Leibniz's examples of knowledge of necessary truths.

Present Locke's argument as an argument map.

We can undermine Locke's argument if we can reject C1. Is there something wrong with Locke's conception of innate knowledge? After all, Plato and Leibniz don't talk of innate knowledge as *conscious*. But if innate knowledge isn't conscious as Locke says, then what can it be? Locke anticipates and objects to four alternative definitions of innate knowledge.

If we define as 'innate' *any* knowledge that we can gain, Locke objects that this is a misuse of the term (§5) – everything we come to know, including through sense experience, will be innate! What we should say is that the *capacity* for knowledge is innate. This is true – we are born with the ability to know things – but it doesn't mean that there is innate *knowledge*. Compare: the capacity to see (vision) is innate, but that doesn't mean that *what* we see is innate as well!

What if we define innate knowledge as what everyone knows and agrees to when they gain the use of reason (§6)? After all, both Plato and Leibniz emphasise the role of reason in innate knowledge. But, Locke presses, why think that what we can discover by reasoning is *innate*? If the knowledge is innate, and so we already have it, why do we need to 'discover' it (§§8–10)? Anyway, even if we grant the definition, there is still no innate knowledge, because children can reason *before* they understand mathematical and logical truths.

To take account of this, we could say that innate knowledge is gained at some point after the use of reason (§13). This is hopeless – it doesn't mark off innate knowledge from all kinds of other knowledge, including what we learn from sense experience.

Finally, what about defining innate knowledge as truths that are assented to promptly as soon as they are understood (§§17–18)? Innate knowledge is 'self-evident'. But there are many such claims that rely on sense experience, e.g. 'white is not black'. So they can't be innate.

Locke concludes that there is no satisfactory definition of 'innate' that can be used to defend the claim that there is innate knowledge.

> Explain the difference between the ability to know and knowledge.

> Explain Locke's arguments against innate knowledge.

LEIBNIZ'S RESPONSE TO LOCKE

LEIBNIZ, *NEW ESSAYS ON HUMAN UNDERSTANDING*, BK 1, CH. 1

Although we presented Leibniz's argument for innate knowledge before discussing Locke's objections, in fact, Leibniz wrote his *New Essays* as a commentary on and response to Locke. Leibniz argues that Locke has not understood the sense in which knowledge can be innate. Locke's theory that ideas must be conscious has misled him. We can know things without being conscious of them. Locke is wrong to claim (P2) that an idea can only be in the mind if we are conscious of it (p. 18). Innate knowledge exists as 'a disposition, an aptitude, a preformation' in the mind towards developing, understanding and knowing certain thoughts (p. 21). In other words, according to Leibniz, *none* of Locke's definitions of 'innate' are quite right. We have innate knowledge in a sense not envisaged by Locke.

Unconscious knowledge

On p. 18, Leibniz picks up the example of 'It is impossible for the same thing to be and not to be', and rejects Locke's claim that this is not universally accepted. Everyone uses this knowledge all the time, but 'without explicitly attending to it'. Indeed, we can't really think without it, since it is needed to distinguish the concept of one thing from the concept of something different. 'General principles [such as the example given] enter into our thoughts, serving as their inner core and as their mortar. Even if we give no thought to them, they are necessary for thought. The mind relies on these principles constantly' (p. 23).

We can see this with Locke's example of the claim that 'white is not black'. Leibniz accepts that claims like 'white is not black' aren't innate. But they are applications of a necessary truth that *is* innate, namely 'It is impossible for the same thing to be and not be', to particular cases and concepts acquired from sense experience. Locke might object that the particular cases, such as 'white is not black', are known *before* the abstract principle. Leibniz responds that in the particular cases, we *unconsciously deploy* our knowledge of the abstract principle that something can't both be and not be at the same time.

Leibniz's theory entails that knowledge can be unconscious. But this shouldn't be controversial. Memory 'stores' ideas and usually, but not always, retrieves them when we need them. This shows two things: we can know things without being conscious of them; and

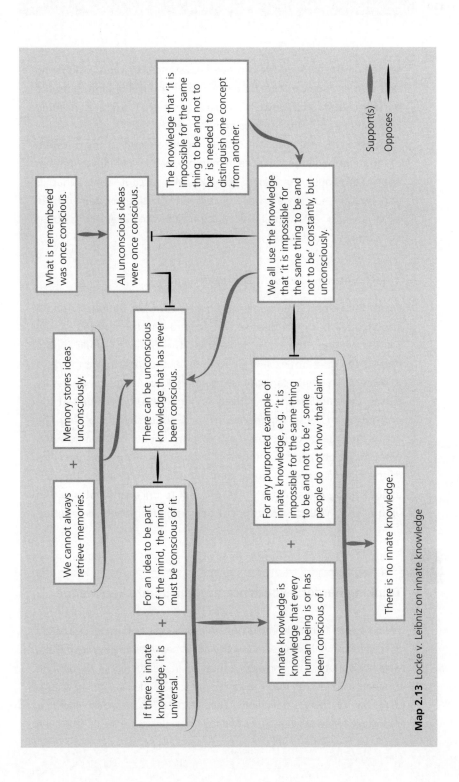

Map 2.13 Locke v. Leibniz on innate knowledge

What is remembered was once conscious.

All unconscious ideas were once conscious.

The knowledge that 'it is impossible for the same thing to be and not to be' is needed to distinguish one concept from another.

We all use the knowledge that 'it is impossible for the same thing to be and not to be' constantly, but unconsciously.

Memory stores ideas unconsciously.

We cannot always retrieve memories.

There can be unconscious knowledge that has never been conscious.

For an idea to be part of the mind, the mind must be conscious of it.

For any purported example of innate knowledge, e.g. 'it is impossible for the same thing to be and not to be', some people do not know that claim.

If there is innate knowledge, it is universal.

Innate knowledge is knowledge that every human being is or has been conscious of.

There is no innate knowledge.

Support(s)

Opposes

retrieving this knowledge can need assistance. So even Locke, who says that an idea can only be part of the mind if it is something the person can be conscious of, must accept that there is nothing impossible about unconscious knowledge.

Locke can reply that this is true, but irrelevant to the question of innate knowledge, because in memory, we are recalling what has been conscious. But, says Leibniz, why accept that what is unconscious must always have once been conscious or gained from experience (p. 20)? Why think that we can know everything about our minds straightaway?

Innate knowledge as a disposition

On p. 20, Leibniz comments on Locke's contrast between 'innate knowledge' as knowledge we can acquire and the innate capacity for knowledge. The contrast restricts the options. While innate knowledge does not exist 'fully formed' or explicitly in our minds, it is more than mere capacity. In gaining knowledge of necessary truths, the mind needs to actively engage with itself, albeit at the prompting of sense experience. Thus, Leibniz says on p. 24, 'The actual knowledge of [necessary truths] isn't innate. What is innate is what might be called the potential knowledge of them, as the veins of the marble outline a shape that is in the marble before they are uncovered by the sculptor'. It takes work to uncover what is within us, but what we uncover, we have not learned from sense experience.

What, according to Leibniz, is innate knowledge?

Thinking harder: experience triggers innate knowledge

We have seen that in defending innate knowledge, Leibniz rejects Locke's conception of what innate knowledge could be. The same is true of Plato, who holds that innate knowledge must be 'remembered' in response to experience. In fact, no major philosopher has defended innate knowledge using one of Locke's definitions. They all reject Locke's claim that it is impossible for knowledge to exist 'in the mind' unless we are or have been conscious of it. Innate knowledge is knowledge *which cannot be gained from experience*, e.g. geometry (Plato) and other necessary truths (Leibniz). Since we are not consciously aware of this knowledge from birth, there is some point at which we first come to be aware of it. And so innatists argue that experience *enables our awareness* of the knowledge.

How is experience 'enabling' knowledge different from simple *learning* from experience? We have already said that, with innate knowledge, experience is necessary but not sufficient. But can we say more than this? One modern version of the theory talks of experience 'triggering' knowledge. The idea of triggering is often used in the study of animal behaviour. For example, in some species of bird, a baby bird need only hear *a little bit* of the bird song of its species before being able to sing the *whole* song itself. There has been far too little experience of hearing the song sung by other birds for the baby bird to learn from experience; rather the experience has triggered its innately given song.

Peter Carruthers notes that there are many developments in our cognitive *capacities* that are genetically determined. For example, infants cannot see further than approximately 12 inches when first born. Within 8 weeks, they can see much further. This development of the eye is genetically encoded. The same could be true for certain types of *knowledge*. At a certain genetically determined point in development, children begin to think in a particular way for the first time, but that way of thinking has not been learned from experience. For example, around 3–4 months, babies *quickly* shift from thinking of objects as existing only while they experience them to thinking of objects as something that can exist outside their experience. So, for example, they begin looking for things they have dropped. Or again, babies *very quickly* relate to other people as having minds – beliefs, desires, intentions, emotions, etc. In both cases, they couldn't have learned this knowledge (that objects exist independent of experience, that other people have minds) from experience. So the knowledge is innate.

Again, this is not to say that experience has no role. A child must be exposed to the relevant stimuli – interactions with objects and people – for the knowledge to emerge. What shows that the knowledge is innate is that it cannot be learned from experience.

Carruthers, *Human Knowledge and Human Nature*, p. 51

Genes always cause their effects through interaction with the environment. For example, there are genes for height, but someone's height also depends on their diet as a child.

Explain the claim that experience 'triggers' innate knowledge.

> The claim is not simply that we have the *capacity* to gain this knowledge, as Locke allowed. Rather, the claim is that our capacities are 'preshaped' or 'predisposed' towards thinking truly about the world in some ways rather than others. So experience merely triggers our knowledge, rather than being the source of the knowledge.

ALTERNATIVE EMPIRICIST ACCOUNTS

The debate over innatism opposed innatism and (classical) empiricism. But many recent philosophers, including Carruthers, have argued that innate knowledge is compatible with the spirit of empiricism and the claim that *ultimately* all our knowledge derives from sense experience. We can provide an empirical explanation of innate knowledge in terms of evolution. Knowledge is innate in the sense of it being encoded genetically that we will develop and use the knowledge at a certain point in cognitive development under certain conditions. Evolution has prepared our minds to form an understanding of the world in terms of mind-independent physical objects and the existence of other minds with beliefs and desires. We can argue that these beliefs constitute knowledge because they are reliable.

See Reliabilism, p. 55.

It is worth noting, though, that claims about physical objects and other minds are contingently true. What can an empiricist say about the kinds of necessary truths Leibniz and Locke discuss, such as '2 + 2 = 4' and 'It is impossible for the same thing to be and not to be'? How could evolution give us knowledge of necessary truths if Leibniz is right that necessary truths cannot be established through experience?

Here an empiricist can provide an alternative account of how we know them. We don't know necessary truths innately; instead, necessary truths are *analytic*. We acquire the concepts involved from experience, and then in understanding the concept, we come to know the necessary (analytic) truths. The knowledge is conceptual, not innate.

Outline the argument that because necessary truths are analytic, knowledge of necessary truths is not innate.

This alternative explanation will only be successful on two conditions. First, the empiricist has to show that the relevant concepts are acquired from experience. If the concepts are innate, then the knowledge will count as innate as well. We will discuss this issue next. Second, the empiricist must show that necessary truths are, in fact, analytic. This issue will underpin much of the debate over THE INTUITION AND DEDUCTION THESIS (p. 150).

Is there any innate knowledge?

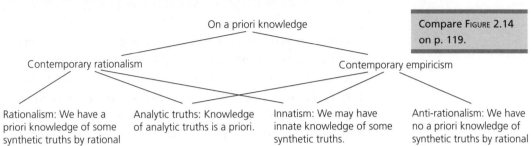

Compare Figure 2.14 on p. 119.

On a priori knowledge

Contemporary rationalism

Contemporary empiricism

Rationalism: We have a priori knowledge of some synthetic truths by rational insight and reasoning.

Analytic truths: Knowledge of analytic truths is a priori.

Innatism: We may have innate knowledge of some synthetic truths.

Anti-rationalism: We have no a priori knowledge of synthetic truths by rational insight and reasoning.

Figure 2.16 Contemporary rationalism and empiricism on a priori knowledge

Locke's argument against innate concepts

The claim that there are innate concepts means that not all concepts are learned from experience (even if experience is necessary to 'trigger' them); some concepts are somehow part of the structure of the mind. If some propositional knowledge is innate, then some concepts must be innate, because propositional knowledge is formulated in terms of concepts. Conversely, if we can show that there are no innate concepts, we will have shown that there is no innate knowledge.

We also discuss whether necessary truths are analytic using the example of mathematics in extension material.

Why does innate knowledge require innate concepts?

LOCKE, *AN ESSAY CONCERNING HUMAN UNDERSTANDING*, BK 1, CH. 4

In Ch. 4, Locke provides this very argument against innate knowledge. To have innate knowledge requires that one has the concepts involved in the proposition one knows (§1). If we first had to acquire the concepts, then the knowledge can't be innate. But there are no innate concepts.

It is an important part of Locke's argument that whatever concepts we have, we are conscious of. Furthermore, he assumes (and everyone in the debate agrees) that innate concepts must be universal – every human being has them. If we put these two thoughts together, an innate concept must be one that every human being is or has been conscious of.

Locke gives three main reasons for rejecting the existence of innate concepts, given his definition of what they are:

See Locke's arguments against innate knowledge, p. 125.

1. If we observe newborn babies, we have no reason at all to think that they have any concepts beyond, perhaps, ones deriving from their experience in the womb, such as WARMTH and PAIN (§2). Certainly, we can't think that such advanced concepts as IDENTITY or IMPOSSIBILITY are concepts babies are familiar with and conscious of. But these concepts are necessary for the knowledge that 'It is impossible for the same thing to be and not to be' (see p. 125 above).

2. Another favourite of innatism at the time of Locke was the concept of GOD. But not only is this not a concept that babies have, it is not a concept that all human beings have – whole societies, historically, have been atheist (§8). The concept of GOD is not innate, but learned by children from their teachers (§13).

3. The only way a concept can be part of the mind without the mind being conscious of it is if it is lodged in memory (§20). To remember something is to have been conscious of it in the past. If you aren't remembering a concept, then it is new to your mind – arising from some impression of sensation or reflection. Innate ideas would have to be neither remembered nor new. How could there be such a thing?

See Descartes' Trademark argument, p. 161.

Explain Locke's argument against innate concepts.

REJECTING LOCKE'S DEFINITION OF 'INNATE CONCEPT'

We noted in Thinking harder: experience triggers innate knowledge (p. 130), defenders of innate knowledge disagree with Locke's definitions of innate knowledge. The same applies to innate concepts. They reject his claim that it is impossible for concepts to exist 'in the mind' unless we are or have been conscious of them. Innate concepts are concepts which cannot be gained from experience, and arguments defending innatism try to show that experience cannot explain how we have or use the concept. Experience is necessary to trigger our development of the concept, but it is not sufficient to explain our having the concept.

The idea of experience 'triggering' the concept needs to be understood carefully. The claim is not that we simply have the *capacity* to form the concept. Rather, we are predisposed to form *just this concept*, which we cannot form on the basis of experience alone.

On this understanding of innate concepts, it is no objection that babies don't have the relevant concept of GOD or IDENTITY – it needs to be triggered by experience before it develops.

What is it for experience to trigger an innate concept?

LEIBNIZ'S DEFENCE OF INNATE CONCEPTS

LEIBNIZ, *NEW ESSAYS ON HUMAN UNDERSTANDING*, BK 1, CH. 3

Leibniz's defence of innate concepts follows his defence of innate knowledge. He accepts Locke's claim that innate knowledge requires innate concepts. Therefore, if we want to say that 'It is impossible for the same thing to be and not be' is innate knowledge, we will have to say that concepts such as IDENTITY and IMPOSSIBILITY are innate (p. 32). But, to answer Locke's first objection, this means that we have, from birth, the disposition to form these concepts. Indeed, they are essential to all thought, even though it takes time for us to make them *explicit* in our thinking.

See LEIBNIZ'S RESPONSE TO LOCKE, p. 127.

In answer to Locke's second objection, Leibniz points out that to lack the *word* for God is not to lack the concept of GOD (p. 33). Some societies have no word for 'being', but that doesn't mean they don't have thoughts that use the concept. Again, it may take considerable work of reflection to develop the concept of GOD (Ch. 1, p. 18). We are disposed, from our experience of nature, to develop the idea of a higher power. But this isn't yet the full concept of GOD as we have it. Our experience enables a concept that goes beyond what we can learn from experience; our minds are 'receptive' to the idea of God.

In answer to Locke's third objection, Leibniz repeats his theory that innate knowledge and concepts exist as dispositions in the mind (p. 33) – so neither new, in the sense of originating outside the mind, nor remembered.

Are Locke's objections to innate concepts convincing?

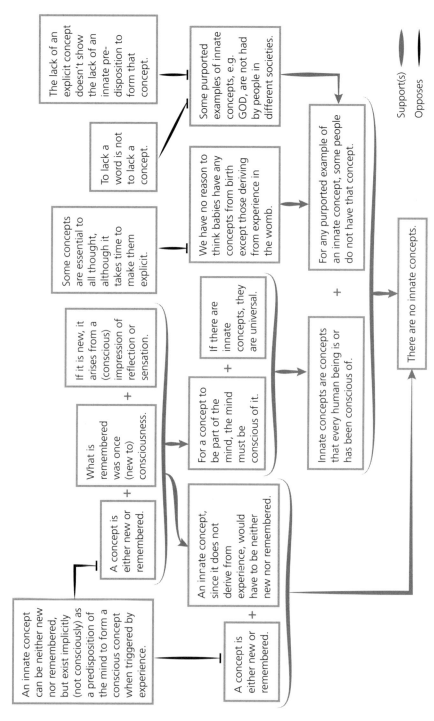

Map 2.14 Locke v. Leibniz on innate concepts

The lack of an explicit concept doesn't show the lack of an innate pre-disposition to form that concept.

Some purported examples of innate concepts, e.g. GOD, are not had by people in different societies.

To lack a word is not to lack a concept.

Some concepts are essential to all thought, although it takes time to make them explicit.

We have no reason to think babies have any concepts from birth except those deriving from experience in the womb.

For any purported example of an innate concept, some people do not have that concept.

If it is new, it arises from a (conscious) impression of reflection or sensation.

What is remembered was once (new to) consciousness.

A concept is either new or remembered.

If there are innate concepts, they are universal.

For a concept to be part of the mind, the mind must be conscious of it.

Innate concepts are concepts that every human being is or has been conscious of.

There are no innate concepts.

An innate concept can be neither new nor remembered, but exist implicitly (not consciously) as a predisposition of the mind to form a conscious concept when triggered by experience.

An innate concept, since it does not derive from experience, would have to be neither new nor remembered.

A concept is either new or remembered.

Support(s)

Opposes

The mind as a 'tabula rasa'

If innatism is false, then we must acquire all our concepts from experience. Whether or not you think that Locke's objections to innatism work, it is worth considering whether this alternative theory can be defended. If it can, then either innatism is false, or at least it has a plausible competitor. If it cannot, that may be a further argument for thinking that innatism is true.

'Tabula rasa' is Latin for 'blank slate'. The phrase recalls the time when children would have slates (or tablets (*tabula*)), like small blackboards, to write on. Until the teacher told them to write something, the slates would be blank.

LOCKE'S TWO SOURCES OF CONCEPTS

LOCKE, *AN ESSAY CONCERNING HUMAN UNDERSTANDING*, BK 2, CH. 1

Locke argues that at birth – or more accurately, since there can be consciousness and thought before birth, prior to any experience – the mind is a '*tabula rasa*' (§2).

It contains no ideas – no thoughts or concepts. If you observe newborn babies, says Locke, you'll find no reason to disagree (§6). All our ideas, then, derive from one of two sources:

1. Sensation (§3): our experience of objects outside the mind, perceived through the senses. This gives us ideas of 'sensible qualities'.
2. Reflection (§4): our experience of 'the internal operations of our minds', gained through introspection or an awareness of what the mind is doing. This provides the ideas of perception, thinking, willing and so on. These ideas may well arrive later in childhood (§8).

See LOCKE'S DISTINCTION BETWEEN PRIMARY AND SECONDARY QUALITIES, p. 80.

What, according to Locke, are the two sources of all ideas?

HUME ON IMPRESSIONS AND IDEAS

Locke's use of the term 'idea' to cover sensations and concepts (and propositional thoughts!) is very confusing (see LOCKE'S ARGUMENTS AGAINST INNATE KNOWLEDGE, p. 125). The *sensation* of yellow isn't the same thing as the *concept* YELLOW. When we see something yellow, this perceptual experience is quite different from the role YELLOW plays in the thought 'If it is yellow, it is coloured'. Hume's terminology is a little clearer, though it still doesn't quite match everyday meanings.

HUME, *AN ENQUIRY CONCERNING HUMAN UNDERSTANDING*, §2

According to Hume, what we are immediately and directly aware of are 'perceptions'. 'Perceptions' are divided into 'impressions' and 'ideas'. Although he doesn't say so explicitly here, Hume, following Locke, divides impressions into those of 'sensation' and those of 'reflection'. Impressions of sensation derive from our senses, impressions of reflection derive from our experience of our mind, including emotions.

Hume distinguishes between impressions and ideas on three grounds. First, there is a difference between the two marked by a difference of 'forcefulness' and 'vivacity' or 'liveliness' (p. 7); impressions relate roughly to 'feeling' (or 'sensing') and ideas to 'thinking'. Think what it is like to see a scene or hear a tune; now, what it is like to imagine or remember that scene or tune. The latter is weaker, fainter. (Thinking, for Hume, works with ideas as images in the same way as imagination and memory.) However, Hume immediately qualifies this claim – disease or madness can make ideas as lively and forceful as impressions. So, second, Hume argues that ideas are 'copies' of impressions. And on p. 9, Hume provides a third distinction between ideas and impressions: we are liable to confuse and make mistakes about ideas, but this is more difficult with impressions.

Just as there are impressions of sensation and reflection, so there are ideas of sensation (e.g. RED) and ideas of reflection (e.g. THINKING). What Hume means by 'idea' here, we can refer to as *concepts*. So his theory of how we acquire ideas is a theory of how we acquire concepts. His claim is that we copy them from impressions.

Identify and explain three differences between impressions and ideas.

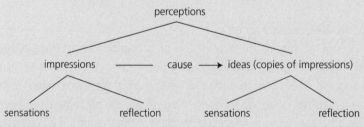

Figure 2.17 Hume on impressions and ideas

So Locke and Hume have slightly different versions of how we first acquire ideas with which we can think (concepts). We start with sense experiences of the physical world and experiences of our own minds; for Locke, this gives us ideas; but this makes it sound as if the experiences themselves are the ideas with which we think. Hume corrects this: it is copies of sensory impressions that we use in thinking.

Explain the claim that experience is the origin of all our concepts.

Why think that all ideas derive from impressions? Hume gives two arguments (p. 8). First, without having a particular type of experience, a person lacks the ability to form an idea of that experience. Thus, a blind man does not know what colour is and a mild man cannot comprehend the motive of revenge. We'll return to this claim in THINKING HARDER: CHALLENGING THE COPY PRINCIPLE (p. 141). Hume's second argument relates to 'simple' and 'complex' ideas.

SIMPLE AND COMPLEX CONCEPTS

LOCKE, *AN ESSAY CONCERNING HUMAN UNDERSTANDING*, BK 2, CH. 2

Locke argues that the basic building blocks of all thought are simple ideas, or more precisely, in Hume's terminology, simple impressions – single colours, single shapes, single smells and so on. For each, there is a corresponding simple idea (for clarity, I shall talk, from now on, about concepts). A simple impression or simple concept 'contains nothing but one uniform appearance or conception in the mind, and is not distinguishable into different ideas' (§1). Of course, we experience many such simple impressions at once, e.g. we hold a toy car that is at once both cold and hard. But there is no confusing the sensation of cold with the sensation of hardness – they are quite distinct.

As the building blocks of thought, simple concepts can be used to construct complex concepts (§2).

1. We can *unite* or *combine* the impressions of the qualities we perceive into the concept of a single object – we identify one and the same thing, a dog, say, as having a particular colour, shape, smell. So we can think of 'that thing', where the concept of 'that thing' is made up of many concepts of colour, shape, smell.

2. We can also form complex concepts by *abstraction*, e.g. the concept DOG doesn't correspond to any one particular dog. When we abstract, we ignore certain specific features and concentrate on others; so to develop the concept DOG, we ignore the different colours and sizes of dogs and pick out features they have in common, such as four legs, tail, bark, hairy.

3. We can put together simple concepts in an original way. While many of us have seen a picture of a unicorn, *someone* had to invent the concept without seeing a picture. They did it by putting together concepts of HORSE and HORN and WHITENESS.

Explain Locke's theory of the origin of concepts.

HUME, *AN ENQUIRY CONCERNING HUMAN UNDERSTANDING*, P. 8

Hume agrees with Locke's claim that all concepts are either simple concepts or complex concepts that have been constructed out of simple concepts. He claims, like Locke, that all concepts can be analysed into simple concepts which each correspond to an impression. (This is his second argument for thinking that all concepts derive from impressions.) Therefore, all concepts ultimately derive from experience and innatism is false.

For example, in direct opposition to Descartes, Hume claims that the concept GOD, based on concepts of PERFECTION and INFINITY, is extrapolated from concepts of IMPERFECTION and FINITUDE: 'The idea of God – meaning an infinitely intelligent, wise, and good Being – comes from extending beyond all limits the qualities of goodness and wisdom that we find in our own minds.'

On Descartes' view, and his response to Hume's claim, see DESCARTES' TRADEMARK ARGUMENT, p. 161.

Issues with the empiricist theory of concepts

Hume and Locke argue that *no* concept, no matter how abstract or complex, is more than a putting together, altering or abstracting from simple concepts, and that all simple concepts derive from impressions. We can show that this theory is false if we can find a counterexample, either a concept that does not derive from an impression or a complex concept that cannot be analysed into simple concepts. We start with a possible example of a concept that does not derive from an impression.

On counterexamples and general claims, see THE PURPOSE AND NATURE OF DEFINITION, p. 32.

Thinking harder: challenging the copy principle

Is it true that without a specific experience, we can't form the relevant concept? Hume notes that there is an exception to this claim. If you present someone with a spectrum of shades of blue with one shade missing, then using their imagination, they will be able to form an idea of that shade. This idea has not been copied from an impression. Hume dismisses the example as unimportant, but it is not. If it is possible that we can form an idea of a shade of blue without deriving it from an impression, is it possible that we could form other ideas without copying them from impressions?

The question is important because Hume uses his 'copy principle' repeatedly in his philosophy. For example, he closes §2 (p. 10) by saying that in metaphysics, we become confused because the ideas we work with, e.g. SUBSTANCE, are 'faint and obscure', so we don't understand them well. Because ideas derive from impressions, we can solve metaphysical debates by asking, of the words used, 'From what impression is that supposed idea derived?' If we can't find the associated impression, we can conclude that the word is used without a proper meaning, and reject the debate. However, if we *can* form ideas without copying them from impressions, then we can't use Hume's copy principle to cut through metaphysical debates as he suggests. So can the copy principle be defended against the counterexample of the missing shade of blue?

See HUME ON SUBSTANCE, p. 145.

Explain the importance of 'the missing shade of blue'.

There are two possible solutions that allow for the case of the shade of blue while maintaining a strong link between ideas and impressions.

1. We can weaken the copy principle to say 'Any ideas that are not (ultimately) copied from impressions are only *meaningful* if they *could* be copied from impressions'. In other words, what the idea is an idea of is something we can encounter in experience. The missing shade of blue clearly meets this condition, but perhaps many metaphysical ideas will not.

2. We can keep the copy principle as it is – 'all ideas are (ultimately) copied from impressions' – but explain how and why the missing shade of blue is an 'exception'. The simple impressions of different shades of blue are related to each other, as they can be arranged according to how they resemble each other (from dark to light, say). From the arrangement, we can form the idea of the missing shade *drawing on other similar impressions we already have*. This only works when impressions are structured by resemblance like this. If we have no relevantly similar impressions which strongly resemble the missing impression, we cannot form the missing idea. This is the same reason that a blind man cannot form an idea of colour, and so it fits well with Hume's theory.

?

Does the missing shade of blue undermine the claim that ideas are copied from impressions?

LEIBNIZ ON 'INTELLECTUAL IDEAS'

LEIBNIZ, *NEW ESSAYS ON HUMAN UNDERSTANDING*, PREFACE AND BK 1

Leibniz gives a number of examples of concepts that he claims are not derived from experience as Locke and Hume claim, but are innate. His longest list is in the Preface. On p. 4, he comments on Locke's division of concepts into those that originate in sensation and those that originate in reflection, which Leibniz calls 'intellectual ideas'. He comments, 'to reflect is simply to attend to what is within us, and something that we carry with us already is not something that came from the senses! So it can't be denied that there is a great deal that is innate in our minds.' Thus, he says the concepts of BEING, UNITY, SUBSTANCE, DURATION, CHANGE, ACTION, PERCEPTION and PLEASURE are all innate, because we are ourselves beings, unities, substances, that endure through time, change, act, perceive and experience pleasure. In fact, all the concepts we acquire through reflection can be called 'innate'. (He reaffirms the claim for BEING on p. 24 and for SUBSTANCE on p. 33.)

> Explain Leibniz's claim that reflection provides us with innate concepts.

Discussion

Locke can rightly respond that reflection upon what I am does not establish innate concepts. My *existence* and my *ability* to perceive are innate, but that doesn't mean that the *concepts* of SUBSTANCE and PERCEPTION are innate. Locke argues that we must first *experience* our own mind and its activities (in reflection) to develop the concepts – hence they are not innate. It is a confusion to argue that because we derive the concepts from our mental activities that we do not therefore derive them from experience.

> Do concepts I gain from reflecting on my own nature count as innate?

However, reflecting on our own nature cannot be a general explanation for all innate concepts, e.g. some concepts involved in necessary truths, such as IMPOSSIBILITY, and concepts from geometry, such as SQUARE. If these are innate, it is not because I am impossible or a square! It must be something to do with their role in innate knowledge. But perhaps these concepts are not innate, and the relevant knowledge claims, e.g. 'it is impossible for the same thing to be and not to be' or 'all squares have four sides' are not innate, but analytic truths as the empiricists argue.

Thinking harder: the concept of substance

The response we gave on Locke's behalf is too quick. Locke allows that I am a substance, and of course my existence is innate, but this doesn't mean that the concept SUBSTANCE is also innate. His position is that we gain the concept of substance from our experience – perhaps our experience of ourselves in reflection. A substance is something that continues to exist as one and the same thing through time, that possesses properties which can change even as it remains the same thing. But, even if we are substances, do we experience ourselves in reflection *as a substance*? To defend his claim that we acquire the concept SUBSTANCE from experience, Locke will need to show that we do. We can apply the same argument concerning physical objects. We have two particular concepts of substance, namely PHYSICAL SUBSTANCE (physical objects) and MENTAL SUBSTANCE (minds or selves). Do we experience physical objects as substances? Do either of these concepts of substance come from experience?

Berkeley on substance

See IDEALISM LEADS TO SOLIPSISM, p. 111.

See also Descartes' argument for THE *COGITO*, p. 155.

See THE IMMEDIATE OBJECTS OF PERCEPTION ARE MIND-DEPENDENT OBJECTS, p. 99.

Berkeley, who was an empiricist, argues that the concept of MENTAL SUBSTANCE or MIND can be derived from our experience of ourselves, but that the concept of mind-independent PHYSICAL SUBSTANCE is incoherent. We start with the first. He claims that I am not only aware of my mental activities, but aware of my mind as that which is active in thinking, perceiving and willing. So I am aware that my mind is not reducible to the activities themselves. So, Berkeley argues, we can derive the concept of MENTAL SUBSTANCE from our own minds, but the concept is not innate, as it is derived from our experience of ourselves.

However, Berkeley argues that we can gain no idea of PHYSICAL SUBSTANCE from sense experience. We do not experience physical substance, only the primary and secondary qualities of physical objects, and both are mind-dependent. That anything exists beyond these changeable properties is not an idea that sense experience supports. But rather than conclude that the concept is innate, we should conclude that it is *confused*.

Berkeley's arguments illustrate the two ways empiricists can respond to proposed counterexamples to their theory of acquiring concepts. First, they can argue that the concept is, in fact, derived from experience. Second, they can argue that the concept is *incoherent*, the result of some kind of mental error. This would explain its origin as neither derived from experience nor innate.

Hume on substance

Hume develops this last objection further, and adds a further argument to those of Berkeley against the concept of PHYSICAL SUBSTANCE. The concept of a PHYSICAL SUBSTANCE is the concept of something independent of experience existing in three-dimensional space. But how can experience show us that something exists independently of experience? I see my desk; a few moments later, I see it again. If my two experiences are of one and the same desk, then the desk existed when I wasn't looking at it. *But I don't experience the desk existing when I'm not looking at it.* So how do I arrive at the idea that it is *one and the same* desk, which has persisted through time even when I wasn't experiencing it?

Hume's diagnosis is this. My experience only provides the information that my two experiences of the desk are *very similar*. The desk as I first experience it is very similar, perhaps exactly similar, to the desk as I experience it the second time. But similarity, even exact similarity, is not quantitative identity. Being *qualitatively* identical is not the same as being *numerically* identical. (For example, two people can sit comfortably on identical chairs, but they can't sit comfortably on *one and the same* chair.) My sense experience can only provide the concept of a physical object that is numerically identical (with itself) *while I am experiencing it*.

Hume applies the same argument to the concept of MENTAL SUBSTANCE. He disagrees with Berkeley (and Descartes): we *don't* experience a continuing mental substance (self) over time, we *only* experience a continually changing array of thoughts and feelings. Even if we experienced thought as active, as Berkeley maintains, this experience doesn't support the claim that I am one and the same active substance, persisting through time and different thoughts.

So far, Hume has argued that we cannot derive the concepts of MENTAL or PHYSICAL SUBSTANCE from our experience. If he is right, then we could argue that both concepts must be innate (see THINKING HARDER: EXPERIENCE TRIGGERS INNATE KNOWLEDGE, p. 130). After all, we *do* have the concept of SUBSTANCE as something that persists through change, and we have the concepts of PHYSICAL SUBSTANCE and MENTAL SUBSTANCE. If we can't learn them from experience, they must be innate.

Hume, *A Treatise of Human Nature*, Bk 1, Pt 4, §2

Hume, *A Treatise of Human Nature*, Bk 1, Pt 4, §5

This objection is also discussed in EMPIRICIST RESPONSES TO THE *COGITO*, p. 157.

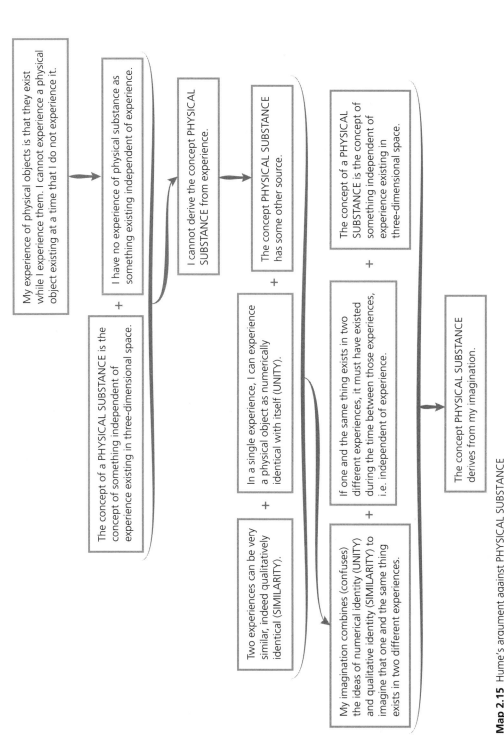

My experience of physical objects is that they exist while I experience them. I cannot experience a physical object existing at a time that I do not experience it.

+

I have no experience of physical substance as something existing independent of experience.

The concept of a PHYSICAL SUBSTANCE is the concept of something independent of experience existing in three-dimensional space.

I cannot derive the concept PHYSICAL SUBSTANCE from experience.

The concept PHYSICAL SUBSTANCE has some other source.

The concept of a PHYSICAL SUBSTANCE is the concept of something independent of experience existing in three-dimensional space.

+

In a single experience, I can experience a physical object as numerically identical with itself (UNITY).

Two experiences can be very similar, indeed qualitatively identical (SIMILARITY).

+

If one and the same thing exists in two different experiences, it must have existed during the time between those experiences, i.e. independent of experience.

My imagination combines (confuses) the ideas of numerical identity (UNITY) and qualitative identity (SIMILARITY) to imagine that one and the same thing exists in two different experiences.

+

The concept PHYSICAL SUBSTANCE derives from my imagination.

Map 2.15 Hume's argument against PHYSICAL SUBSTANCE

But Hume takes his argument to show that both concepts of SUBSTANCE are *confused* rather than innate. In coming up with the concept of a PHYSICAL SUBSTANCE that exists independently of my experiences, I have confused similarity with identity. How does this happen? Our perceptions of physical objects exhibit constancy: if I look at my desk and then shut my eyes and open them again, the desk looks exactly as it did before. On the basis of this similarity, the mind simply has a tendency to *imagine* that what I see after I opened my eyes is not just similar but identical to what I saw before I closed my eyes. The origin of the idea that the two experiences are of something identical – something that exists between and independent of perceptions – is the imagination. The imagination creates the idea of identity from similarity and unity (the idea of an individual thing, being 'one'), both of which we can derive from experience. But there is nothing in experience that matches the concept of PHYSICAL SUBSTANCE.

A similar story applies in the case of MENTAL SUBSTANCE. We've confused the similarity of our thoughts and feelings from one moment to the next with the identity of a 'thing' to which such mental states belong. The concept is not innate, it is confused.

We can object that Hume's theory makes our common-sense idea of the world wrong. If we are to avoid scepticism, we must either find a way to derive these concepts from experience or accept that they are innate.

Explain Hume's arguments that we cannot derive a concept of SUBSTANCE from experience.

Discussion

We began our discussion of the empiricist theory of concepts (p. 137) by saying that we could show the theory to be false if we can find a counterexample – a simple concept that is either not copied from an impression or a complex concept that we cannot analyse into simple concepts that are copied from impressions. If the concept of SUBSTANCE isn't a genuine counterexample to empiricism, then perhaps some other concept will be. For instance, we might argue that attempts to analyse philosophical concepts like KNOWLEDGE, TRUTH and BEAUTY into their simple constituents have all failed to produce agreement. A good explanation for this is that they don't have this structure, and Locke and Hume's theory of the origin of concepts is wrong. Another example is GOD, and we will look at Descartes' proposal that this concept is innate in DESCARTES' TRADEMARK ARGUMENT (p. 161).

On the concept of knowledge, see THE TRIPARTITE VIEW, p. 37, and RESPONSES, p. 50.

Are there any innate concepts?

We noted (p. 132) that the empiricist argument against innatism not only required that there are no innate concepts, but also that necessary truths are analytic. This is an issue to which we will return in our next topic.

Key points: innatism

- Innatism about knowledge claims that we have some propositional knowledge, not derived from experience, already 'built into' our minds.
- Plato argues that learning is a form of remembering, and provides an example of a boy discovering a geometrical truth just by being asked questions. As he is not taught anything, the questions must have helped him recover knowledge he already had.
- Leibniz argues that experience cannot give us knowledge of necessary truths, and so this knowledge is a priori. Because we discover their truth by attending to what is in our minds, it is also innate.
- Locke argues that there is no innate knowledge. He provides several definitions of innate knowledge, and rejects them all. In particular, there is no knowledge that everyone has, whether from birth or when gaining the use of reason.
- Leibniz argues against Locke's view that we can only have ideas of which we are conscious. Innate knowledge exists as a disposition towards developing and using knowledge of necessary truths. Memory shows that knowledge can be unconscious.
- Supporters of innatism generally understand innate knowledge as knowledge which can't be gained from experience, but which is triggered by experience.
- Some recent defenders of innate knowledge offer an explanation of how we have innate knowledge in terms of evolution.
- Empiricists argue that other purported examples of innate knowledge, e.g. necessary truths, can be explained as knowledge of an analytic proposition, so the knowledge is conceptual, not innate.
- Innatism about concepts claims that some concepts are not derived from experience, but already part of the structure of the mind.
- Locke rejects innate concepts for three reasons: babies have almost no concepts, and those they have are derived from experience; no concept, even GOD, is possessed by all human beings; any idea must be either new to the mind or remembered.

- Defenders of concept innatism reject Locke's understanding of innate concepts, arguing instead that they are concepts that cannot be learned from experience, though experience may be necessary to trigger them.
- Leibniz argues that this understanding of innate concepts defeats Locke's first objection. He also argues that human beings are universally disposed to form the concept of GOD, and that understanding innate concepts as dispositions to think in particular ways explains how an idea can be neither new nor remembered.
- Classical empiricism argues that all concepts derive from experience. In Locke's terms, all concepts derive from either sensation (sense experience) or reflection (experience of our minds). Prior to experience, the mind is a *tabula rasa*.
- Hume claims that simple concepts are (fainter) copies of impressions. We cannot form ideas without the relevant experience (e.g. a blind man and colour).
- Locke and Hume argue that complex concepts are created out of simple concepts by combining and abstracting from them.
- Hume allows that some simple ideas, e.g. a particular shade of blue, don't have to be derived from sense impressions. We can make Hume consistent by saying that an idea does not need to be copied from an impression, but it is only meaningful if there is a possible impression it could be copied from. Alternatively, we can explain why the shade of blue is a very specific exception that cannot be generalised.
- Leibniz takes all concepts that are derived from reflection to be innate. However, empiricists can object that such concepts are not innate, but derived from the experience of our own minds.
- Berkeley and Hume argue that PHYSICAL SUBSTANCE is not a concept that can be derived from experience but is not innate.
- Hume argues that both PHYSICAL SUBSTANCE and MENTAL SUBSTANCE derive from a confusion between similarity and identity; we experience similarity, but we imagine identity. Both are therefore not innate, but confused.
- We can object that Hume's analysis leads to scepticism. If he is right that these concepts don't derive from experience, this is a good reason to think that the concepts are innate.
- We can object to empiricism that there are some complex concepts, e.g. KNOWLEDGE or BEAUTY, that cannot be analysed in terms of simpler concepts.

B. The intuition and deduction thesis

Rationalism and empiricism revisited

We noted in DEFINING RATIONALISM, EMPIRICISM AND INNATISM (p. 117) that there were two debates over whether reason is a source of knowledge. Because a posteriori knowledge comes from sense experience by definition, the debates concern a priori knowledge. The first debate concerned whether any a priori knowledge is innate (innatism v. empiricism). The second concerns whether any a priori knowledge is gained through rational insight and reasoning (rationalism v. empiricism).

We noted that, historically, 'classical rationalists' connected these two rational sources of knowledge. Descartes is one of those philosophers. Our interest in this section will be his defence of knowledge gained through rational insight and reasoning. But we will see that certain moves in his arguments require innate knowledge (and concepts) as well.

THE MEANING OF 'INTUITION' AND 'DEDUCTION'

See DEDUCTIVE
ARGUMENT, p. 7.

First, however, we need to understand the terms in the heading above. The form of reasoning Descartes presents is intended to be deductive. So if the premises are true, then the conclusion *must* be true if the argument is valid. In this case, we say that the conclusion is entailed by the premises. If the premises are true but the conclusion could be false, then the deduction has failed. The advantage of using deduction is that it is a way of *proving* the conclusion from the premises. If we can be confident that the premises are true and the inference is correct, we can be confident that the conclusion is true.

What about 'intuition', which I've also been referring to as 'insight'? This *doesn't* mean a 'gut feeling' or 'instinct'. It refers to *rational* intuition. For example, when you consider a deductive argument, do you understand why, if the premises are true, then the conclusion must be true? Take the example, 'Socrates is a man and all men are mortal. Therefore, Socrates is mortal.' How is it that you can 'see' the conclusion follows – that it *must* be true if the premises are true? This grasping of rational truths takes us towards the idea of 'rational intuition', though it covers much more than deductive reasoning. Another example is necessary truth. How do you understand that 2 + 2 not only equals 4, but must equal 4? Or that it is impossible for the same thing to be and not to be? At the heart of rational intuition is *discovering the truth of a claim just by thinking about it*. Very often, what we discover in rational intuition is that the claim is true because it must be true.

Descartes puts the two methods together: we know a number of claims by rational intuition, and we can use these as the premises in deductive arguments to gain knowledge of further claims. We will see that he argues that using these methods, we can gain knowledge of our own existence as mental substances, of the existence of God, and of the existence and nature of physical objects.

Explain the concepts of rational intuition and deduction.

EMPIRICIST ALTERNATIVES

Whether we have rational intuition in this sense is disputed by empiricists. As we noted in DEFINING RATIONALISM, EMPIRICISM AND INNATISM (p. 117), everyone can agree that we can know analytic propositions a priori (just by thinking about them). However, empiricists can argue that knowledge of analytic propositions isn't a function of 'rational intuition', but a form of conceptual knowledge. To know an analytic truth, one simply needs to understand the concepts involved. As long as the concepts are learned from experience, knowledge of analytic truths is no threat to the empiricist claim that all knowledge ultimately derives from experience.

Empiricists also allow that we can, of course, know our own mental states 'just by thinking about them'. The origin of this knowledge isn't rational intuition either, but impressions of reflection.

See THE MIND AS A *TABULA RASA*, p. 137.

The real debate between empiricism and rationalism, then, concerns whether we can have a priori knowledge of any synthetic propositions that don't concern our own mental states. We can use this to sharpen our definitions of rationalism and empiricism:

> *Rationalism (2.0)*: Rationalism claims that we have some a priori knowledge of synthetic propositions about the world external to our minds.
> *Empiricism (2.0)*: Empiricism (about knowledge) claims that there is no a priori knowledge of synthetic propositions about the world external to our minds (whether this is innate or gained from rational intuition and deduction).

Given this, for any claim that rationalists offer as an example of knowledge through rational intuition and deduction, empiricists have four possible responses:

1. that the proposition is analytic, not synthetic;
2. that the proposition is about our own minds, known from impressions of reflection;
3. that knowledge of the proposition is a posteriori, not a priori; or
4. that we can't know the proposition at all.

As we go through Descartes' arguments for knowledge from intuition and deduction, we need to bear in mind these alternative empiricist explanations of the knowledge he claims. But first, an elaboration of an empiricist theory of knowledge from Hume.

Hume's fork

HUME, *AN ENQUIRY CONCERNING HUMAN UNDERSTANDING*, §4, PT 1

Hume argues that we can have knowledge of just two sorts of claim: the relations between ideas and matters of fact. He uses two related criteria to make the distinction, though it is easier to grasp what he means by taking them in a different order:

1. Relations of ideas 'can be discovered purely by thinking, with no need to attend to anything that actually exists anywhere in the universe' (p. 11). Matters of fact, by contrast, are 'propositions about what exists and what is the case' (p. 12).
2. Relations of ideas are statements that are 'either intuitively or demonstratively certain' (p. 11). Hume gives the example of 3 × 5 = 30/2 – a statement about the relations of numbers. Relations of ideas that are demonstratively certain are known by deduction. Matters of fact, by contrast, are not known by deduction, because they are statements that can be *denied without contradiction*.

The second point needs explanation. First, a contradiction both asserts and denies something. For example, a true analytic proposition cannot be denied without contradiction. To say that vixens are not foxes is a contradiction in terms; it is to say that female foxes are not foxes. Second, in a deductive argument, if you assert the premises, but deny the conclusion, then you contradict yourself, e.g. '3 × 5 = 15 and 30 ÷ 2 = 15, but 3 × 5 ≠ 30 ÷ 2'. Hume is claiming that we gain knowledge of relations of ideas through merely understanding concepts and through deductive inference from such understanding. To deny any claims we know this way would involve a contradiction.

(We can also use deduction to infer matters of fact from other matters of fact, e.g. Socrates is a man and all men are mortal, so Socrates is mortal. But 'Socrates is mortal' isn't known by deduction in Hume's sense, since the premises rely on sense experience.)

We can now connect the two criteria. What we know that is intuitively or demonstratively certain is also what can be discovered purely by thinking – relations of ideas. On the other hand, propositions about what exists – matters of fact – we cannot know by a priori reasoning. Hume goes on to argue that we can know them through experience.

The history of philosophy is full of debate about what qualifies as relations of ideas in Hume's sense. As we shall see, Descartes argues that a great deal can be known through rational intuition and demonstration, while Hume rejects many of Descartes' claims. So we need to interpret Hume in line with empiricism, as saying that a priori knowledge (relations of ideas) is either analytic (and what can be deduced from analytic truths) or only about my own mind, while all knowledge of synthetic propositions about the world beyond my mind (matters of fact) is a posteriori.

Outline and explain the key differences between relations of ideas and matters of fact.

Matters of fact

While the main focus of debate between rationalism and empiricism concerns a priori knowledge, it is worth briefly describing Hume's theory of our a posteriori knowledge of matters of fact. The foundation of knowledge of matters of fact, Hume argues, is what we *experience* here and now, or can remember (p. 12). We gain it by using observation and employing induction and reasoning about probability. All knowledge that goes beyond what is present to our senses or memory rests on *causal inference*. We take our experience to be an effect of whatever fact we infer. If I go out in the morning and all the streets are wet when they were dry yesterday evening, I'll infer that it rained in the night. I do this because I think that rain causes the streets to become wet, and if the whole area is wet, not just small part, I'll believe the cause is rain (rather than liquid spilling or some other explanation).

And how do I know all this? How do I know what causes what? Not by a priori reasoning or deduction. If you encounter some object that you've never experienced before, you cannot work out what effects it will have just by examining it. Just by examining a magnet – having never experienced one before – could you deduce what effect it will have on metal? Just by examining bread, could you work out that it doesn't nourish tigers (p. 13)? Just by seeing a billiard ball roll towards another billiard ball, could you conclude that the second one will move away? Even if you imagine that this is what will happen, that's arbitrary, groundless.

It is only our *experience* of what causes what that enables us to make causal inferences in particular cases. It is only our experience that enables us to infer from the existence of some cause to its effect, or from some effect to its cause. I have experienced rain wetting the streets around me and spillages wetting smaller areas. Reason can impose some order on the particular causal relations we discover through experience. For example, reason can simplify our causal principles, for instance by identifying different instances (the movements of billiard balls and the vibrations of molecules, say) as examples of the same kind of thing (kinetic energy). But reason can do no more than this (p. 14).

See Hypothetical reasoning, p. 9.

Explain Hume's theory of our knowledge of matters of fact.

Descartes' theory of rational intuition

Descartes' *Meditations* provide an extended study in establishing knowledge through rational intuition and deduction. We focus on three central claims: his '*cogito*', the existence of God, and the existence of physical objects in the 'external world' (i.e. the world outside the mind). We begin by looking at his 'cogito' and his elaboration of the idea of rational intuition through his concept of 'clear and distinct' ideas.

DESCARTES, *MEDITATIONS* II (PP. 3–6), III (PP. 9–10)

The *cogito* (*Meditation* II, pp. 3–6)

At the start of *Meditation* II, we find Descartes supposing that all that he perceives and remembers is an illusion; that he has no body or senses at all; that in believing anything else, he is being deceived by a 'supremely powerful and cunning deceiver', an 'evil demon'. How did he get into this state?!

The full story is discussed in DESCARTES' SCEPTICAL ARGUMENTS (p. 189). But for now, we can note that Descartes is seeking to find out what he can know as true. To achieve this, he has decided to avoid believing anything that is not 'completely certain and indubitable' (*Meditation* I, p. 1). He then argues that he can doubt his senses, his memory and even that he has a body (note that these are all a posteriori claims we would use perception to establish). The demon could make it seem that he sees a tree when he doesn't, that he has a body when he doesn't, and so on. The question now, at the start of *Meditation* II, is whether he can know anything at all.

Descartes begins by arguing that, even if the evil demon is deceiving him about his senses and so on, 'he will never bring it about that I am nothing while I think I am something' (p. 4). Why not? Descartes cannot doubt that he exists: if he were to doubt that he exists, that would prove he does exist – as something that thinks (doubting is a kind of thinking). He cannot be deceived that he thinks. So he knows that he exists as something that thinks. The *cogito*, Latin for 'I think', is Descartes' first stepping stone to knowledge.

However, Descartes can't know that he exists *as a body* – his sense perception of his body, and of bodies in general, could be something he is deceived about. The demon could make it seem that he has a body when in fact he does not. Could he nevertheless *be* a body, without knowing it? Descartes can't say, but at least his

> On knowledge as certain, see INFALLIBILISM, p. 53.

> Explain Descartes' argument for the *cogito*.

Descartes discusses
this further in
Meditation VI. See
Metaphysics of
Mind, SUBSTANCE
DUALISM, p. 179.

So Descartes adopts
a type of sense-data
theory of perception.
At this point,
Descartes is an
idealist (see THE
IMMEDIATE OBJECTS OF
PERCEPTION ARE
MIND-DEPENDENT OBJECTS,
p. 99), but once he
accepts the existence
of physical objects he
becomes an indirect
realist (see INDIRECT
REALISM, p. 78).

knowledge of what he is can't *depend* on his being a body, since he knows he exists whether or not he has a body. What he is, is a thinking thing, 'a thing that doubts, understands, affirms, denies, wants, refuses, and also imagines and senses' (p. 5). Furthermore, he knows which type of thought he is engaging in: he can't mistakenly think that he is imagining when he's conceiving, can't think he's doubting when he's willing, and so on.

The last activity of the mind that Descartes lists is 'senses'. But doesn't sense perception involve having a body? So doesn't the fact that he senses establish the existence of physical objects? No, because, Descartes notes, he has sensory experiences in his dreams as well, when he is not seeing or hearing at all. 'Sensing' is just having sensory experiences. Understood like this, independent of their cause, these experiences are nothing more than a form of thinking, and so don't depend on having a body.

Clear and distinct ideas (*Meditation* III, pp. 9–10)

At the start of *Meditation* III, Descartes reflects on the *cogito*. He finds that his certainty in it rests on how the idea presents itself to his mind. So he argues (p. 9),

P1. 'In this first item of knowledge there is simply a clear and distinct perception of what I am asserting.'
P2. If clarity and distinctness do not guarantee truth, then I cannot know that I exist.
P3. I do know that I exist.
C1. Therefore, 'as a general rule … whatever I perceive very clearly and distinctly is true'.

This argument lays the foundations for Descartes' theory of *rational intuition*. Descartes has defended the *cogito* as a claim that he knows to be true just by thinking about it. He knows because it is an idea that is 'clear and distinct'.

What does this mean? Descartes doesn't say in the *Meditations*, but gives this definition in his *Principles of Philosophy* (Pt 1, §45): an idea is clear 'when it is present and accessible to the attentive mind – just as we say that we see something clearly when it is present to the eye's gaze and stimulates it with a sufficient degree of strength and accessibility'. An idea is distinct if it is clear and 'it is so sharply separated from all other ideas that every part of it is clear'. In the *Meditations*, again drawing on an analogy with vision, Descartes connects clear and distinct ideas to what he calls 'the natural light': 'Things that are revealed by the natural light – for example, that *if I am doubting then I exist* – are not open to any doubt, because no other faculty that might show them to be false could be as trustworthy as the natural light' (p. 11). So, for Descartes, rational intuition is the 'natural light', our ability to know that clear and distinct ideas are true.

In what sense are clear and distinct ideas 'indubitable'? Just saying 'I can't doubt it, so it must be true' is clearly not good enough. The fact that you can't doubt something may just be a psychological fact about you (cp. 'I'm sure he told the truth. I can't believe he would lie to me' – and yet he did …). Things that we cannot doubt in this sense are not yet a good guide to the truth.

But this subjective sense of 'indubitable', a *feeling* of certainty, is not what Descartes means. He means that when I, as a rational thinker, using my best, most careful judgement, consider a proposition, I judge that it is impossible that it should be false. It is necessarily true that when I think of the proposition, it is true. When I think the thought 'I think', then that thought, 'I think', must be true. The indubitability of the proposition is an epistemological fact about the proposition, not a psychological fact about me.

> What, according to Descartes, is a 'clear and distinct' idea?

EMPIRICIST RESPONSES TO THE *COGITO*

What does it mean to say 'I exist' or 'I think'? Descartes claims that he is a thinking *thing*. He is the *same* thing from one thought to another. But can Descartes know this? The evil demon may deceive him: perhaps there is only *a succession of thoughts*, nothing that persists between thoughts which is a *single* thing.

As we saw in THINKING HARDER: THE CONCEPT OF SUBSTANCE (p. 143), Hume develops the argument as follows: we don't experience a continuing mental

> *Treatise of Human Nature*, Bk 1, Pt 4, §5

substance over time, we *only* experience a continually changing array of thoughts and feelings. So what is the basis for thinking that there is a *thing* that thinks? In coming up with the idea of a 'thinking thing' – a mental substance – we confuse *similarity* with *identity*. We've confused our experience of the similarity of our thoughts and feelings from one moment to the next with the idea that there is one identical 'thing' persisting through such thoughts and to which they belong.

See IDEALISM AND GOD, p. 104.

Descartes' response to this objection, in an appendix to the *Meditations* called 'Objections and Replies', is to say that thoughts logically require a thinker. (Berkeley might respond similarly: thoughts are passive – they must *be* thought by something.) But is this something Descartes could be deceived about?

Explain Hume's objection that Descartes' *cogito* does not establish knowledge of a self.

Perhaps it is true that there can't be a thought unless something thinks it. But that doesn't entail that the 'thinker' is a subject that persists from one thought to another. Hume argues that even if we experience thinking as active in this way, how does our experience enable us to move to the claim that I am one and the same active substance, persisting through time and different thoughts? As soon as Descartes says that to be a thinker is to doubt, will, imagine and so on, he assumes we can say these activities belong to the *same* subject, that he (the same thinker) does all this. But perhaps the evil demon is simply creating a series of false thoughts, among which is the thought that a thinker, a substance, an 'I', exists. Descartes' claims about *what* he is could be false.

Is the *cogito* an example of knowledge by rational intuition? Descartes will argue that it is, because it is a clear and distinct idea. But first, we have just questioned whether it is clear and distinct that I am a mental substance. Second, Hume argues that we can know immediately about our minds through impressions of reflection. This will be a priori knowledge and intuitively certain, but impressions of reflection don't provide us with knowledge of our existence as a mental substance. Berkeley disagrees, and thinks our experience of our mental activities does allow us to infer that we exist as mental substances. I know I exist because I experience myself, not because of anything about 'clear and distinct' ideas being certainly true.

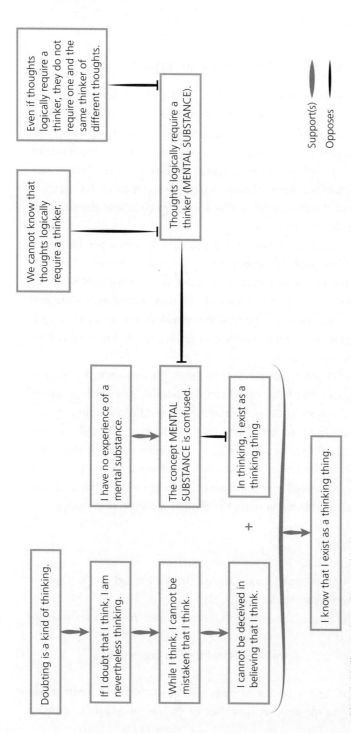

Even if thoughts logically require a thinker, they do not require one and the same thinker of different thoughts.

We cannot know that thoughts logically require a thinker.

Thoughts logically require a thinker (MENTAL SUBSTANCE).

I have no experience of a mental substance.

The concept MENTAL SUBSTANCE is confused.

In thinking, I exist as a thinking thing.

Doubting is a kind of thinking.

If I doubt that I think, I am nevertheless thinking.

While I think, I cannot be mistaken that I think.

I cannot be deceived in believing that I think.

+

I know that I exist as a thinking thing.

Support(s)

Opposes

Map 2.16 The *cogito* and some objections

CLEAR AND DISTINCT IDEAS AND GOD

DESCARTES, *MEDITATION* III (PP. 10, 17)

What, apart from the *cogito*, is clear and distinct? Our perceptions of physical objects can *seem* clear and distinct, but in fact, they are not (p. 10). On reflection, Descartes sees that what was clear was 'merely the ideas', i.e. the sensory experiences, but not what causes them. So as perceptions of physical objects (if that is what our sensory experiences are), they are not clear and distinct. By contrast, mathematical claims, such as '2 + 3 = 5', are clear and distinct, and Descartes cannot doubt them.

More precisely, he can only doubt such a claim when he thinks not about the claim, but about the power of an evil demon (or God) to deceive him. So, *at the time we consider it*, a thought which is clear and distinct we must believe to be true. But when we are not focusing on it, in order to be sure that the clear and distinct thought really is true, we need to know that we are not being deceived by an evil demon (or God).

And so Descartes undertakes to prove the existence of God, and then to show that God would not deceive us. We will look at his attempted proofs of God's existence next, but before doing so, it is worth looking at the argument that if God exists, God would not deceive us, and so we are secure in our knowledge of clear and distinct ideas. Descartes provides this argument on p. 17 (here and below, I have added in missing premises in brackets, some of which Descartes assumes because he has argued for them previously):

P1. God exists.
P2. By definition, God is supremely perfect.
P3. 'The natural light makes it clear that all fraud and deception depend on some defect' (p. 17).
P4. (By definition, something that is supremely perfect can have no defects.)
C1. Therefore, it is not possible for God to deceive us.

By this conclusion, Descartes does not mean that we cannot make mistakes! He means that God 'has given me the ability to correct

We discuss an objection to Descartes' theory of the relation between clear and distinct ideas and God in extension material.

any falsity there may be in my opinions' (*Meditation* VI, p. 30). We are assured that once we have done all we can to avoid error, and form beliefs on the basis of clear and distinct ideas, then we will not go wrong. But we are not assured of anything more than this.

Descartes doesn't spell it out, but God's existence is enough to rule out deception by an evil demon as well.

P1. God is supremely powerful.

P2. If God is supremely powerful, then an evil demon could only deceive me if God allowed it.

P3. If an evil demon is deceiving me, then I have no way of correcting my false opinions.

P4. If I have no way of correcting my false opinions, then God is a deceiver.

C1. Therefore, if God permits an evil demon to deceive me, then God is a deceiver.

P5. God is not a deceiver.

C2. Therefore, God will not permit an evil demon to deceive me.

But can we know what God will or won't do or allow? Descartes allows that we cannot know God's purposes (*Meditation* IV, p. 19), but we don't need to. If we have no way of correcting our false beliefs, this would frustrate what we are, namely rational minds seeking the truth using clear and distinct ideas. We don't need to know what God's purposes are in order to know that this would amount to God being a deceiver, which is contradictory to being supremely perfect.

> Explain Descartes' argument for the claim that we are not being deceived, first in prose, then using an argument map.

Descartes' Trademark argument

Descartes provides three arguments for the existence of God, his Trademark argument, a cosmological argument (p. 168), and an ontological argument (p. 171). In the Trademark argument, Descartes tries to prove the existence of God from just the idea of GOD as a being that is, among other things, supremely powerful and supremely perfect. He argues that the concept of GOD is innate, like a 'trademark' that our creator has stamped on our minds (p. 17).

DESCARTES, *MEDITATION* III, PP. 10–14, 17

Descartes begins by identifying three possible sources of any idea (p. 10):

On innate concepts, see LOCKE's ARGUMENT AGAINST INNATE CONCEPTS, p. 133.

1. The idea derives from something outside my mind, such as I experience in sense perception.
2. I have invented it.
3. It is innate. (Descartes explains this as 'it derives from my own nature', but he also uses the usual innatist argument that it can't be learned from experience (or invention). See REJECTING LOCKE's DEFINITION OF 'INNATE CONCEPT', p. 134.)

Explain Descartes' three sources of ideas.

We cannot in general be certain which of the three types of cause an idea has (p. 11). Which is the source of the concept GOD?

Before answering that question, Descartes embarks on a long defence of the claim that a cause must have at least as much 'reality' as its effect, and that the cause of an idea must have as much reality as what the idea is an idea *of*. Both the claim and the argument are very puzzling, so we set them aside to explore further below. For now, here is a common-sense example: if we discover a picture of a sophisticated machine, even though it's just a *picture*, we think it must be the product of an advanced society or a highly fertile imagination. It is what it is a picture *of* that makes us think the cause is sophisticated. Where could the 'sophistication' of the machine in the picture come from except a mind that is itself just as sophisticated? The cause must have as much 'reality' as the machine in the picture.

See THINKING HARDER: DEGREES OF REALITY, p. 165.

Bernard Williams, *Descartes*, pp. 138–9

With this in place, Descartes argues:

P1. I have the concept GOD.
P2. The concept GOD is a concept of something infinite and perfect (pp. 11–12).
P3. As a mind, a thinking substance, I can think up (create) many ideas, including ideas of people and physical objects (pp. 13–14).
P4. But I am finite, while the concept GOD is a concept of something infinite (p. 14).

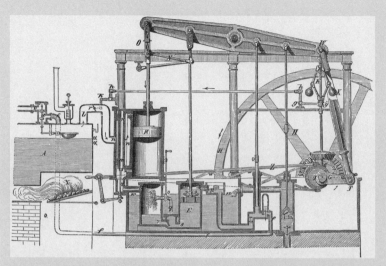

Figure 2.18 What can we infer about the cause of this diagram?

C1. Therefore, it is a concept of something with more reality than my own mind.

P5. The cause of the concept GOD must have as much reality as what the concept is of.

C2. Therefore, my mind could not have created it.

P6. The only possible cause is God.

C3. Therefore, God exists.

Descartes considers and rejects an objection to (P4), namely that I have all the perfections I attribute to God, and so could invent the concept (p. 15). But given that I am in doubt, I clearly do not have infinite knowledge – I am not infinite, but finite.

How could we have acquired the concept GOD? Descartes has argued that he couldn't have invented it. On p. 16, he adds that it does not derive from sense experience (it isn't something that arises 'unexpectedly' as do other ideas of sense). So by elimination, the concept GOD must be innate, built into the structure of our minds by God.

Outline Descartes' Trademark argument.

Explain why, if the Trademark argument succeeds, it provides an example of knowledge through rational intuition and deduction.

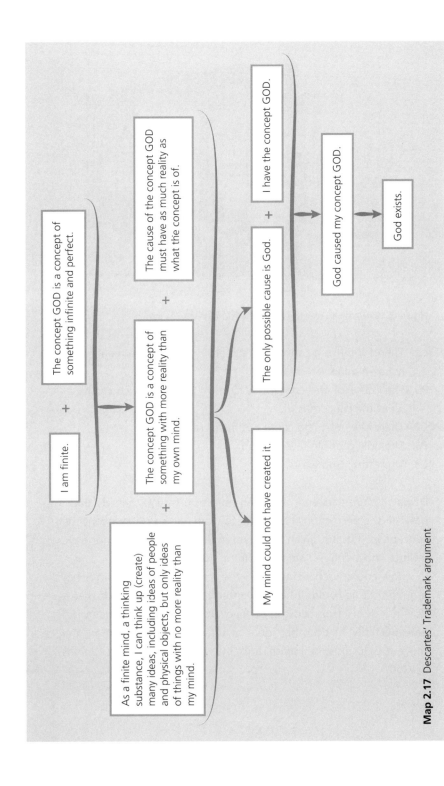

Map 2.17 Descartes' Trademark argument

Thinking harder: degrees of reality

Descartes' argument rests on claims (C1) and (P5), but these are difficult and highly controversial. The idea of 'degrees of reality' is strange to us, but was a standard part of medieval metaphysics.

1. A 'substance' is defined as something that can exist independently, such as the mind, God and physical objects.
2. An 'attribute' is a property of a substance – the attribute of mind is thought, while extension (having spatial dimensions) is an attribute of physical objects.
3. A 'mode' is a particular determination of a property. So ideas are modes of the mind – specific ways of thinking. Being specific sizes or shapes are modes of physical objects.

A substance has more reality than an attribute, because a property cannot exist without a substance, and so is dependent on it. There can be no thoughts without a thinker. Modes, therefore, also have less reality than substances. Ideas are modes of the attribute 'thought', which is possessed by thinking substances.

Descartes applies these thoughts to cause and effect. He simply takes it to be a clear and distinct idea that the cause of something must contain at least as much reality as its effect (p. 12). From this, he derives the claim that something can't come from nothing (p. 13). But in fact, it is easier for us to understand this the other way around – something can't come from nothing, and so whatever is part of the effect must have originated in the cause. For instance, a stone can only be created by or from something that contains the qualities of the stone (what is needed to make a stone). Or again, something hot can't derive its heat from something cold.

Ideas are more complicated. As modes of thought, the 'intrinsic reality' of all ideas is the same, and less than the reality of my mind, which is a substance. But ideas also represent something, e.g. an object, a size, a tune, a mind, God. Some of these things – object, mind, God – are substances; others – a size, a tune – are modes. The degree of reality of the thing that the thought is about determines the idea's 'representative reality' (p. 11). Just as we need to able to explain where the heat in something hot comes from, so we need to be able to explain the representative reality of an idea. Just as heat comes from something hot, so an idea with a certain representative reality must come from something with at least as much intrinsic reality (p. 12). So ideas of substance can only be caused by substances; ideas of modes can be caused by either modes or substances.

We can now apply this to the concept GOD. As a concept, it is a mode of thought, and so it seems my mind – a substance – could cause it, just as my mind causes many other ideas. But the special features of what GOD is a concept *of*, namely something infinite and perfect, mean that it has a representative reality *greater* than the intrinsic reality of my mind. If I invented the concept, GOD would contain things – infinity and perfection – that are not in its cause, because I am imperfect and finite. But this is impossible – there must be as much reality in the cause as in the effect. So only God, being perfect and infinite, could create a concept of something perfect and infinite.

What does Descartes mean by 'representative reality'?

EMPIRICIST RESPONSES TO THE TRADEMARK ARGUMENT

Empiricists will reject Descartes' Trademark argument as it claims both that the idea of GOD is innate, and that we can prove the existence of God using rational intuition and deduction. We noted above that claims (C1) and (P5) are particularly problematic, and it is these claims that empiricist objections focus upon. We can use Hume's discussion of the concept of GOD and his 'fork' to present challenges to these claims.

Is the concept of GOD innate?

As we saw in HUME, AN ENQUIRY CONCERNING HUMAN UNDERSTANDING (p. 140), Hume rejects the claim that the concept GOD cannot be created by our minds. We can form this concept by starting from ideas of finitude: 'The idea of God – meaning an infinitely intelligent, wise, and good Being – comes from extending beyond all limits the qualities of goodness and wisdom that we find in our own minds'. In 'extending beyond all limits' the ideas of finite goodness and wisdom we have from experience, we create an abstract negation of what is finite. Thus, we create ideas of what is NOT-FINITE (INFINITE) and NOT-IMPERFECT (PERFECT).

However, Descartes considers and rejects just this proposal (p. 14). The idea of imperfection or lack depends upon an idea of perfection; we can't recognise that we are imperfect *unless* we have an idea of perfection with which to compare ourselves.

This argument seems to work in other cases, e.g. REAL and REALITY. It is intuitively plausible that our concept REAL is not an abstraction from NOT-UNREAL – how could we first have experiences of what is unreal on which UNREAL is based? Our experiences are fundamentally of what is real, so REAL is the primary concept. But this is not as clearly true for the cases of PERFECTION and INFINITY – we could first experience limits and then create a new concept UNLIMITED and then use this concept to create the concepts PERFECTION and INFINITY.

Furthermore, PERFECTION and INFINITY – if they mean more than 'not imperfect' and 'not finite' – are arguably challenging and unclear concepts. What is it, exactly, to think not merely of the *absence of limits*, but of something for which there could be no limits? Yet Descartes claims that we have a very powerful – clear and distinct – positive idea of God as perfect and infinite, and not some hazy notion of something indefinitely great. Yet he also accepts that, as a finite mind, he cannot 'grasp' this thought, but he merely 'understands' it (p. 14). With this admission, his claim that the concept of GOD is both clear and distinct and involves a positive conception of God's infinity and perfection is unpersuasive.

> Explain Hume's argument that the concept GOD is derived from experience and Descartes' response.

Knowledge of causes

We can use HUME'S FORK (p. 152) to challenge a number of Descartes' assumptions about causation. Descartes assumes that all ideas have a cause. But as Hume argues elsewhere, *must* everything (every idea) have a cause? The claims 'everything has a cause' and 'something cannot come out of nothing' are not analytically true. 'Some things do not have a cause' is not a *contradiction in terms* like 'Some bachelors are married' is. Of course, from our experience, we have good reason to think that everything has a cause, but this is still only a contingent truth; it may be false. We cannot show that it holds without exception.

Second, if we can't know that it is impossible for something to come out of nothing, then we can't know, either, that a cause must contain at least as much 'reality' as its effect. What causes what is something we must discover from experience; we cannot know it by a priori reason.

> *A Treatise of Human Nature*, Bk 1, Pt 3, Ch. 3

> Does Descartes' Trademark argument show that we can know that God exists through rational intuition and deduction?

Descartes' cosmological argument

COSMOLOGICAL ARGUMENTS are studied further in Metaphysics of God, p. 95.

Descartes' second argument for the existence of God is a 'cosmological' argument. Cosmological arguments for God's existence start from (some version of) the question 'Why does anything exist?'

See THE COGITO, p. 155.

DESCARTES, *MEDITATION* III, PP. 15–16

At this point in the *Meditations*, the only thing that Descartes knows to exist is himself. So Descartes asks what causes *his* existence. As the argument is long and complicated, I have divided it into sections.

P1. If I caused my own existence, I would give myself all perfections (omnipotence, omniscience, etc.).
P2. I do not have all perfections.
C1. Therefore, I am not the cause of my existence.

P3. A lifespan is composed of independent parts, such that my existing at one time does not entail or cause my existing later.
P4. My existence is not uncaused.
C2. Therefore, some cause is needed to keep me in existence.
P5. I do not have the power to cause my continued existence through time.
C3. Therefore, I depend on something else to exist.

P6. I am a thinking thing and I have the idea of God.
P7. There must be as much reality in the cause as in the effect.
C4. Therefore, what causes my existence must be a thinking thing and have the idea of God.

P8. Either what causes me is the cause of its own existence or its existence is caused by another cause.
P9. If its existence is caused by another cause, then the point repeats: this second cause is in turn either the cause of its own existence or its existence is caused by another cause.
P10. There cannot be an infinite sequence of causes.

On (P7), see THINKING HARDER: DEGREES OF REALITY, p. 165.

C5. Therefore, some cause must be the cause of its own existence.

P11.What is the cause of its own existence (and so, directly or indirectly, the cause of my existence) is God.

C6. Therefore, God exists.

Descartes adds a further argument, picking up (P3) and (C2).

C2. Some cause is needed to keep me in existence.

P12.There cannot be an infinite chain of causes because what caused my existence also causes my continued existence in the present.

P13.My parents, or any other supposed cause of my existence, do not keep me in existence.

P14.The only cause that could keep me in existence is God.

C7. Therefore, God exists.

Outline Descartes' cosmological argument.

The cause of continued existence

Why does Descartes say that not only the start of his existence, but his continued existence through time, needs to be caused (C2)? For instance, we might object that my continued existence doesn't require a cause, because *nothing changes* – I simply continue to exist. If I cease to exist, *that* requires a cause.

But this misunderstands both causation and continued existence. I am sitting on a chair – nothing is changing. But there is a cause of this continued state of affairs, namely gravity and the rigidity of the chair. Should either of those *standing conditions* change, then I would no longer be sitting on the chair. I'd either be floating (no gravity) or sitting on the ground (collapsed chair). That people don't die at any given instant is the result of whatever it is that keeps them alive. Therefore, we should accept that my continued existence does require a cause. It is worth noting that what causes my continued existence must itself continue to exist – it can't be a cause in the past, since my continued existence must be caused from moment to moment (just as my sitting on a chair is).

We might object, however, that my continued existence is simply dependent on the immediately preceding state of affairs, and so we don't need to say that what caused me to exist in the first place also keeps me in

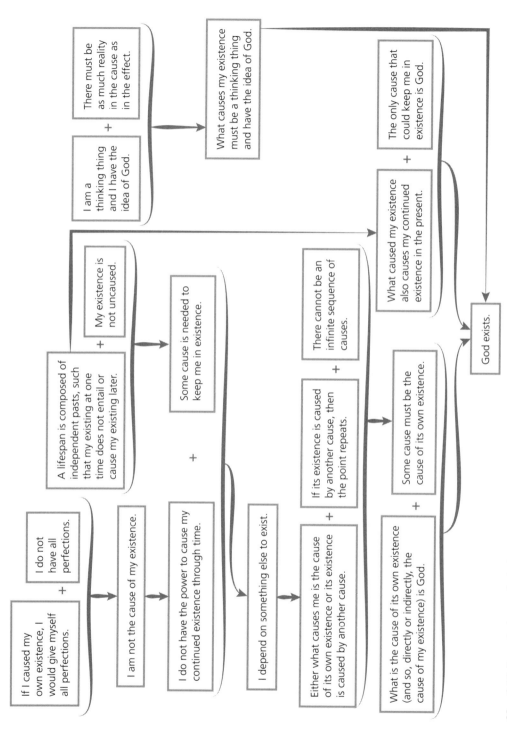

Map 2.18 Descartes' cosmological argument

existence. For instance, my bodily processes keep me alive at any moment, but they didn't give me life. But this forgets that Descartes is talking about his *self*, which is his mind, not his body.

See THE *COGITO*, p. 155.

So what keeps a mind in existence through time? If it was something in his mind itself, he would know, he claims. And it can't be his parents – they only gave existence to him originally, but don't keep him in existence. Whatever it is, it must either be caused by something else or cause itself. And so Descartes deduces that God exists as the only thing that causes its own existence.

Explain why Descartes claims that his continued existence requires a cause.

EMPIRICIST RESPONSES TO DESCARTES' COSMOLOGICAL ARGUMENT

Descartes' cosmological argument shares the assumptions about causation made by his Trademark argument. We saw in EMPIRICIST RESPONSES TO THE TRADEMARK ARGUMENT (p. 166) that empiricists may use Hume's fork to object to these assumptions. To (P4) and (C2), we may object that we cannot know that everything has a cause. It is possible that Descartes' existence is uncaused; we cannot show otherwise by rational intuition and deduction. What causes what is a matter of fact, and this can only be established by experience. To (P7), we can object that we cannot know that a cause must have as much 'reality' as its effect. What the cause of a 'thinking thing' is we must discover through experience, and cannot know a priori.

A third objection based on Hume's fork is aimed at (P10). We don't know that an infinity of causes is impossible. As with 'everything has a cause', it isn't analytic; but in addition, we can't have experience of this matter. It seems conceivable, therefore, that something has always existed, and each thing in turn caused the next. We cannot infer, then, that something that is its own cause – God – exists and is the cause of everything else.

These objections are discussed further in Metaphysics of God, TWO ISSUES FOR ARGUMENTS FROM CAUSATION, p. 109.

Descartes' ontological argument

Descartes' third argument for God's existence is an 'ontological' argument. Ontological arguments claim that we can deduce the existence of God from the concept of God. But unlike the Trademark argument, ontological arguments don't appeal to the *cause* of the concept. Rather, they argue that once we understand the concept GOD, we understand that a being corresponding to this concept, God, must exist.

ONTOLOGICAL ARGUMENTS are studied further in Metaphysics of God, p. 57.

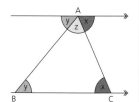

Figure 2.19 The internal angles of a triangle always equal 180 degrees

Explain Descartes' claim that we can know that clear and distinct ideas are true.

See Necessary/ contingent truth, p. 116.

DESCARTES, *MEDITATION* V

Descartes' argument relies heavily on his doctrine of Clear and distinct ideas (p. 156). He opens *Meditation* V by explaining how we can explore our concepts in thought to gain knowledge. For example, you may think that there can be triangles whose internal angles don't add up to 180 degrees, but reflection proves this impossible. Our thought is *constrained* in this way. The ideas we have determine certain truths, at least when our ideas are clear and distinct. Once you make the idea of a triangle (the concept TRIANGLE) clear and distinct, you understand that the internal angles of a triangle add up to 180 degrees, and this shows that this is, in fact, true.

We can now apply this method to the concept of GOD. Descartes' argument is very brief:

The idea of God (that is, of a supremely perfect being) is certainly one that I find within me ... and I understand from this idea that it belongs to God's nature that *he always exists.*

We can understand this passage either in terms of rational intuition of the clear and distinct idea of GOD or as a very short deduction from such a clear and distinct idea. Understood the first way, Descartes is arguing that careful reflection on the concept of GOD reveals that to think that God does not exist is a contradiction in terms, because it is part of the concept of a supremely perfect being that such a being has existence. Thus, we can know that it is true that God exists.

In fact, it shows that God must exist. A contradiction in terms does not just happen to be false, it *must* be false. So to say 'God does not exist' *must* be false; so 'God exists' must be true. As in the case of the triangle, it is not *our thinking it* that makes the claim true. Just as the concept TRIANGLE forces me to acknowledge that the internal angles of a triangle add up to 180 degrees, so the concept GOD forces me to acknowledge that God exists.

Furthermore, I cannot simply *change* the concept in either case; I can't decide that triangles will have two sides, nor that it is no part of the concept of a supremely perfect being that such a being exists. I haven't invented the concept of GOD. I discover it in my mind, because it is *innate* (as argued in the Trademark argument).

One striking puzzle is why Descartes thinks that the concept of a supremely perfect being includes the thought that such a being exists. Spelling this out (P4 below) gives us a short deductive argument:

P1. I have the idea of God.
P2. The idea of God is the idea of a supremely perfect being.
P3. A supremely perfect being does not lack any perfection.
P4. Existence is a perfection.
C1. Therefore, God exists.

But why should we accept (P4)? In the main body of the *Meditations*, Descartes doesn't say. However, in an appendix to the *Meditations*, known as 'Objections and Replies', Descartes explains that God's existence is entailed by the other perfections of God. For example, a supremely perfect being is omnipotent, possessing all power it is logically possible to possess. An omnipotent being cannot depend on any other being for its existence, since then it would lack a power, namely the power to cause its own existence. An omnipotent being has this power and so depends on nothing else to exist. Such a being exists eternally, never coming into being or going out of being. As a supremely perfect being, God is omnipotent by definition, and so God must exist.

God is the only concept that supports this inference to existence, because only the concept of God (as supremely perfect) includes the concept of existence (as a perfection). We can't infer the existence of anything else this way.

See Metaphysics of God, OMNIPOTENCE, p. 30.

Explain Descartes' ontological argument.

EMPIRICIST RESPONSES TO DESCARTES' ONTOLOGICAL ARGUMENT

Once again, empiricists may apply HUME'S FORK (p. 152) to argue that Descartes' ontological argument fails. Hume provides such an argument on the grounds that 'God does not exist' is not a contradiction in terms.

Dialogues Concerning Natural Religion, Pt 9, p. 39

P1. Nothing that is distinctly conceivable implies a contradiction.

P2. Whatever we conceive as existent, we can also conceive as non-existent.

C1. Therefore, there is no being whose non-existence implies a contradiction.

We can put the argument another way. If 'God does not exist' is a contradiction, then 'God exists' is an analytic truth. But this can't be right, because claims about what exists are matters of fact, synthetic propositions.

Descartes could respond in either of two ways. He could claim that 'God exists' is a synthetic truth, but one that can be known by a priori reflection. Or he could claim that 'God exists' is an analytic truth, though not an obvious one. Because he doesn't have the concepts 'analytic' and 'synthetic' (they were invented 150 years later, by Kant), he doesn't, of course, say either. Instead, he defends his claim as the product of rational intuition (and perhaps deduction).

On these grounds, he rejects Hume's (P2). Because our minds are finite, we normally think of the divine perfections, such as omnipotence and necessary existence, separately and so we don't notice that they entail one another. But if we reflect carefully, we shall discover that we cannot conceive of one while excluding the other. It *is* a contradiction to deny that God exists.

Explain Hume's argument that no being exists necessarily and Descartes' reply.

Descartes' proof of the external world

We have looked at Descartes' use of rational intuition and deduction to attempt to establish the *cogito* and the existence of God. The third claim we shall consider is that an 'external world' of physical objects exists.

In his arguments leading up to the *cogito*, Descartes presents a series of sceptical arguments (see DESCARTES' SCEPTICAL ARGUMENTS, p. 189). He argues that we cannot know from perception that physical objects exist. While we can know that we have sensory experiences, those experiences don't give us the knowledge that their causes are physical objects.

See also SCEPTICISM ABOUT THE EXISTENCE OF MIND-INDEPENDENT OBJECTS, p. 83.

If perception doesn't show that physical objects exist, then in order to prove that they exist, we need to undertake a number of preliminary steps.

1. We need to understand our *concept* of a physical object – what is it that we think exists?

2. We need to show that this is a *coherent* concept, not something self-contradictory (like the concept of a round square).

3.   We need to show that it is *possible* that physical objects exist.

With all that in place, we can then argue that

4.   Physical objects do, in fact, exist, and we can know this.

We start with (1) and (2).

DESCARTES, *MEDITATIONS* II, V, VI

The concept of a physical object (*Meditation* II, pp. 6–8)

Descartes discusses the concept of PHYSICAL OBJECT when discussing the nature of his mind. He has argued that 'sensing' is just having sensory experiences – whether physical objects are the cause of these experiences is not clear and distinct. This is puzzling, so he considers perceptual experiences further, focusing on the example of perceiving a piece of wax (p. 6). His question is, 'exactly what is it that I think a piece of wax, as a physical object, is?' (In the argument that follows, 'imagination' is the faculty that deals with images, including those derived from sense experiences.)

P1.   When I melt a piece of wax, it loses all of its original sensory qualities (the particular taste, smell, feel and shape it has).

P2.   Yet I believe it is the same wax.

C1.   Therefore, what I think of as the wax is not its sensory qualities.

P3.   What I think is the wax is what remains through the changes of its sensory qualities.

P4.   This is a body, something that is extended – i.e. has size and shape and takes up space – and changeable, i.e. its sensory and spatial properties can change (p. 7).

P5.   I know that the wax can undergo far more possible changes, including changes in its extension, than I can imagine.

C2.   Therefore, my concept of the wax as extended and changeable does not derive from my imagination (and therefore it does not derive from perceptual experiences).

C3.   Therefore, I comprehend the wax as what it is (as opposed to its sensory qualities) by my mind alone.

C4. Only this thought of the wax, and not the perceptual experience of it, is clear and distinct.

Explain Descartes' concept of PHYSICAL OBJECT, first in prose, then using an argument map.

Descartes finishes by commenting that the wax he comprehends by his understanding is the same wax that is presented by images from the senses. Although we say we 'see' the wax (through vision), in fact we judge (through understanding) that it is present from what we see.

  Descartes' question is not about the wax itself, but about his experience, knowledge and concept of it. This is shown by his comment, on p. 8, that '[w]hat I see might not really be the wax; perhaps I don't even have eyes with which to see anything'. He doesn't, in *Meditation* II, know that there are physical objects. But he knows he has experiences of them. And it is this – his concept of what he experiences – that he is exploring.

  (The argument also shows that the concept of PHYSICAL OBJECT does not derive from sense experience, but is part of the understanding. This means that it is not learned from experience, but is innate. For other discussions of the concept of PHYSICAL OBJECT (SUBSTANCE), see Thinking harder: the concept of substance, p. 143.)

  Descartes turns to the question of whether anything corresponds to our concept of PHYSICAL OBJECT in *Meditation* V. He argued, in *Meditation* III, that whatever is clearly and distinctly perceived is true. His concept of PHYSICAL OBJECT, refined by the wax argument to mean a body that is extended and changeable, is clear and distinct. Therefore, it is a coherent concept and if physical objects exist, then they are indeed extended and changeable.

Compare and contrast Descartes and Hume on the origin of the concept of PHYSICAL SUBSTANCE.

Thinking harder: the existence of physical objects (*Meditation* VI)

Having established the coherence of our concept PHYSICAL OBJECT (see (1) and (2) on p. 174), Descartes turns his attention to whether physical objects are possible and exist (see (3) and (4) on p. 175). His argument that they are possible is straightforward:

P1. I have a clear and distinct idea of what a physical object is.
P2. (God exists and is supremely powerful.)
P3. The only reason for thinking that God cannot make something is that the concept of it is contradictory.
C1. Therefore, God can make physical objects.
C2. Therefore, (if God exists) it is possible that physical objects exist.

To prove that physical objects in fact exist, Descartes first considers two arguments that aim to show that THE EXISTENCE OF THE EXTERNAL WORLD IS THE BEST HYPOTHESIS (see p. 84) to explain our experience. But he is dissatisfied because neither of them gives us certainty, which he thinks is necessary for knowledge (see INFALLIBILISM, p. 53).

The first argument is from imagination (p. 27). Descartes begins by showing that the faculty of imagination is different from the faculty of understanding.

P1. The imagination uses images, e.g. imagining a triangle. But the understanding does not. We cannot imagine a chiliagon, a two-dimensional figure with 1,000 sides. But we can work mathematically with it, e.g. working out its internal angles.
P2. Imagining takes more effort than understanding.
C1. Therefore, imagination and understanding are different.
P3. Imagination is not essential to me, while understanding is. I cannot be me (a thinking thing) without understanding, but I can be me without imagination.
P4. The best explanation for all these differences is that imagination depends upon having a body. (Imagination draws its ideas from the body, which makes its ideas sensory images and difficult to

Critically compare Descartes' arguments below with Russell's argument.

Explain Descartes'
argument from
imagination for the
existence of physical
objects.

work with, and makes imagination not essential to a thinking thing. Being purely mental, understanding draws its ideas from itself, making them non-imagistic and easy to work with, and understanding is essential to a thinking thing.)

C2. Therefore, it is probable that the body (a physical object) exists.

It is, however, only *probable*, so the argument doesn't give us knowledge of the existence of physical objects.

Descartes' second argument is from perception (p. 28). It is natural to think that we know that physical objects exist because we perceive them. Our perceptions are both involuntary and 'much more lively and vivid' than imagination or memory. One explanation is that they are caused by physical objects that exist independent of our minds. But Descartes reminds us of his sceptical arguments (see DESCARTES' SCEPTICAL ARGUMENTS, p. 189): perception does not give us knowledge of the causes of our perceptual experiences. The *mere fact* that perceptual experiences are vivid and involuntary isn't enough to show that they are caused by mind-independent physical objects.

It does, however, provide the starting point for his next argument (p. 30).

In support, note that
Berkeley identifies
exactly these
features to
distinguish
perception from
imagination, but he
is an idealist. See
ARGUMENTS FROM
ILLUSION AND
HALLUCINATION, p. 110.

On P2, see THINKING
HARDER: DEGREES OF
REALITY, p. 165.

P1. I have involuntary perceptual experiences of physical objects.

P2. (These experiences are caused by some substance.)

P3. If the cause of my perceptual experiences is my own mind, my perceptual experiences are voluntary.

P4. Because I know my mind, I would know if my perceptual experiences are voluntary.

C1. Therefore, because I know that my perceptual experiences are involuntary, I know that the cause of my perceptual experiences is not my own mind.

C2. Therefore, the cause must be some substance outside me – either God or physical objects.

P5. If the cause is God, then God has created me with a very strong tendency to have a false belief (that physical objects exist) that I cannot correct.

P6. If God has created me with such a tendency, then God is a deceiver.

P7. (God is perfect by definition.)

C3. (Therefore,) God is not a deceiver.

C4. (Therefore, God did not create me with a tendency to have false beliefs that I cannot correct.)

C5. (Therefore, if God exists, I do not have such a tendency.)

C6. Therefore, if God exists, the cause of my perceptual experiences of physical objects is the existence of physical objects.

P8. (God exists.)

C7. Therefore, there is an external world of physical objects that causes my perceptual experiences.

This argument is one of the best examples of the use of rational intuition and deduction. It is surprising to think that we cannot know from sense experience that physical objects exist. It is even more surprising to be told that we can nevertheless know that physical objects exist using a priori reasoning.

See Clear and distinct ideas and God, p. 160.

On P8, see Descartes' Trademark argument, p. 161, Descartes' cosmological argument, p. 168, and Descartes' ontological argument, p. 171.

Outline Descartes' argument for the existence of physical objects.

EMPIRICIST RESPONSES TO DESCARTES' PROOF OF THE EXTERNAL WORLD

Descartes' argument for the existence of physical objects depends on his arguments for the existence of God. If these fail, then he hasn't shown that physical objects exist. Therefore, the same empiricist objections that were brought against his arguments for the existence of God can be made to undermine his argument for the existence of physical objects by arguing that Descartes has not established the existence of God (P8).

Hume's arguments concerning causation (see Empiricist responses to the trademark argument, p. 166) also target (P2). It is possible that our perceptual experiences of physical objects have *no* cause. This is not to argue that 'for all we know', there is no cause of our perceptual experiences. Rather, Hume's arguments claim that we cannot know a priori that they have a cause. It is no contradiction (though it is very strange!) to suppose that they are uncaused.

We have seen that other empiricists present different arguments for our knowledge of the existence of physical objects. Locke and Russell provide inductive arguments for the claim that the existence of physical objects is the best explanation of our perceptual experience (Scepticism about the existence of mind-independent objects, p. 83). As we have seen, Descartes rejects such

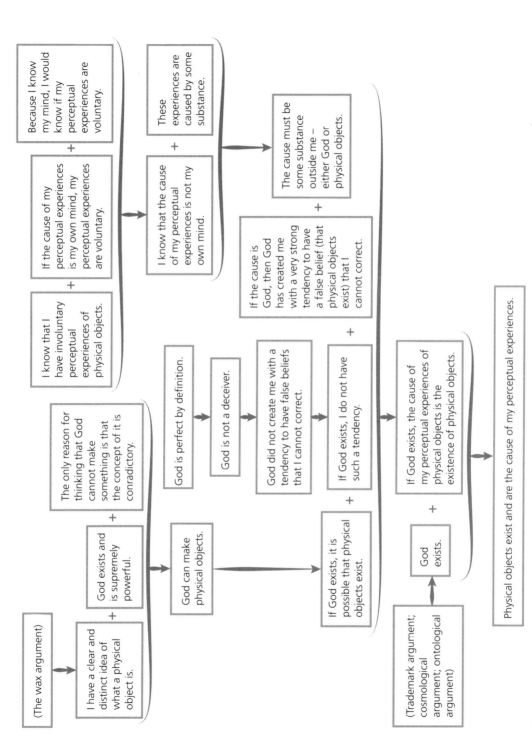

Map 2.19 Descartes' proof of the external world

(The wax argument)

I have a clear and distinct idea of what a physical object is.

+

God exists and is supremely powerful.

+

The only reason for thinking that God cannot make something is that the concept of it is contradictory.

God can make physical objects.

If God exists, it is possible that physical objects exist.

+

God is perfect by definition.

God is not a deceiver.

God did not create me with a tendency to have false beliefs that I cannot correct.

If God exists, I do not have such a tendency.

+

If the cause is God, then God has created me with a very strong tendency to have a false belief (that physical objects exist) that I cannot correct.

If God exists, the cause of my perceptual experiences of physical objects is the existence of physical objects.

+

(Trademark argument; cosmological argument; ontological argument)

God exists.

I know that I have involuntary perceptual experiences of physical objects.

+

If the cause of my perceptual experiences is my own mind, my perceptual experiences are voluntary.

+

Because I know my mind, I would know if my perceptual experiences are voluntary.

I know that the cause of my perceptual experiences is not my own mind.

+

These experiences are caused by some substance.

The cause must be some substance outside me – either God or physical objects.

Physical objects exist and are the cause of my perceptual experiences.

arguments as unsatisfactory as the conclusion lacks certainty. But perhaps inductive arguments are as good as we can get, as no deduction of the existence of physical objects is possible. Berkeley would reject both deductive and inductive arguments for (mind-independent) physical objects, since he argues that the very concept is incoherent (see THE IMMEDIATE OBJECTS OF PERCEPTION ARE MIND-DEPENDENT OBJECTS, p. 99). By contrast, direct realists would argue that no argument for the existence of physical objects is needed once we understand that perception is an open awareness of physical objects (see DIRECT REALISM, p. 67). Descartes goes wrong when thinking that his perceptions are sense-data (see WHAT ARE SENSE-DATA?, p. 79), capable of existing as mental things independently of the physical objects he perceives.

> **?**
>
> Does Descartes establish that we have any knowledge through rational intuition and deduction?

Key points: the intuition and deduction thesis

- Deduction is a form of reasoning in which the premises are intended to entail the conclusion, i.e. if the premises are true, the conclusion must be true.
- Rational intuition involves discovering the truth of a claim just by thinking about it. Very often we discover that the claim must be true.
- Empiricism can allow that we know analytic truths 'just by thinking about them' since they are a form of conceptual knowledge. We can also know about our own minds 'just by thinking'. But empiricism claims that there is no a priori knowledge of synthetic propositions about the world external to our minds (whether innate or from reasoning).
- By contrast, rationalism claims that we have some a priori knowledge of synthetic propositions about the world external to our minds.
- Hume's 'fork' states that we know only 'relations of ideas' and 'matters of fact'. Relations of ideas are established by pure thought and are 'intuitively and demonstratively certain'. This is because to deny a relation of ideas is a contradiction. Matters of fact are about the world and are known through experience and induction, especially causal inference.
- Descartes uses rational intuition and deduction to argue for the existence of himself, God and physical objects.
- He argues that he cannot doubt his own existence, and that he is a thinking thing. 'I think', the *cogito*, is Descartes' first item of knowledge.
- Descartes' theory of 'clear and distinct' ideas is an account of rational intuition. A clear idea is 'present and accessible to the attentive mind'; a

distinct idea is clear and also sharply separated from other ideas so that every part of it is clear.

- Empiricists can object that Descartes cannot know that thoughts require a thinker as something that persists between thoughts. Hume argues that in coming up with the idea of a mental substance, we confuse similarity (of thoughts) for identity (of thinker).

- Empiricists may also argue that the *cogito* is not known by rational insight, but from impressions of reflection.

- Descartes argues that we can know that an idea that is clear and distinct is true while we consider it. We can only know that all ideas that are clear and distinct are true once God's existence is proven.

- Descartes argues that we know that God is not a deceiver, because we know that God is perfect. This does not mean that God guarantees every belief we have. It means that we have the means to correct any mistakes we make. If we believe only what we can clearly and distinctly perceive to be true, we will not go wrong.

- Because God is not a deceiver, and God is omnipotent, God would not let an evil demon deceive us.

- In his Trademark argument, Descartes identifies three sources of ideas: outside my mind, invented, and innate.

- He claims that all causes must have at least as much reality as their effects. The cause of an idea must have as much reality as what the idea represents.

- He argues that only God has as much reality as what the concept GOD represents, namely something infinite and perfect. The concept can't be invented by me and doesn't derive from experience. Therefore, it is innate.

- Empiricists can object to Descartes that we invented the idea of God by negating ideas of imperfection and finitude.

- Descartes replies that our idea of God is of something that is positively, not negatively, infinite and perfect. We can object that this isn't persuasive.

- Empiricists can also object to his claim that the cause of an idea must have 'as much reality' as its object, and his assumption that all ideas have a cause.

- In his cosmological argument, Descartes argues that he depends on something else to exist, and as a thinking thing with the idea of God, his cause must also be a thinking thing with the idea of God. He also rejects the possibility of an infinite series of causes, and concludes that there must be something whose existence is not caused by anything else – God.

- As before, empiricists can object to the assumption that everything has a cause, but also to the assumption that an infinity of causes is impossible. These claims can only be established, if at all, by experience, and experience doesn't show that they are true.

- Descartes' ontological argument claims that it is impossible to think coherently of God, a supremely perfect being, as lacking existence.

- Empiricists can respond that there is no contradiction in thinking of any being as non-existent. Claims about what exists are synthetic propositions, and denying a synthetic proposition is not a contradiction.

- Descartes argues that our concept of a physical object, e.g. a piece of wax, cannot be derived from its sensory properties, because these can change, while we think the object is the same object. Furthermore, we understand that the object can go through more changes than we can imagine.

- Our concept of a physical object is of something extended and changeable. This concept is part of the understanding. It is clear and distinct, and so physical objects are possible.

- But do physical objects exist? Imagination uses images deriving from the senses and requires effort. These are reasons to think bodies exist, but not a proof. Or again, we have involuntary sensory experiences of bodies. But this is also not enough to show that bodies exist.

- However, because sensory experiences are involuntary, we can know that they are not caused by our own minds. Because God is not a deceiver, we also know that they are not caused by God, but by physical objects themselves. Therefore, we know that physical objects exist.

- Empiricists may again object to the assumption that our sensory experiences must have a cause. They can also argue that the existence of physical objects is the best explanation for our sensory experiences, and this is enough for us to know that they exist.

Summary: reason as a source of knowledge

In this section on reason as a source of knowledge, we have looked at the debates over whether any knowledge is innate or gained by rational intuition and deduction. The debate is between:

1. Empiricism: our knowledge is limited to what can be derived from sense experience and analytic truths, and our concepts all derive from sensation or reflection;
2. Rationalism: there is, in addition, a priori knowledge of synthetic truths that we gain from rational insight and deduction; and
3. Innatism: we have some a priori knowledge of synthetic truths, and therefore of some concepts, innately.

In the classical debate, rationalism and innatism joined together to oppose empiricism.

In our discussion and evaluation of these theories, we have looked at the following issues:

1. What is the distinction between analytic and synthetic propositions? What is the distinction between a priori and a posteriori knowledge? What is the distinction between necessary and contingent truths? And how are the distinctions linked to each other?
2. Why and how do Plato and Leibniz argue for innate knowledge, and why and how does Locke reject it?
3. How, according to Locke and Hume, are all concepts derived from experience? Do any concepts, such as the concept of substance, present counterexamples?
4. If some concepts cannot be derived from experience, are such concepts innate or incoherent?
5. What is it to say that experience 'triggers' innate knowledge or concepts?
6. What is Descartes' theory of rational intuition? Can we use rational intuition and deduction to gain a priori knowledge? If so, are the truths we know always analytic?
7. How does Descartes argue for the existence of his mind, God and physical objects?
8. What is Hume's fork and how can it be applied to form objections to Descartes' arguments?

IV. The limits of knowledge

A. Philosophical scepticism

The particular nature of philosophical scepticism

In THE TRIPARTITE DEFINITION OF KNOWLEDGE (p. 37), we noted that there is a distinction between belief, even true belief, and knowledge. According to the tripartite view, at least, knowledge requires a justification. Scepticism is the view that our usual justifications for claiming our beliefs amount to knowledge are inadequate, so we do not in fact have knowledge. Scepticism can target knowledge from any source, including the two sources we have discussed, perception and reason. And so it challenges both empiricism and rationalism.

But before saying more about the nature of philosophical scepticism, let's look at a famous example.

AM I A BRAIN IN A VAT?

Thought experiments are a philosophical method designed to test a hypothesis or philosophical claim through imagining a hypothetical situation, and coming to a judgement. In GETTIER'S OBJECTION: ARE THE CONDITIONS JOINTLY SUFFICIENT?, p. 47, we saw that Gettier cases are thought experiments that test the claim that knowledge is justified true belief. Here is a thought experiment that tests whether we have any knowledge at all.

Suppose that I am not a walking, talking human being, but simply a brain in a vat. Connected to my brain is a supercomputer that feeds in just the right impulses to generate the illusion of reality as I experience it now. All of my sensory experiences are being produced in my brain by electrical signals from the supercomputer. I'm living in a virtual reality. Since I think that the reality I experience is one of physical objects and other people, I'm being deceived.

Here is the sceptical challenge: I cannot know that I am not a brain in a vat. If I were, things would seem *exactly the same* as if I am a walking, talking person. If I were a brain in a vat, my experiences would be qualitatively indistinguishable from the experiences I have if I am not. So I can't have any evidence that I am not a brain in a vat. So I can't know, therefore, whether I am, in fact, a brain in a vat or not. But if I am a brain in a vat, all my beliefs about what I experience are false; I have no body, I'm not sitting at a

Figure 2.20 A brain in a vat

computer, I'm not hearing the sounds of keys clicking, etc. More importantly, even if I'm not a brain in a vat, and reality is as I think it is, my true belief *lacks justification*. I don't have any reason to believe that reality is as I think it is rather than to believe that I am a brain in a vat. But if my belief that reality is as I think it is, is not justified, then it isn't knowledge. I don't know that I'm not just a brain in a vat.

Let's extend the thought experiment. The supercomputer feeds me not only sense experiences, but also 'memories'. So I cannot trust my memories, because the computer could create 'memories' of things that never happened. So I cannot know anything about the past, including whether it happened at all. Perhaps I only just came into existence, and all my memories are false.

Let's take it one step further. Perhaps even my *thoughts* are being fed to me by a supercomputer. Isn't it possible that every time I think '2 + 2 = ?', the computer makes me think '4' when the answer is actually 5? Can I know that this isn't happening? How? If I can't, then my belief that 2 + 2 = 4 isn't justified. And so I can't know that 2 + 2 = 4.

Explain the brain in a vat thought experiment and its challenge to our knowledge.

THE DISTINCTION BETWEEN PHILOSOPHICAL SCEPTICISM AND NORMAL INCREDULITY

Reflecting on the thought experiment of being a brain in a vat helps us understand some peculiar features of philosophical scepticism and how it differs from normal incredulity, our normal everyday doubts about whether some claim is true or not.

Philosophical scepticism can get started by reflecting on *how* we know what we think we know. Take the belief that I have two hands. I think I know that I have two hands. But how do I know this? Well, I can feel them, I can see them. But, says the sceptic, couldn't my experience – what I feel and what I see – be just the same if I were a brain in a vat? If I don't know I'm not a brain in a vat, do I really know that I have two hands? In fact, do I know that a world exists outside my mind at all? How do I know that appearance is a reliable guide to reality?

Philosophical doubts are peculiar. They don't make sense in everyday circumstances. Of course, if I've just been in an accident, and can't feel my left arm, doubting whether I have two hands does make sense! But the sceptic is not interested in these propositions when we have an 'everyday reason' to doubt them. The sceptic's reason for doubting them does not arise from a particular context – it is a general doubt about their justification. The sceptic admits that there is no everyday reason to doubt whether I have two hands or whether there is an external world. But that doesn't mean there isn't *any* reason to doubt these things.

Is this sort of sceptical doubt *doubt*? It has no practical consequences, and a philosophical sceptic is not a very cautious person! Yet the sceptic insists that sceptical doubts are relevant – we *should* know that we are not a brain in a vat wired up to a supercomputer if we are to know that 'This is a hand'.

Outline and explain two differences between philosophical scepticism and normal incredulity.

THE ROLE/FUNCTION OF SCEPTICISM WITHIN EPISTEMOLOGY

The effect of philosophical scepticism is not 'We can't be *certain* of our everyday judgements, although they are *probably* true.' It is to put the whole idea of our usual justifications into question. If these sceptical possibilities were true, we would have *absolutely no reason* to hold on to our usual beliefs. If I were wired up to a supercomputer, things would *seem* exactly the same, but the reality would be completely different. Sceptical arguments aim to completely undercut our usual justifications.

We might think that it is 'unreasonable' to have such doubts. But this misunderstands the role or purpose of doubt. While some philosophers have understood philosophical scepticism as a kind of theory, it is better to understand it as a kind of challenge. The sceptic doesn't suggest that there is any reason to *believe* in sceptical possibilities of thought experiments, but requests that we *rule them out* as possibilities. In trying to meet the sceptic's challenge, we can discover what we know and how we know it.

Scepticism is sometimes taken as the claim that nothing is known. But this is not a good definition of philosophical scepticism, for it must then defend the claim that we can know nothing, which is trivially self-defeating anyway (because then we would know that we know nothing – so there is something we know). Likewise, scepticism is not the claim that our beliefs are all false. For this is not logically coherent. For instance, my beliefs that 'I am not at the South Pole' and that 'I am not at the North Pole' can't both be false (obviously, both can be true).

Scepticism is best understood as the claim that our usual justification for claiming our beliefs amount to knowledge is inadequate. Doubt based on challenging us to rule out the *possibility* of very unlikely situations is called 'hyperbolic' doubt. And the purpose of this doubt is to help us find what we *can* know, if anything.

What is the role of scepticism in epistemology?

LOCAL AND GLOBAL SCEPTICISM

Local scepticism is scepticism about some specific claim, or more commonly, about some area/branch of supposed knowledge. We might doubt whether we can know how many planets exist in the universe (without doubting astronomy in general). Or more broadly, we might doubt whether there can be any knowledge about God's existence and nature (without doubting, say, scientific knowledge). Our normal incredulity is always local – we have specific reasons for doubting specific claims, and in our philosophical 'moods', we may doubt knowledge about religion, ethics and so on.

Global scepticism extends doubt without limit. The brain in a vat provides an example. If we can't know whether or not we are brains in vats, and cannot even trust our reasoning, then it seems all our knowledge comes into question. Global scepticism has focused especially on having no knowledge of an external world of physical objects, and this is how we shall discuss it here, setting aside questions about knowledge of God, ethics and other branches of knowledge. If we can secure knowledge of such a mind-independent world, we will have defeated global scepticism, whatever conclusions we reach about the other branches of knowledge. Descartes' first meditation provides the most famous example of how philosophical scepticism can begin from local scepticism to become global, and we turn to this next.

Explain the difference between local and global scepticism.

Descartes' sceptical arguments

Descartes begins his *Meditations* by presenting three arguments that support scepticism, sometimes called the 'three waves of doubt'. In the first, he presents a version of THE ARGUMENT FROM ILLUSION (p. 71) to begin to question his knowledge from sense experience. In the second, he questions whether he can know whether he is awake or asleep. This challenges empirical knowledge more robustly. In the third, he presents his version of the 'brain in a vat' thought experiment: can he know that he is not being deceived in all his experience and thought by a powerful, malicious demon?

DESCARTES, *MEDITATION* I

On doubt and certainty

Descartes begins *Meditation* I by declaring that he has known for a long time that in order to establish anything 'in the sciences that was stable and likely to last' (p. 1), he would have to start from the foundations. He does not need to reject as *false* everything he thinks he knows, but he needs to avoid believing things 'that are not completely certain and indubitable'. To establish this certainty, he seeks to test his beliefs by doubting them. He adopts philosophical scepticism as his starting point. As he tries to call his beliefs into question, he repeatedly asks how he can *know* they are true. So he understands knowledge in terms of what is 'completely certain and indubitable'. If we can doubt a belief, then it is not certain and so it is not knowledge. This procedure for establishing what we can know to be true is Descartes' 'method of doubt'.

On knowledge as certain, see INFALLIBILISM, p. 53. On what Descartes means by 'indubitable', see CLEAR AND DISTINCT IDEAS, p. 156.

   If Descartes doubted each belief in turn, this would take forever. So he decides to question the principles on which his beliefs are based. We can understand this as his calling into question the general justifications we offer for our beliefs.

Explain Descartes' method of doubt and its purpose.

An argument from illusion

So what can we doubt? Descartes begins by presenting an argument from illusion as many of his beliefs are based on his sense experience. He notes that he has, in the past, been deceived by his senses – things have looked a way that they are not (p. 1). Things in the distance look small, for instance. Or again, a pencil half-submerged in water looks crooked.

But, Descartes remarks, such examples from unusual perceptual conditions give us no reason to doubt all perceptions, such as that I am looking at a piece of paper with writing on it. More generally, we might say that perceptual illusions are *special cases* (and ones we can frequently explain). Otherwise we wouldn't be able to talk about them as illusions. So they don't undermine perception generally.

The argument from dreaming

Descartes then doubts whether he knows he is awake (p. 1). Sometimes when we dream, we represent to ourselves all sorts of crazy things. But sometimes we dream the most mundane things. I could be dreaming that I'm looking at a piece of paper. I could even have the thought, while I'm dreaming, that I'm not dreaming! There is no reliable way to tell whether I'm awake or asleep.

This argument attacks all sense perception, even the most mundane and most certain. I cannot know that I see a piece of paper because I cannot know that I am not dreaming of seeing a piece of paper. It questions whether we can tell what reality is like from what we experience, since those experiences could be no more than a dream.

We can object that there *are* reliable ways of distinguishing waking perception from dreaming, such as the far greater coherence of perception. But what Descartes means is that I cannot know, of my perception now, whether I am awake or asleep. The objection assumes that I can rely on my memory of what I have experienced to compare it with my dream. But what if I'm dreaming that I remember this?

Descartes then claims that even if he were dreaming, and maybe imagining particular physical objects, dreams are constructed out of *basic ideas* and these must correspond to something real – ideas of body, extension, shape, quantity, size, motion and time. And so the truths of geometry seem secure, as do truths of arithmetic, such as '2 + 3 = 5'. Even if he is dreaming, this seems impossible to doubt.

The evil demon

But Descartes then casts doubt on even these claims of mathematics by questioning whether God may have deceived him (p. 2). Is it possible that he could go wrong in adding two and three? To the objection that God is good and wouldn't deceive Descartes like this, Descartes introduces a further doubt. Suppose that God does not exist. Suppose, worse, that all my experiences are produced in me by an evil demon who wants to deceive me (p. 3). If this were true, I wouldn't know, because my experiences would be exactly the same (just as with the brain in the vat thought experiment). So I cannot know that I am not being deceived by an evil demon.

Descartes uses the evil demon supposition to make sure that he doesn't believe anything he can't know. It seems that he can't know anything – that there is an external, physical world or even the basic truths of mathematics. Unless he can rule out the possibility that he is being deceived by an evil demon, then he can't be certain of anything. He has reached the point of global scepticism.

Descartes' list here is a list of primary qualities, and matches Locke's, with the addition of time. See LOCKE'S DISTINCTION BETWEEN PRIMARY AND SECONDARY QUALITIES, p. 80.

Why does Descartes' argument from dreaming cast doubt on more knowledge than his argument from illusion?

Explain Descartes' use of philosophical scepticism to reach global scepticism.

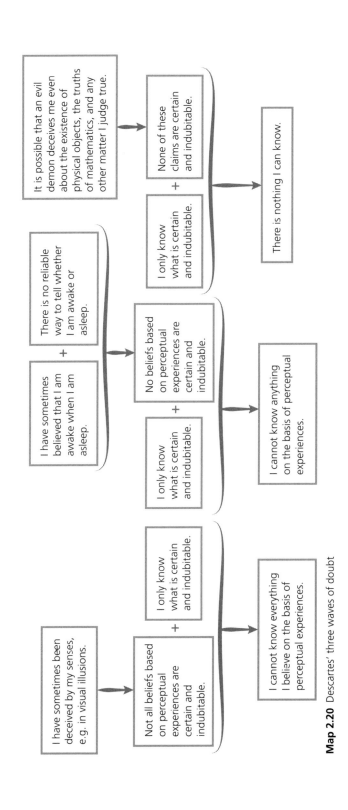

Map 2.20 Descartes' three waves of doubt

Key points: philosophical scepticism

- Scepticism challenges whether our usual justifications for what we think we know are adequate. For example, a popular sceptical thought experiment argues that if we were brains in vats, our experiences could be exactly as though we weren't. So we don't know whether we are brains in vats.

- Sceptical doubt is odd: it is not interested in everyday reasons for doubting a proposition, it has no practical consequences, and it invents very unlikely situations that we have no reason to think are actually true. But it insists that it is legitimate – we should know that sceptical possibilities, e.g. that I am a brain in a vat, are not true in order to know the things we claim to know.

- Scepticism does not claim that we know nothing, nor that all our beliefs are false. It challenges our usual justifications, bringing into question whether we know what we claim to know.

- Local scepticism is scepticism about some particular branch of knowledge. Global scepticism extends the sceptical challenge to knowledge without limit, and especially to the question of whether there is a world beyond the individual's mind.

- Descartes presents three sceptical arguments, sometimes called the three waves of doubt. His argument from illusion throws doubt on always believing what our senses tell us. His argument from dreaming throws doubt on all sense perception, but he allows that the ideas from which his dreams are constructed must reflect something real. His argument from the evil demon brings even this last claim and the truths of mathematics into question, leading to global scepticism.

B. Responses to scepticism

Descartes' own response

Descartes' response to the global scepticism at the beginning of *Meditation* II is to use rational intuition and deduction. He begins with THE *COGITO* (p. 155). He argues that even if an evil demon is deceiving him, Descartes can know that he exists and that he thinks. He can know about his own mind and the thoughts he has. He then builds on this by developing his theory of CLEAR AND DISTINCT IDEAS (p. 156). This enables him to argue that the truths of mathematics are indubitable, and so he can know these as well.

However, he still has no certainty about the causes of sense perception, and so the existence of a world of mind-independent physical objects. He has sensory experiences in his dreams as well, when he is not seeing or hearing at all. However, by exploring his ideas, he is able to know that his concept of a physical object is a concept of something extended in space (see DESCARTES' PROOF OF THE EXTERNAL WORLD, p. 174), but that is all for now. At this point, Descartes cannot move beyond idealism.

See DESCARTES'
TRADEMARK ARGUMENT,
p. 161, DESCARTES'
COSMOLOGICAL ARGUMENT,
p. 168, and DESCARTES'
ONTOLOGICAL ARGUMENT,
p. 171.

Descartes' next move in reconstructing what he can know is to attempt to prove the existence of God relying just on the concept of GOD and other clear and distinct ideas, e.g. concerning causation. Not only can God's existence be known from the concept of GOD, but also a number of other truths about God's nature. Among these, one of the most important for Descartes' project is that God is not a deceiver and God is omnipotent. It is on this basis that Descartes meets the challenge of scepticism head on.

Because God is not a deceiver, then God would not allow *incorrigible* errors, but has given me the ability to form true beliefs (see CLEAR AND DISTINCT IDEAS AND GOD, p. 160). And so I can dismiss the possibility of the evil demon – if an evil demon were deceiving me, I would have no way of correcting my beliefs about the world. Among these beliefs is that physical objects exist and are extended in space. Because God can bring about anything that corresponds to a clear and distinct idea, and is not a deceiver, I can know that there are such physical objects, which I experience in perception.

But how do I know that I am not dreaming? At the very end of the *Meditations*, Descartes also uses God's not being a deceiver to solve this objection. He accepts that we can tell the difference between dreaming and being awake, because memory connects up perceptions coherently, but not dreams, and because we can confirm our perceptions using different senses (p. 34). This response is only available *now* (and not in *Meditation* I) because he has established that God is not a deceiver. Without that, we couldn't rely on memory in this way.

We must nevertheless be careful about what we claim to know through perception. Our sense perceptions are not 'reliable guides to the essential nature of the bodies located outside me, for on that topic they give only very obscure and confused information' (p. 31). We can and do continue to make mistakes about what we perceive. Our individual perceptual judgements will not qualify as certain in the way clear and distinct ideas do. In particular, we shouldn't think that our perceptions of physical objects as having properties of colour, smell, taste, temperature, and so on, resemble the objects themselves. The essential nature of physical objects is given not through sense experience, but through an a priori analysis of our concept of PHYSICAL OBJECT. Thus, Descartes ends up adopting INDIRECT REALISM (p. 78), drawing a distinction between primary and secondary qualities and defending the claim that we can know that physical objects have primary qualities but we cannot know that they have secondary qualities.

Does Descartes successfully defeat global scepticism?

Empiricist responses

As we saw in RATIONALISM AND EMPIRICISM REVISITED (p. 150), empiricists deny that there is any a priori knowledge of synthetic propositions. This can be understood as a form of local scepticism. They restrict the knowledge that we have to

1. (a priori) knowledge of analytic propositions and what can be deduced from them;
2. (a posteriori) knowledge of synthetic propositions about the world outside one's minds; and
3. knowledge of our own minds, derived from impressions of reflection.

Any claim that does not fall under one of these three categories, we do not know.

One objection to empiricism is that this restriction on knowledge is too severe. It leads to local scepticism across many branches of supposed knowledge. For example, can we know that God exists? If 'God exists' is a synthetic claim, according to empiricism, we could only know that God exists from sense experience. But can we? Hume argued that we can't – the reasoning involves claims that sense experience cannot establish. So we can't know whether God exists.

These arguments are studied in Metaphysics of God. See ARGUMENTS RELATING TO THE EXISTENCE OF GOD, p. 56.

Another example is morality. Moral claims, such as 'Murder is wrong', don't *appear* to be analytic. But could we know them through *sense* experience? Which of our senses pick up on 'wrongness', and how? If

See MORAL ANTI-REALISM, p. 380.

empiricists can't show that moral claims are either analytic or a posteriori, then they will be forced to conclude that there is no moral knowledge either.

We put these local scepticisms aside to ask how empiricists respond to global scepticism and the attack on knowledge from sense experience. We have seen that Descartes argues that we must turn to rational intuition and deduction to show that we can gain knowledge from experience.

We considered two alternative empiricist responses in SCEPTICISM ABOUT THE EXISTENCE OF MIND-INDEPENDENT OBJECTS (p. 83) and THE IMMEDIATE OBJECTS OF PERCEPTION ARE MIND-DEPENDENT OBJECTS (p. 99). As indirect realists, Locke, Russell and Trotter Cockburn agree with Descartes that we only immediately perceive sense-data and we must infer the cause of our sense experiences. They defend the claim that an external world of physical objects is that cause, on the grounds that it is the best explanation of our experience, in particular, that it is involuntary, coherent between different sense modalities (vision, hearing, etc.), and that it is systematic.

However, there are two objections that may be raised to this argument understood as a response to scepticism. First, Descartes argues that the existence of the external world remains a *hypothesis* – we cannot know with certainty that physical objects exist. But we can respond that Descartes sets the standard for knowledge too high – knowledge does not require certainty (see INFALLIBILISM, p. 53). If the existence of physical objects is the best explanation of our sense experience, this is sufficient justification for us to know that they exist (if the belief is also true). Rather than respond to scepticism by appealing to rational intuition and deduction to meet the demand for certainty, this response rejects the demand for certainty.

The second objection challenges the claim that the existence of physical objects *is* the best explanation for our sense experience. If we are brains in vats, then our sense experience is exactly as it is now – involuntary, coherent, systematic – and yet the world is nothing like what we experience it as being. (Ok, so a physical object, the supercomputer, exists, but this is hardly the result Russell and others were after!) Our experience provides *no* reason to prefer the hypothesis of physical objects over the hypothesis of being a brain in a vat. Both explanations of our experience are equally good. So inference to the best explanation cannot show that we can rule out the possibility of being brains in vats. So it doesn't meet the challenge of global scepticism.

Berkeley takes a completely different approach. He removes the challenge of scepticism by rejecting the distinction between appearance and reality. What we experience is reality. Idealism has no need to discover how

Explain one argument for the claim that we cannot know that physical objects exist by inferring them from our sense experience.

our perceptions of physical objects relate to reality. In experiencing ideas, we are experiencing what exists.

One interesting point about Berkeley's argument is that his understanding of the relation between our minds and God as the source of our perceptions is rather similar to the relation between our brains and the supercomputer in the brain in a vat thought experiment. Berkeley infers that something outside my mind must cause my perceptions, and given the complexity of my experience, that something must be God. But could it be a supercomputer instead?! Berkeley would, of course, respond that a supercomputer is a physical object (as is a brain), and we have no reason to think that physical objects can exist independent of minds. The thought experiment is incoherent.

The responses we have discussed in this section are from classical empiricists (and Russell). But empiricism may be combined with reliabilism (as well as other theories of knowledge). So the response that follows next can also count as empiricist as it defends our ability to gain knowledge from sense experience.

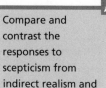

Compare and contrast the responses to scepticism from indirect realism and idealism.

Thinking harder: reliabilism

RELIABILISM (p. 55) disputes the theory of knowledge that scepticism assumes. Our true beliefs do not need to be justified to count as knowledge, reliabilism claims, they only need to be produced by a reliable cognitive process. Suppose I am not a brain in a vat. Then perception is a reliable process – most of the beliefs I form on the basis of sense experience are, in fact, true. That is enough to say that I gain knowledge from sense experience – my beliefs are true and produced by a reliable cognitive process. I do not need, in addition, to *justify* my beliefs, e.g. to have evidence that perception is reliable. In particular, I do not need to know that I am not a brain in a vat. If I am not a brain in a vat, then, because perception is a reliable process, I know that there are physical objects.

This can sound very counter-intuitive. If I am a brain in a vat, then I don't know that there are physical objects. Even the reliabilist agrees with that: if I am a brain in a vat, how I form beliefs is very unreliable, and most of them are false. So surely I need to know that I am *not* a brain in a vat, and that my beliefs are caused by a reliable process, in order to know that there are physical objects.

But as an objection to reliabilism, this point is confused. First, reliabilism can respond that there is a difference between *knowing that p* and *knowing that I know that p*. Suppose that I don't know whether I am a brain in a vat. If that's true, then I don't know whether perception is reliable or not. So since I don't know whether perception is reliable, I can't know that I know that there are physical objects. This is all true, but why does any of this matter? If I'm not a brain in a vat, then – whether I know it or not – perception is reliable, and so I know that there are physical objects.

Why should we think that in order to know that *p*, I must also know that I know that *p*? It could be that the cognitive process that produces beliefs about *p* is reliable, but the cognitive process that produces beliefs about what I know is unreliable. In such a case, I can know that *p* without knowing that I know that *p*. For instance, animals can gain knowledge through perception, but they can't even *think* about whether they are brains in vats, let alone having *reliable* thoughts about such matters. Reliabilists reject the sceptical claim that we cannot know about physical objects through perception unless we know that we are not brains in vats.

Is there a satisfactory response to the challenge of philosophical scepticism?

Key points: responses to scepticism

- Descartes argues that even if the evil demon is deceiving him, he can know truths through rational intuition and deduction. By this means, he tries to prove the existence of God. If he can show that God exists and is not a deceiver, he can then argue that physical objects exist and are the causes of his sense experiences and that he is not dreaming.
- Empiricists argue that we can only know about the world outside our minds through sense experience. All a priori knowledge is of analytic propositions. We may object that empiricism will lead to scepticism about God and morality.
- Many empiricists who are indirect realists argue that we can know that physical objects exist because their existence is the best explanation of our sense experience. Scepticism challenges this claim, e.g. that we are brains in vats could be an equally good explanation.

- Berkeley denies the distinction between appearance and reality – because only minds and ideas exist, the content of our sense experiences is what reality is.
- Reliabilism rejects scepticism's assumption that our beliefs must be justified to be knowledge. As long as our beliefs about physical objects are caused by a reliable process, then we know such objects exist. We do not even need to know that they are caused by a reliable process. So we do not need to know that we are not brains in vats in order to have knowledge about the world.

Summary: the limits of knowledge

In this section on the limits of knowledge, we have looked at the challenge of scepticism to our claims to knowledge. In particular, we have looked at the following issues:

1. What is scepticism, and how does it differ from 'normal incredulity'?
2. How does the brain in a vat thought experiment challenge our claims to knowledge?
3. What are Descartes' arguments in support of scepticism, and how does he seek to answer them?
4. In what ways do empiricists try to meet the challenge of scepticism?
5. How might we defend our knowledge against scepticism by appealing to reliabilism?

Chapter 3

Moral philosophy

Plato, *The Republic*, 352d

Please see the ADDITIONAL FEATURES (p. 3) for an explanation of the different kinds of marginal boxes and what they mean. Please see CHAPTER 1 HOW TO DO PHILOSOPHY (p. 6) for explanations of philosophical argument and how to understand argument maps.

I shall make no distinction between the terms 'ethics' and 'morality'.

'How should one live?' It is not a trivial question, Socrates says. Perhaps uniquely among animals, we human beings not only act, we also consider how we *should* act. We think that there are better and worse ways of acting, we reflect on our experience of making mistakes, and try to improve things. Much of this, of course, relates to our own self-interest – meeting our needs, successfully achieving our personal goals, and so on. But that is not all. We are social creatures, we live together, and our lives and actions affect the lives and actions of other people. How should we relate to one another, how should we treat one another? We are concerned not only for ourselves, but for other people as well, and how other people treat us is critical to our own happiness. How should each of us live so that each of our lives goes 'best'? What is 'good' in life and how may we go about trying to attain it?

These questions form the basis for moral philosophy. We can approach them in three different ways. First, we can try to answer them 'in general', developing and defending theories about what people care about or what makes their lives go well. This approach is called *normative ethics*, and aims to give us general guidance on what is morally right or wrong, what is good or bad. Second, we can try to answer very specific questions about how we should live or act, such as when it is right to go to war or what kind of sexual relations between people are best. This is the domain of *practical* or *applied ethics*, which considers particular issues in real life and asks what is the right thing to do. Third, we can ask more about the questions and answers themselves. For example, do we think that these questions have a correct answer, which we must then try to discover? Or are we exploring our personal attitudes towards life and other people? Or perhaps each society – each group of people living together – decides what it will accept for itself? This approach leads us into *metaethics*, the philosophical study of what morality is.

In this chapter, we will consider all three approaches to moral philosophy. We shall begin by looking at three theories in normative ethics. The first theory argues that questions about how we should live and act should be answered by focusing on the consequences of the action, the second asks us to focus on the motive, and the third on what it is to be a good person. We will then turn to four issues in applied ethics, seeing how each of our three normative theories answers questions about stealing, eating animals, lying and simulated killing (pretending to kill in plays, films, video games, etc.). We will end by looking at a range of theories in metaethics in the debate over whether or not moral judgements, such as 'stealing is wrong', can be said to be objectively true or false, whether what we are doing in normative and applied ethics is trying to discover the truth or no more than exploring our attitudes about a key concern of human life – how to live.

By the end of the chapter, you should be able to analyse, explain and evaluate a number of arguments for and objections to theories about what is right/wrong, good/bad, and apply these theories to a number of practical issues. You should also be able to analyse, explain and evaluate a number of arguments for and objections to metaethical theories about whether moral judgements can be objectively true or false.

Syllabus checklist ✓

The AQA AS and A level syllabus for this topic is:

I. Normative ethical theories

✓ The meaning of good, bad, right, wrong within each of the three approaches specified below
✓ Similarities and differences across the three approaches specified below

A. Utilitarianism

- ✓ The question of what is meant by 'utility' and 'maximising utility', including:
  - Jeremy Bentham's quantitative hedonistic utilitarianism (his utility calculus)
  - John Stuart Mill's qualitative hedonistic utilitarianism (higher and lower pleasures) and his 'proof' of the greatest happiness principle
  - Non-hedonistic utilitarianism (including preference utilitarianism)
- ✓ Act utilitarianism and rule utilitarianism

Issues, including:
- ✓ Whether pleasure is the only good (Nozick's experience machine)
- ✓ Fairness and individual liberty/rights (including the risk of the 'tyranny of the majority')
- ✓ Problems with calculation (including which beings to include)
- ✓ Issues around partiality
- ✓ Whether utilitarianism ignores both the moral integrity and the intentions of the individual

B. Kantian deontological ethics

- ✓ Immanuel Kant's account of what is meant by a 'good will'
- ✓ The distinction between acting in accordance with duty and acting out of duty
- ✓ The distinction between hypothetical imperatives and categorical imperatives
- ✓ The first formulation of the categorical imperative (including the distinction between a contradiction in conception and a contradiction in will)
- ✓ The second formulation of the categorical imperative

Issues, including:
- ✓ Clashing/competing duties
- ✓ Not all universalisable maxims are distinctly moral; not all non-universalisable maxims are immoral
- ✓ The view that consequences of actions determine their moral value

✓   Kant ignores the value of certain motives, e.g. love, friendship, kindness
✓   Morality is a system of hypothetical, rather than categorical, imperatives (Philippa Foot)

C. Aristotelian virtue ethics

✓   'The good' for human beings: the meaning of eudaimonia as the 'final end' and the relationship between eudaimonia and pleasure
✓   The function argument and the relationship between virtues and function
✓   Aristotle's account of virtues and vices: virtues as character traits/dispositions; the role of education/habituation in the development of a moral character; the skill analogy; the importance of feelings; the doctrine of the mean and its application to particular virtues
✓   Moral responsibility: voluntary, involuntary and non-voluntary actions
✓   The relationship between virtues, actions and reasons and the role of practical reasoning/practical wisdom

Issues, including:
✓   Whether Aristotelian virtue ethics can give sufficiently clear guidance about how to act
✓   Clashing/competing virtues
✓   The possibility of circularity involved in defining virtuous acts and virtuous people in terms of each other
✓   Whether a trait must contribute to eudaimonia in order to be a virtue; the relationship between the good for the individual and moral good

II. Applied ethics

Students must be able to apply the content of Normative ethical theories and Metaethics to the following issues:
✓   Stealing
✓   Simulated killing (within computer games, plays, films, etc.)
✓   Eating animals
✓   Telling lies

III. Metaethics

✓ The origins of moral principles: reason, emotion/attitudes, or society
✓ The distinction between cognitivism and non-cognitivism about ethical language

A. Moral realism

✓ There are mind-independent moral properties/facts
  ● Moral naturalism (cognitivist) – including naturalist forms of utilitarianism (including Bentham) and of virtue ethics
  ● Moral non-naturalism (cognitivist) – including intuitionism and Moore's 'open question argument' against all reductive metaethical theories and the 'naturalistic fallacy'

Issues that may arise for the theories above, including:
✓ Hume's 'fork' and A. J. Ayer's verification principle
✓ Hume's argument that moral judgements are not beliefs since beliefs alone could not motivate us
✓ Hume's is–ought gap
✓ John Mackie's argument from relativity and his arguments from queerness

B. Moral anti-realism

✓ There are no mind-independent moral properties/facts
  ● Error theory (cognitivist) – Mackie
  ● Emotivism (non-cognitivist) – Ayer
  ● Prescriptivism (non-cognitivist) – Richard Hare

Issues that may arise for the theories above, including:
✓ Whether anti-realism can account for how we use moral language, including moral reasoning, persuading, disagreeing, etc.
✓ The problem of accounting for moral progress
✓ Whether anti-realism becomes moral nihilism

I. Normative ethical theories

How should I live? This is a central question that we all face. Morality is intended to assist us in thinking about the question. 'Normative ethics' is the branch of philosophy that discusses theories of how to live and what we should do. We will discuss three normative ethical theories, utilitarianism, Kantian deontological theory, and Aristotelian virtue ethics.

A. Utilitarianism

In its simplest form, utilitarianism is defined by three claims.

1. What is right? Actions are morally right or wrong depending on their consequences and nothing else. An act is right if it maximises what is good. This is 'act consequentialism'.
2. What is good? The only thing that is good is happiness, understood as pleasure and the absence of pain. This is 'hedonism'.
3. Who counts? No one's happiness counts more than anyone else's. This is a commitment to equality.

This is known as hedonistic act utilitarianism. If we put (1) and (2) together, we see that the theory claims that an action is right if it *maximises* happiness, i.e. if it leads to the greatest happiness of all those it affects. Otherwise, the action is wrong. Our actions are judged not 'in themselves', e.g. by what *type* of action they are (a lie, helping someone, etc.), but in terms of what *consequences* they have. Our actions are morally right if they bring about the greatest happiness.

'Greatest happiness' is comparative (great, greater, greatest). If an action leads to the greatest happiness of those it affects, no other action taken at that time could have led to greater happiness. So an action is right only if, out of all the actions you could have done, this action leads to more happiness than any other. Just causing *some* happiness, or more happiness than unhappiness, isn't enough for an act to be morally right.

Act utilitarianism seems to provide a clear and simple way of making decisions: consider the consequences of the different actions you could perform and choose that action that brings about, or is likely to bring about,

What is hedonistic act utilitarianism?

the greatest happiness. It makes complicated decisions easy and avoids appeals to controversial moral intuitions. The only thing that matters is happiness, and surely everyone wants to be happy. We can figure out empirically how much happiness actions cause, and so we can solve moral issues by empirical investigation.

Bentham's quantitative hedonistic utilitarianism

BENTHAM, *AN INTRODUCTION TO THE PRINCIPLES OF MORALS AND LEGISLATION*, CHS 1, 4

'The principle of utility' (Ch. 1)

Jeremy Bentham is considered the first act utilitarian. He defended the 'principle of utility', also known as the 'greatest happiness principle'. It is 'that principle which approves or disapproves of every action whatsoever, according to the tendency which it appears to have to augment or diminish the happiness of the party whose interest is in question'. Or again, 'that principle which states the greatest happiness of all those whose interest is in question, as being the right and proper … end of human action' (§2). So Bentham claims that in judging actions to be morally right or wrong, we should take into account only the total amount of happiness that the action may produce. Likewise, in our own actions, we should aim to produce the greatest happiness we can.

What is the principle of utility?

The meaning of 'utility'

Utilitarianism is so-called because it is concerned with 'utility'. In §3, Bentham explains what he means by 'utility', making the connection between utility and happiness:

> By utility is meant that property in any object, whereby it tends to produce benefit, advantage, pleasure, good, or happiness (all this in the present case comes to the same thing) or (what comes again to the same thing) to prevent the happening of mischief, pain, evil, or unhappiness to the party whose interest is considered.

In §5, he clarifies what he means by 'interest':

> A thing is said to promote the interest, or to be *for* the interest, of an individual, when it tends to add to the sum total of his pleasures: or, what comes to the same thing, to diminish the sum total of his pains.

So, something has 'utility' if it contributes to your happiness, which is the same as what is in your interest. And happiness is pleasure and the absence of pain. The claim that pleasure, as happiness, is the only good is known as hedonism. In Ch. 5, Bentham goes on to list fourteen 'families' of pleasure, such as sensory pleasure, the pleasures of exercising one's skills, the pleasures of having power, the pleasures of memory, and the pleasures of benevolence. He also lists twelve families of pain, many deriving from similar sources as pleasure.

Explain what Bentham means by 'utility'.

'Measuring pleasure and pain' (Ch. 4)

Bentham argued that we can measure pleasures and pains and add them up on a single scale by a process he called the 'felicific calculus' ('felicity' means happiness), also known as the 'hedonic calculus' or 'utility calculus'. If a pleasure is more intense, will last longer, is more certain to occur, will happen sooner rather than later, or will produce in turn many other pleasures and few pains, it counts for more. In thinking what to do, you also need to take into account how many people will be affected (the more you affect positively, and the fewer you affect negatively, the better). The total amount of happiness produced is the sum total of everyone's pleasures produced minus the sum total of everyone's pains. As this demonstrates, Bentham took a *quantitative* approach to happiness.

Briefly explain the central claims of Bentham's utilitarianism.

The reasons to believe utilitarianism rest in its intuitive appeal. Everyone cares about happiness (Bentham claims that the *only* things that motivate people are pleasure and pain). Morality is about how to act, so it better be about what motivates us. So it is about happiness. If happiness is good, then

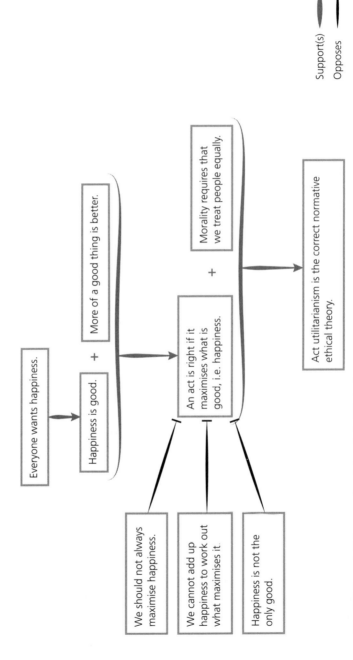

Everyone wants happiness.

Happiness is good.

+ More of a good thing is better.

An act is right if it maximises what is good, i.e. happiness.

We should not always maximise happiness.

We cannot add up happiness to work out what maximises it.

Happiness is not the only good.

Morality requires that we treat people equally.

+

Act utilitarianism is the correct normative ethical theory.

Support(s)

Opposes

Map 3.1 Some initial reasons for and against utilitarianism

surely it is reasonable to think that more happiness is better. So we should maximise happiness. And until we have a good reason to think otherwise, treating people as equal is an appealing moral starting point.

However, Bentham's normative ethical theory may also strike us as too simple. For example, is happiness the *only* thing that matters morally, i.e. is hedonism the correct theory of what is good? Should we really bring about the greatest happiness in all situations, even when we have to violate someone's rights to do so? Or again, 'more' happiness might be better than 'less', but can we really 'add up' how much happiness an action will cause? So even if we think that morality has *something* to do with happiness, we might want to reject utilitarianism. We will look at these objections and more, but before we do, we look at how John Stuart Mill developed and deepened Bentham's theory.

Mill on utilitarianism

MILL, *UTILITARIANISM*, CHS 1, 2

John Stuart Mill begins his book on utilitarianism by remarking on how surprising it is that, with all the developments in knowledge over the last two millennia, there is still little agreement on the criterion for right and wrong. In science, we start from particular observations and work out the laws of nature from them. But our usual method of empirical induction doesn't work in ethics. Part of the difficulty is that we can't easily infer the principles of morality from particular cases, because we first need to know the principles in order to judge whether an action is right or wrong.

However, we shouldn't exaggerate the disagreement. Many philosophers agree that morality involves moral laws and they agree on what many of these laws are (e.g. concerning murder, theft, harming others, betrayal, etc.), even if they disagree about why these are moral laws. Mill then remarks that people's moral approval and disapproval is, as a matter of fact, strongly influenced by the effects of actions on their happiness. So the principle of utility has played a significant role in forming moral beliefs, even if this hasn't been recognised.

When Mill wrote *Utilitarianism*, there was a lot of misunderstanding of what utilitarians actually believed. Ch. 2 clarifies what utilitarianism is – what it really claims – by considering and replying to eleven objections which Mill argues arise from misunderstanding the theory. We will be able to consider only some of these in any detail, but it is worth setting them all out briefly here:

1. 'Utility' means what is useful, not what is pleasurable. Utilitarianism therefore ignores the value of pleasure.
   Reply: Obviously a misunderstanding. Mill reasserts Bentham's central claims. First, 'actions are right in proportion as they tend to promote happiness, wrong as they tend to produce the reverse of happiness'. Second, '[b]y happiness is intended pleasure, and the absence of pain; by unhappiness, pain, and the privation of pleasure'. Third, 'pleasure, and freedom from pain, are the only things desirable as ends'. Like Bentham, then, Mill accepts and defends hedonism.
2. Utilitarianism values only pleasure. It does not recognise the 'higher' things in life or the dignity of human beings.
3. Happiness is unattainable.

We will discuss these two objections in Mill's QUALITATIVE HEDONISTIC UTILITARIANISM, next (p. 212).

4. We do not need happiness and many wise and noble people have lived without it.
   Reply: True, but what have noble people sacrificed their happiness for? Surely, it is the happiness of others. If not, then what a wasted sacrifice! Utilitarianism recognises the virtue of sacrificing your happiness for others – the aim remains to increase the total happiness in the world.
5. Utilitarians make right and wrong depend upon the agent's happiness.
   Reply: Another obvious misunderstanding. It is the happiness of everyone that is the criterion of right action. For this reason, we should organise society and raise children in such a way that

each person feels that their own happiness is bound up with the happiness of others, that they are made happy by making others happy.

6. Utilitarianism is too idealistic, expecting people to be motivated by everyone's happiness in general.
7. Utilitarianism makes people cold and unsympathetic to others, considering only their actions and not their personal qualities.

We return to these two objections in PARTIALITY (p. 234) and MORAL INTEGRITY AND THE INDIVIDUAL'S INTENTIONS (p. 237).

8. Utilitarianism is a godless theory.
    Reply: It isn't. Utilitarianism can easily be made compatible with Christian teachings about God. (Given his social context, Mill mentions only Christianity.)
9. Utilitarianism will lead to people sacrificing moral principles for 'expedient' immoral action.
    Reply: 'Expedient' usually means either what is in the person's own interest or in the short-term interest, as when someone lies to get out of a tricky situation. Where an action is 'expedient' in this sense and sacrifices the greater happiness of people generally, then utilitarianism condemns it. We will return to this issue in MILL ON JUSTICE (p. 231).

For Mill's view on lying, see TELLING LIES, p. 339.

10. It is not possible to work out the consequences of an action for human happiness.
11. Utilitarians will be tempted to make exceptions to the rules.

We discuss these two objections in PROBLEMS WITH CALCULATION (p. 225) and RULE UTILITARIANISM DEVELOPED (p. 241).

Having provided an overview of Ch. 2, we turn to one of its main themes – the nature of happiness.

Mill's qualitative hedonistic utilitarianism

What is happiness? Mill agrees with Bentham that happiness is pleasure and the absence of pain. But the exact relation between pleasure and happiness needs further clarification. Happiness is not 'a continuity of highly pleasurable excitement', a life of rapture, 'but moments of such, in an existence made up of few and transitory pains, many and various pleasures, with a decided predominance of the active over the passive, and having as the foundation of the whole, not to expect more from life than it is capable of bestowing'. Thus variety, activity and realistic expectations play an important role in how our pleasures make up our happiness.

Is happiness, understood like this, attainable (objection (3))? Yes, says Mill, many people can experience it. The main obstacles are a poor education and poor social arrangements that lead to lack of opportunity and inequality. Of course, we can't expect good fortune all the time – we will all experience disease and the loss of people we love. But the main sources of human suffering are things that we can diminish over time.

Does utilitarianism degrade human beings in valuing only pleasure (objection (2))? In his essay on Bentham, Mill sympathises with the objection applied to Bentham's view of happiness. Bentham didn't really understand human nature, Mill argues; 'If he thought at all of any of the deeper feelings of human nature, it was but as idiosyncrasies of taste'. According to Bentham's felicific calculus, 'quantity of pleasure being equal, push-pin is as good as poetry' (push-pin was a very simple child's or gambler's game). Mill rejects the view that pleasures and pains are all equally valuable, and in *Utilitarianism*, he provides an alternative account of human nature that answers the objection.

Higher and lower pleasures

Mill argues that the claim that utilitarianism degrades human beings misunderstands what human beings take pleasure in. Some types of pleasure are 'higher' than others, more valuable, more important to human happiness, given the types of creatures we are and what we are capable of.

We consider Aristotle's theory of happiness in EUDAIMONIA, p. 271.

Why is it important to utilitarianism as a theory that we can achieve happiness?

Aristotle's theory of pleasure is discussed in EUDAIMONIA AND PLEASURE, p. 294.

Which pleasures? How can we tell if a type of pleasure is more valuable (quality) than another, rather than just more pleasurable (quantity)? The answer has to be to ask people who know what they are talking about. If everyone (or almost everyone) who has experience of two types of pleasure prefers one type to the other, then the type that they prefer is more valuable. To ensure that they are considering the quality and not quantity of the pleasure, we should add another condition. A pleasure is higher only if people who have experience of both types of pleasure prefer one even if having that pleasure brings more pain with it, or again, even if they would choose it over a greater quantity of the other type of pleasure.

Explain Mill's test for higher pleasures.

Mill argues that, as long as our physical needs are met, people will prefer the pleasures of thought, feeling and imagination to pleasures of the body and the senses, even though our 'higher' capacities also mean we can experience terrible pain, boredom and dissatisfaction. For example, ''Tis better to have loved and lost than never to have loved at all'. We can say the same about intelligence and artistic creativity – better to have the pleasures that they bring, even though they cause us pain and distress, than to be unintelligent or lack creativity.

Tennyson, 'In Memoriam A.H.H.'

Thus Mill compares a human being with a pig (objection (2) claims that valuing only pleasure is a 'doctrine worthy only of swine'). As human beings, we are able to experience pleasures of deep personal relationships, art and creative thought that pigs are not. We can experience new and deeper kinds of pain as a result. Yet we don't think that the possibility of pain would be a good reason for choosing to be a well-looked-after pig, rather than a human being. 'It is better to be a human being dissatisfied than a pig satisfied'. This preference, Mill thinks, derives from our sense of dignity, which is an essential part of our happiness.

In introducing this distinction between higher and lower pleasures, Mill rejects the felicific calculus, and adds the element of quality to the quantitative analysis of happiness that Bentham puts forward.

Explain Mill's distinction between higher and lower pleasures.

It is important to note that if Mill's prediction here is wrong – if people with the relevant experience do not prefer the pleasures of thought, feeling and imagination to other pleasures, then these are not higher pleasures. So we can object that people do *not* reliably pursue the 'higher' pleasures of thought, feeling and imagination instead of the 'lower' pleasures related to the body and the senses.

Mill accepts the point, but argues that it is no objection. First, there is a difference between preference and action. We can choose what we know to be less good, whether from weakness of will or laziness or other factors. We still recognise that what we did not choose is more valuable.

Second, appreciating the higher pleasures can be more demanding. Our ability to experience higher pleasures can be undermined by hard work, lack of time, infrequent opportunities to experience them, and so on. We may seek lower pleasures simply because those are more readily available to us.

Not just anyone's preference counts as deciding whether a pleasure is 'higher' or 'lower'. As with any question, we need to consult people who know what they are talking about. Having been to an art gallery once doesn't count as having experienced the pleasures of art, and listening to just one pop song doesn't count as having experienced the pleasures of pop music. Mill says that one pleasure is higher than another if almost everyone who is 'competently acquainted' with both prefers one over the other.

Compare and contrast Bentham and Mill on happiness.

Is pleasure the only good?

SMART ON HEDONISTIC AND NON-HEDONISTIC UTILITARIANISM

SMART, *UTILITARIANISM*, CH. 3

As we have seen in the case of Bentham and Mill, utilitarians can disagree about what is good, and so about which consequences or 'states of affairs' are best. Bentham thinks that we should concern ourselves only with the quantity of happiness caused while Mill thinks matters are more complicated, and we need to take into account the quality of happiness as well (higher v. lower pleasures). This question of what is good is the focus of Smart's discussion. Is only pleasure good? Is only happiness, understood as involving both quantity and quality of pleasure, good? Is anything other than pleasure or happiness good? In connection with the last option, Smart mentions G. E. Moore, who thought that some other states of mind, aside from pleasure, are also good, such as knowledge. Smart calls Moore an 'ideal' utilitarian, as opposed to the 'hedonistic' utilitarianism of Bentham and Mill.

How might Bentham respond to Mill's distinction between higher and lower pleasures? He could say that our preference for higher pleasures is not because such pleasures are qualitatively better, but because they are more 'fecund' – they are likely to produce *more* pleasure either for others or for ourselves in the long term. For example, if we enjoy thought, then we may produce greater benefits for society, e.g. through scientific research.

Yet, Smart claims, Mill seems right that pleasures are not all equal – if they were, a contented sheep would be as good as a contented human, so perhaps, to maximise happiness, we should decrease the human population and increase the number of cared-for sheep! It seems that most of us, at least, do prefer the pleasures of thought, feeling and imagination – perhaps because human beings are intellectual creatures: we owe our survival in evolutionary terms to our intellect, not our bodily strength or speed.

To try to understand our preferences for certain pleasures further, Smart asks us to imagine a scenario in which someone is wired up to electrodes in his brain, so that just by pressing a button, he could give himself intense sensual pleasure reliably and with no ill-effects. What should we say if he came to prefer this to anything else, and spent all his spare time doing this? What if we knew that most people would feel the same if they were wired up? Is this a picture of a good or happy life, one we should bring about as the maximisation of happiness?

Figure 3.1 Is this a picture of the good life?

Smart argues that while we can understand that the electrode operator is *contented*, and even that we would be contented if we became electrode operators, we simply don't want to become electrode operators. We want to do more with our lives than that, to achieve things, and if someone were to force us to become electrode operators, we would not now thank them for it, but be made unhappy by the prospect. The same applies to Mill's dictum 'Better to be Socrates dissatisfied than a fool satisfied'. Socrates would not want to be a fool, even knowing that after he became a fool, he would be contented.

Smart argues that our responses here are not a matter of the quality of the pleasure, as Mill thinks, but our *attitude* towards it. To say that someone is *happy*, and not just contented, is to express approval of their pleasures. Because we think a life as an electrode operator is wasted, we do not think such a person 'happy', only contented, and we would not want such a life for ourselves. Of course, Mill rejects this analysis: he says that when we judge pleasures as higher or lower, we should put aside all considerations of morality, of whether we *ought* to prefer the pleasure to another. Smart claims we don't do this – we prefer certain pleasures to others and our approval of them is an aspect of this.

Smart concludes that Mill's position is not a form of *pure* hedonism after all. Pure hedonism recognises pleasure as the only good and sole criterion for what we ought to bring about. Such a view can only defend the place of higher pleasures in terms of their fecundity; they are not 'higher' at all. But Mill's concept of happiness is evaluative, because happiness is pleasure of which we approve. And so it is not pure hedonism.

Mill and Bentham agree that pleasure is always good. But imagine a world in which there is just one person, who believes (falsely) that elsewhere in the world, other people are being tortured. This thought delights him a great deal; he is a sadist. Is his pleasure bad? Would the world be a morally better place if this belief caused him sadness?

Smart defends the hedonist position: it is good that he feels pleasure at the thought of their suffering, because at least he is happy, and no one else is, in fact, suffering. Our difficulty in accepting this is that in the real world, sadistic thoughts and pleasures often cause *actual* suffering. In other words, they lead to morally bad consequences. But we need to separate this from whether they are bad in and of themselves, 'intrinsically'. No pleasure, Smart claims, is intrinsically bad; it is only ever bad if it causes pain (to the person themselves or others).

> Explain Smart's interpretation of the distinction between higher and lower pleasures.

> Is pleasure ever bad 'in itself' or only ever bad because it leads to bad consequences?

NOZICK'S EXPERIENCE MACHINE

In his discussion of the electrode machine, Smart contrasts our desire for pleasure with our desire for achievements, and then talks of happiness as not only contentment, but approving of our contentment. We can question whether this really gets to the bottom of our desire for achievement.

Robert Nozick asks us to imagine being faced with the chance of plugging in to a virtual reality machine. This machine will produce the experience of a very happy life, not only with many and various pleasures and few pains, but (the experience of) many successful achievements. If we plug in, we will not know that we are in a virtual reality machine. We will believe that what we experience is reality. However, we must agree to plug in for life or not at all.

> 'The experience machine', *Anarchy, State and Utopia*

Nozick argues that most of us would *not* plug in. We value being in contact with reality, even if that makes us less happy, even if we experience fewer achievements. But we can't understand this in terms of the 'pleasure' of being in touch with reality, or a preference for certain types of pleasure

Figure 3.2 Which would you prefer? Why?

Explain Nozick's 'experience machine' and the objection to hedonism he draws from our response to it.

over others, because if we were in the machine, we would still experience this pleasure (we would believe we were in touch with reality). Instead, what we want is not a *psychological state* at all; it is a *relation* to something outside our minds. Smart is right that we want achievements; but we want *real* achievements, not just the psychological state of experiencing an achievement. Nozick concludes that we cannot understand what is good just in terms of our subjective psychological states, such as pleasure.

PREFERENCE UTILITARIANISM

One solution to the complications around pleasure and happiness facing hedonistic utilitarianism is offered by preference utilitarianism. Preference utilitarianism is a form of non-hedonistic utilitarianism that argues that what we should maximise is not pleasure, but the *satisfaction of people's preferences (desires)*.

1. If Nozick is right, we prefer to be in touch with reality, but not because it brings us pleasure. Having this preference satisfied is valuable. For a preference to be satisfied, it must be satisfied in reality. It is not enough that the person thinks their preference is satisfied.
2. We can also appeal to preferences to explain Mill's claims about higher and lower pleasures. He defends the distinction in terms of what people prefer. However, rather than talk about the value or quality of types of pleasure, we could argue that whatever people prefer is of more value to them – whether or not most people would prefer pleasures related to thought, feeling and imagination.

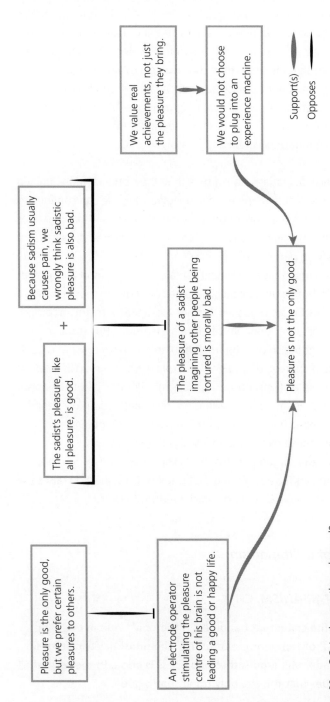

Pleasure is the only good, but we prefer certain pleasures to others.

An electrode operator stimulating the pleasure centre of his brain is not leading a good or happy life.

The sadist's pleasure, like all pleasure, is good.

Because sadism usually causes pain, we wrongly think sadistic pleasure is also bad.

+

The pleasure of a sadist imagining other people being tortured is morally bad.

Pleasure is not the only good.

We value real achievements, not just the pleasure they bring.

We would not choose to plug into an experience machine.

Support(s)

Opposes

Map 3.2 Is pleasure the only good?

3. The satisfaction of many of our preferences will bring us pleasure, but many will not. For instance, Bentham and Mill do not distinguish between producing happiness and decreasing pain. But are these morally equivalent? If people more strongly prefer not to suffer pain than to be brought pleasure, then that would explain the thought that it is more important not to cause harm. Or again, we can also argue that people have preferences about what happens after their death, e.g. to their possessions, and it is important to satisfy these as well, even though this cannot bring them any pleasure.

Explain preference utilitarianism and one argument for it.

In sum, preference utilitarians can argue that they offer a more unified account of what is valuable than hedonist utilitarianism. We can continue to claim that happiness is the only good if we now understand happiness as one's desires being satisfied. Pleasure is important, when it is, because it results from satisfying people's preferences.

They can also argue that they simplify Smart's theory. Smart argues that happiness is good, but he understands happiness in terms of those pleasures we approve of. But Smart offers no further explanation of this approval. People simply do or don't approve of certain pleasures. But shouldn't we approve of what is good? In other words, shouldn't a theory of what is good say what we *should* approve of, rather than explain what is good in terms of what we *do* approve of (with no further reason)? Preference utilitarianism can say that what is good is maximising the satisfaction of people's preferences. That many people prefer certain pleasures to others is enough reason to prioritise those pleasures; approval isn't relevant.

But what is the argument for the claim that satisfying people's preferences is good and the only thing that is good? This question raises the issue of how we know what is good, which we turn to next.

Mill's 'proof' of utilitarianism

MILL, *UTILITARIANISM*, CH. 4

Mill defends the claim that happiness is the only value in Ch. 4, his famous 'proof' of the principle of utility. The proof has two stages. In the first stage, Mill argues that happiness is good. In the second stage, he argues that it is the only thing that is good.

Stage 1: happiness is good

Mill argues that you can't strictly 'prove' that something is good or not. That is, it is not something that you can deduce from other premises. This is normal for 'first principles' in any area of knowledge, and a claim about what is ultimately good is a first principle in ethics. Nonetheless, we can give a reasoned argument about what is good.

First, some terminology. What is good is what we should aim at in our actions and lives. So what is good is an 'end' – the purpose – of our actions. Philosophers understand actions in terms of means and ends. Ends are why you do what you do; means are how you achieve your ends. So I might cross the street to post a letter. My end is posting the letter, my means is crossing the street. Now, of course, my posting a letter is also a means to an end, the end of communicating with someone. This, too, may be a means to an end. Perhaps I am asking them for a favour. So I cross the street in order to post the letter in order to ask someone a favour. What is the end of asking them for a favour? What am I ultimately aiming at?

What we *should* aim at is what is desirable, says Mill. So what he wants to show is, first, that happiness *is* desirable, and second, that *only* happiness is desirable. If he is right, then the answer to our previous question about why I am asking for a favour will be 'happiness'.

Since we can't deduce what is good, we have to appeal to evidence. Mill's argument that happiness is good has three parts.

1. 'The only proof capable of being given that an object is visible is that people actually see it … In like manner … the sole evidence … that something is desirable is that people do actually desire it …'
2. 'No reason can be given why the general happiness is desirable, except that each person … desires his own happiness'.
3. 'This, however, being a fact, we have not only all the proof the case admits of, but all which it is possible to require, that happiness is a good: that each person's happiness is a good to that person, and the general happiness, therefore, a good to

Mill here appears to adopt MORAL REALISM (see p. 351). By contrast, Smart defends a form of NON-COGNITIVISM (p. 348), claiming that moral judgements are expressions of subjective attitudes and so can't be established by reason.

Briefly explain Mill's argument that happiness is good.

the aggregate of all persons …' Put more clearly, each person takes their own happiness to be good, and so, adding each person's happiness to that of others, the happiness of everyone – the general happiness – is good for people in general.

(Continued below)

See UTILITARIANISM AS NATURALISM, p. 355.

CLARIFYING THE ARGUMENT

G. E. Moore objected that Mill commits the fallacy of equivocation in this argument, confusing two meanings of a word. The word 'desirable' has two meanings. Its usual meaning is 'worthy of being desired'. Anything desirable in this sense is good. This is the sense it has in (2), since Mill is arguing that the general happiness is good. But another meaning could be 'capable of being desired'. To discover what is capable of being desired, look at what people desire. This is the sense it has in (1), it seems, since Mill links what is desirable to what people desire. But what people actually desire is not the same as what is *worthy* of being desired (good). People want all sorts of rubbish! Mill has assumed that what people desire just is what is good; he hasn't spotted that these are distinct meanings of 'desirable'.

Explain Moore's objection to Mill's proof.

But Moore's objection misinterprets Mill's argument. Mill is asking 'What *evidence* is there for thinking that something is worthy of being desired?' He argues that people *in general* desire happiness. Unless people *in general* desire what is not worth desiring, this looks like good evidence that happiness is desirable. Is there anything that *everyone* wants that is not worth wanting? If we look at what people agree upon in what they desire, we will find evidence of what is worth desiring. Everyone wants happiness, so it is reasonable to infer that happiness is desirable (good).

Other philosophers have objected that Mill commits the fallacy of composition in (3). This is a fallacy of inferring that because some part has a property, the whole of which it is a part also has that property. Mill seems to be saying that because each person desires their own happiness, everybody desires everybody's happiness (the general happiness). But this doesn't follow. For example, suppose that every girl loves a sailor (substitute 'own happiness'). From the fact that for each girl, there is some sailor that she loves ((b) in FIGURE 3.3), we cannot infer that there is one sailor (substitute 'general happiness') which every girl loves ((a) in FIGURE 3.3).

Explain the objection that Mill's proof commits the fallacy of composition.

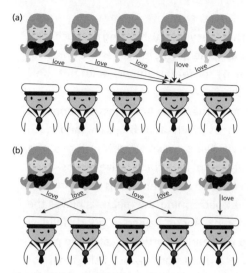

Figure 3.3 Every girl loves a sailor

But this is also a misinterpretation of Mill's argument. At no point does Mill feel that he needs to defend the idea of impartiality in ethics. He simply assumes that ethics is concerned with what is good in general. He is not trying to infer that we ought to be concerned for others' happiness. Having argued that happiness is good, it follows from his assumption that ethics is impartial that we should be concerned with the general happiness.

> Explain Mill's argument for the claim that happiness is good. Can you construct an argument map for it?

MILL, *UTILITARIANISM*, CH. 4 (*continued from above*)

Stage 2: only happiness is good

The claim that happiness is good is relatively uncontroversial. It is much more controversial to claim that it is the *only* good. Mill must argue that everything of value – truth, beauty, freedom, etc. – derives its value from happiness.

Now if people only ever desired happiness, he could use the previous argument to show that happiness is the only good. But clearly, people desire many different things. Of course, we may desire many things as a means to happiness, such as buying a nice house or having a good job. But it isn't obvious that everything we desire is a means to happiness. For example, in NOZICK'S EXPERIENCE

MACHINE (p. 217), we argued that we want truth (being in touch with reality) and not because it has some psychological effect on us. So going by the evidence, many different things, and not only happiness, are good.

Mill's response is to clarify further what happiness is. Happiness has many 'ingredients', such as truth and freedom, and each ingredient is desirable in itself. We can explain this in terms of a distinction between 'external means' and 'constitutive means' to an end. We usually think of the relation between means and end as an instrumental relation, i.e. that performing the means achieves the further, independent end. Think about having a good holiday. Suppose you have to get up very early in order to catch the plane. You do this in order to have a good holiday, but it isn't part of having a good holiday. Getting up early is an external means to the end. But there is also another relation between means and ends, a constitutive relation. Later on, you are lying on the beach in the sun, listening to your favourite music. Are you doing this 'in order' to have a good holiday? Not in the same sense. This just *is* having a good holiday at the moment. Lying on the beach is a constitutive means to the end of having a good holiday. Having a good holiday is not something 'further' or additional that you achieve by lying on the beach. In these circumstances, here and now, it is what 'having a good holiday' amounts to.

The same applies to happiness, Mill argues. For example, when someone desires to know the truth 'for its own sake', their knowing the truth doesn't cause their happiness as some further and separate thing. Rather, in this situation, their happiness *consists in* their knowing the truth. Knowing the truth for its own sake is part of happiness for them. So, Mill claims, whatever we desire for its own sake is part of what happiness is, for us.

Why believe this? Mill argues that to desire something *just is* to find it pleasant. It is, he says, 'physically and metaphysically impossible' to desire something that you don't think is a pleasure. As pleasure is happiness, we only desire happiness, and happiness is the only good.

Explain the distinction between external and constitutive means.

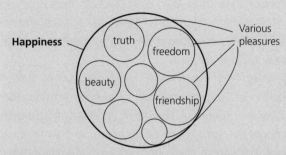

Figure 3.4 The constitutive means to happiness

However, we have seen that both preference utilitarianism and Smart provide alternative accounts of happiness and the good. Preference utilitarianism allows that, if we understand pleasure as a psychological state (which we should), we can desire something without desiring it 'as pleasant'. What we desire is part of our happiness because happiness is the satisfaction of desires, not because happiness is pleasure which is caused by the satisfaction of desires. Smart adds an evaluative element to happiness. We are made happy by knowing the truth because we approve of knowing the truth, and not simply because it brings us pleasure (in the sense of contentment).

> 1) Explain Mill's argument for the claim that happiness is the only good. 2) Does Mill succeed in showing that the only good is happiness?

Issues for (act) utilitarianism

We have considered whether and how utilitarianism can defend the claim that pleasure or happiness is the only good. In this section, we will look at four further objections to act utilitarianism.

> We will consider these issues in relation to rule utilitarianism in RULE UTILITARIANISM DEVELOPED, p. 241.

PROBLEMS WITH CALCULATION

On p. 205, we noted that act utilitarianism seems to offer a clear and straightforward way of discovering what is right and wrong. We need to consider how much happiness an action will cause. But the tenth objection Mill considers (see p. 211) is that it is not possible to work out the consequences of an action for human happiness. How can we know or work out the consequences of an action, to discover whether it maximises happiness or not? Surely this will be too difficult and too time-consuming for us to do. Bentham's felicific calculus (p. 207) is, in practice, mind-boggling, and we just can't get the relevant information (how intense each affected person's pleasure or pain will be, how long it will last, what other pleasures or pains it might cause in turn, etc.).

Preference utilitarianism might try to claim another advantage here. It is easier to know whether someone's preference has been satisfied than how much pleasure someone experiences. But this is very little improvement if we still need to compare the strength of different people's preferences, whether satisfying one preference leads to further preferences being satisfied, and so on.

However, the objection misrepresents what utilitarians say. Bentham does not say that an action is right if it *actually* maximises happiness. He says it is right according to 'the tendency which it appears to have' to maximise happiness. We don't need to be able to work out the consequences precisely. An action is right if we can reasonably expect that it will maximise happiness. He also says that the felicific calculus need not be 'strictly pursued' before each decision or moral judgement. It just needs to be 'kept in view'.

This still means we must be able to work things out roughly. Mill thought this was still too demanding. Happiness is 'much too complex and indefinite' a standard to apply directly to actions. But we don't need to try, he claims, because over time, people have automatically, through trial and error, worked out which actions tend to produce happiness. This is what our inherited moral rules actually are: 'tell the truth', 'don't steal', and 'keep your promises' are embodiments of the wisdom of humanity that lying, theft and false promising tend to lead to unhappiness.

Mill calls these moral rules 'secondary principles'. It is only in cases of conflict between secondary principles (e.g. if by telling the truth you break your promise) that we need to apply the greatest happiness principle directly to an action. We shouldn't attempt to calculate happiness directly unless we have such a conflict. Only in cases of conflict will there be genuine exceptions to these rules.

Of course, our inherited morality still makes mistakes in what it thinks will or won't contribute to general happiness. So we can improve on the rules that we have. But saying this is quite different from saying that we have to consider each action from scratch, as though we had no prior moral knowledge.

Explain the difference between saying that an act is morally right if it actually maximises happiness and saying an act is morally right if it appears to have a tendency to maximise happiness.

Explain the problem of calculation and Mill's solution to it.

Which beings' happiness should we include?

A number of these issues about calculation, and whether Mill's responses really solve the problem, come into sharp relief when we consider which beings we should include in calculating the happiness or unhappiness caused by an action. Bentham was aware that his identification of happiness as the only good had some radical implications. He argued that the question of who or what to consider when looking at the consequences of our actions is not 'Can they *reason*? nor, Can they *talk*? but, Can they *suffer*?' Utilitarianism says that happiness is good, not just that the happiness of humans is good. If happiness is good, then it is good no matter what creature feels it. There is nothing in the theory that gives us a reason to privilege human happiness over the happiness of non-human animals. So it seems that the logic of utilitarianism requires us to take as much account of beings that are not human as of human beings. The third condition of act utilitarianism (see p. 205) – that the happiness of each matters *equally* – does not stop at the boundary between human and non-human.

We return to this issue in Eating animals, p. 327.

An Introduction to the Principles of Morals and Legislation, Ch. 17

This line of thought has been more recently developed by Peter Singer. We do not think that it is right to treat women worse than men just because they are women (this is sexism), nor to treat one race worse than another (this is racism). Likewise, it is wrong to treat animals as unequal just because they are not human. This is 'speciesism'.

Animal Liberation

We can object that with women and men, and different races, there is no difference in those important capacities – reason, the use of language, the depth of our emotional experience, our self-awareness, our ability to distinguish right and wrong – that make a being a person. But there is a difference between human beings and animals with all of these.

Singer responds that these differences are not relevant when it comes to the important capacity that human beings and animals share, namely sentience, the basic consciousness needed to experience pleasure and pain. For a utilitarian, an act (or rule) is wrong if it produces more *suffering* than an alternative. Who is suffering is irrelevant. When it comes to suffering, animals should be treated as equal to people.

If the happiness of every being that can feel pleasure or pain, or can have preferences that are satisfied or not, makes a difference to whether an action is morally right or not, the problem of calculation is intensified. If it is difficult to compare the happiness of different people, it is much more difficult to compare the happiness of a person with that of, say, a pig or a

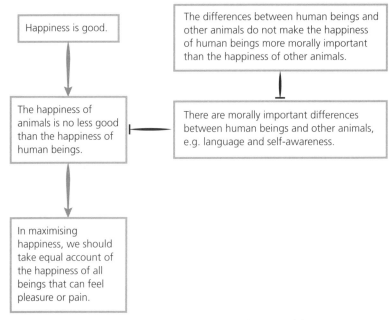

Map 3.3 Whose happiness should we consider in making moral decisions?

bird. But this will be relevant if we ask whether we should eat meat or whether we should destroy wild habitats to make new farms to grow crops for people.

Furthermore, in response to Mill, we can argue that our inherited morality isn't much help here. Many cultures do not take much moral notice of animals beyond prohibiting deliberately inflicting pain on them for no good reason. Apart from that, they allow treating them simply as tools to be used to make human lives happier, e.g. as food, as clothing, as beasts of burden, as objects of experiment, and so on. So we cannot use our existing moral rules, since they do not take account of the happiness of creatures other than humans, and yet we cannot calculate the effects of our actions on the happiness of non-human animals with any degree of accuracy.

Singer can respond that a new customary morality is needed. We will need to work out, together and as best we can, drawing on whatever evidence we can, the tendencies our actions have to affect the happiness of other creatures, and then create secondary principles concerning how we treat animals. It may not be perfect, but it is the best we can do.

Explain Bentham and Singer's argument that utilitarianism requires us to take account of the happiness of non-human animals, and one implication of this requirement.

FAIRNESS, INDIVIDUAL LIBERTY AND RIGHTS

Questions of fairness, liberty and rights are questions of justice. As we shall see again in JUSTICE (p. 307), justice is the principle that each person receives their 'due'. Justice requires that we treat equals equally, and if what someone is due depends on some quantifiable attribute (e.g. ability in some area), we should treat differences proportionally. In other words, justice is fairness. A situation is unjust, for instance, if someone has more or less than their 'fair share', if they are favoured or unfavoured in some way that they do not deserve. Utilitarianism requires us to take each person's happiness into account equally. It may therefore seem that it respects fairness. But is this so?

'The tyranny of the majority'

In *On Liberty*, Mill was concerned with how, in a democracy, policies that lead to the greatest happiness for the majority could have a very negative affect on the minority. When a government is making laws, should it take into account what the majority of people want and simply *overrule* the interests or happiness of the minority? This may seem to be the basic principle of democracy, but if this is how laws should be made, then the majority have a form of absolute power. Suppose the majority want to enforce a system of very harsh punishment, e.g. the death penalty for theft, or outlaw homosexuality? Utilitarianism says we should do *whatever* brings about the greatest happiness. But should there be *constraints* on what the majority can do to the minority? For instance, should individuals have certain rights, e.g. to freedom of movement, freedom of thought, and freedom of expression, that protect them from such absolute power? Or is it morally permissible to remove these freedoms from some people (which would seem unfair) if it would lead to the greatest happiness overall?

Mill notes that there are two ways that the majority can exercise its power over minorities leading to a 'tyranny of the majority' unless its power is constrained. First, as just noted, it can do so through democratic government. For example, a democratic government could pass a law forbidding people to criticise a particular form of religious belief, or alternatively, a law forbidding them to practice it, if that is what the majority of people in society wanted. He argues that the powers of democratic government need to be limited by a respect and recognition for individual rights and liberties, but, we might think, utilitarianism has no place for these moral concepts.

Mill is also concerned about a second way the majority can exercise power, namely through the 'tyranny' of social opinion, 'the tendency of society to impose … its own ideas and practices as rules of conduct on those who dissent from them'. Everyone thinks that their way of doing things, what they like and dislike, should be the standard for everyone else. Think of the disapproval of other religious practices, of other cultures' traditions, of homosexuality, of standards of music and taste; think how quick people are to 'take offence' and think 'something should be done about it', and how such attitudes are communicated in the tabloid press. This disapproval, when socially expressed and endorsed, affects how people think and what they do; they are not free to think, feel and live as they please – even if there is no law preventing them from doing so.

Take, for example, the relationship between men and women. In Mill's day, it was simply 'understood' that women were not equal to men. Women's place was in the home, looking after the children. This made it very difficult for women who didn't want to live like this – if they seriously tried to live 'as men', they faced strong public censure. Much of this 'understanding' has now, fortunately, been left behind, and a utilitarian can condemn it because women equal men in number – happiness is not maximised under sexism. But imagine now a society in which it is 'understood' that the place of people of some minority race in a society should be to serve those of the majority race. The majority of people are happy, albeit at the expense of the happiness of the minority. How could utilitarianism condemn such a practice (assuming that this policy creates the greatest happiness, i.e. any attempts to make the minority happier would lead to less happiness for the majority)?

Briefly outline the objection that act utilitarianism will lead to the tyranny of the majority.

This contrasts with KANTIAN DEONTOLOGICAL ETHICS, p. 248.

Rights and liberties

The obvious unfairness of the tyranny of the majority arises from the fact that act utilitarianism does not rule out any type of action as immoral. There are no constraints on pursuing the greatest happiness. For example, if torturing a child produces the greatest happiness, then it is right to torture a child. Suppose a group of child abusers only find and torture abandoned children. Only the child suffers pain (no one else knows about their activities). But they derive a great deal of happiness. So more happiness is produced by torturing the child than not, so it is morally right. This is clearly the wrong answer.

Many rights involve restrictions placed on how people can treat each other. For instance, I have a right that other people don't kill me (the right to life). I also have a right to act as I choose as long as this respects other people's rights (the right to liberty). One of the purposes of rights is to protect individual freedom and interests, even when violating that freedom would produce greater happiness. For example, my right to life means that no one should kill me to take my organs, even if doing so could save the lives of four other people who need, respectively, a heart, lungs, kidneys and a liver. Utilitarianism, we may object, doesn't respect individual rights or liberty, because it doesn't recognise any restrictions on actions that create the greatest happiness.

Some utilitarians simply accept this. We have no rights. But, they argue, as long as we consider situations *realistically*, then whatever brings about the greatest happiness is the right thing to do. For example, in the case of the tortured child or killing me to use my organs, in real life, other people would find out and become very upset and fearful that the same could happen to them or their children. So these actions wouldn't lead to the greatest happiness. Counterexamples that appeal to very unlikely scenarios are unhelpful, because they have little to do with real life. In real life, act utilitarianism gives us the correct moral answer.

However, even if this is true (which we may question), the theory still implies that *if* it was very unlikely that anyone would find out, then it would be right to torture children (in the circumstances described). But other people finding out isn't what *makes* torturing children wrong. By leaving out rights, utilitarianism misses something of great moral importance, so it can't be the right theory of morality.

> Explain the objection that utilitarianism doesn't recognise individual rights.

Mill on justice

MILL, *UTILITARIANISM*, CH. 5

Mill discusses the problem of whether utilitarianism can give a plausible account of justice, which he calls 'the only real difficulty in the utilitarian theory of morals', in Ch. 5 of *Utilitarianism*.

First, he analyses what justice is and argues that at its heart, it is about the moral rights of the individual. We think of each of the following kinds of action as a violation of justice:

1. violating someone's legal rights;
2. violating someone's moral rights (laws are sometimes wrong, so their legal rights are not always the rights they should have in law);
3. not giving someone what they deserve, in particular failing to return good for good and evil for evil;
4. breaking a contract or promise;
5. failing to be impartial when this is required, e.g. in relation to respecting rights, what people deserve or cases of public interest;
6. treating people unequally.

What is distinctive about justice is that it relates to actions that harm a specific, identifiable individual, who has the right that we don't harm them in this way. Duties of justice are 'perfect' duties. We must always fulfil them, and have no choice over when or how, because someone else has the right that we act morally. (There are other cases of wrongdoing, e.g. not giving to charity, in which no *specific* person can demand this of us. Instead, we have some choice in how we fulfil the obligation to help others. These are 'imperfect' duties.)

But *why* do we have the rights that we have? Mill says that '[w]hen we call anything a person's right, we mean that he has a valid claim on society to protect him in the possession of it, either by the force of law, or by that of education and opinion'. And the reason why society should protect us in this way is the *general happiness*. The interests that are protected as rights are 'extraordinarily important'. They are interests concerned with security. We depend on security for protection from harm and to be able to enjoy what is good without fearing that it will be taken from us. The rules that prohibit harm and protect our freedom are more vital to our interests than any others. And so we protect these interests with rights, and these become the subject of justice. *This contributes most to happiness in the long term*. Hence, Mill says, 'I account the justice which is grounded on utility to be the chief part, and incomparably the most sacred and binding part, of all morality'.

Explain Mill's concept of justice.

How does Mill try to resolve the conflict between utilitarianism and rights?

Discussion

On Mill's view, we only have a right if our having that right contributes to the greatest happiness in the long run. We may wonder whether the rights that we usually take ourselves to have (e.g. related to individual liberty) really do this. For example, would society be more happy if people had less freedom in some cases? This is an important debate in political philosophy.

A clearer objection is that Mill's theory of rights doesn't offer a strong defence of individual rights in particular cases. Suppose there is an occasion where violating my rights will create more happiness than not. As we said above, a right protects the individual's interest against what may compete with it, e.g. the greater happiness on this occasion. Hence, my right to life prevents my being murdered to save the lives of many others. But if the ground of rights is the general happiness, this protection seems insecure. On the one hand, we have the demands of the greatest happiness, e.g. we can create more happiness if we kill one person to save five. On the other hand, we have the individual's right, but this turns out to be just the demands of the greatest happiness as well. If my rights are justified by general utility, then doesn't the happiness created by overriding my rights justify violating them? Utilitarianism can't offer any other reason to respect my right in this particular instance.

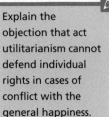

Explain the objection that act utilitarianism cannot defend individual rights in cases of conflict with the general happiness.

Mill can respond that this approach to conflicts between rights and happiness in individual cases doesn't understand utilitarianism in the right light. We need to consider happiness 'in the largest sense'. Rights protect our permanent interests, and thus serve the general happiness considered over the long term. We should establish that system of rights that would bring the most happiness, and then defend these rights. (Compare what Mill says regarding 'secondary principles' above, p. 226.)

But now we can object that Mill has given up on *act* utilitarianism. Mill seems to recommend that we don't look at the consequences of each act taken individually to see whether it creates the greatest happiness. He recommends that we create rights, which are a kind of *rule*, and enforce them even when they conflict with happiness in certain situations. Thus, he says,

> [j]ustice is a name for certain classes of moral rules, which concern the essentials of human well-being more nearly, and are therefore of more absolute obligation, than any other rules for the guidance of life; and the notion which we have found to be the essence of the idea of justice,

that of a right residing in an individual, implies and testifies to this more binding obligation.

Can act utilitarianism respect fairness?

When rights are involved, the right action is not the one that creates the greatest happiness, but the one that respects the right. It seems that, in the end, Mill must adopt RULE UTILITARIANISM (p. 240) to provide his account of rights and justice.

PARTIALITY

Many of the things that we do to make people happy are aimed at *specific* other people, namely our family and friends. We do them favours, buy them presents and generally spend our time and money on them. In other words, we are *partial* towards them. We are not impartial in how we treat everyone, we are not equally concerned with the happiness of everyone. But act utilitarianism argues that in our decisions, we need to consider the greatest happiness that our actions could create, and this requires us to consider the happiness of *each person equally*. In other words, we should be impartial.

So if act utilitarianism is right, it seems we should spend much less time with the particular people we love and more time helping people who need help, e.g. through voluntary work. Likewise, we should spend less money on the people we love and give much more money to charity. This would lead to greater happiness, because people who really need help will be made much more happy by the same amount of money or effort than people who don't really need anything. But is this correct? Is it morally permissible to be partial or is impartiality always required of us?

There are different ways we can develop this conflict between utilitarianism and our natural partiality towards some people into an objection. For instance, we can argue that utilitarianism is too idealistic, expecting people to give priority to needy strangers over those they know and love – to be motivated by the general happiness, rather than the happiness of those they are close to. Or again, we can argue that utilitarianism misses something morally important in counting each person equally. In the abstract, each person is equal, but *to me*, each person does not and should not count equally. It is morally right and good (or at least, not morally wrong) to show partiality towards those people one knows and loves.

Figure 3.5 *Must* we *always* maximise happiness?

One response, which Mill gives in *Utilitarianism*, Ch. 2, is simply to say that there are very few opportunities any of us have to benefit people 'in general'. And so only considering and contributing to the happiness of a few people is absolutely fine, and utilitarianism does not require more. While impartiality is required in principle, in practice we serve the greatest happiness by showing partiality. Utilitarianism is not too idealistic.

But there are two objections to this response. First, if it was true in Mill's day that people could not often benefit people 'in general', that no longer seems true today. There are many charities that work around the globe and welcome volunteer fundraisers, and the news makes us continually aware of many different causes of suffering around the world. It is perfectly possible, therefore, to dedicate much of one's time and money to helping others 'in general', and there are many opportunities to do so. So it seems that utilitarianism does demand more impartiality than we usually show.

Second, Mill's response doesn't address the objection that utilitarianism simply fails to understand the moral importance of partiality. It is not just that partiality should be *allowed*. Suppose a woman visits a friend in hospital. The friend thanks her. She replies, 'It was nothing, I was just doing my duty, maximising the general happiness in the world'. The friend can feel upset – the visit isn't personal, it is just a *means* to create happiness. If some other action would have created more happiness, being completely impartial, the woman would have done that instead of visiting the friend. If the general

Michael Stocker, 'The schizophrenia of modern ethical theories'

happiness is the ultimate end that we should seek in our action, then we should think of our friendships as a way to maximise the general happiness. This doesn't seem right.

Bernard Williams, 'Persons, character and morality'

Or again, suppose a man is in a boating accident with both his wife and a stranger. Neither can swim, and he can only rescue one. We might think that he should simply rescue his wife. But if he thinks, 'rescuing my wife will lead to greater happiness than rescuing the stranger', this seems to miss the particular importance that being married has, including its moral importance. The man has 'one thought too many', and we (and his wife!) can object to his way of thinking about what to do.

Friendship requires that the friend is valued as the individual person that they are, and that we act out of love for them. The partiality that we show towards our friends seems to rule out a utilitarian understanding of morality. Doing something for a friend is morally good, not wrong because it fails to be impartial, nor even just 'permitted' as a way of maximising happiness. Furthermore, attachments of love and friendship are central to our happiness, indeed to wanting to stay alive at all. But again, these attachments motivate actions that are not impartial between everyone's happiness. Utilitarianism fails to recognise the moral importance of partiality.

Some utilitarians have replied that morality does require us to be impartial and so it is just much more demanding than we like to think. Can you defend spending money on your friends, rather than helping others through charity, when much of the world is in poverty or at war? Rather than objecting to utilitarianism, we should side with utilitarianism in objecting to our usual, partial morality.

However, Mill's discussion of justice (see p. 231) explicitly allows for partiality, and enables us to give a different response. In making the objection, we are considering utilitarianism in the wrong way again. People have learned that having partial relationships is central to happiness, and so it does not maximise happiness to require people to give them up in favour of promoting the general happiness all the time.

Explain the objection to utilitarianism from partiality and one response to it.

To this response we may repeat the objection, made on p. 233, that Mill is giving up on *act* utilitarianism. Instead, he is appealing to general rules about living, and considering which of these rules would maximise happiness. And this is rule utilitarianism.

MORAL INTEGRITY AND THE INDIVIDUAL'S INTENTIONS

Thinking harder: moral integrity

Having integrity involves acting according to your own values, sticking to them especially in the face of temptation or other situations that would make it easier to do something you consider wrong. Just as our actions are guided by our concern for particular other people (partiality), they are also guided by our values. But just as utilitarianism appears to require us to set aside our partiality, it can also seem to require that we set aside our moral values in order to maximise happiness. In other words, utilitarianism attacks our moral integrity.

Imagine George, who has just completed his PhD in chemistry and is looking for a job. He isn't having much luck, and with only his wife working and small children to look after, the situation is causing a lot of stress. This is having a damaging effect on everyone, but especially the children. An older chemist says he can get George a job in a laboratory that does research developing chemical weapons. George is strongly opposed to chemical warfare and so wants to refuse the job. But his colleague points out that refusing the job will simply leave the vacancy for someone else, someone who will pursue the research with enthusiasm and so develop more chemical weapons faster and more effectively than George will.

Utilitarianism says that George should take the job. Suppose we add to Williams' example, and say that George not only has scruples about chemical weapons, he went into chemistry in order to develop ways of counteracting chemical weapons. He came to this decision after travelling abroad, during which time he came across an awful scene in a village that had suffered a chemical attack. All this makes little difference to utilitarianism. That George would be made unhappy by taking the job is already taken into account in calculating the greatest happiness; his unhappiness in acting against his moral values is outweighed by the prevention of significant unhappiness to others.

Utilitarianism requires George to take a value he holds dear, a commitment he has made, one that bestows meaning on his life for him, and treat it as simply one preference among others because of the situation he finds himself in. It sees the situation this way: if George refuses to take

Bernard Williams, 'A critique of utilitarianism'

the job, a consequence of his action will be that *someone else* will bring about significant harm (in chemical weapons research) that George can prevent by taking the job, and so George should take the job.

But can it make sense to think about George and how he chooses to live his life in this way? Why should George be responsible for what *someone else* does? Williams comments that

> [i]t is absurd to demand … that he should just step aside from his own project … and acknowledge the decision which utilitarian calculation requires. It is to alienate him in a real sense from his actions and the source of his action in his own convictions … It is thus … an attack on his integrity.

For each of us, our relation to what we each do is special. I am not responsible for what you do in the same way that I am responsible for what I do. But, if what you do is a consequence of what I do, utilitarianism treats them both the same. It doesn't respect the way that my actions are expressions of who I am and the values I hold. Utilitarianism cannot understand or respect integrity.

For a third time, a utilitarian such as Mill could respond that integrity is central to happiness. It doesn't maximise happiness to require people to act against their integrity. But for a third time, we may repeat that in this response, the utilitarian gives up on act utilitarianism and appeals to a rule.

Explain the objection to act utilitarianism from integrity.

Intentions

Act utilitarianism claims that an action is right if it leads to the greatest happiness. It does not, therefore, recognise the moral value of our *intentions* in acting as we do. (By contrast, we will see in THE GOOD WILL (p. 249) that Kant makes our intentions the foundation of morality.) We could capture this point by saying 'it is the thought that counts'. Whether someone intends to harm us or not – whether or not they do harm us – makes a big difference to how we respond to their action. Trying to harm someone and failing – so they are unharmed – is (usually) still blameworthy; trying not to harm someone and failing – so they are accidentally harmed – is not. But how can this be if all that matters are consequences, not intentions?

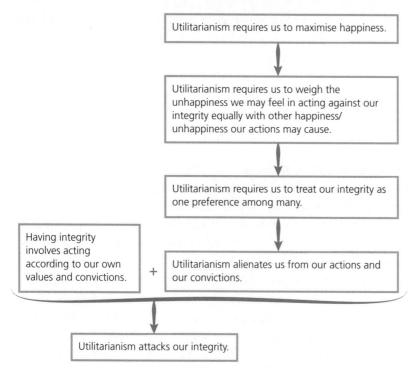

Map 3.4 The objection to utilitarianism from integrity

Mill discusses these points briefly in *Utilitarianism*, Ch. 2, when replying to objections (6) and (7) (see p. 211). It is correct to say that utilitarianism considers people's intentions as irrelevant to whether the action is morally right or not. However, that does not mean that it thinks intentions have nothing at all to do with morality. They are relevant when considering whether someone is a morally good person. And a utilitarian can say that an intention that tends to produce morally wrong actions, such as intending to harm someone, is itself a bad intention, while intentions to produce happiness are good intentions. But we need to separate the judgement of whether an action was right or wrong from the judgement of whether the intention was good or bad.

Good intentions can contribute to the greatest happiness in another way. Having good intentions is one of the 'ingredients' of happiness. In MILL'S 'PROOF' OF UTILITARIANISM (p. 220), he argues that the desire to do good is one of those things that is desirable (good) for its own sake. For people who desire to do good because it is good, it is *part* of their happiness that they

Explain how an act utilitarian can recognise the moral importance of intentions.

1) Is Mill's account of the moral importance of intentions correct?
2) Is an action morally right if it maximises happiness?

have this motive. Doing good is, in itself, pleasant to them. If we desire to do good, and nothing prevents us, then we also intend to do good. So good intentions are also part of a good person's happiness. For the utilitarian, this is the best possible psychology to have. What is good is maximising happiness, and here is someone who aims at and gets happiness from maximising happiness – what could be happier!

Is Mill's response adequate? The objection was that someone's intentions make a moral difference to their *action*, e.g. that an action can be wrong because of the individual's intentions, whatever the consequences of the action. Mill continues to deny this, and claims it only makes a moral difference to how we evaluate them as a person. Suppose someone lied to you but you saw through it – would you only think that they were a bad person or would you also think that they had done something wrong? Or again, suppose two scientists develop a genetically modified disease. One does so in order to kill people and deliberately releases it in a crowded city, wreaking havoc. The other does so in order to understand how the disease works, and takes many precautions to prevent the modified disease from escaping. But it does escape, in a crowded city, wreaking havoc. Did both scientists do equally wrong actions, or should we blame the evil scientist more than unfortunate one?

Rule utilitarianism

As we have seen, act utilitarianism judges the rightness or wrong of an act by its consequences. By contrast, rule utilitarianism claims that an action is right if, and only if, it complies with those rules which, if everybody followed them, would lead to the greatest happiness (compared to any other set of rules). In other words, rule utilitarians do not look at the consequences of individual actions, but at the consequences of people following rules. A rule is morally right if following it leads to greater happiness than following an alternative rule. An action is morally right if it complies with a rule that is morally right.

We will look at reasons in favour of rule utilitarianism, but first, an objection to the theory from Smart.

Explain the difference between act and rule utilitarianism.

SMART ON RULE UTILITARIANISM

SMART, *UTILITARIANISM*, CH. 2

Smart objects that rule utilitarianism amounts to 'rule worship'. The point of the rules is to bring about the greatest happiness. If there is a situation in which breaking the rule will lead to more happiness than following the rule, what reason could we have for following the rule? If I know e.g. that lying in a particular situation will produce more happiness than telling the truth, it seems pointless to tell the truth, causing unhappiness. The whole point of the rule was to bring about happiness, so there should be an exception to the rule in this case. The alternative to 'everyone obeys the rule' is not 'no one obeys the rule'. Clearly, the best course of action is for some people to break the rule sometimes, in those situations in which breaking the rule leads to more happiness than following the rule.

Rule utilitarians could respond by saying that we should amend the rule to allow the exception in such cases. For example, 'Don't lie' should become 'Don't lie unless telling the truth will hurt someone's feelings'. However, life is complicated. *Whenever* a particular action causes more happiness by breaking the rule than by following it, we should do that action. Smart points out that if we keep amending the rules like this, there is no difference between what an act utilitarian would recommend and what a rule utilitarian would recommend. Furthermore, and more seriously for rule utilitarianism, if we try to add all the possible amendments to the rules in order to make acting on them always produce the greatest happiness, we will end up with just one rule, namely to maximise the greatest happiness. Because there are so many situations in which breaking a rule might lead to greater happiness than following it, no other rule can be certain of maximising happiness. And so rule utilitarianism collapses into act utilitarianism. It isn't a distinct theory at all.

Explain Smart's argument against rule utilitarianism, first in prose, then in an argument map.

RULE UTILITARIANISM DEVELOPED

To answer this objection, rule utilitarians can do two things. First, they could provide some reason for following rules even when doing so doesn't maximise happiness. Second, they could argue that despite recommending that we follow rules when doing so doesn't maximise happiness, it is still a better theory than act utilitarianism. In fact, rule utilitarians have provided arguments that support both points at once.

Their first argument is that morality should be understood as a set of rules. It needs to provide general guidance over the long term, a way of thinking that people can remember and rely on. So rather than considering actions individually, we need to take in the bigger picture when thinking about right and wrong. This is just a reflection on what morality must be, psychologically speaking. Since we are to have rules, then the aim of these rules should be to maximise happiness. And so actions are right when they follow a rule that maximises happiness overall – even when the action itself doesn't maximise happiness in this particular situation.

Second, rule utilitarians argue that their theory has a number of advantages over act utilitarianism, which we can see by considering how rule utilitarians respond to the objections raised to act utilitarianism.

1. PROBLEMS WITH CALCULATION (p. 225): We don't have to work out the consequences of each act in turn to see if it is right. We need to work out which rules create the greatest happiness, but we only need to do this once, and we can do it together. This is what Mill says human beings have done over time, giving us our customary moral rules ('secondary principles', p. 225). Rule utilitarianism gives rules a *formal* place in its theory of whether an action is right.
2. FAIRNESS, INDIVIDUAL LIBERTY AND RIGHTS (p. 229): A rule forbidding torture of children will clearly cause more happiness if everyone followed it than a rule allowing torture of children. So it is wrong to torture children. More generally, individuals have rights, which are rules, because if people have to follow these rules (respect people's rights), that leads to the greatest happiness. Rules requiring fairness and justice will produce greater happiness in the long run than rules that do not, and these constraints will prevent the tyranny of the majority. Mill's argument is correct, but it entails rule utilitarianism, not act utilitarianism.
3. PARTIALITY (p. 234): A rule that allows partiality to ourselves, our family and friends will create more happiness than a rule that requires us to be impartial all the time. This explains the moral importance of partial relationships – they are necessary to happiness. Of course, we shouldn't be completely partial. We still need to consider the general happiness, but we only need to act in such a way that, *if everyone acted like that*,

would promote the greatest happiness. For example, in the case of charity, I only need to give as much to charity as would be a 'fair share' of the amount needed to really help other people. This combination of partiality and impartiality respects both our natural inclinations and the demands of morality.

4. MORAL INTEGRITY (p. 237): The rule utilitarian may provide a similar argument for integrity as for partiality. The best rule, perhaps, will be one that allows exceptions to other rules, i.e. a rule that allows people not to follow other rules if they conflict with one's integrity.

5. INTENTIONS (p. 238): What is it for an action to comply with a rule? It is not just a matter of what its consequences are. For example, a person kills someone else. But was this murder or manslaughter or something else again? If the person *intended* to kill someone, and that is what they wanted to bring about, that is very different than if the killing was accidental or if the person was only intending to defend themselves against an attack. A rule prohibiting murder is not a rule prohibiting self-defence, even if self-defence may lead to death. So whether an action complies with a rule or not depends, at least in part, on the individual's intention in performing the act. Two actions may have the same consequences, and yet one is right and one is wrong, because they are different types of action and fall under different moral rules, because the person's intention in each was different. And so rule utilitarianism can recognise that the thought does count.

These developments in the theory enable the rule utilitarian to respond to Smart's objection. If people try to follow act utilitarianism, this will lead to less happiness in the long term. For instance, people will make mistakes in working out what the consequences of their action for happiness will be. They will no longer feel secure in their rights and there will be pressure on personal relationships to be given up in favour of impartiality. And we will fail to make important distinctions between different types of action. So we may have to give up some happiness here and now to be more certain of the greatest happiness overall. Following rules provides this certainty.

All this provides reasons to follow rules even when doing so doesn't lead to the greatest happiness on occasion. An act is not made right by maximising happiness but by being in accordance with a rule. If there is a conflict between following the rule and maximising happiness (e.g. telling a lie when 'no harm is done'), there should be no temptation for the utilitarian

Outline and explain how rule utilitarianism meets *two* objections to act utilitarianism.

Is it right to follow a rule that generally produces the greatest happiness, even where breaking that rule would cause more happiness in this situation?

to say that we should break the rule. Even if the act does maximise happiness, this doesn't make it right. (This also responds to objection (11) on p. 211.)

OBJECTIONS

We may question whether the replies that rule utilitarianism gives above are persuasive.

First, we can object that rule utilitarianism still fails to understand what is important about partiality. Rule utilitarianism *permits* partiality and it *encourages* it insofar as partiality contributes to happiness. But partiality is good, according to rule utilitarianism, because it contributes to the *general* happiness. The importance of the *individual*, and making someone happy just for their sake, still seems to be missing. For instance, if I form friendships because this maximises happiness, does that respect and value my friends for themselves, as the particular people they are? If the man who rescues his wife thinks 'Rescuing my wife is in accordance with a rule that will lead to greater happiness than a rule that requires me to rescue the stranger', this is still one thought too many.

Second, a rule that protects integrity could prove very problematic. If what someone values goes strongly against promoting the greatest happiness, then morality itself may seem in conflict with their integrity. Is it possible, for instance, that someone finds meaning in their life through making as much money as possible, without constraints? The rule utilitarian must insist that people's values, and so their integrity, are broadly in line with what the set of rules that maximises happiness generally requires. Put another way, morality itself probably needs to be part of people's commitments for rule utilitarianism to respect their integrity. But now, is this an objection any more? Or simply a recognition of the legitimate demands that morality makes upon us?

Rule utilitarianism also faces the very first objection we raised to act utilitarianism, IS PLEASURE THE ONLY GOOD? (p. 214). Suppose morality is a set of rules. Should that set of rules aim to maximise happiness (the balance of pleasure over pain), or are there other important values, such as telling the truth, that matter independent of the pleasure they bring (or preferences they satisfy)? This is an objection that Kant will develop in his theory of THE GOOD WILL (p. 249).

A new objection that rule utilitarianism faces, which act utilitarianism doesn't, is whether all of morality can be summed up by rules. Isn't life too complicated for this? If so, we will need a different theory to explain what the right thing to do is when there are no rules that apply. This is an objection that ARISTOTELIAN VIRTUE ETHICS (p. 268) will develop. The rule utilitarian has a simple answer to this objection, though we can question whether it is adequate. One of the rules is 'When no other rules apply, do that action that maximises happiness'.

> **?**
>
> Does rule utilitarianism provide the correct definition of a right action?

Key points: utilitarianism

- In its simplest form, act utilitarianism claims that an act is right if, and only if, it maximises happiness, i.e. if it creates more happiness than any other act in that situation.
- Bentham defends hedonism, claiming that happiness is the only good, and that happiness is pleasure and the absence of pain. He develops the 'felicific calculus' to work out how much happiness an act creates.
- Mill defends a more complex form of hedonism. While happiness is still the only good and comprised of pleasure and the absence of pain, Mill argues that some pleasures ('higher' pleasures) are more valuable than others. One pleasure is higher than another if almost everyone who has experience of both prefers one pleasure, even if there is less of it or it is accompanied by more pain.
- Mill argues that the pleasures of thought, feeling and imagination are higher than the pleasures of the body and the senses, and give dignity to human happiness.
- Smart argues that to defend the distinction between higher and lower pleasures, we must appeal to our attitude toward different pleasures. If we do not approve of someone's pleasures, we say that he is contented but not happy.
- We may object that pleasure is not always good or the only good. Is pleasure at someone else's pain good? Nozick argues that we also value being in touch with reality. This is not a psychological state, but a relation to something outside our minds.
- Preference utilitarianism argues we should maximise preference satisfaction. This theory claims to explain why pleasure is not the only good thing and the distinction between higher and lower pleasures.
- Mill argues that happiness is desirable. The evidence for this is that everyone desires happiness.

- Moore objects that Mill confuses two senses of 'desirable', while other philosophers object that Mill commits the fallacy of composition when arguing that the general happiness is good. But we can reply that both objections misinterpret Mill's argument.
- Mill argues that happiness is the only good. It has many 'ingredients', which are constitutive means to happiness. An external means brings about a distinct end; a constitutive means constitutes that end in part (e.g. in a particular situation).
- How do we know which act will create the most happiness? Bentham replies that an act is right if we can reasonably expect that it will cause the greatest happiness, while Mill argues that our common-sense moral rules ('secondary principles') are a guide to what maximises happiness.
- Bentham argued that we should consider the pleasure and pain of non-human animals in our calculations for maximising happiness. Singer argues that not to do this is 'speciesism'. But this makes calculating which actions produce the greatest happiness much more difficult, and our common-sense morality doesn't offer guidance on this issue.
- Justice is fairness, giving each person their 'due'. Utilitarianism may lead to the 'tyranny of the majority', in which a minority are treated very unfairly because this maximises the happiness of the majority. Mill argues that to avoid such tyranny, people need protection in the form of rights and liberties.
- However, we can object that utilitarianism cannot respect people's rights because it does not rule out any type of action as immoral. It says that *whatever* maximises happiness, even torturing children for pleasure, is right.
- Some utilitarians accept that we don't have rights, but we can't test utilitarianism by unrealistic examples.
- Mill analyses justice as involving actions that relate to individual rights. These duties are 'perfect' in that we must always fulfil them. Imperfect duties, by contrast, leave us some room for choosing how to fulfil the duty, and they are not owed to specific individuals.
- Mill argues that we have rights because this produces the greatest happiness over the long term. Our rights protect what is most important to our happiness.
- We can object that if my rights are based on the general happiness, then in a situation in which the general happiness conflicts with my rights, there is no reason to respect my rights.

- If Mill argues that in such cases, we should still respect my rights, it seems he defends rule utilitarianism, not act utilitarianism.
- We can object that utilitarianism is too idealistic in requiring us to be impartial about whose happiness we promote. It also misunderstands the moral importance of partiality, e.g. in friendship, in claiming that the reason why partial relations are good is because they maximise the general happiness – utilitarianism loses sight of the importance of the individual.
- We can object that utilitarianism asks us to set aside our moral values in order to maximise happiness. This is an attack on moral integrity. It is absurd to require people to count their commitments as just one preference among many in deciding what to do. In particular, we are not responsible for what other people choose to do as a consequence of our actions in the same way that we are responsible for our own actions.
- We can object that utilitarianism fails to recognise the importance of intentions to right action. Mill responds that utilitarianism is about right action, not all of morality. Good intentions are important in helping us do what is right, namely maximising happiness.
- Rule utilitarianism claims that an act is morally right if, and only if, it complies with rules which, if everybody follows them, lead to the greatest happiness.
- Smart objects that rule utilitarianism leads to 'rule worship'. If breaking a rule would create more happiness on that occasion, we should break it. Rule utilitarians respond that people need to trust that others will abide by the rules, so we shouldn't break it. Following the rules will lead to the greatest happiness in the long run.
- Rule utilitarianism has strong replies to many objections to act utilitarianism, such as problems with calculation, individual rights, and the role of intentions in right action.
- Rule utilitarianism continues to face other objections to utilitarianism in general, namely whether pleasure is the only good and the moral value of partiality. We can also question whether morality can be summed up by rules.

B. Kantian deontological ethics

Deontology

Deontologists believe that morality is a matter of duty. We have moral duties to do things which it is right to do and moral duties not to do things which it is wrong to do. Whether something is right or wrong doesn't depend on its consequences. Rather, an action is right or wrong *in itself*.

Deon (Greek) means 'one must'.

Contrast
UTILITARIANISM, p. 205.

Most deontological theories recognise two classes of duties. First, there are general duties we have towards anyone. These are mostly prohibitions, e.g. do not lie; do not murder. But some may be positive, e.g. help people in need. Second, there are duties we have because of our particular personal or social relationships. If you have made a promise, you have a duty to keep it. If you are a parent, you have a duty to provide for your children. And so on.

We each have duties regarding our *own* actions. I have a duty to keep *my* promises, but I don't have a duty to make sure promises are kept. Deontology claims that we should each be most concerned with complying with our duties, not attempting to bring about the most good. In fact, all deontologists agree that there are times when we *should not* maximise the good, because doing so would be to violate a duty. Most deontologists also argue that we do not have a duty to maximise the good, only a duty to do *something* for people in need. As this illustrates, many deontologists think our duties are quite limited. While there are a number of things we *may not* do, we are otherwise free to act as we please.

Deontology says that certain types of action are right or wrong. As we saw in INTENTIONS (p. 238), we can distinguish types of action, morally speaking, on the basis of the individual's intention. For example, a person may kill someone else. A conventional description of the action is 'a killing'. But not all 'killings' are the same type of action, morally speaking. If the person *intended* to kill someone, i.e. that is what they aimed to bring about, that is very different than if the killing was accidental or if the person was only intending to defend themselves against an attack.

1) Explain why the relation between intention and action is important in deontology. 2) Explain similarities and differences between deontology and rule utilitarianism.

Actions are the result of choices, and so should be understood in terms of choices. Choices are made for reasons, and with a purpose in mind. These considerations determine what the action performed actually is. So deontology argues that we do not know what type of action an action is unless we know the intention. We should judge whether an action is right or wrong by the agent's intention.

Kant's account of the good will and duty

Kant is a deontologist. To understand Kant's moral philosophy, we need to explain a couple of terms and assumptions. First, Kant believed that, whenever we make a decision, we act on a *maxim*. Maxims are Kant's version of intentions. They are our personal principles that guide our decisions, e.g. 'to have as much fun as possible', 'to marry only someone I truly love'. All our decisions have some maxim or other behind them. Second, morality is a set of principles that are the same for everyone and that apply to everyone. Third, Kant talks of our ability to make choices and decisions as 'the will'. He assumes that our wills are rational; that is, we can make choices on the basis of reasons. We do not act only on instinct. We can act on choice, and we can consider what to choose using reasoning.

> What, according to Kant, is a 'maxim'?

KANT, *FOUNDATIONS OF THE METAPHYSICS OF MORALS*, CHS 1, 2

Kant argues that the fundamental principle of morality is this: 'Act only on that maxim through which you can at the same time will that it should become a universal law'. Why does he come to this conclusion, and what does it mean?

The good will

Kant begins his argument by reflecting on whether anything is morally good 'without qualification'. He argues that only the 'good will' is. Anything else can either be bad or contribute to what is bad. For instance, intelligence and self-control are good – but they can enable someone to do clever or difficult bad things, if that is what they choose. Power can be good, but it depends on what use we put it to. Nor is happiness good without qualification. If someone is made happy by hurting others, their happiness is morally bad. So we evaluate happiness by morality. Having a morally good will is a precondition to *deserving* happiness.

Kant then makes a second claim. What is good about the good will is not what it *achieves*. It doesn't derive its goodness from successfully producing some good result. Rather, it is good 'in itself'.

Figure 3.6 Not all clever, happy people are good!

See Fairness, individual liberty and rights, p. 229.

Why does Kant say
that only the good
will is good without
qualification?

If someone tries their hardest to do what is morally right but they
don't succeed, then we should still praise their efforts as morally good.

The distinction between acting in accordance with duty and acting out of duty

What is our conception of the morally good will? We can understand
it in terms of the concept of duty. Kant argues that to have a good
will is to be motivated by duty. This is best understood through an
example. Suppose a shopkeeper sells his goods at a fixed price,
giving the correct change, and acting honestly in this way. Of course,
this is the morally right thing to do, he shouldn't cheat people. But
it doesn't show that he has a good will, since acting like this is just
in his self-interest. If all he cares about is keeping his customers, and
that is the only reason he is honest, then even though he does the
right thing, he does it because it will benefit his business, not
because it is the right thing to do. Such a person, we may suspect,
would quite happily start acting dishonestly, cheating his customers,
if it benefited his business to do so.

The shopkeeper is acting *in accordance* with duty – he does the
right thing. To act in accordance with duty is simply to do what is
morally right, whatever one's motive for doing so. But the
shopkeeper isn't *motivated by* duty, i.e. he doesn't act *from* or *out
of* duty. To act out of duty is to do what is morally right because it
is morally right. To have a good will is to act out of duty, to be
motivated by the fact that doing this action is your duty.

Kant controversially claims that this distinction applies not only
in cases where the action benefits ourselves, but when it benefits
other people. Suppose you help or please someone else just because
that is what you want to do and enjoy doing, e.g. because you like
them. Kant says that this is right and should be praised and
encouraged (it is in accordance with duty), but your actions don't
necessarily have moral *worth*, because you are helping them just
because you want to, and not because it is morally right to do so
(you are not acting out of duty). Could you act on both your desire
to help and because it is right to help? Yes, that's possible. But
because you want to help someone else, it is *unclear* whether you

are acting out of duty or not. By contrast, if someone were to help someone else even when they didn't want to, but just because they believe that it is the morally right thing to do, *that* would show that they have a good will.

Explain the distinction between acting in accordance with duty and acting out of duty.

Thinking harder: the good will again

So to have a good will is to do one's duty (what is morally right) *because* it is one's duty (because it is morally right). But what *is* morally right? What does a good will will? Here, things get tricky. A good will isn't good because it aims at certain ends, because there are no ends that are good without qualification. We can't, for instance, say that the good will aims at the general happiness, because happiness isn't always morally good. So the good will must, in some way, be good 'in itself', just on the basis of what it is like as a will. What makes a will good is something about the maxims it adopts. However, it can't be *what* the maxims say, i.e. what they aim at. A puzzle …

Another puzzle arises if we consider this in terms of motives. What is it to want to do one's duty because it is one's duty, if we can't say what one's duty is? It can only be the thought of doing one's duty 'as such', i.e. to think of it as 'one's duty' rather than, say, to help others or not to steal. But what does this thought amount to?

To solve these puzzles, we need to recall Kant's assumptions. Maxims are principles of choice. They are subjective – you have yours, I have mine. What makes them different is what they are about, what they aim at and why. But what they have in common is that they are all principles. Now, morality is a set of principles for everyone. So the concept of duty is the concept of a principle for everyone. So, somehow, the good will is a will that chooses what it does, motivated by the idea of a principle for everyone. This is 'not an expected result', Kant says.

Briefly outline Kant's concept of the good will.

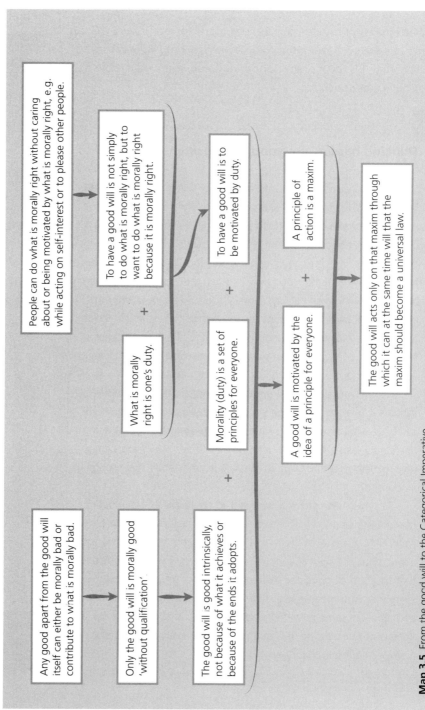

Map 3.5 From the good will to the Categorical Imperative

Any good apart from the good will itself can either be morally bad or contribute to what is morally bad.

Only the good will is morally good 'without qualification'.

The good will is good intrinsically, not because of what it achieves or because of the ends it adopts.

What is morally right is one's duty.

Morality (duty) is a set of principles for everyone.

A good will is motivated by the idea of a principle for everyone.

People can do what is morally right without caring about or being motivated by what is morally right, e.g. while acting on self-interest or to please other people.

To have a good will is not simply to do what is morally right, but to want to do what is morally right because it is morally right.

To have a good will is to be motivated by duty.

A principle of action is a maxim.

The good will acts only on that maxim through which it can at the same time will that the maxim should become a universal law.

The Categorical Imperative

Kant has arrived at the principle, 'Act only on that maxim through which you can at the same time will that it should become a universal law'. He later calls this principle the 'Categorical Imperative'. How can this idea serve as a motive or criterion for the good will? Kant rephrases it: to have a good will, I should act only on maxims that I can also will everyone to act on. I can adopt this principle itself as a maxim, a principle of choice. I choose only to make choices on the basis of maxims that everyone could act on. But this maxim doesn't specify any particular end or goal (such as happiness). It only mentions the idea of a principle for everyone, a universal law.

We need to understand the Categorical Imperative in more detail. But first, an example: suppose I am tempted to make a promise with no intention of keeping it; e.g. I might borrow money (because I want the money) on the promise to pay it back, but I don't intend to pay it back. We can show that this is wrong. Suppose everyone acted on this maxim. Then everyone would know that everyone acts on this maxim. In that situation, making a false promise like this would be impossible. No one would trust my promise, and I can't make a promise unless someone believes it. So I can't will my maxim to be universal.

Explain Kant's argument from the concept of the good will to the Categorical Imperative.

Hypothetical and categorical imperatives

An 'imperative' is just a command, a statement of what one should or ought to do. 'Hypothetical imperatives' are statements about what you ought to do, on the assumption of some desire or goal. They specify a means to an end. So 'if you want to see the show, you ought to get to the theatre at least 15 minutes early' is a hypothetical imperative. In this example, the assumed desire or goal is explicit: the imperative is presented as a conditional, with the desire described in the antecedent ('you want to see the show'), and the command in the consequent ('get to the theatre at least 15 minutes early'). But hypothetical imperatives can leave the assumed desire or goal implicit, e.g. 'Eat at least five portions of fruit and vegetables a day' (if you want to stay healthy).

Why can't I just say 'I want to see the show but refuse to get there early' or 'I want to be healthy but refuse to eat fruit and vegetables'? Why *ought* I to do these things, given what I want? Because these are the means to my end. Kant argues that willing the end *entails* willing the means. It is an analytic truth that someone who wills the end wills the means. To will an end is to will an effect. But the concept of an effect contains the concept of a cause. Hence, to will an effect, you must will the cause. The cause is the means. (It is important here that you don't merely *want* the end, but actually will it.)

Hypothetical imperatives can be avoided by simply giving up the assumed desire or goal. Suppose I don't want to see the show – then I don't need to get to the theatre early. Suppose I don't want to be healthy – then the imperative to get my 'five-a-day' doesn't apply to me. (Of course, it is odd not to want to be healthy, and we may wonder if I really do not want to be healthy. Perhaps I do want to be healthy, but I can't be bothered. If this is the case, I want to be healthy, but I don't will it.) In other words, it is possible to 'opt out' of a hypothetical imperative.

This isn't true of morality, we usually think. Moral duties are not hypothetical. They are what we ought to do, full stop. They are your duty regardless of what you want. They are 'categorical'. Kant has also argued that moral duties aren't a means to some further end, because what makes an action good is that it is willed by the good will. All categorical imperatives – our moral duties – are derived from one, *the* Categorical Imperative: 'Act only on that maxim through which you can at the same time will that it should become a universal law'.

How are categorical imperatives possible? Why is there something that we ought to do, regardless of what we want? Kant argues that moral duties depend just on our being rational. We need to understand further just what this means.

Explain the distinction between a hypothetical and a categorical imperative.

Thinking harder: contradiction in conception and contradiction in will

There are two different ways in which we could fail to be able to will our maxim to become a universal law.

1. 'Contradiction in conception': the situation in which everyone acts on that maxim is somehow self-contradictory. We saw an example of this in the case of making a false promise, above. Another example: suppose you want a gift to take to a party, but you can't afford it, so you steal it from the shop. Your maxim is something like: 'To steal something I want if I can't afford it'. This can only be the right thing to do if everyone could do it. However, if we could all just help ourselves to whatever we wanted, the idea of 'owning' things would disappear. Now, by definition, you can't steal something unless it belongs to someone else. Stealing presupposes that people own things. But people can only own things if they don't all go around helping themselves whenever they want. So it is logically impossible for everyone to steal things. In other words, it is inconceivable – a contradiction in conception – for everyone to steal things. We can't conceive of the maxim 'To steal something I want if I can't afford it' being a universal law, so we can't rationally will it to be a universal law. And so stealing (at least stealing just because one wants something) is wrong.

2. 'Contradiction in will': this is more difficult to understand. The maxim is not self-contradictory when universalised, but there is another way in which we cannot rationally will it. Consider a refusal to help other people, ever. It *is* logically possible to universalise the maxim 'not to help others in need'. The world would not be a pleasant place, but this is beside the point. Kant does *not* claim that an action is wrong because we *wouldn't like* the consequences if everyone did it (many philosophers and students have misinterpreted Kant on this point). His test is

Kant notes that contradiction in conception defines 'perfect' duties (duties of justice) while contradiction in will defines 'imperfect' duties. See MILL ON JUSTICE, p. 231.

Why, according to Kant, is it wrong to steal?

whether we can rationally will that our maxim be a universal law. Willing and wanting (or liking) are different. Someone can want something that they don't will – they don't choose to act on their desire, e.g. such as cheating on their husband or wife with someone they find very attractive. And someone can will something they don't want, such as going to the dentist for surgery. Kant is concerned with willing not wanting. He argues that we *cannot will* that no one ever help anyone else. How so?

P1. A will, by definition, wills its ends (goals).

P2. As we said above, to truly will the ends, one must will the necessary means.

C1. Therefore, we cannot rationally will a situation in which it would be impossible for us to achieve our ends. To do so is to cease to will the necessary means to one's ends, which is effectively to cease to will any ends at all. This contradicts the very act of willing.

P3. It is possible that the only available means to our ends, in some situations, involves the help of others.

C2. We cannot therefore will that this possibility is denied to us.

C3. Therefore, we cannot will a situation in which no one ever helps anyone else.

Explain Kant's tests of 'contradiction in conception' and 'contradiction in will', first in prose, then using argument maps.

Morality and reason

As the contradiction in conception and contradiction in will show, disobeying the Categorical Imperative involves a self-contradiction, according to Kant. He argued that it is not just morally wrong to disobey the Categorical Imperative, it is also irrational. Through the Categorical Imperative, *reason* both determines what our duties are and gives us the means to discover them. Furthermore, we intuitively think that morality applies to *all and only* rational beings, not just human beings.

In Douglas Adams' *The Hitchhiker's Guide to the Galaxy*, Arthur Dent protests to the Vogons, rational aliens who are going to

Figure 3.7 The alien, but not the dog, is subject to the Categorical Imperative

destroy the Earth, that what they are doing is immoral. Dent's protest makes sense, even though he isn't protesting about the actions of human beings. But morality doesn't apply to beings that can't make rational choices, such as dogs and cats (pets misbehave; they don't act *morally wrongly*).

With this link, we can explain the nature of morality in terms of the nature of reason. Morality is universal, the same for everyone; so is reason, says Kant. Morality and rationality are categorical; the demands to be rational and moral don't stop applying to you even if you don't care about them. Neither morality nor rationality depend on what we want.

The second formulation of the Categorical Imperative

Kant gives a second formulation of the Categorical Imperative, known as the Formula of Humanity: 'Act in such a way that you always treat humanity, whether in your own person or in the person of any other, never simply as a means, but always at the same time as an end'. Why does he say this, and what does it mean?

Let us return to the idea of the good will. Only the good will is good without qualification. Another way of saying this is that it is the only thing of unconditional value. Everything else that is valuable depends, in some way, on the good will. For instance, intelligence is valuable for all sorts of purposes. In other words, it is valuable as a means to an end. Its value, then, depends on the value of its end. What gives its end value? We do, says Kant. Something is only an end if it is adopted by a will. It is our adopting something as an end that gives it value. Because I have desires and purposes, various things in the world are valuable *to me*.

So far, value is subjective. What is valuable is valuable because it is valuable to someone; and what is valuable to me may not be valuable to you. However, this does not apply to other people (or rational beings generally). Your value is not simply your value *to me* as a means in relation to some purpose or desire I have. It is not even your value to you (you might have very low self-esteem, and wrongly underestimate your value). We have 'intrinsic worth', which Kant identifies as 'dignity'. What gives us this dignity is our rational will. The will has unconditional value *as the thing which gives value to everything else*. So in the second formulation above, by 'humanity', Kant means our ability to rationally determine which ends to adopt and pursue.

Kant says that because people are ends in themselves, we must always treat them as such, and never 'simply' as a means. Note that he does not say we cannot use people as a means, but that we can't use them *only* as a means. We rely on other people in many ways as a means of achieving our own ends; e.g. people serving me in a shop are a means of getting what I want to buy. What is important, says Kant, is that I also respect them as an end.

To treat someone simply as a means, and not also as an end, is to treat the person in a way that undermines their power of making a rational choice themselves. So the Second Formula means, first, that we should appeal to other people's reason in discussing with them what to do, rather than manipulating them in ways they are unaware of. Coercing someone, lying to them or stealing from them all involve not allowing them to make an informed choice. If they are involved in our action in any way, they need to be able to agree (or refuse) to adopt our end as their own.

Second, treating someone as an end also means leaving them free to pursue the ends that they adopt. The value of what people choose to do lies in their ability to choose it, not just in what they

Explain Kant's reason for claiming that people have intrinsic worth.

have chosen. So we should refrain from harming or hindering them. This is to respect their rationality.

Third, someone's being an end in themselves means that they are an end for others. We should adopt their ends as our own. What this means is that we should help them pursue their ends, just as we pursue our own ends. In other words, the second formulation requires that we help other people. This should be one of our ends in life.

Explain what Kant means by the claim that we must treat people as ends in themselves.

Issues for Kantian deontological ethics

UNIVERSALISABILITY AND MORALITY

Is Kant right to think that acting on maxims that are universalisable is morally right or permissible, while acting on maxims that are not universalisable is morally wrong? Are there counterexamples? Let's start by asking whether there could be a case of acting on a universalisable maxim that is morally wrong. We might think that this is just a matter of phrasing the maxim cleverly. In the example of stealing the gift above, I could claim that my maxim is 'To steal gifts from large shops and when there are seven letters in my name (Michael)'. Universalising this maxim, only people with seven letters in their name would steal only gifts and only from large shops. The case would apply so rarely that there would be no general breakdown in the concept of private property. So it would be perfectly possible for this law to apply to everyone.

Kant's response is that his theory is concerned with my *actual* maxim, not some made-up one. It is not actually part of my choice that my name has seven letters, or perhaps even that it is a *gift* I steal. If I am honest with myself, I have to admit that it is a question of my taking what I want when I can't afford it. For Kant's test to work, we must be honest with ourselves about what our maxims are.

Can we find a counterexample of this kind? Suppose I am in dire straits. I really need money to get food and shelter, and the situation is growing urgent. But I am too proud to ask people for help. So I con them instead: I borrow money on the promise of repaying it, but I don't intend to keep my promise. I wouldn't do this unless things were desperate. Is my maxim universalisable? It seems so. If, as a matter of law, everyone made promises they didn't intend to keep whenever they wanted something, *that* would be impossible. People would no longer believe promises; and you can't make a promise unless someone accepts it! But my maxim is much more specific, because it is 'to make a promise I don't intend to keep rather than ask for help, but only in the face of such desperate circumstances'. This can be universalised, it seems, as it wouldn't occur often enough for promise-making to become impossible.

But now, is what I do wrong? If we think it is not, then this example is no counterexample – my maxim can be universalised, and my act is not wrong. But if conning people in this situation, rather than asking for help, is wrong, then this is an action that is wrong, and yet the maxim is universalisable.

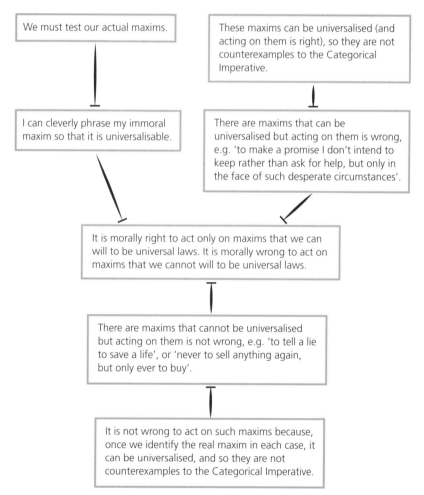

Map 3.6 Objections to the Categorical Imperative as the standard of morality and replies

Kant's Categorical Imperative fails to give us the right answer. It is not always right to do something where the maxim is universalisable.

Another possible counterexample is furnished by one of Kant's own examples. Suppose someone comes to your house to seek refuge from someone who wants to murder them. Soon after they have hidden, the would-be murderer arrives and asks you where they are. *Even in this situation*, Kant says, you should not lie. Lying is *always* wrong, because we cannot universalise the maxim to deceive people. Most people would disagree, and argue that lying in such a situation is the right action. But perhaps Kant is wrong about our maxim in this case. Perhaps the maxim is 'to tell a lie to save a life', and this can be universalised.

Are there any clearer counterexamples of maxims where acting on them is not morally wrong, but the maxim is not universalisable? Say I am a hard-working shop assistant, who hates the work. One happy Saturday I win the lottery, and I vow 'never to sell anything to anyone again, but only ever to buy'. This is perhaps eccentric, but it doesn't seem morally wrong. But it cannot be universalised. If no one ever sold things, how could anyone buy them? It is logically impossible, which makes it wrong according to Kant's test. So Kant's Categorical Imperative again gives us the wrong answer. It is not always wrong to do things which require other people do something different.

CONFLICTS BETWEEN DUTIES

Kant argues that our moral duties are absolute. A duty is absolute if it permits no exceptions. Nothing can override a moral duty, because it is categorical. All other ends have their worth in relation to the good will. But the good will is motivated by duty.

This causes problems in cases in which it seems that two absolute duties conflict with each other. Should I break a promise or tell a lie? Should I betray a friend to save a life? If I am faced with a situation in which I must do one or the other, then Kant's theory implies that whatever I do must be wrong.

One response is to say that a *real* conflict of duties can never occur. If there appears to be a conflict, we have misunderstood what at least one duty requires of us. If duties are absolute, we must formulate our duties very, very carefully to avoid them conflicting. As we will see when discussing TELLING LIES (p. 339), Kant himself thought that some of our duties are very straightforward; e.g. our duty not to lie is simply that – *never* lie. But you can believe the rest of Kant's theory and not accept his view that duties are simple like this. For example, you could argue that 'don't lie' isn't a duty. Our

Kant, 'On a supposed right to lie from altruistic motives'

We discuss this example and Kant's reasoning further in TELLING LIES, p. 339.

Does the Categorical Imperative determine what we ought to do?

Briefly explain the objection to Kantian deontology from conflicts between duties.

duty could be something like 'don't lie unless you have to lie to save a life'. There will always be *some* maxim you can act on which you will be able to universalise. So it will always be possible to do your duty.

We can object that it is more realistic simply to say that (most) duties are not absolute. For instance, there is a duty not to lie, but it may be permissible to lie in order to save someone's life. Less important duties can 'give way' to more important ones. In cases of conflict, one will give way and no longer be a duty in that situation. This understanding is at odds with Kant's theory of morality. His whole analysis of duty is that it is categorical. It is difficult to see how his understanding of why morality is rationally required could allow that duties can give way to each other.

Do duties ever really conflict?

THE VIEW THAT CONSEQUENCES OF ACTIONS DETERMINE THEIR MORAL VALUE

Utilitarians object that Kantian deontology is confused about moral value. If it is my duty not to murder, for instance, this must be because there is something bad about murder. But then if murder is bad, surely we should try to ensure that there are as few murders as possible. If I *know* that unless I kill someone deliberately, many people will die, how can I justify *not* killing that person? Surely it is only my duty not to kill because death is bad. So I should prevent more deaths, and so in this case, I have a duty to kill, because I would be killing in order to save lives. What makes a will good is that it wills good ends.

See THE GOOD WILL, p. 249.

Kant's response, of course, is that there are no ends that are good without qualification, even happiness. So this cannot be the right analysis of the good will.

But the disagreement goes deeper. Utilitarianism understands all practical reasoning – reasoning about what to do – as *means–end* reasoning: it is rational to do whatever brings about a good end. The utilitarian thinks it is just *obvious* that if something is good, more of it is better, and we ought to do what is better. Kant disagrees and offers an *alternative* theory of practical reasoning. Means–end reasoning is appropriate for hypothetical imperatives, but this is not all there is to practical reason. It is also irrational to act in a way that not everyone could act in. If rationality were only about means–end reasoning, then we couldn't say that any ends – such as other people – are obligatory. Morality becomes hypothetical. You only ought to do your duty *if* you want to be morally good. This treats morality like just another desire or purpose which we may or may not have.

Is happiness always good?

Mill's response to this, of course, is that happiness is the only desirable end. But, once again, Kant has argued that happiness is not always good.

MORALITY IS A SYSTEM OF HYPOTHETICAL IMPERATIVES

But is Kant's view of practical reasoning correct? Are there, in fact, any categorical imperatives, rules we must follow on pain of being irrational if we don't? Philippa Foot argues that there are not, and that what it is rational for someone to do depends on what they want.

FOOT, 'MORALITY AS A SYSTEM OF HYPOTHETICAL IMPERATIVES'

As we saw in HYPOTHETICAL AND CATEGORICAL IMPERATIVES (p. 253), an imperative for Kant is something that ought to be done. Hypothetical imperatives state that you should or need to do the action as a means to something you want. Here 'want' has a wide meaning, covering not just passing or occasional desires, but also your long-term projects and plans. For example, if you are committed to getting a good education, then you should study hard, even when you don't feel like it. Categorical imperatives present the action as something you should or must do, full stop, 'without regard to any other end'. Kant argues that they are 'objective', that acting on them is a matter of being rational rather than fulfilling a subjective desire.

Foot notes that we do commonly contrast moral judgements with hypothetical imperatives in this sense. We find two uses of 'should' or 'ought' in how we use language. In the first use, if we discover the person doesn't want what the imperative assumes, or we discover the action isn't a suitable means, then we no longer say they should act on it. For example, 'you should take the third left if you are going to the restaurant': if you are not going to the restaurant, or the third left is a dead-end, then we no longer say that you should take the third left. But we also use the words 'should' and 'ought' when we don't withdraw our claim that 'you should do *x*'. 'You shouldn't lie', 'But I don't care about the truth, I really want to trick him', 'That's irrelevant; you shouldn't lie'. You can't rebut or escape the requirement to act just by showing that it doesn't help you get what you want.

However, so far, this point is only about language, and it isn't enough to show that Kant is right that moral judgements are categorical in the sense he means. To see this, think of the rules of etiquette or the rules of a club. For example, in the UK, handshakes should be brief (so Debrett's guide to etiquette tells us). If ... what? The imperative doesn't mention something you want. We might try to spell it out, e.g. adding 'if you want to fit in' or 'if you want people to think well of you', but this isn't how etiquette works. Even if someone doesn't care what others think, it is *still* a breach of etiquette for them not to release another person's hand after shaking it. Likewise, in Foot's (now old-fashioned) example, if the club rules say, 'Do not take ladies into the smoking room', there isn't a hidden assumption 'if you want to remain part of the club'. Suppose someone doesn't want to remain part of the club, thinking it fusty and sexist, and he will quit tomorrow for good. Is he now allowed to take ladies into the smoking room? No. In these examples, we don't withdraw the 'should' depending on what someone wants.

These are examples of *non-hypothetical* imperatives. Clearly, they are not unconditional or inescapable in the sense that Kant thinks moral judgements are. They are not categorical in Kant's sense because *by themselves* they don't give us a reason to act. Whether you have *reason* to observe the rules of etiquette or the rules of the club will depend on what you want. If you don't like the rules of the club, don't join – nothing wrong in that.

Moral judgements are also non-hypothetical imperatives in this sense. But this fact does not yet show that they are categorical in the sense of giving everyone and anyone a reason to act in accordance with them. To show this would be to show that immorality is irrational, which is just what Kant argues. But, claims Foot, this is because Kant assumes that acting immorally involves disregarding a rule that you have accepted (e.g. that no one should lie) or again that it is inconsistent to want other people to act in a way you don't intend to (e.g. that they should tell the truth while you lie). But this is simply not so. 'Irrational actions are those in which a man in some way defeats his own purposes', and acting immorally need not involve this (although it may, e.g. by making enemies of people you may later need as friends).

Why do we think that the rules of morality are categorical when the rules of etiquette are not, even though both are non-hypothetical? Foot argues that the answer lies in our feelings about morality. The 'binding force' of morality is simply the feeling that moral judgements are inescapable. And our feelings are the result of how moral rules are taught. The rules of morality are taught and enforced much more stringently than the rules of etiquette. As a result of how we as children are trained to behave in morally right ways, we feel that we 'must do' what is morally right, whatever our desires or plans. There is no other meaning we can sensibly give to the idea that morality is 'categorical'.

Foot recognises two possible objections to her view. First, if she is right, then what does 'acting out of duty' amount to? If moral judgements are not categorical, it seems that doing what is right 'because it is right' no longer gives us a reason to act. Foot's response is that Kant is mistaken in thinking that the motive of duty is the only morally good motive. We genuinely care about others' good quite apart from thoughts of duty. We can understand 'doing the right thing because it is the right thing to do' as being motivated by morally good concerns. This looks like moral action on the basis of hypothetical imperative, e.g. you are helping because you want to help. This isn't wrong, but 'wanting to help' needn't be a passing desire. A virtuous person is one who is *dedicated* to moral ends, not someone who acts morally just so long as they 'feel inclined'.

Second, doesn't Foot's view undermine morality? In particular, what can we say to people who simply don't care about morality ('amoralists')? Isn't it true they *ought* to care? And isn't this a contrast with the case of someone who doesn't want to join the club? Foot responds that amoralists could accept that the moral 'ought' is non-hypothetical, but still not think it gives them a reason to live by moral rules. Amoralists take themselves to have no reason to be moral. We can say that they may well be mistaken, and could spoil their own lives. But there is no more that we can say than this, for the moral 'ought' has no magical force to give everyone a reason to be moral, irrespective of what they want in life.

Figure 3.8 Why should someone who doesn't care about morality be moral?

See THE VALUE OF CERTAIN MOTIVES below.

Is it irrational to be immoral?

The value of certain motives

In PARTIALITY (p. 234), we looked at two variations of an objection that utilitarianism does not take account of the importance of relationships in which we show partiality to someone, such as friendships. The first variation was that utilitarianism makes morality too demanding by requiring us to be impartial between our friends/family and people we don't know. Kantian deontology doesn't require this. While we are required to help others, we are not required to be completely impartial or maximise happiness. There is no contradiction in maxims that show partiality to some people. (And there is no contradiction in a maxim which aims to help others but not maximise happiness.) However, the second variation of the objection, concerning how we should understand the moral worth of motives involved in relationships of love and friendship, does apply to Kant's theory as it did to utilitarianism. So it is not partial relationships themselves, but the typical motives involved, that Kant's theory struggles with.

Kant makes the motive of duty, acting out of duty, doing your duty because it is your duty, the *only* motive that has moral worth, and says that doing something good for someone else because you *want* to is morally right, but not morally good. But consider again the example of visiting a friend in hospital (p. 235). If the visitor protests to her friend that she is just doing her duty, that her motive is simply to do what is morally right, then her friend can object. Kant seems to say that we have to want to benefit people because it is our duty to do so, not because we like them. But surely, if I do something nice for you because I like you, that is a morally good action.

This applies as much outside relationships of partiality. I may act to help a stranger, moved by kindness, sympathy and compassion. My action may well be in accordance with duty, but because I am motivated by my feelings and not by a concern to do the right thing because it is the right thing to do, Kant would say that my action has no moral worth. My feelings are *instrumentally* valuable, because they motivate me to act in accordance with duty. But they are not themselves morally valuable. And yet much of the time, we do good things because we feel warmly towards the people we benefit. We can object that putting the motive of duty above feelings as the source of good action is somehow inhuman.

Explain the objection that Kant does not recognise the value of being motivated by love or kindness.

Kant can respond that he is not trying to *stop* us from being motivated by our feelings. His point is that, when we are choosing what to do, how we feel should not be as important as what it is morally right to do. Our feelings shouldn't *decide* the matter, our motive to do what is morally right should. But when you do something for a friend, should you think 'I'll do this because he is my friend; and it is morally right to do so'? Consider again the man rescuing his wife from drowning (p. 236). If he thinks 'She's my wife and it is morally permissible that I rescue her', he has 'one thought too many'. His commitment to his wife means that he should stop at 'She's my wife.'

Perhaps Kant can reply that you don't actually need to have such a thought. His theory, after all, is how we can tell whether something is right or wrong, not how we should actually think all the time. So we can say that to be morally good, you only need to be willing to refuse to help your friend if that involved doing something morally wrong. And likewise for the man and his wife.

1) Is an action only morally good if it is motivated by duty?
2) Should you act only on that maxim through which you can also will that it become a universal law?

Key points: Kantian deontological ethics

- Deontology claims that actions are right or wrong *in themselves*, not depending on their consequences. It identifies different types of action, and so judges whether they are right or wrong, on the basis of the agent's intention.
- Our duties are concerned with *our* actions, not attempting to bring about the most good. It can be against our duty to do what maximises the good.
- Kant argues that choices are made according to maxims, and that morality is a set of principles everyone can follow.
- He argues that only the good will is good without qualification. No end, not even happiness, is always good.
- Acting in accordance with duty is doing what is morally right, whatever one's motive. Acting out of duty is doing what is morally right because it is morally right.
- The good will is motivated by duty. To have a good will is to do one's duty because it is one's duty.
- Kant argues that it is morally right to 'Act only on that maxim through which you can at the same time will that it should become a universal law' (the Categorical Imperative). Acting on a maxim that does not pass this test is morally wrong.
- A hypothetical imperative tells you what you ought, rationally, to do, assuming a certain desire or goal. A categorical imperative tells you what you ought to do, irrespective of what you want.
- A maxim can fail the test of the Categorical Imperative in two ways: 1) contradiction in conception: it cannot be consistently universalised, because a situation in which everyone acted on it is impossible; 2) contradiction in will: it cannot be willed in a universal form, because a situation in which it was universally followed undermines the operation of the will.

- As the test shows, Kant bases morality on reason. Reason and morality are categorical, apply to all rational beings, and are independent of our desires.
- Kant reformulated the Categorical Imperative as the Formula of Humanity: 'Act in such a way that you always treat humanity, whether in your own person or in the person of any other, never simply as a means, but always at the same time as an end'. This requires us to respect others' ability to make rational choices, and to help them achieve their ends.
- We can object that the Categorical Imperative delivers some counter-intuitive results. There are maxims that can be universalised, but which it is wrong to act on. And there are maxims that cannot be universalised, but which are not wrong to act on.
- We can also object that Kantian deontology cannot allow duties to conflict, but in the real world, they do conflict.
- Utilitarians argue that an action is right if it brings about what is good, so the moral value of an action depends on its consequences. Kant replies that this can't be true, as nothing is good without qualification except the good will.
- Utilitarians also argue that it is irrational not to maximise what is good. Kant replies that it is irrational to act on a maxim that not everyone could act on.
- Foot argues that while moral judgements are non-hypothetical because we don't withdraw them depending on what someone wants, they are not categorical in Kant's sense, giving everyone a reason to follow them. To act irrationally, she claims, is to act in a way that defeats one's own purposes, and acting immorally need not involve this.
- We can object that Kant does not recognise the moral value of motives other than duty, such as friendship and kindness. One response is that Kant only requires us not to act on such motives if they conflict with our duty.

Points from Julia Annas, 'Virtue ethics', are incorporated throughout the discussion of Aristotle's virtue ethics.

C. Aristotle's virtue ethics

Utilitarianism and Kantian deontology focus on morally *right actions* – what is the right thing to do, and why? On these views, to be a good person is to be motivated to do morally right actions. By contrast, virtue ethics starts with what it is to be a *good person*. From this, it then derives an account of what a morally right action is, which it understands in terms of what a good person would do. An important claim of virtue ethics is that there is more to the moral life than actions. Annas notes that some form of virtue ethics or other has been the 'default form' of ethical theory in Western philosophy until the last few hundred years. Its 'classical' version is stated most clearly by Aristotle, and other forms developed by rejecting or adding to some elements of Aristotle's theory.

The good for human beings

ARISTOTLE, *NICOMACHEAN ETHICS*, BK 1 (§§1–5, 7–10, 13)

Aristotle begins the *Nicomachean Ethics* with the question 'What is the good for human beings?' What is it that we are aiming at, that would provide a successful, fulfilling, good life? His discussion is very similar to MILL's 'PROOF' OF UTILITARIANISM (p. 220). Or more accurately, since Aristotle got there first, and Mill was very familiar with Aristotle – Mill's proof resembles Aristotle's argument.

Our different activities aim at various 'goods'. For example, medicine aims at health; military strategy aims at victory. For any action or activity, there is a purpose (a 'why') for which we undertake it – its end. An analysis of the purposes for which we do things is an analysis of what we see to be 'good' about them. An answer to 'Why do that?' is an answer to 'What's the point?' – and 'the point' is what is worthwhile about doing that.

Now, complex activities, such as medicine, have many component activities, e.g. making pharmaceuticals, making surgical implements, diagnosis, etc. Where an activity has different components like this, the overall end (health) is better – 'more preferable' – than the end of each subordinate activity (successful drugs, useful implements, accurate diagnoses). This is because these activities are undertaken for the sake of the overall end.

We undertake actions and activities either for the sake of something further or 'for their own sake'. Suppose there is some end for whose sake we do *everything* else. Suppose that this end we desire for its own sake, not the sake of anything else. Then this end

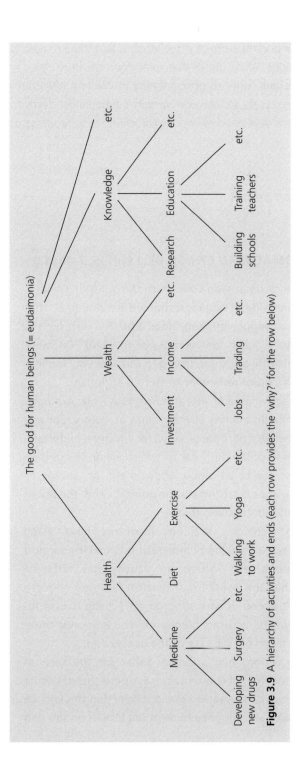

Figure 3.9 A hierarchy of activities and ends (each row provides the 'why?' for the row below)

would be *the* good for us (§2). As Annas comments, in thinking about why we do what we do, we end up thinking about how to live one's life well as a whole.

Eudaimonia

People generally agree, says Aristotle, that this is *eudaimonia*. What does he mean by this?

Eudaimonia is the good for a human life. It is often translated as 'happiness' but Aristotle says it is 'living well and faring well'. We have some idea of what it is when an animal or plant is living and faring well – we talk of them 'flourishing'. A plant or animal flourishes when its needs are met in abundance and it is a good specimen of its species. Gardeners try to enable their plants to flourish; zookeepers try to enable the zoo animals to flourish. So eudaimonia is 'the good' or the 'good life' for human beings as the particular sort of being we are. To achieve it is to live as best a human being can live.

There are a number of contrasts we can draw with our usual idea of 'happiness'.

1. We can talk of people being happy as a psychological state, and in particular – perhaps a result of the influence of utilitarianism – we think of it as pleasure. But eudaimonia is not a state of mind. It characterises an activity – the activity of living. A good life is one that realises the full potential that a human life has.
2. Eudaimonia is not something subjective, but objective. To say someone is or was eudaimon is to make an objective judgement about their life as a good human life. It is not to say anything (directly) about their state of mind; nor is it a judgement the person themselves has any special authority over. By contrast, if someone says they are happy or unhappy, it is difficult to correct them or know better.
3. Eudaimonia is not something easily changed. It does not come and go as happiness (in the usual sense) can. For it is an evaluation of a person's life (a life lived well) as a whole. This is a very stable judgement.

Explain three differences between eudaimonia and happiness.

Mill responds by distinguishing HIGHER AND LOWER PLEASURES, p. 212.

However, we still don't know just what eudaimonia is – what sort of life is a good or flourishing life? Aristotle notes that people disagree on whether it involves pleasure, wealth, honour or something else again (§§4, 5). But, says Annas, if we start from the idea that it characterises *the activity of living* one's life, it can't be about passive states of mind, such as pleasure. Another reason it can't be just pleasure per se, Aristotle argues, is because we share pleasure with animals and we're after the good for human beings. Eudaimonia also can't be about money or wealth. First, notes Annas, having wealth isn't an activity. Second, if eudaimonia is a final end, then it can't be an instrumental good. But money is only useful as a means to an end, it isn't an end in itself. Aristotle argues that it can't be honour either, since to have honour, others must honour you. What is it you want to be honoured (recognised, rewarded, praised) *for*? Whatever the answer, achieving *that* must be what is good.

Aristotle briefly raises the suggestion that the wise person wants to be honoured for their virtues. (We'll consider what a virtue is below.) But just *having* virtues, e.g. courage or intelligence, can't be enough for a good life, for two reasons. First, you can have virtue while asleep. Such inactivity isn't our end in life. Second, having virtue is compatible with suffering great misfortune in life. But this isn't a good life either. So we still don't know yet what eudaimonia is.

Final ends

Is there such a thing as *the* good for human beings? Given that we think pleasure, honour, or again, knowledge, are all good, how could eudaimonia be *the* good, our *only* good (§7)?

Call an end that we desire for its own sake a 'final' end. We can't give some further purpose for why we seek it. If there is just one end for the sake of which we do everything else, that is the good. If there is more than one end, there are various final ends, each of which is good. If pleasure, honour and knowledge are final ends, doesn't that show that eudaimonia is not our only good?

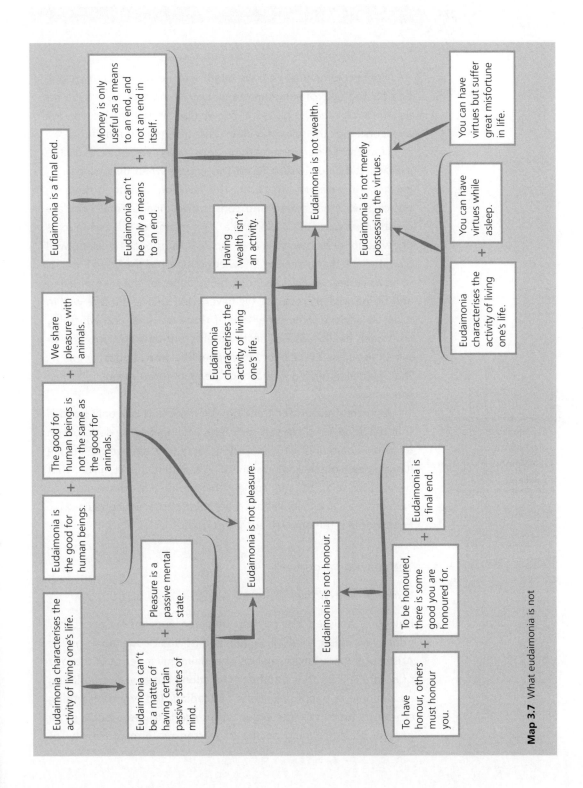

Map 3.7 What eudaimonia is not

Not yet. Some final ends we might seek *both* for their own sake *and* for the sake of something else. Everything that we pursue for its own sake – such as pleasure, knowledge, honour and so on – we also pursue for the sake of eudaimonia, of living a good life.

How can we pursue something *both* for its own sake and for the sake of eudaimonia? We faced this puzzle when discussing MILL'S 'PROOF' OF UTILITARIANISM (p. 220). The solution was to distinguish between external means and constitutive means. Final ends are constitutive parts of eudaimonia. For example, we can pursue knowledge for its own sake and pursue it for the sake of living well if we believe that acquiring knowledge is part of the good life.

Everything we do, says Aristotle, is done for the sake of living and faring well. By contrast, we never want to live and fare well in order to achieve some *other* end. If there is a final end which we *never* seek for the sake of anything else, but only ever for its own sake, this will be a final end 'without qualification'. Annas comments that if eudaimonia is our final end, then it must be 'complete' in just this sense.

A further reason for thinking eudaimonia is our only good is that the good should be self-sufficient; i.e. it makes life desirable on its own. Eudaimonia is the most desirable thing, and we can't make it more desirable by adding something else to it. In fact, given what we've just said, to add some other goal, e.g. knowledge, to eudaimonia is just to make that other thing part of your eudaimonia. Eudaimonia is the only self-sufficient good.

Explain Aristotle's argument that eudaimonia is our final end.

The function argument

'Function' and 'virtue'

Having established the relation between eudaimonia and other goods, we need to think again about what eudaimonia is. So Aristotle embarks on an analysis of eudaimonia in terms of the idea of *ergon*. This is often translated 'function', but as with translating *eudaimonia* as happiness, this is misleading. The ergon of a thing *can* be its function – the ergon of an eye is to see – but a more general account would be the 'characteristic form of activity' of something. 'Function' here is better understood in relation to 'functioning' rather than 'purpose'.

The 'characteristic activity' of something provides an insight into what type of thing it is (otherwise in what sense would the activity be 'characteristic'?). It thereby provides an evaluative standard for that thing: something is a good x when it performs its characteristic activity well. If the ergon of a knife is to cut, a good knife cuts well; a good eye sees well; a good plant flourishes (it grows well, produces flowers well, etc., according to its species).

In order to fulfil its ergon, a thing will need certain qualities. An *arête* is a quality that aids the fulfilment of a thing's ergon. It can be translated generally as an 'excellence', or more specifically, a 'virtue'. So sharpness is a virtue in a knife designed to cut. Good focus is a virtue in an eye.

Explain Aristotle's concepts of 'function' and 'virtue'.

The argument

Aristotle applies this entire account to human beings. Virtues for human beings will be those traits that enable them to fulfil their ergon. So, first, what is the 'characteristic activity' of human beings? At the most general level, we are alive. But this isn't distinctive of just us. So we shouldn't identify 'life' as our characteristic activity. We are a type of animal, rather than plant. We are conscious, have sense perception, etc. But again, we share this with many animals. But we want to know what the good for human beings, distinctively, is.

A human life is distinctively the life of a being that can be guided by *reason*. We are, distinctively, rational animals. Many commentators misunderstand Aristotle to be claiming that reason*ing* is our ergon. But Aristotle makes a deeper point – what is characteristic of us is that whatever we do, we do for reasons. All our activities – not just 'reasoning' – are, or can be, guided by reasons. Being guided by reasons is, of course, a matter of our psychology, and so Aristotle talks of the activity of the soul (*psyche*).

Now, we said above, that a good x (eye, knife, etc.) is one that performs its characteristic activity well, and that it will need certain qualities – virtues – to enable it to do this. Our ergon is living as a rational animal, i.e. living in accordance with reason, and the virtues

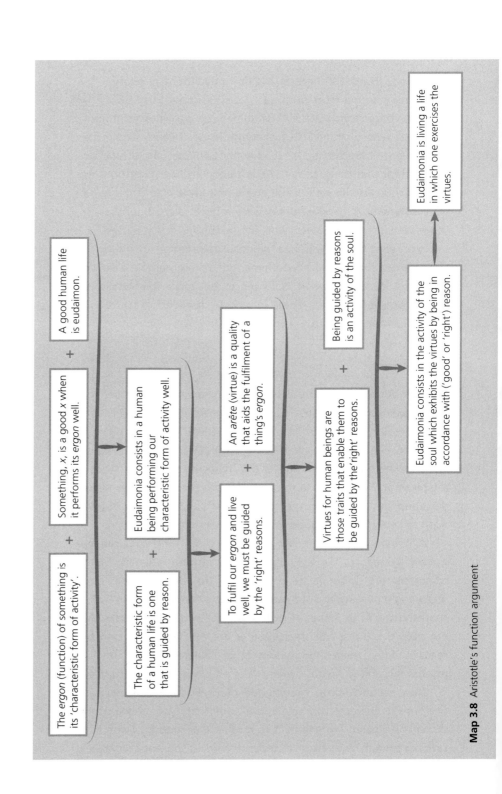

The *ergon* (function) of something is its 'characteristic form of activity'.

+

Something, *x*, is a good *x* when it performs its *ergon* well.

+

A good human life is eudaimon.

The characteristic form of a human life is one that is guided by reason.

+

Eudaimonia consists in a human being performing our characteristic form of activity well.

To fulfil our *ergon* and live well, we must be guided by the 'right' reasons.

+

An *arête* (virtue) is a quality that aids the fulfilment of a thing's *ergon*.

+

Virtues for human beings are those traits that enable them to be guided by the 'right' reasons.

Being guided by reasons is an activity of the soul.

+

Eudaimonia consists in the activity of the soul which exhibits the virtues by being in accordance with ('good' or 'right') reason.

Eudaimonia is living a life in which one exercises the virtues.

Map 3.8 Aristotle's function argument

of a human being will be what enables us to do this. To fulfil our ergon and live well, we must be guided by the 'right' reasons – good reasons, not 'bad' reasons. So eudaimonia consists in the activity of the soul which exhibits the virtues by being in accordance with ('good' or 'right') reason. Eudaimonia is living a life in which one exercises the virtues. Finally, we must add – as noted earlier – that this must apply to a person's life as a whole. A day or even a year of living well doesn't amount to a good life.

Outline and explain Aristotle's function argument.

Testing the analysis

The next question might be 'But what is it to live in accordance with right reason?' The rest of the *Nicomachean Ethics* can be understood as an answer to this question. But before moving on to that issue, it is worth double-checking that this is a plausible account of eudaimonia. In §8, Aristotle argues that it is indeed consistent with other things we want to say about what is good for human beings.

1. There are three types of thing that are good for us – goods of the mind (e.g. intelligence, courage, etc.), goods of the body (e.g. strength, health, etc.) and 'external' goods (e.g. wealth, food, etc.). People generally agree that the goods of the mind are worth more than the others. We often think of the others as additional to, but not comprising, a good life. This agrees with the analysis; eudaimonia centrally concerns goods 'of the soul'.
2. We have said that eudaimonia is living well. The analysis agrees, and spells out what it is to live well.
3. We can return to the suggestions (p. 272) that eudaimonia involves virtue, pleasure and wealth, and now explain the truth in each.
    a. Virtue: as we said, to possess virtue is not enough; eudaimonia requires that one *acts* on it as well. The employment of virtues and the achievement of good purposes are better than simply having the virtues.
    b. Pleasure: people find pleasant whatever it is that they love. A virtuous person loves living virtuously – you shouldn't call someone 'just', for instance, if they dislike doing what is just. But that means that the life of the virtuous person will also be pleasant. Eudaimonia is therefore both good and pleasant.

See also Eudaimonia and pleasure, p. 294.

Explain Aristotle's claim that eudaimonia involves virtue, pleasure and prosperity.

c.   Wealth: in order to *live* virtuously (e.g. to be generous), we will also need a certain amount of external goods. And so, enough good fortune is needed for a fully good life.

In §10, Aristotle raises a puzzle. If eudaimonia relates to the *whole* of someone's life, then can you call someone eudaimon while they are still alive? Their life is not yet finished – something terrible may yet happen that would lead us to say that theirs was not a good life. On the other hand, it is absurd to say that they *are* eudaimon after they have died. We could say, once they are dead, that they *were* eudaimon, but then it is strange that we cannot say that they *are* eudaimon before they have died.

Aristotle's solution is to say that fortunes change, but living virtuously has a much greater permanence. A virtuous person deals with bad fortune in the best possible way, so only very rarely and through terrible circumstances, can someone virtuous fail to lead a good life. Now we understand that virtue is central to leading a good life, we can call someone who is virtuous 'eudaimon' while they live, if they have sufficient external goods.

Thinking harder: the rational 'soul'

We now have the outline of an answer to the question 'what is the good for human beings?' It is living in accordance with reason, and this requires the virtues. So what are the virtues?

Because our ergon is the activity of the soul in accordance with reason, a virtue is a trait of a person's 'soul' – we would perhaps say 'mind' or 'self'. In §13, Aristotle provides an analysis of the soul. We can divide it into an arational part and a rational part (at least in analysis, even if there aren't literal 'parts'). The arational part can be further divided in two – the part that is related to 'growth and nutrition' (Aristotle thought that all life has soul) and the part related to desire and emotion. The desiring part we share with other animals, but in us, it can be responsive to reason. For instance, suppose someone wants to use all their money to buy things they want, but they recognise that it is good to share their wealth with others, and so they do so, their desire gives way. Someone with the virtue of generosity has reshaped their desires, and is not even tempted to try to spend their money on themselves, but happily provides for other people's needs and desires. What they want 'speaks with the same voice' as their reason.

We can talk about the rational part of the soul having two parts as well. There is, again, the desiring part which can respond to reasons and there is the part with which we reason, which has reason 'in itself'. Virtues are traits that enable us to live in accordance with reason. They are, therefore, of two kinds – virtues of the intellect (traits of the reasoning part) and virtues of character (traits of the part characterised by desire and emotion).

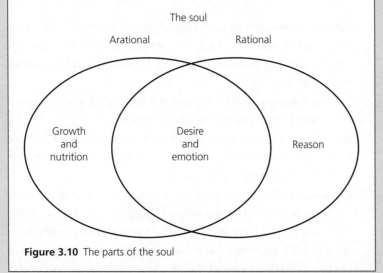

Figure 3.10 The parts of the soul

Aristotle's account of virtues

As we have seen, a virtue is a trait of mind or character that helps us achieve a good life, which Aristotle has analysed as a life in accordance with reason. There are two types of virtue – intellectual virtues and moral virtues. The central intellectual virtue for leading the good life, we will see, is PRACTICAL WISDOM (p. 288). In Bk 2, Aristotle concentrates on moral virtues, traits of character.

ARISTOTLE, *NICOMACHEAN ETHICS*, BK 2 (§§1–7)

Aristotle thought that the list of virtues isn't a miscellaneous collection, but grounded in a general, reasoned account of what virtues are.

Virtues as character traits

Aristotle says that anything that is part of the soul (the mind) is either a passion, a faculty or a state (trait) of character. So since virtues are part of the soul, they must be one of these.

1. Passions: Aristotle's term 'passions' covers our bodily appetites (for food, drink, sex, etc.), our emotions, and any feelings accompanied by pleasure or pain. But these can't be virtues for three reasons.
    a. Just having a particular passion – feeling hungry or angry – doesn't make you a good or bad person.
    b. We don't choose our passions, but virtues are related to the choices we make. We cannot generally, just by an act of will, choose what we feel or want.
    c. Virtues concern how we are *disposed* to feel and act; they are not desires that actually motivate us.
2. Faculties: faculties are things like sight or the ability to feel fear. Virtues can't be these, since we have these naturally but we have to *acquire* virtue (see THE ROLE OF EDUCATION IN THE DEVELOPMENT OF A MORAL CHARACTER, p. 285).
3. So virtues must be states of character.

Aristotle defines states of character as 'the things in virtue of which we stand well or badly with reference to the passions'. Character involves a person's *dispositions* that relate to what, in different circumstances, they feel, how they think, how they react, the sorts of choices they make, and the actions they perform. So someone is short-tempered if they are disposed to feel angry quickly and often; quick-witted, if they can think on their feet; intemperate, if they get drunk often and excessively. What we find pleasant also reveals our character.

Character has a certain stability and longevity. Character traits last much longer and change less easily than many 'states of mind', such as moods and desires. But character can change, and so it is less stable and long-lived than personal identity. Yet it is central to being the person one is. Annas comments that my virtues are dispositions of *me*, and so they are connected to my life as a whole. Aristotelian virtue theory assumes that there is a sense in which I can think about my life as a 'unity'.

What kind of state of character is a virtue? Some traits of character, such as being short-tempered or greedy, stop us from leading a good life – these are vices. Other traits of character, such as being kind or courageous, help us to lead a good life – and these are the virtues. Any virtue makes the thing which has it good and able to perform its characteristic activity well. So, in us, a virtue of character is a disposition to feel, desire and choose 'well', which is necessary if we are to live well and so achieve eudaimonia.

This last point – choosing well – is important. Annas notes that virtues in the fullest sense aren't simply dispositions to behave in certain ways, like being clumsy is a disposition to have accidents. They are expressed in the choices we make and the reasons for which we act, and a virtue involves a commitment by the person to an ethical value. And so, as we will see further in PRACTICAL WISDOM (p. 288), practical reason is central to having and exercising the virtues.

Virtues, the doctrine of the mean, and the importance of feelings

What is involved in choosing and living well? Aristotle compares living well with other activities, such as eating well or physical training. In these cases, the good nutritionist or good trainer needs to avoid prescribing too much food or exercise or too little. We achieve health and physical fitness by following an 'intermediate'

'Temperance' is the virtue relating to pleasure, especially our desires for food, drink and sex.

What is a trait (or state) of character?

What, according to Aristotle, is a moral virtue?

course of action, which Aristotle calls the 'mean'. However, what this is differs from person to person. A professional sportsman needs more food and exercise than most people. The mean, what is neither too much nor too little, is relative to each individual. (This 'mean' is not a mathematical quantity, an 'objective' mean halfway between the two extremes, as 6 is halfway between 2 and 10.)

Now, in the 'art of living', so to speak, something similar applies. We can feel our passions either 'too much' or 'too little' – and here we see the importance of feelings in virtue. Virtue involves being disposed to feeling in an 'intermediate' way, neither too much nor too little. Some people feel angry too often, over too many things (perhaps they take a critical comment as an insult), or maybe whenever they get angry, they get very angry, even at minor things. Other people feel angry not often enough (perhaps they don't understand how people take advantage of them). To be virtuous is 'to feel [passions] at the right times, with reference to the right objects, towards the right people, with the right motive, and in the right way' (§6). This is Aristotle's 'doctrine of the mean'.

It is important to note that Aristotle's doctrine of the mean does *not* claim that when we get angry, we should only ever be 'moderately' angry. We should be as angry as the situation demands, which can be very angry or only slightly irritated. Given the very close connection between what we feel and how we choose to act, virtues are dispositions of choice as well, and there is a 'mean' for actions as well as for feelings.

Annas expands on this. We need to do the right thing for the right reasons and in an appropriate way. This appropriate way involves both affective and intellectual aspects. Our action needs to be accompanied by the right feelings. This isn't merely a matter of self-control, but wholeheartedness. As in our example of justice above (p. 277), doing the right thing but grudgingly, or while controlling one's temptation to do the wrong thing, although better than doing the wrong thing (!), is not virtuous, according to Aristotle.

The intellectual aspect of virtuous action involves understanding that this action is the right thing to do. What the right action, time, object, person and so on is, for both feeling and action, PRACTICAL

Explain Aristotle's doctrine of the mean.

WISDOM (p. 288) helps us to know. (We won't complete our account of virtue, therefore, until we have understood what practical wisdom is.) Practical wisdom is a virtue of reason. Our passions, we noted, are susceptible to reason. There can be right and wrong ways to feel passions, and the right way to feel passions is determined by reason. If we feel our passions 'irrationally' – at the wrong times, towards the wrong objects, etc. – then we don't live well. Likewise, we can choose the right or wrong actions and act for the right or wrong reasons, usually as a result of whether the feelings that help influence our choices are themselves rational or irrational. So, Aristotle concludes, a virtue is 'a state of character concerned with choice, lying in the mean, i.e. the mean relative to us, this being determined by a rational principle, and by that principle by which the person of practical wisdom would determine it' (§6).

The application of the doctrine of the mean to particular virtues

The doctrine of the mean entails that we can (often, if not always) place a virtue 'between' two vices. Just as there is a right time, object, person, etc., at which to feel fear (or any emotion), some people can feel fear too often, about too many things, and towards too many people, or they get too afraid of things that aren't that dangerous. Other people can feel afraid not often enough, regarding too few objects and people. Someone who feels fear 'too much' is cowardly. Someone who feels fear 'too little' is rash. Someone who has the virtue relating to fear is courageous. The virtue is the 'intermediate' state between the two vices of 'too much' and 'too little'.

In §7, Aristotle presents the following examples. For many states of character, he notes, we don't have a common name.

We discuss courage and temperance in detail in extension material available on the companion website.

Table 3.1 Virtue as the 'mean'

Passion/concern	Vice of deficiency	Virtue	Vice of excess
Fear	Cowardly	Courageous	Rash
Pleasure/pain	'Insensible'	Temperate	Self-indulgent
Giving/taking money	Mean	Liberal ('free')	Prodigal ('spendthrift')
Spending large sums of money	Niggardly	'Magnificent'	Tasteless
Important honour	Unduly humble	Properly proud	Vain
Small honours	'Unambitious'	'Properly ambitious'	'Overambitious'
Anger	'Unirascible'	Good-tempered	Short-tempered
Truthfulness (regarding oneself)	Falsely modest	Truthful	Boastful
Humour	Boorish	Witty	Buffoonish
Pleasant to others	Quarrelsome, surly	Friendly	Obsequious
Shame	Shy	Modest	Shameless
Attitude to others' fortune	Spiteful (rejoicing in others' bad fortune)	Righteously indignant (pained by others' undeserved good fortune)	Envious (pained by others' good fortune)

Work through the table, working out what state of character each word refers to. Use a dictionary if you need to.

Obviously, Aristotle notes, not all *types* of actions or states of character can pick out a mean. For example, being shameless is not a mean, but a vice, while murder is always wrong. Furthermore, we often oppose a virtue to one of the two vices, either because it forms a stronger contrast with that vice (e.g. courage–cowardice) or because we have a natural tendency towards that vice, so need to try harder to resist it (e.g. temperance–self-indulgence).

But we can wonder whether virtues and virtuous actions are always 'intermediate' in any meaningful sense. We will return to this issue in GUIDANCE ON HOW TO ACT (p. 310).

Can you think of a virtue that is not 'intermediate'?

The role of education in the development of a moral character

We now know what virtues are. But how do we acquire them? Virtues are necessary for eudaimonia, but because they are dispositions towards feeling passions, and passions are not under the direct control of the will, we can't simply choose to become virtuous. In §§1–4, Aristotle argues that we acquire virtues of character through 'habit', in particular the habits we form during our upbringing. We need to develop virtue because, Aristotle argues, we are not virtuous just by nature. He points out that for what we can do naturally, we first have the 'potentiality' and then exhibit the activity. For example, you don't acquire sight by seeing; first you have sight, then you can see. But for the virtues, you must first practice acting in a virtuous way – courageously, generously, kindly, etc. – before you can be virtuous. We are not naturally virtuous, but we are naturally capable of becoming virtuous.

> 'Ethics' comes from the ancient Greek word for a virtue of character, *ethiké*, which is a variant on the word for habit, *ethos*.

The skill analogy

We can understand how we acquire virtues by an analogy with acquiring practical skills, such as carpentry, cookery or playing a musical instrument. There are two parts to the analogy.

The first part regards how the development of the skill/virtue begins. We come to form dispositions to feel and behave in certain ways by what we *do*. The same is true for practical skills. You cannot learn cookery or a musical instrument just by studying the theory, by merely acquiring knowledge about how to cook or play; you have to practice the activity. Likewise, being told how to be good is not enough to become good; you have to actually practice being good: 'the virtues we get by first exercising them, as also happens in the case of the arts as well [e.g. learning to play a musical instrument]. For the things we have to learn before we can do them, we learn by doing them'. Hence, 'by doing the acts that we do in our transactions with other men we become just or unjust, and by doing the acts that we do in the presence of danger, and by being habituated to feel fear or confidence, we become brave or cowardly' (§1).

It can seem that there is a puzzle in what Aristotle says. In order to become just, we have to do just acts. But how can we do just acts unless we are already just? The puzzle is solved by distinguishing between actions which are 'in accordance with' justice and just acts, properly so called (§4). The actions that we do when learning to become just are acts in accordance with justice. But a just act is an act that is not only in accordance with justice, but also done *as the just person does it*.

This takes us to the second part of the skill analogy, which Annas draws out. While we first learn from others, this is only half the process. As with practical skills, the aim in moral education is to get the child/student to learn to think for themselves. This involves two related skills.

See THE DISTINCTION BETWEEN ACTING IN ACCORDANCE WITH DUTY AND ACTING OUT OF DUTY, p. 250, for a similar distinction drawn by Kant.

First, the expert progresses from simply following rules to developing a highly attuned sensitivity to how each situation is different, and how to respond to those differences appropriately. So a good carpenter responds and works with the knots and grain in the wood; a good chef checks the seasoning of each dish by tasting it, and adjusts each element of a meal in light of the others. Likewise, in growing in virtue, we become better able to recognise situations in which action is called for and what to do in response.

Second, just as in developing a practical skill, we understand why this way rather than that is better – why this screwdriver, why this spice, and not that one – so, in its development of virtue, the child comes to reflect on the reasons for acting this way rather than that. He or she tries to make their moral judgements and practice more coherent and unified, and is able to justify their choices. In all this, our appreciation of what is virtuous may change. For example, we may first associate courage just with physical courage, particularly in fighting. But then, with reflection and greater experience, we come to identify it in dealing with emotional challenges, with loss, in friendships and speaking truth to power. We may come to rethink whether certain types of action that we thought exemplified courage, e.g. in Hollywood blockbusters, really are courageous at all or a form of masculine competition. Thus as we develop in virtue, we understand, in a practical way, more about what is good. All this is part of our developing PRACTICAL WISDOM (p. 288).

Explain the skill analogy in Aristotle's theory of how we acquire virtues.

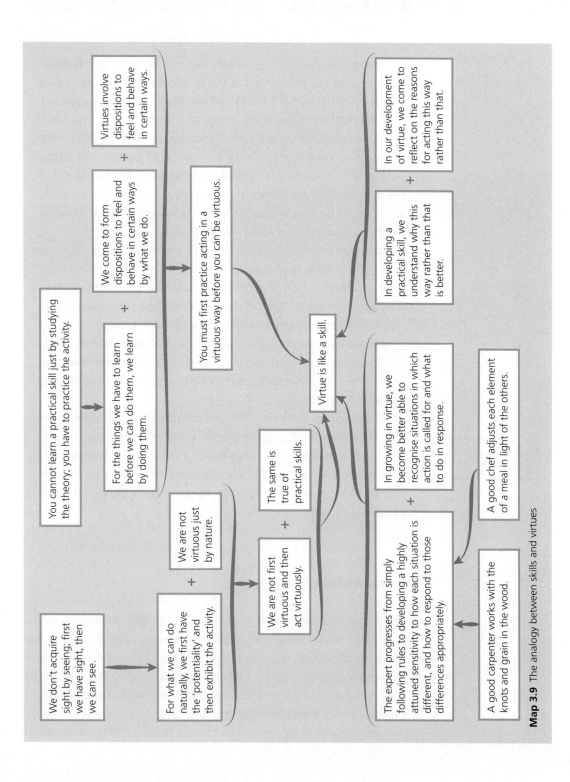

Map 3.9 The analogy between skills and virtues

We don't acquire sight by seeing; first we have sight, then we can see.

For what we can do naturally, we first have the 'potentiality' and then exhibit the activity.

You cannot learn a practical skill just by studying the theory; you have to practice the activity.

For the things we have to learn before we can do them, we learn by doing them.

We come to form dispositions to feel and behave in certain ways by what we do.

+

Virtues involve dispositions to feel and behave in certain ways.

You must first practice acting in a virtuous way before you can be virtuous.

+

We are not virtuous just by nature.

We are not first virtuous and then act virtuously.

+

The same is true of practical skills.

Virtue is like a skill.

In developing a practical skill, we understand why this way rather than that is better.

+

In our development of virtue, we come to reflect on the reasons for acting this way rather than that.

In growing in virtue, we become better able to recognise situations in which action is called for and what to do in response.

+

The expert progresses from simply following rules to developing a highly attuned sensitivity to how each situation is different, and how to respond to those differences appropriately.

A good chef adjusts each element of a meal in light of the others.

A good carpenter works with the knots and grain in the wood.

And so, Aristotle argues, a fully virtuous action is one in which the agent knows what they are doing, chooses the act for its own sake (i.e. for the end at which the relevant virtue aims, e.g. justice), and makes their choice from a firm and unchangeable character. Until it has moved from the early learning stage to the development of a richer expertise, a child may do what is just (such as not taking more than its fair share) because it is told to do so, or because it likes the person it is sharing with, or because it wants to please an adult, and so on. It neither truly understands what justice *is* nor does the child choose the act *because* the act is just.

Annas notes that there are limits to the skill analogy. First, we don't have to pursue the ends of a particular skill, such as creating beautiful furniture or tasty food, e.g. we may lose interest in that activity or its rewards. But virtues pursue our final end – eudaimonia – and we can't opt out of having that end, we can't want to live at all and cease to want to live a good life. Second, many practical skills can be developed without involving our emotions, but the development of our emotional dispositions is central to developing virtue.

Aristotle concludes that whether or not we can lead a good life depends a great deal on the habits we form when we are young – in our childhood and early adulthood. Furthermore, because our character is revealed by what we take pleasure in, we need to learn to take pleasure in the things that we should take pleasure in, and be pained by what should pain us.

See EUDAIMONIA AND PLEASURE, p. 294.

Practical wisdom

We saw that Aristotle defines eudaimonia as activity of the soul which exhibits the virtues by being in accordance with reason, and virtue as 'a state of character concerned with choice, lying in the mean, i.e. the mean relative to us, this being determined by a rational principle, and by that principle by which the person of practical wisdom would determine it'. These definitions and the account of moral development make clear the centrality of practical reason to virtue and living a good life. In order to complete our accounts of eudaimonia and virtue, we need to understand what practical reason and practical wisdom are.

ARISTOTLE, *NICOMACHEAN ETHICS*, BK 6, §§1, 2, 5, 8, 9, 12, 13

Practical wisdom (*phronesis*) is an intellectual virtue, a virtue of practical reasoning. Aristotle draws a distinction between theoretical reason and practical reason (§1). Roughly, theoretical reason investigates what we can't change and aims at the truth. Practical reason investigates what we can change and aims at making good choices. Reasoning about what we can change is deliberation, so practical reason is expressed in deliberation. To make good choices, not only must our reasoning be correct, but we must also have the right desires (§2).

For more detail, see CHOICE AND DELIBERATION, p. 303.

The person with practical wisdom deliberates well about how to live a good life (§5). So practical wisdom is 'a true and reasoned state or capacity to act with regard to the things that are good or bad for man'.

The role of practical wisdom

Practical wisdom differs from other sorts of knowledge both because of its complexity and its practical nature. Aristotle claims that it involves

1. a general conception of what is good or bad, related to the conditions for human flourishing;
2. the ability to perceive, in light of that general conception, what is required in terms of feeling, choice and action in a particular situation;
3. the ability to deliberate well; and
4. the ability to act on that deliberation.

So it involves general knowledge, particular knowledge, an ability to reason towards a choice, and an ability to act on that choice. There are different ways in which we can fail to deliberate well (§9).

What, according to Aristotle, is practical wisdom?

a. We can deliberate with the wrong end. Our starting point is wrong, and so our choice is wrong. Our general knowledge of the good is faulty.
b. We can have the right end, and perhaps even achieve it. However, we don't understand the right means to the end, and so if we achieve our end, this is accidental or lucky. Either our knowledge of the particular circumstances or our reasoning is faulty.
c. We can fail to deliberate when we should or take too long.

So practical wisdom means deliberating with a good end, identifying the right means, and doing so in a timely way. In its fullest sense, practical wisdom involves deliberating from the most unqualified end, eudaimonia itself.

Point (2) above says that practical wisdom involves understanding what is required in a particular situation in light of a general understanding of what is good. The question that faces us on any occasion is how to achieve what is good – what the good life involves – in the here and now, in this situation. But there are no *rules* for applying knowledge of the good life to the current situation. What is right on a particular occasion is in accordance with 'right reason', but Aristotle has argued that this can vary from one occasion to another. Furthermore, this kind of insight is inseparable from making a good decision: we must not only understand the situation (which can involve considerable sensitivity), but also understand how to act well in it.

This makes it impossible to make generalisations about right and wrong, good and bad, that are true in all cases. Practical wisdom intuitively 'grasps' the particular facts involved in the case. This does not make ethics subjective, as there is a truth of the matter to be discovered. However, proving the truth of one view against another is not possible by argument alone. If you are blind, I may not be able to convince you of the colour of moonlight; if you lack insight into what is good, I may not be able to convince you of the goodness of being kind. If you can't understand the situation we are facing, I may not be able to convince you that the right thing to do on this occasion is to be generous.

THE ROLE OF EDUCATION IN THE DEVELOPMENT OF A MORAL CHARACTER, p. 285.

And so, Aristotle argues, practical wisdom is not something that can be *taught*, for what can be taught is general, not particular (§8). Rules and principles will rarely apply in any clear way to real situations. Instead, moral knowledge is only acquired through experience.

The relation between practical wisdom, virtue and action

How does practical wisdom relate to virtue and virtuous action? We can imagine this objection: living a good life is a matter of being good, and this involves the virtues. So what use is practical wisdom?

A first, simple answer (§12) is this: the virtues (justice, courage, generosity, etc.) set our ends. Because we are virtuous, we aim at the good life, and we have a reliable conception of what this is (it involves justice, courage, generosity, etc.). But that isn't enough to live a good life, because it doesn't tell us what is good (courageous, etc.) *in this particular situation*. For that, we need practical wisdom to identify the (constitutive) means to our virtuous ends.

Further reflection tells us more. In THE ROLE OF EDUCATION IN THE DEVELOPMENT OF A MORAL CHARACTER (p. 285), we drew a distinction between acting in accordance with a virtue and doing a fully virtuous action. A fully virtuous action is one in which the agent knows what they are doing and chooses the act for its own sake. Both this knowledge and this kind of choice depend on having practical wisdom. The knowledge involves understanding what is good in this situation, and choice depends upon deliberation, and good deliberation involves practical wisdom. So acting virtuously requires practical wisdom.

So Aristotle draws a distinction between 'natural' virtue and 'full' virtue (§13). He allows that we can have good dispositions from birth; e.g. someone might be naturally kind. But this doesn't amount to 'full virtue'. A naturally kind child doesn't fully comprehend the nature of their action, and could easily be misled into being kind for the wrong reasons or at the wrong time. Without practical wisdom, we can't have full virtue.

1) Explain why Aristotle claims that practical wisdom is not merely knowledge of moral rules. 2) Compare Aristotle and Kant on the nature of practical reason.

Explain why
Aristotle claims that
practical wisdom
requires virtue and
virtue requires
practical wisdom.

But practical wisdom also depends on virtue (§12). It is possible to deliberate from the wrong ends. A bad person can be very clever in achieving what they want. But cleverness is not practical wisdom, because practical wisdom also involves having general knowledge about what is good. This depends upon being virtuous, because what appears good to someone depends on their character traits. So on Aristotle's theory, we become both good and practically wise *together*.

Key points: Aristotelian virtue ethics (I)

- All our activities aim at some good. If there is one good that all activities aim at in the end, this is the good for human beings.
- Aristotle argues that this good is eudaimonia, sometimes translated 'happiness', but better understood as 'living well and faring well' or 'flourishing'. Eudaimonia is not a psychological state, but an objective quality of someone's life as a whole.
- We seek final ends for their own sake, and eudaimonia is a final end. Wealth is an instrumental good, so eudaimonia can't be a matter of wealth. There are other final ends, such as pleasure and honour, but we seek these also for the sake of eudaimonia. Eudaimonia is the only final end that we seek *only* for its own sake.
- Something's *ergon* is its function or characteristic activity. Something is good when it performs its ergon well. An *arête* – a virtue – is a quality that enables a thing to fulfil its ergon.
- Our characteristic activity is to live our lives guided by reason. Virtues are qualities that enable us to live according to reason. Our good, therefore, is the activity 'of the soul' which exhibits the virtues by being in accordance with right reason.
- Eudaimonia involves virtuous activity, pleasure (because we enjoy what we love doing) and wealth (because we need some good fortune for virtuous activity).
- The soul has three parts – an arational part, a part characterised by desires and emotions that is responsive to reason, and the rational intellect.

- Moral virtues are traits of character, dispositions to feel, desire and choose in accordance with reason. A virtue lies 'in the mean', a disposition to feel passions neither too much nor too little, but 'at the right times, with reference to the right objects, towards the right people, with the right motive, and in the right way' and to choose actions in accordance with reason. And so a virtue is 'a state of character concerned with choice, lying in the mean, i.e. the mean relative to us, this being determined by a rational principle, and by that principle by which the person of practical wisdom would determine it'.
- To choose the right act for the right reasons and to act in an appropriate way, wholeheartedly, involves both feelings and reason. A fully virtuous act is one in which the agent knows what they are doing, chooses the act for its own sake, and makes their choice from a firm and unchangeable character.
- Character traits, and therefore virtues, are acquired through the habits we form when growing up. As with learning practical skills, we acquire virtue not by being told what is right, but by doing acts in accordance with virtue. However, as with practical skills, the idea is to develop an expertise that goes beyond following rules to making one's own judgements on the basis of good reasons and sensitive to each situation.
- Practical wisdom is a virtue of practical reason. It is 'a true and reasoned state or capacity to act with regard to the things that are good or bad for man'. It involves insight into what is good or bad in general, insight into what is good in a particular situation, and the abilities to deliberate well and act on that deliberation.
- There is no set of rules for applying general knowledge of what is good to particular situations. Practical wisdom simply grasps the particular relevant facts directly.
- So knowledge of what to do is practical so it can't be taught, but requires experience.
- To do a fully virtuous action, we must aim at the right end. This is set by being virtuous. But we must also know what we are doing, understood as a means to that end. This is provided by practical wisdom.
- We cannot have virtue without practical wisdom, since virtue involves fully virtuous action. We cannot have practical wisdom without virtue, since practical wisdom involves general knowledge of what is good, and this requires virtue.

Eudaimonia, pleasure and philosophy

We have in place the three most important concepts in Aristotle's ethical theory, namely eudaimonia, virtue and practical wisdom. We turn now to look at three issues, the relation of eudaimonia to pleasure and reason, the nature of voluntary action and moral responsibility, and the nature of justice. The first provides some important points of comparison between Aristotle's theory and utilitarianism, the third provides an account of the place of deontology in Aristotle's theory, and both the second and third will prove important resources to draw upon when we turn to think about APPLIED ETHICS (p. 321).

EUDAIMONIA AND PLEASURE

In his account of eudaimonia, Aristotle has emphasised the importance of virtue and reason. But many people think that pleasure is central. UTILITARIANISM (p. 205), for example, holds that happiness (composed of pleasure and the absence of pain) is the only good, and so the best life must be a life of pleasure. What place does Aristotle give to pleasure in his account?

We discuss temperance further in extension material.

ARISTOTLE, *NICOMACHEAN ETHICS*, BKS 7.12–13, 10.1–5

Is pleasure good?

Like Mill, Aristotle claims that pleasure is good, and that eudaimonia involves pleasure. To defend his view, he needs to answer objections that reject the goodness of pleasure, and to clarify just how and when pleasure is good. He does this in Bks 7.12–13 and 10.2. (We will not discuss all the objections he considers, as some are difficult and technical.)

1. *Objection*: The temperate person avoids pleasure.
    Reply: Not true. What the temperate person avoids is an *excess* of certain *bodily* pleasures.
2. *Objection*: The practically wise person doesn't seek pleasure, but only avoids pain.
    Reply: Not true. The practically wise person does seek pleasure, but in accordance with reason. Furthermore, the fact that they avoid pain (in accordance with reason) shows that pleasure is good. As pain is bad and to be avoided, the contrary of pain, pleasure, is good and to be pursued.

3. *Objection*: Pleasure interferes with thought.

   Reply: Not true. The pleasures of thinking don't interfere with thinking, but assist it. It is pleasures that arise from other sources that interfere with thinking. It is generally true of pleasurable activities that each interferes with the others (see PLEASURE, VIRTUE AND FUNCTION, p. 296).

4. *Objection*: Not *all* pleasures are good, for example bodily pleasures or taking pleasure in something bad or disgraceful. (Aristotle doesn't provide an example, but voyeurism – an invasion of someone's privacy, especially sexual privacy – provides a fairly clear example.)

   Reply: If we say bodily pleasures are not good, then how can we explain that their opposite, bodily pains, are bad? It is only *excess* of pleasure here that is bad. Disgraceful pleasures are not good, agreed. To explain this, we could say any of three things:

   a. Disgraceful pleasures are not really pleasures, but only pleasant to bad people. All real pleasures are good, though.

   b. The kind of pleasure involved in something disgraceful is a pleasure (e.g. looking at an attractive naked body), and so it is good in general. But such pleasure is not good when it is caused by or involves something disgraceful (such as an intrusion on privacy).

   c. Pleasures are of different kinds, and only some pleasures are good. We will look further at this below.

Do we have any positive reasons for thinking that pleasure is good? Aristotle considers four arguments from another philosopher, Eudoxus, for the claim that pleasure is the *only* good (§10.2). He argues that Eudoxus is right that pleasure is a good, but not that it is the only good. (We will see further arguments from Aristotle in the next section.)

1. Every creature aims at pleasure. This is a good indication that it is, for each thing, the good. And what is good for all things is *the* good.

Is there any good reason to think that pleasure is not good?

This argument is almost identical to the first part of MILL'S 'PROOF' OF UTILITARIANISM, p. 220.

Aristotle agrees that this is the strongest reason for thinking that pleasure is good. However, he argues that pleasure is not the *only* thing that we aim at, it is not our only end (§10.3). There are other things which we seek out, such as seeing, knowing, being virtuous, that we would seek out even if they brought us no pleasure. The pleasure they bring is not *why* we seek them. They are FINAL ENDS (p. 272), not a means to pleasure.

With the next three arguments, Aristotle agrees that they show that pleasure is good, but not that it is the only good.

2. Everything avoids pain, so its contrary, pleasure, is good.
3. We choose pleasure for its own sake, not for some further purpose.
4. Adding pleasure on to any good makes it more desirable.

So, we should conclude that pleasure is good, but not the only good.

Explain why Aristotle claims that pleasure is not the only good.

In Metaphysics of Mind, such feelings are known as PHENOMENAL PROPERTIES/ QUALIA, p. 173.

Thinking harder: pleasure, virtue and function

What *is* pleasure? We naturally think of it as a kind of subjective feeling, which we can only define by how it feels. But Aristotle argues that it is the unimpeded activity of our faculties (§7.12). This is a very difficult claim to understand, but we can start by thinking about being 'in the zone', as we say now. Start with the activities of the senses, such as seeing (§10.4). Pleasure in the activity of a sense is caused most when that sense is at its best (e.g. when you can see well) and active in relation to its 'finest' object. Aristotle doesn't define this, but we can think of it as something on which we can really exercise that sense. So with vision, this is something that is (at least) interesting to look at, that we can explore and engage with through sight. Works of art and beautiful landscapes might provide examples. Looking at such things gives us (visual) pleasure. The same can be said of activities of thought – there is pleasure here in grappling with something that *exercises* our thought, but which *doesn't impede* it, e.g. through being too difficult to understand. We can extend this analysis to all our activities.

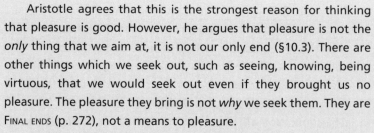

Figure 3.11 Psychologists define being 'in the zone' as marked by automatic activity, focused concentration, *and enjoyment*

But pleasure is not something simply *caused* by, and separate from, such unimpeded activity. It 'completes' the activity. It is part of it, not a separate end, nor a state produced by the activity, as deliberating might produce a decision or looking might produce finding. The pleasure is *in* the activity itself and intensifies and supports it. Thus, when we enjoy an activity, we throw ourselves into it, and we enjoy it less if our attention is distracted. If this is the correct analysis of what pleasure is, we can explain how pleasures can be good or bad, and how they relate to virtue and eudaimonia. Each kind of activity – eating, thinking, running, listening to music – has a corresponding kind of pleasure. So there are different kinds of pleasure. A pleasure is good when the activity that produces it is good and bad when the activity is bad.

In THE FUNCTION ARGUMENT (p. 274), we said that 'function' is best understood as 'characteristic activity'. Aristotle claims that different animals have different characteristic activities, and so they enjoy different pleasures. The pleasures that are most suited to human beings are, therefore, those that relate to our characteristic activity, namely living in accordance with reason. Now, it is the virtuous person who has the traits and the practical wisdom that enable them to perform this characteristic activity and this constitutes the good life for human beings. So what is 'truly' pleasant is what is pleasant to the virtuous person. It is these pleasures that form part of eudaimonia. People who are not virtuous may get pleasure from other activities, but such pleasure is not good or 'truly' pleasant.

Explain Aristotle's analysis of what pleasure is.

Compare and contrast Aristotle and Mill on pleasure.

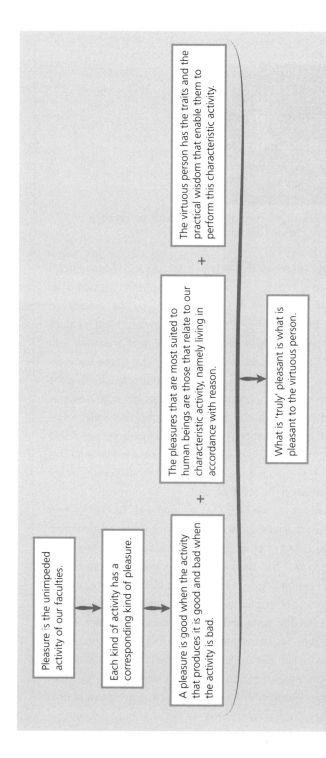

Pleasure is the unimpeded activity of our faculties.

Each kind of activity has a corresponding kind of pleasure.

A pleasure is good when the activity that produces it is good and bad when the activity is bad.

The pleasures that are most suited to human beings are those that relate to our characteristic activity, namely living in accordance with reason.

+

The virtuous person has the traits and the practical wisdom that enable them to perform this characteristic activity.

+

What is 'truly' pleasant is what is pleasant to the virtuous person.

Map 3.10 On pleasure and virtue

EUDAIMONIA AND PHILOSOPHY

In PRACTICAL WISDOM (p. 288), we saw that Aristotle divides reason into practical reason and theoretical reason. We have discussed the place and role of practical reason in eudaimonia, and claimed that virtue, which is necessary for eudaimonia, is impossible without practical reason. But we have said nothing about theoretical reason. What part does this play in eudaimonia? In the second half of Bk 10, Aristotle completes his account of eudaimonia.

ARISTOTLE, *NICOMACHEAN ETHICS*, BK 10.6–8

Before we turn to the role of theoretical reason, what has already been said (§6)?

1. Eudaimonia is not a state, but an activity (EUDAIMONIA, p. 271). You don't live the best life by being asleep or suffering such misfortune that you can do very little.
2. It is desirable for its own sake and it is self-sufficient (FINAL ENDS, p. 272).
3. It involves virtuous actions, as these are desirable for their own sake (THE ROLE OF EDUCATION IN THE DEVELOPMENT OF A MORAL CHARACTER, p. 285).

Aristotle has also just argued that eudaimonia involves pleasure. But we shouldn't make the mistake of thinking that the best life is one of pleasant *amusements*, even if this is what people with power and wealth spend time doing. People find different activities pleasant depending on their character. What is truly pleasant is what is pleasant to the good person, and this is a life of virtuous activity, not a life of mere amusement.

So, to theoretical reason. Theoretical reason – the contemplation of truth – is what is 'highest' about human beings, Aristotle argues. Animals have a form of practical wisdom, in that they consider and act on what is best for themselves. But they do not contemplate general truths. This ability is our share in 'divinity'. Eudaimonia, therefore, must include excellent activity of theoretical reason, which is philosophy.

P1. This activity is best, because theoretical reason is the best thing in us and with it, we contemplate what is best (the greatest, most wonderful and most divine things in the universe), not merely what is best *for us* (as in practical wisdom).

P2. We are able to undertake this activity more continuously than any other activity, so it leads to the most continuously happy life.

P3. It is the most pleasant activity – at least, its pleasures are most pure and enduring, unlike pleasures of the body.

P4. It is the most self-sufficient activity. Nothing further arises from it (it is knowledge for its own sake), while in other virtuous activities, we normally gain something (honour, gratitude, friendship, power, etc.) beyond doing the action. We need fewer external goods for this than for any other virtuous activity. (To be generous, you need money. To be courageous, you need power. To be temperate, you need opportunities …)

P5. We are active in order to have leisure. 'Leisure' is undertaking those activities we wish to undertake. The virtues of politics aim at creating space for leisure, just as we only undertake war in order to achieve peace. They serve the activity of reason.

P6. Finally, theoretical reason is what we most *are*, it is our characteristic activity.

C1. Therefore, the best and most pleasant life for us, given our nature, will be a life of reason. The life of the philosopher (or more generally, a life dedicated to knowledge) will be the best life.

Aristotle concludes that we should strive to live such a life of theoretical reasoning as far as possible, to live in accordance with the best thing in us. But we are human, and require more than this. Hence the life of virtue more broadly is also part of eudaimonia, as he has argued all along. Having passions, having a body, living with others – these are all characteristically human too. Furthermore, the life of virtue doesn't require a great deal of external goods, and so while these are necessary, they are not central.

Explain Aristotle's claim that the best life is the life of a philosopher.

Voluntary action, choice and moral responsibility

There are two reasons to study the concepts of voluntary action, choice and moral responsibility. The first is that they are central to APPLIED ETHICS (p. 321). As Aristotle observes, we praise and blame what is voluntary, but not what is involuntary (Bk 3.1). So if we make judgements about people's actions, we must take into account whether they acted voluntarily and by choice or not. The second is that Aristotle has said that both virtue and practical reason are concerned with choice, so we can deepen our understanding of these central concepts by understanding the concept of choice. Aristotle discusses these issues in the first half of Bk 3.

ARISTOTLE, *NICOMACHEAN ETHICS*, BK 3.1–5

Voluntary and involuntary actions

There are two things that render our actions involuntary – force and ignorance. When we act voluntarily, by contrast, we know what we are doing, and we bring it about ourselves. Contrast three cases of standing on a train and stepping on someone's foot:

1. The train lurches, you lose your balance, and accidentally step on someone's foot. Stepping on their foot is involuntary, caused by force.
2. You shuffle your feet to get comfortable, and put your foot down on someone's foot without looking. Although moving your feet is voluntary, stepping on someone's foot is involuntary, caused by ignorance (that their foot was there).
3. You deliberately and knowingly bring your foot down on top of someone else's. This is voluntary.

Force

We can be forced to do things not only by physical forces but also by psychological pressure (such as threat of pain). Where no one could withstand such pressure, we don't blame someone for what they do. This shows that what they do is involuntary. However, the psychological pressure must be negative not positive. We don't think of the prospect of something good or pleasant as 'forcing' us to act. Giving in to temptation is not acting involuntarily! When we act involuntarily, we do so with pain and regret.

Now, some actions that we do, we don't want to do. These might be called voluntary or involuntary. Aristotle gives the example of sailors throwing goods overboard in a storm. They want to save the boat, but they don't want to lose the goods. Such actions, he argues, should be called voluntary. First, actions which we do to avoid a greater evil or in order to secure some good end are the right actions to *choose*. Second, we praise people for such actions, and we noted above that praise and blame attaches to what is voluntary.

So, the distinction between voluntary and involuntary actions relates to the *moment of action* in the particular circumstances one is in, not whether the action is generally desirable.

Ignorance

Some actions done as a result of ignorance are involuntary, some are simply 'not voluntary'. The difference lies in whether the action is one that causes us pain or regret. Suppose, again, you step on someone's foot while shuffling your feet. If you regret this, then stepping on their foot is involuntary. But if you don't care, then it is simply non-voluntary.

The kind of ignorance that makes an act involuntary relates to the particular circumstances of the action. You know what you are aiming at (you aren't ignorant of the end, e.g. 'to get comfortable'), and you can know relevant general truths (e.g. people have feet). But you don't know the particular circumstances of the action, e.g. what you are actually doing (stepping on someone's foot); or in other cases, what its consequences will be, what tools you are using to act with, or how (in what manner) you are acting (e.g. you might think you are gently helping, when you are actually annoyingly hindering).

We should also distinguish acting *in* ignorance from acting as a result of ignorance. When drunk or really angry, you may do something without fully understanding just what you are doing. Here we say that your action is a result of your drunkenness or rage,

Explain Aristotle's distinction between voluntary and involuntary action.

rather than your ignorance, and we may still blame you for your actions. But your drunkenness or rage puts you in a state of ignorance. So you act in ignorance, but not from ignorance.

See THINKING HARDER: MORAL RESPONSIBILITY, p. 305.

Voluntary action

Voluntary action, then, is action that you bring about, in the knowledge of what you are doing.

Sometimes people say that actions done from desire or emotion aren't voluntary. But this is a mistake for four reasons.

1. If it were true, we would have to say that neither animals nor children ever act voluntarily.
2. There are many good actions that we can do from desire and emotion (such as being kind), and we ought to do them. It would be strange to say that what we ought to do is not voluntary.
3. Actions done from desire or emotion are pleasant, not painful. But we said involuntary actions are painful, while the prospect of what is pleasant does not force us to act.
4. Our desires and emotions are no less part of *us* than our reason. Acting on them is something *we* do.

Choice and deliberation

We need to distinguish what is voluntary from what we choose (§2). Everything we choose to do is voluntary, but not everything voluntary is chosen. For instance, spontaneous actions and the actions of young children and animals are voluntary, but not chosen in the sense intended here. So what is choice?

1. It isn't desire – someone who gives in to temptation acts with desire, but not from choice, while someone who resists temptation acts on choice, but against their desire.
2. It isn't 'wish', since you can wish for what is impossible and things you can do nothing about, but choice relates to what we can actually do. What we wish for is also an end, something we are aiming at. What we choose are not ends, but the means to achieve our ends.

See Practical wisdom, p. 288.

3. It isn't a kind of opinion – opinions are true or false, but choices are good or bad.
4. Instead, choice relates to voluntary action, where this is done on the basis of *deliberation*.

So what is deliberation (§3)? We don't deliberate about what we can't change, such as the facts – we investigate these (theoretical reasoning). We only deliberate about things that we can change (practical reasoning). In fact, we only deliberate when we need to act differently on different occasions. You don't deliberate about how to make a cup of tea (once you've learned) – you just get on and do it! So deliberation is a kind of reasoned thought about what we can change by our efforts, and where we need to act differently on different occasions.

Aristotle also claims that we don't deliberate about ends. But is this right? For instance, I might study in order to get a good grade (my end). But I might well deliberate about whether to get good grades; for example whether it is worth the effort. Or again, I may have two ends that conflict – being a good friend and telling the truth – and I deliberate about which end to pursue.

However, what Aristotle probably means is that we don't deliberate about ends as ends. When we deliberate, we always have some end in view, and whatever we are considering is as a means to that end. If I deliberate about whether to get good grades, I am considering this in light of some further end, such as going to university. If I deliberate about being a good friend or telling the truth, I do so in light of my final end – leading a good life.

We can now say what choice is. Choice is what we decide upon as a result of deliberation. So it is a deliberate desire regarding something that is in one's power.

Explain Aristotle's theory of choice and deliberation.

Thinking harder: moral responsibility

When are we morally responsible for what we do? This question is important to applied ethics. We are generally happy to say that people who do good actions are morally responsible for what they do, and we praise them accordingly. But do people who are bad do bad things voluntarily and by choice? Before Aristotle, Socrates had argued that they do not. Everyone aims at what they believe is good. All bad action is acting from ignorance of what is truly good, so it is not voluntary. Aristotle accepts that bad people are ignorant of the good, but maintains that they still act voluntarily.

Free will and responsibility are also discussed in Metaphysics of God, MIDGLEY ON FREE WILL, p. 132.

To know fully what the right act is involves understanding *why* it is right. Someone who is bad might know, as a child does, that action *x* shouldn't be done. But if they don't understand why, they don't really know what they ought to do. Put another way: given that we all aim at eudaimonia, what is good is the 'proper' object of wish – what is truly desirable (§4). This is, in fact, what the good person desires. Bad people desire what is not truly desirable, but they don't realise this. Most errors of this kind are caused by pleasure. What is bad can seem desirable if we think it is pleasant. And different states of character find different things pleasant; e.g. the just person finds justice pleasant, but the unjust man does not.

However, the fact that bad people are ignorant of what is good does not entail that bad people act involuntarily. Aristotle offers four arguments for this claim.

1. We noted that choice relates to the means, the actions that we take. What it is in our power to do, it is also in our power not to do. So we can choose to do either good or bad actions. So bad people do bad actions voluntarily.
2. We encourage people not to do bad actions, yet we don't encourage people not to do things that are out of their power. That would be pointless. So bad actions are done voluntarily.

To these arguments, we might respond that there is a *sense* in which bad people choose to do bad actions. But still they are not *morally responsible* for them, because they are pursuing what seems good to them. They do not know what is truly desirable, and it is this ignorance that influences their choices.

Aristotle's third argument responds to this objection.

3.   Bad people became bad as a result of their choices. Therefore, they are responsible for becoming bad, and thus becoming ignorant of what is good.

Why believe this? In THE ROLE OF EDUCATION IN THE DEVELOPMENT OF A MORAL CHARACTER (p. 285), we noted that we acquire a particular state of character by acting in a corresponding way. For example, we become just by acting in accordance with justice. Thus, we are partly responsible for our character traits. We can choose how to act, knowing that how we act will make us good or bad people. A person, through choosing to act badly, becomes a bad person, and at that point, they have become ignorant of what is good.

Rather like becoming drunk, and then not knowing what you are doing, or becoming ill through ignoring medical advice, or ugly through lack of care and exercise, we are responsible for becoming bad through the choices we made. We can't, when drunk, choose to be sober; or when ill, choose to be healthy; or when ugly, choose to be beautiful – so when bad, we can't simply choose to become good. Yet despite this, our condition is voluntary and we are morally responsible for it. What appears good or pleasant depends on one's character traits. If the bad person is mistaken about what is good, this is as a result of their character traits. But as they are responsible for their character traits, they are responsible for their lack of knowledge of what is truly good. So the fact that they are doing something bad, thinking that it is good, does not count as the kind of ignorance involved in involuntary action (acting *from* ignorance), but as the kind of blameworthy ignorance (acting *in* ignorance) involved in drunkenness.

Construct an argument map of Aristotle's argument for the claim that bad people are responsible for becoming bad.

4. If we reject this argument, and claim that the bad person is not responsible for what they think is good, then we must apply the claim generally – *no one* is responsible for what seems good or bad to them.

    P1. If the bad person is not responsible for their bad actions, and these are not done voluntarily, then the good person is not responsible for their good actions, and these are not done voluntarily.

    P2. But we said earlier that what is good cannot force us to act, and that what is involuntary is painful and causes regret.

    C1. So good actions are done voluntarily.

    C2. Therefore, so are bad actions.

Of course, actions and character traits are not voluntary in the same way. Voluntary actions are under our control from start to finish. But with the development of character traits, it is only at the beginning – in choosing the actions that lead to certain character traits – that they are fully voluntary. After this, we gradually become a certain sort of person, and then we cannot simply choose to be a different sort of person.

> Outline and explain Aristotle's defence of the claim that bad people are morally responsible for their bad actions.

JUSTICE

As discussed in Fairness, individual liberty and rights (p. 229), issues of justice are central to how we treat other people. Because justice often involves the thought that there are constraints on what we may do to others – that there are some things we simply may not do – justice is most naturally explained using deontological ethics. Looking at Aristotle's account of justice provides us both with a point of comparison between Aristotle, Kant and Mill, as well as useful ideas when thinking about applied ethics (p. 321).

In his analyses of most virtues, such as courage or temperance, Aristotle understands what it is to act in the right way, e.g. courageously or temperately, by reflecting on the virtue. In a sense, the virtue defines the act. The courageous act is the act that a courageous person would do. When it comes to justice, exceptionally, the analysis runs more in the opposite direction – the act defines the virtue. Justice, the virtue, is understood as the disposition to do what is just, to act justly and wish for justice. And we can provide a substantial account of what is just without referring back to the character trait of justice. Aristotle's account is largely deontological.

ARISTOTLE, *NICOMACHEAN ETHICS*, BK 5

Aristotle argues that 'justice' has two meanings (§1).

1. In the 'wide' sense of justice, anything legal is just, and anything illegal is unjust. On his account of the law (but perhaps not ours today), the law instructs us to be virtuous (courageous, temperate, good-tempered, etc.) and prohibits us from being vicious. In this wide sense, then, justice is equivalent to virtue, at least in relation to how we treat other people. We shall put this meaning of justice to one side and focus on its narrow sense.
2. In its narrow sense, justice is fairness, and to be unjust is to act 'graspingly' (§2). Justice is concerned with those goods, such as money, safety or happiness, in which we can obtain some advantage relative to other people. To be unjust is to seek to gain more than one's fair share of something good or avoid one's fair share of something bad. Justice is the principle that each person receives their 'due'. There are two kinds of justice as fairness.
    a. Justice in the distribution of what is good and bad (who gets what). Here, justice requires us to treat equals equally (§3). If people are unequal (e.g. what people are due depends on how well they do something), then we should treat their differences proportionally. So people should receive goods according to their merit (however merit is to be identified).
    b. Justice in rectification. Here, some injustice needs to be set right or corrected (§4). The focus, then, is not on the people involved, who are treated as equals, but on the injustice. What is unequal needs to be made equal. For example, if two people have signed a contract, and one breaks the contract by taking more than their share of a profit, justice

will require that the wrongdoer returns the illicit profit and makes some recompense. If one person has injured another, the victim has suffered. Justice in rectification compensates for this suffering and inflicts some form of suffering on the wrongdoer, removing their unjust 'gain' of avoiding suffering.

Justice, then, is intermediate between acting unjustly (having too much) and being unjustly treated (having too little). This virtue, unlike the others, *does* relate to an intermediate 'amount' of something (§5).

> **?**
>
> What is justice, according to Aristotle?

Development

We need to clarify what it is to act unjustly and what it is to be unjustly treated.

Aristotle distinguishes between unjust states of affairs, unjust acts, acting unjustly and being unjust (§8).

1. In an *unjust state of affairs*, there is an unjust distribution – someone has more or less than they should – but this is not the result of anything that anyone has *done*. For example, you may suffer some illness that means that you cannot work for a long time and end up poorer than other people.
2. An *unjust act* is an act which results in injustice (someone has more or less than they should). It is merely unjust, and no more, if the person is acting involuntarily (e.g. they act from ignorance).
3. However, to do an unjust act voluntarily is to *act unjustly*. One acts unjustly, but is not an unjust person, if the unjust act is voluntary but not done by choice. In this case, the person acts with knowledge but has not deliberated. An example would be injuring someone through anger. Such a person is not a bad person, but they do act unjustly.

1) Explain Aristotle's account of the relation between justice and voluntary action. 2) Compare Aristotle and Mill on justice.

4.   However, to do an unjust act by choice is to *be unjust*. In other words, the unjust person knows what they are doing (it is not from ignorance) and has deliberated about what to do (§5.8). This is the worst form of unjust act.

To be unjustly treated, the unjust action must be against your wishes (§9). You cannot be treated unjustly voluntarily – if you agree to the action, you are not unjustly treated. Nor can you treat yourself unjustly – if what you do is voluntary, then even if it harms you, you haven't acted against your wishes, so you haven't acted unjustly against yourself. So, for instance, if you give away a great deal of wealth or you accept more than your share of suffering, you do no injustice to yourself.

Issues for Aristotelian virtue ethics

We compare Aristotle's theory of virtue ethics with other theories in extension material, raising some of these questions there.

There are many issues that we may raise with Aristotle's virtue ethics, and the theory of human nature that underpins it. We can question his analysis of particular virtues. We can question whether he is right about pleasure. We can question whether theoretical reason is the 'highest' thing in us. And much more. However, the specification directs us to four issues, and it is these that we will discuss here.

GUIDANCE ON HOW TO ACT

A first issue is whether Aristotle's virtue ethics can provide us with any helpful guidance on how to act. Utilitarianism offers us the principle of maximising happiness and Kant offers us the test of the Categorical Imperative. What does Aristotle say that can help us decide what to do?

Many philosophers have thought that Aristotle's doctrine of the mean should function in this way. But it isn't much help. First, 'too much' and 'too little' aren't quantities on a single scale. The list of 'right time, right object, right person, right motive, right way' shows that things are much more complicated than that. Second, it gives us no help with understanding, for example, how often we should get angry, and how angry we should get. Just about anything could be 'in the mean' if the circumstances were right!

But it is unlikely that Aristotle intended the doctrine of the mean to be helpful in this way. We can't 'figure out' what it is right to do by applying a rule like the doctrine of the mean; we must have practical wisdom. Aristotle says explicitly that what is in the mean is 'determined by the person of practical wisdom'. And life is complicated; so practical wisdom isn't about applying easy rules either. It's about 'seeing' what to do, which requires virtues of character and lots of experience.

Explain the objection that the doctrine of the mean provides no guidance on how to act.

But then does Aristotle's theory of practical wisdom provide any guidance about what to do? If I have practical wisdom, it seems that I simply know what to do. But if I do not have practical wisdom, what then? Knowing that the right action is what a virtuous person would do doesn't help me, because I don't know what the virtuous person would do! Aristotle seems to admit as much when he says that practical wisdom requires virtue. Without a good character, I cannot understand what is truly good. But this means that knowledge of the good is not within everyone's reach. Either Aristotle's theory provides no guidance to anyone who isn't virtuous, or his theory is wrong because we are all sufficiently rational to understand what is right and wrong.

Explain the objection that Aristotle's virtue ethics provides no guidance to someone who is not already virtuous.

Aristotle argues that this is too simple. In discussing moral responsibility (see Thinking harder: moral responsibility p. 305) and whether bad action can be voluntary (and therefore blameworthy), we saw that knowledge of the good can come in degrees, and that we can improve or destroy our ability to know what is good by the kind of character we develop. If someone has a completely depraved character, perhaps they really don't know what is good or bad. But most people will have enough understanding of the good to make moral decisions. Furthermore, people can improve their knowledge of what is good by becoming more virtuous people.

Annas argues that virtue ethics assumes that each of us already has a life by the time we start to reflect on which action is the right one. This has two implications. First, we already have some general guidance from the culture in which we grew up, but reflection will reveal that our traditional ethical views are inadequate in some way or other. Our desire to do what is right is an expression of our striving to be better people. Second, we are each at different stages in ethical development and have different aims and ideals in life. Reflecting on what to do, therefore, can't be a matter of following an algorithm, like learning to use a computer. There simply cannot be a specification of the 'right action' that is universal, the same for everyone and available to everyone regardless of what they are like as people already.

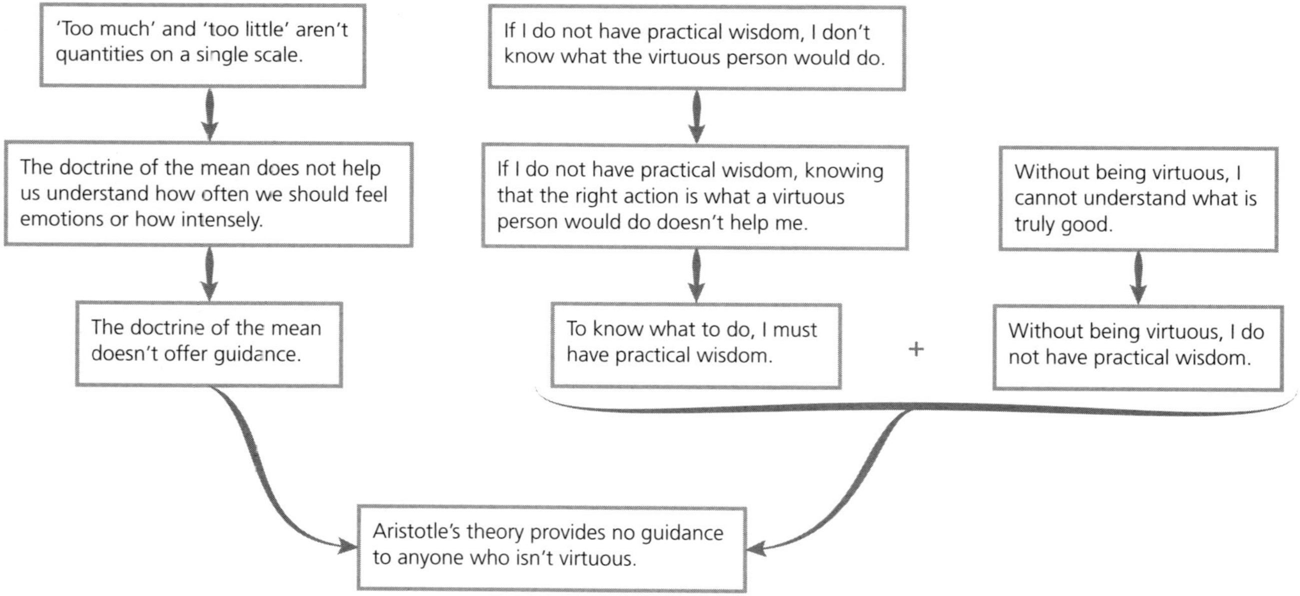

'Too much' and 'too little' aren't quantities on a single scale.
The doctrine of the mean does not help us understand how often we should feel emotions or how intensely.
The doctrine of the mean doesn't offer guidance.
If I do not have practical wisdom, I don't know what the virtuous person would do.
If I do not have practical wisdom, knowing that the right action is what a virtuous person would do doesn't help me.
To know what to do, I must have practical wisdom.
+
Without being virtuous, I cannot understand what is truly good.
Without being virtuous, I do not have practical wisdom.
Aristotle's theory provides no guidance to anyone who isn't virtuous.

Map 3.11 Does Aristotle's virtue ethics offer guidance?

As we saw in THE ROLE OF EDUCATION IN THE DEVELOPMENT OF A MORAL CHARACTER (p. 285), becoming virtuous takes experience and practice. No teacher or book can make you virtuous ('follow these simple rules, and you will achieve eudaimonia').

The objection that virtue ethics can't provide guidance on how to act is thinking of guidance too much in terms of *rules*. Just because practical wisdom is not a set of rules, that doesn't mean it provides no guidance at all. Aristotle's theory suggests we think about situations in terms of the virtues. Rather than ask 'could everyone do this?' (as Kant suggests) or 'what will bring about the best consequences?' (as utilitarianism suggests), we can ask a series of questions: 'would this action be kind/courageous/loyal …?' or again, since I am deciding how I should act, not how anyone should act, 'what would I do if I were more kind/courageous/loyal …?' Thinking about what to do in this way could be very helpful.

> **Can virtue ethics provide guidance when thinking about what to do?**

CONFLICTS BETWEEN VIRTUES

A second issue for Aristotle's virtue ethics regards cases of conflict between virtues. For example, can we show justice and mercy, or do we have to choose? Here, Aristotle's theory is in a similar position to Kant's deontology. Aristotle denies that conflicts between virtues ever take place. You need practical wisdom to understand what each virtue actually requires you to do in this particular situation. With such understanding, you will be able to discover a path of action which satisfies the demands of each virtue that is relevant to the situation. If you think that mercy requires injustice, or that justice demands being merciless, then you have misunderstood what justice or mercy actually mean in this situation. For example, perhaps we are motivated towards mercy in rectifying an injustice when someone appeals to difficult circumstances or ignorance of the effects of what they did. On Aristotle's analysis, such factors are directly relevant to judging the injustice of the act (whether it is unjust, or done unjustly, or done by an unjust person). So they are relevant to what justice in rectification requires of us.

See CONFLICTS BETWEEN DUTIES, p. 261.

One advantage that Aristotle's theory has over Kant's is that Aristotle explicitly rejects the claim that morality involves absolute or universal rules. It is all a matter of context and judgement, and the idea that we are always pursuing the final end of eudaimonia provides a framework in which to make such judgements. Virtues don't make demands of their own accord, but provide us with various means to achieve eudaimonia. All this makes it easier to resolve potential conflicts.

Nevertheless, whether the theory is convincing in all cases can only be judged by looking at possible counterexamples. For example, could loyalty to a friend ever require you to be dishonest?

THE POSSIBILITY OF CIRCULARITY INVOLVED IN DEFINING VIRTUOUS ACTS AND VIRTUOUS PEOPLE IN TERMS OF EACH OTHER

A third issue relates to Aristotle's accounts of virtuous action and the virtuous person. A simple reading, which causes the problem, is this:

Can virtues ever conflict? What implications follow from your answer for Aristotelian virtue ethics?

1. an act is virtuous if it is an act that would be done by a virtuous person in this situation;
2. a virtuous person is a person who is disposed to do virtuous acts.

The difficulty with these definitions is that, taken together, they do nothing to clarify what a virtuous act is or what a virtuous person is. For instance, if we substitute the definition of a virtuous person in (1), we get 'an act is virtuous if it is an act that would be done by a person who is disposed to do virtuous acts in this situation'. The definition is circular, because we have used the term 'virtuous act' to define what a virtuous act is! We get the same problem if we substitute the definition of a virtuous act in (2): 'a virtuous person is a person who is disposed to do acts that would be done by a virtuous person'.

An exception here is justice, which Aristotle defines in terms of the qualities of the act. See Aristotle on JUSTICE, p. 307.

One way to solve the problem is to pay closer attention to Aristotle's definitions. A (fully) virtuous act is indeed an act that a virtuous person does, when they know what they are doing and choose the act for its own sake (see THE ROLE OF EDUCATION IN THE DEVELOPMENT OF A MORAL CHARACTER, p. 285). However, a virtuous person is not simply someone who does virtuous actions. A virtuous person has the virtues, which are traits, including states of character and excellences of reason, that enable them to achieve eudaimonia. States of character relate to our choices and actions, but they are equally concerned with our passions and with what we find pleasure in (VIRTUES AS CHARACTER TRAITS, p. 280). And eudaimonia is defined not in terms of virtuous actions, but in terms of many activities 'of the soul', including feeling, thinking and choosing. So while (1) is correct, (2) is too simple.

Explain the problem of circularity involved in defining virtuous acts and the virtuous person.

We could press the objection a different way. We can't *tell* whether an act is virtuous without knowing whether a virtuous person would do it. And we can't tell whether someone is virtuous without seeing whether they do virtuous acts.

In reply, first, it is true that the criterion for an act being virtuous is that it is an act that a virtuous person would do. But we have a good *idea* of what a virtuous person is without being able to *name* particular individuals as virtuous or not. When considering 'what the virtuous person would do', we need not have any specific virtuous person in mind. So to judge whether an act is virtuous, we don't need to first judge that person *A* is virtuous and then figure out what *A* would do.

Second, it is true that we infer that someone is virtuous from what they do. But again, this is not the only evidence we have. Virtue is also expressed in emotional responses and pleasure, as well as the quality of someone's thinking. So there is no circularity in establishing whether an act or a person is virtuous.

Annas provides a different, and much simpler, line of response. Virtue ethics does provide an account of virtuous action by appealing to what the virtuous person would do. But this shouldn't be understood (as it is in (1) above) as a *definition* of 'virtuous action' that uses some *independent definition* of 'virtuous person'. Instead, as we saw above, the account encourages us to think of what I should do in my situation (virtuous action) in terms of what I would do if I were more virtuous (virtuous person). Instead of thinking of the matter from the 'third person' ('what is the definition?', 'how can we tell a virtuous action?'), we should think of it from the first person ('what should I do?').

> Can Aristotle answer the objection that virtuous actions and the virtuous person are defined circularly?

Thinking harder: virtue and eudaimonia

Aristotle argues that the good life for human beings is eudaimonia. In developing his theory, he doesn't draw a distinction between a life that is *good for me* and a life that is *morally good*. But we do commonly draw a distinction between what is in our self-interest and what is morally required, and many people feel that the two can come into conflict. Morality can require self-sacrifice; sometimes the morally right thing to do – and so the thing that the virtuous person would do – requires me to give up something good for myself, and perhaps even harm myself. For example, giving to charity is important, but how does it contribute to a good life *for me*? Or again, if someone lives under an unjust dictatorship, courage and justice may lead them to stand up for what is right but be imprisoned or killed as a result.

It seems, then, that eudaimonia and the morally good life can come apart. If so, this is an objection to Aristotle's theory. This objection leads to a second. Is his account of virtue, as a trait that contributes to the individual's eudaimonia, correct? Can there be virtues that are not in our self-interest? Christine Swanton provides some potential counterexamples to Aristotle's theory of virtue. A woman works as a medic in a foreign country, ceaselessly saving lives and relieving suffering, often far from civilisation and under difficult circumstances. She is often ill and tired, and doesn't experience joy in her work, just the conviction that it is needed. She dies prematurely from a virus. Her life looks like a morally good life, one which demonstrates many virtues – of kindness, compassion, generosity, perhaps justice – but not one in which she, personally, 'flourishes' or 'lives well'. Another example: A man is dedicated to preserving the environment. He works hard to publicise the dangers of our current way of life, but finds that other people simply won't listen to him. He becomes very stressed and dies, in despair, of a heart attack. His commitment to a good cause looks virtuous and he practices honesty and justice, yet he hasn't flourished.

Swanton argues that we shouldn't require virtues to contribute to the eudaimonia of the person who has them. There are other values (other 'final ends'), including the good of others, the environment, knowledge, art and so on. Virtues are dispositions to respond to and pursue these values in appropriate ways. Because sometimes these values call on us to sacrifice our own well-being, Aristotle is wrong to think virtues are traits that contribute to one's own eudaimonia.

Virtue Ethics, Ch. 4

Explain the objection that Aristotle is wrong to think that a trait must contribute to the individual's eudaimonia in order to be a virtue.

Figure 3.12 More than 120 aid workers died from the Ebola virus while helping others in the outbreak in 2014. Does a morally good life always involve flourishing as an individual?

Annas provides an extended response to these objections, arguing that they misunderstand the concept of eudaimonia. Our contemporary concept of 'self-interest', like 'happiness', is far too narrow. If we read Aristotle as equating eudaimonia and self-interest, then the claim that eudaimonia is our final end is a form of egoism. And philosophers have mistakenly objected that Aristotle makes ethics self-centred, all about the 'best life for me'. But in Aristotle, we don't have an account of what eudaimonia – flourishing – is for human beings *before* considering the virtues. We can't first specify what it would be to live 'a good life for me' and then investigate whether having virtues would enable this life or not. Aristotle's argument is that living in accordance with the virtues gives us the best account of what *counts* as a flourishing life. If someone else claims that eudaimonia involves getting what you want, having money and power, then they haven't agreed with Aristotle about eudaimonia but disagreed about whether the virtues are necessary – they have a different conception of eudaimonia to start with.

To aim at getting what you want without concern for the interests of others is egoism. On Aristotle's virtue-based account of what it is to flourish, aiming at eudaimonia isn't egoism. Someone who aims to live in a fair, generous, courageous, just way isn't self-centred. Having these virtues means being committed to other people's well-being, and having these commitments is part of what it is to flourish. To live this best life, you must treat people in certain, morally good ways. We can illustrate this with friendship. It is a very important part of leading a good, happy life that one has friends. But someone who is a friend just out of self-interest is not a real friend. He will miss out on the good things – the feelings, the character, the state of mind – that come from being a real friend. On the other hand, someone who does not find friendship a beneficial and important part of their life – who is a friend without feeling that they gain from it – is also missing out on what is important in friendship.

Aristotle's theory entails that the flourishing life involves commitments to values beyond one's own interests, narrowly defined. Each person aims at their own flourishing, says Annas, just in the sense that each person *leads their own life*. It makes no sense to think of your eudaimonia as the final end of my life. Eudaimonia isn't a state of person that someone else can bring about, but a quality of the activity of living life. Only you can *live* your life and I can live only my life. But in pursuing (my) eudaimonia, I

Explain how, according to Annas, Aristotle understands the relationship between the good for the individual and the moral good.

1) Must a trait contribute to eudaimonia in order to be a virtue? 2) Is Aristotelian virtue ethics the right way to think about how to live?

needn't privilege my interests above those of others, and being virtuous may well lead one to stand up for what is right when it doesn't 'benefit' oneself in any narrow sense.

Does this answer the objections? We have a general account of Aristotle that answers the questions 'what is good for me?' and 'what is morally good?' together, so that any supposed example of eudaimonia that doesn't involve the virtues simply begs the question. But the counterexamples still retain some force – aren't there virtuous lives that don't involve the person's flourishing? One response is that the unhappy medic and environmentalist both live lives of *integrity*. It would be a mistake to say that their lives would be better for them if they *hadn't* acted on the values that they hold most dear.

But, pressing the objection, surely they still *lose* something good from their lives by living as they do; we still have an idea that their lives could have gone better *for them*. Integrity is not the same as flourishing. Perhaps what Swanton's objection shows is that, given the different things that are good, what is *really* wrong with Aristotle's notion of eudaimonia is that 'the good life for human beings' is not a coherent unitary whole. There is no single, complete final end. Virtues can pull in different directions, and flourishing in one sense may lead to not flourishing in another sense.

Key points: Aristotelian virtue ethics (II)

- The strongest reason to think that pleasure is good is that every creature aims at pleasure for its own sake. However, pleasure is not our only final end, so it is not the only good.
- Pleasure is the unimpeded activity of a faculty. It is not a *separate* psychological state caused by such activity, but part of the activity, a 'completion' and intensification of it.
- A pleasure is good if the activity which produces it is good. The pleasures most suited to human beings are those produced by living in accordance with reason. Therefore, what is truly pleasant is what is pleasant to the virtuous person.

- Theoretical reason is the best activity, the most pleasant and self-sufficient. Therefore, the best life is the life of the philosopher. However, eudaimonia is more generally the life of virtue as well.

- Voluntary action is action that you bring about, in the knowledge of what you are doing. Involuntary action is action that is forced or done from ignorance of what one is doing.

- Actions that are chosen are voluntary actions done on the basis of a decision resulting from deliberation.

- Deliberation is reasoned thought about what we can change. We do not deliberate about ends as ends, but always deliberate about the means to some assumed end.

- Bad people lack full knowledge of what is good. They desire what is not truly desirable, but what they find pleasant. However, they act *in* ignorance not *from* ignorance, because they are morally responsible for becoming bad people through choosing to do bad actions.

- Aristotle normally defines virtuous action in terms of the virtue. Exceptionally, justice is defined in terms of just acts, rather than the other way around. In its wide sense, justice is simply virtue in relation to others. In its narrow sense, justice is fairness in either distribution or rectification. It involves each person receiving their 'due'.

- Aristotle distinguishes between unjust states of affairs (not brought about by anyone's action), unjust acts (that are involuntary), acting unjustly (voluntarily but not by choice) and being an unjust person.

- We can object that Aristotle's doctrine of the mean is of little use in helping us discover what is virtuous, since the mean is not the 'middle' nor the 'average' nor the 'moderate'. Aristotle can reply that the doctrine on its own isn't intended to be practically helpful in this way. Practical wisdom is needed to apply it.

- We can object that Aristotle's virtue ethics generally provides no guidance to anyone who isn't virtuous. Aristotle can argue that virtue comes in degrees, and many people have at least some knowledge of what is good, which they can use to become more virtuous.

- Annas argues that there is no simple specification of the 'right action' for everyone, as we must take account of each person's stage of moral development and ideals in life. Virtue ethics provides guidance not in the form of rules, but as advice to think about what one would do if one were a little more virtuous.

- We can object that virtues can conflict. Aristotle argues that they don't, and if you think they do, you have misunderstood what the virtues require. Practical wisdom is needed to recognise this.
- We can object that Aristotle defines a virtuous act as something a virtuous person does, and a virtuous person as someone who does virtuous acts. This is circular and uninformative. But Aristotle's account of a virtuous person is much richer than simply someone who does virtuous acts. A virtuous person is someone who has the virtues, which are defined in terms of reason, eudaimonia, feeling and thinking, as well as choosing an action.
- To tell whether an act is virtuous, we do not first need to identify a virtuous person and then reflect on what they would do. We have an abstract conception of 'what the virtuous person would do' which we can use.
- Annas argues that virtue ethics doesn't try to provide a definition of 'virtuous action'. Instead, saying that a virtuous action is one that a virtuous person would do is intended to guide our thinking about what to do were we more virtuous.
- We can object that Aristotle's theory of eudaimonia is wrong, because the good life for the individual and the morally good life can come apart. We can also object that virtues need not contribute to the individual's eudaimonia – a virtuous life may, in some cases, be one in which the individual doesn't flourish.
- Annas responds that we don't have an independent conception of eudaimonia, a good life for the individual, before considering the virtues. Aristotle's argument is that a virtuous life helps us understand what counts as a flourishing life.
- We can press the objection to argue that living a virtuous life may still lead to some loss of other things that are good for the individual. Perhaps this shows that eudaimonia is not a single, complete final end.

Summary: normative ethical theories

In this section on normative ethical theories, we have considered three theories:

1. Utilitarianism: the theory that only happiness is good, and the right act (or rule) is that act (or rule) that maximises happiness

2. Kantian deontology: the theory that one should act only on that maxim through which one can, at the same time, will that it be a universal law
3. Aristotelian virtue ethics: the theory that the good life for human beings is eudaimonia, which is the activity of the soul exhibiting the virtues and in accordance with reason.

In our discussion and evaluation of these theories, we have looked at the following issues:

1. What is good? Is only one thing good?
2. What is happiness? Is it pleasure? What is pleasure?
3. Is an action right or wrong depending on its consequences, its motive, or its place in a virtuous life?
4. What is the nature of practical reason? Is it means–end reasoning, a matter of what we can universalise, or insight into particular situations? Can the imperatives of reason be categorical?
5. Does morality require us to be impartial? What is the moral value of personal relationships, such as friendships, and personal integrity?
6. What is justice? What is the relationship between rights, justice and utility?
7. What is it to treat someone as an end in themselves?
8. What is a virtue?
9. Can duties or virtues conflict?
10. Is a virtuous life a happy life? And must a happy life be virtuous?
11. What is it for an action to be voluntary?
12. What guidance can we expect or receive from normative moral theories?

II. Applied ethics

We will consider the relation between METAETHICS AND APPLIED ETHICS on p. 401.

We said that ethical theories are intended to guide us in knowing and doing what is morally right (p. 205). It is therefore very useful to consider theories in relation to practical issues, in order to understand the theories and their implications better. On each of the four issues we will discuss, there is much more to be said, but our primary purpose is to think about how the three theories we have examined – utilitarianism, Kantian deontology and Aristotelian virtue ethics – would deal with them.

We look at how to think about issues in applied ethics philosophically in extension material.

Stealing

To steal is to take someone else's property with no intention of returning it and without their permission (or without the legal right to do so). To own property involves a system of rights. I own my books, for instance. This means that I am free to use them (read them, keep them where I want, etc.), but no one else is free to use them unless I say so. And so because property involves individual rights, whether or not we may steal is a matter of justice, of what each person is 'due'. I am 'owed' what I own, e.g. it should be returned to me if borrowed, and so to deprive me of my property through stealing or refusing to return it looks like a violation of justice. We start from the presumption that stealing is wrong, but arguments might overturn that presumption. What do our three theories say?

See FAIRNESS, INDIVIDUAL LIBERTY AND RIGHTS, p. 229, and JUSTICE, p. 307.

UTILITARIANISM

A simple act utilitarianism does not phrase the rightness or wrongness of an action in terms of justice. If stealing, on some occasion, creates greater happiness than not stealing, then it is morally right on that occasion. Otherwise, it is morally wrong. It may well be that stealing usually leads to more unhappiness in the world, on balance, so it is usually wrong.

But we also recognise that it can be morally permissible to steal in certain situations. For instance, we might say that it is okay to steal in order to save a life or when we are in dire need, and especially if we steal from someone who is wealthy and so won't be significantly harmed by the loss of their property. Or again, we may think that it is okay to steal from the wealthy where property is unjustly distributed, especially if we intend to benefit the poor – a 'Robin Hood' kind of stealing. Furthermore, we may argue that it would be right to steal something that the owner intended to use for harm, e.g. stealing a gun from someone planning a murder. Act utilitarianism can argue that it recognises these intuitions – these are all occasions on which stealing would lead to greater happiness than not doing so.

However, a society in which stealing was permitted whenever it increased happiness could indirectly lead to greater unhappiness. People would become afraid that others will steal from them whenever the thief convinced himself that it would bring about greater happiness. In such a society, people would cease to trust each other, and so overall, the act-utilitarian approach to stealing would diminish happiness.

In his discussion of justice (p. 231), Mill recognises the importance of property rights and the importance of rights to feeling secure. Having and respecting property rights contributes most to happiness in the long term, and Mill comments that justice is the 'most sacred and binding part of all morality'. This suggests that we should never violate someone's rights for some other purpose, e.g. maximising happiness on this occasion, and so we should never steal. But the examples given above, of Robin Hood or stealing in dire need, indicate that such a strict rule is counter-intuitive. There need to be exceptions.

How would rule utilitarianism deal with this? Perhaps there should be no property – perhaps the world would be a happier place if no one owned anything? If so, rule utilitarianism would say that we should have a rule forbidding ownership. However, this isn't relevant to whether *stealing* is morally right. Stealing assumes that there is property – no property, no theft. You can't steal something if it doesn't belong to someone else. If we want to bring about a world without property, stealing is not the way to do so – we will need new laws. Meanwhile, while there is property, people become very upset if it is stolen from them. So we cannot justify stealing by arguing that the world would be better off without property. We can only argue that a world in which stealing is impossible would be happier than a world in which there is property. But if there is property, the rule 'Do not steal' creates more happiness than a rule that allows stealing freely.

Is there a better rule regarding stealing, one that allows exceptions? Like Mill, rule utilitarians look at the long-term consequences, and following a clear, simple rule will probably lead to better consequences overall than trying to build in lots of exceptions. Although the simple rule won't lead to the best consequences in every case, exception clauses may tempt people to think that their situation is 'exceptional' and lead them to steal when they should not – and so a rule with exceptions won't, in practice, lead to the best consequences in every case either, because people won't follow it.

One solution for rule utilitarianism is to keep the simple rule against stealing, but add another, 'general purpose' rule: 'in circumstances in which not doing something will lead to significant and immediate harm, then do that thing even if that means breaking some other rule'. This would allow stealing to prevent significant and immediate harm.

Explain how a utilitarian might justify a case of stealing.

KANTIAN DEONTOLOGY

In CONTRADICTION IN CONCEPTION AND CONTRADICTION IN WILL (p. 255), we discussed the case of stealing as an example of contradiction in conception. We said that the maxim 'To steal something I want if I can't afford it' leads to a contradiction when universalised. If we all took whatever we wanted when we wanted it, the idea of owning things would disappear. There would be no property. But you can't steal something unless it is someone else's property. This is a contradiction in conception, and so stealing is wrong. (As argued above, the objection that a world without property involves no contradiction in conception or will is irrelevant.)

However, does this apply to all stealing? For instance, the maxim 'To steal in order to save a life' would not, if universalised, lead to the end of property, because it is rare that anyone would need to steal for this purpose. However, it is unlikely that Kant would agree with this amendment (see the discussion of Kant's view of lying, p. 340). Our maxim is still 'To steal', and it is this that causes the contradiction in conception, so perhaps the purpose for stealing isn't relevant. Stealing to save a life is still stealing, it is the same *kind of action* as stealing because one wants something.

Actually, this last claim can be challenged. Perhaps the maxim of stealing to save a life is actually 'To save a life, even if by stealing'. Kant's Categorical Imperative obviously allows that we should pursue good ends, such as saving lives; indeed, it is a contradiction in will not to help others (p. 256). But the whole idea of justice and rights is that there are constraints on *how* we pursue good ends. Kant agrees – the duties of justice are more stringent than the duties of virtue (doing good). So we should not steal.

Figure 3.13 Would Kantian deontology allow someone to steal in certain circumstances?

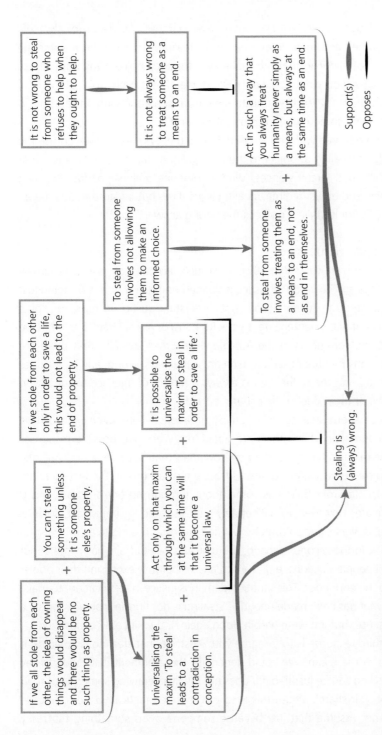

It is not wrong to steal from someone who refuses to help when they ought to help.

It is not always wrong to treat someone as a means to an end.

Act in such a way that you always treat humanity never simply as a means, but always at the same time as an end.

To steal from someone involves not allowing them to make an informed choice.

To steal from someone involves treating them as a means to an end, not as end in themselves.

If we stole from each other only in order to save a life, this would not lead to the end of property.

It is possible to universalise the maxim 'To steal in order to save a life'.

You can't steal something unless it is someone else's property.

Act only on that maxim through which you can at the same time will that it become a universal law.

Stealing is (always) wrong.

If we all stole from each other, the idea of owning things would disappear and there would be no such thing as property.

Universalising the maxim 'To steal' leads to a contradiction in conception.

Support(s)

Opposes

Map 3.12 Is stealing wrong, according to Kantian deontology?

Turning to THE SECOND FORMULATION OF THE CATEGORICAL IMPERATIVE (p. 257), we find another argument that rules out stealing. To steal from someone involves not allowing them to make an informed choice. Why not just ask them to give you what you want? Of course, that is preferable. But what if they refuse? Is it always wrong to steal from someone who, in refusing to help, is doing something that is morally wrong?

If we disagree with the answers Kant's theory gives us, we can use the example of stealing to object to the theory. For instance, we can object that in morally bad circumstances, where someone will die or we live in a repressive and unjust regime, stealing is justified, but because Kant's theory doesn't recognise this, it gives us the wrong answers.

> **Does Kantian deontology prohibit stealing? Do you agree with the answer it gives?**

ARISTOTELIAN VIRTUE ETHICS

As discussed in JUSTICE (p. 307), Aristotle's account of justice is largely deontological. The virtue of justice is defined primarily in terms of doing just actions. Although Aristotle does not understand justice in terms of rights (the concept was invented later by the Romans) or as constraints on what we may do, he comments in the *Nicomachean Ethics*, Bk 2.6, that there are some actions that are never in the mean, but always wrong, and he includes stealing among them. Stealing is always a matter of injustice, of depriving someone of their 'due' or 'fair share'.

What about stealing in an unjust situation, where some people have more than is fair while others are poor? There are two possible responses Aristotle might offer, depending on how the situation came about. Aristotle distinguishes unjust states of affairs from unjust actions. In the first scenario, an unjust state of affairs has come about through no one's action. This is unfortunate. However, to deliberately choose to do an unjust act, such as stealing, is worse, and so can't be justified just by appealing to an unjust state of affairs. In the second scenario, the unjust state of affairs has come about through people's actions, e.g. the rich are deliberately exercising their power to keep the poor poor. This situation demands justice in rectification, to make equal what has been made unequal. Stealing is not normally an act of justice in this sense, but if it were (Robin Hood again?), then it could be justified.

A third response is to disagree with Aristotle that stealing is an act that is never in the mean. We could generalise the argument just made to say that stealing can be justified if it does not involve depriving someone of their 'due' or 'fair share'. When this is so will require practical wisdom, but we should not assume that just because someone owns something that they own it 'fairly'. Or again, we may argue that even if stealing does (appear to) violate justice, it may be justified by appealing to some other virtue, such as kindness in saving someone's life. CONFLICTS BETWEEN VIRTUES (p. 313) must be resolved by practical wisdom.

A final way of thinking about stealing, which is available to rule utilitarianism, Kantian deontology and Aristotelian virtue ethics, is to revisit property rights. Property rights are not 'absolute'. I cannot do *whatever* I want with my books, e.g. I can't start a fire inside a cinema with them, I can't throw them at people, I can't withhold them from the government if I haven't paid my tax, and I can't keep them if they were stolen from someone else. There are limitations to ownership.

How does this help? To steal something from someone, that person must own it, i.e. their property rights over it must be legitimate. If someone steals your phone, you aren't stealing if you take it back without their permission. If, in the tales of Robin Hood, the rich did not own their wealth because they had literally stolen it from the poor, then we could say that Robin Hood didn't steal from the rich at all. He simply returned to the poor what was stolen from them. But perhaps a better description is that the rich did not own their wealth according to *just* laws of ownership, e.g. the taxes that it came from were *clearly* exploitative and so unjust. Robin Hood did steal from them, but if their ownership was unjust, then perhaps his stealing was no violation of justice, and so not wrong.

There remains the question of which theory can best explain this thought.

> Explain how Aristotle's theory of justice may be applied to stealing.

> Is it always wrong to steal?

Eating animals

UTILITARIANISM

Bentham was aware that his identification of happiness – understood as pleasure and the absence of pain – as the only good has some radical implications. As we saw in WHICH BEINGS' HAPPINESS SHOULD WE INCLUDE? (p. 227), one is that animals are morally important. The question of who or what to consider when looking at the consequences of our actions is not 'Can they *reason*? nor, Can they *talk*? but, Can they *suffer*?' We saw that Singer developed the argument to claim that failing to treat animals as equal with human beings when it comes to looking at the consequences of an action for happiness is 'speciesism'.

Does this mean that eating animals is always wrong? Not necessarily. First, there is the question of whether stopping the practices of farming, slaughtering and eating animals would reduce the amount of (animal) suffering in the world more than it would increase (human) suffering. It may seem obvious that it would, but the point must be considered carefully. Second, the utilitarian position only objects to suffering, *not to killing*. Although it can seem very strange to think about it in this way, if you painlessly kill an animal and bring another animal into being, you haven't reduced the total amount of happiness in the world. According to Singer, we need only ensure that animals are happy when they are alive, and slaughtered painlessly. This would make eating meat much more expensive, because animals would have to be kept in much better conditions. Eating meat is only wrong when animals are not treated as well as they could be. The way in which we rear animals for food at present means that eating meat is wrong.

Outline the implications of utilitarianism for whether we should eat meat.

KANTIAN DEONTOLOGY

According to THE CATEGORICAL IMPERATIVE (p. 253), we should act only on maxims that it is possible for everyone to will. 'Everyone' here refers to 'everyone with a rational will'. On this, Kant argues that there is a sharp distinction between human beings and animals. Animals do not have a rational will. They have desires, but to have a will is to be able to stand back from one's desires and reflect on whether or not one's desires are good and whether or not to act on them. And so it seems that *any* maxim that concerns how we treat animals can be universalised. In particular, there is no contradiction, either in conception or in the will, in universalising the maxim to eat meat.

We find the same result when we turn to THE SECOND FORMULATION OF THE CATEGORICAL IMPERATIVE (p. 257). Because of our capacity for practical reason, human beings are ends in themselves. We have a rational will and can adopt ends. This is the only thing that is unconditionally good, and for everything else that is good, its goodness depends upon being adopted by a will. Animals do not have rational wills and are therefore not ends in themselves, and can therefore be treated as means to our ends. We may therefore eat them.

Despite these results, Kant argued that we may *not* treat animals in any way we want. He starts from the idea that we have the duty to others (and to ourselves) to be virtuous. We have a duty to protect and develop our ability to have a good will and to do our duty. He then argues that if we lack kindness towards animals, we may become unkind towards other people –

and this would be morally wrong. Therefore, we need to treat animals in such a way that we don't damage our own abilities to be virtuous. So while we have no duties *to* animals, we do have duties *concerning* animals, but these are indirect duties to ourselves and other people.

Explain Kant's views on how we should treat animals.

We can object that Kant's theory is very counter-intuitive, and fails to account for what is wrong about treating animals badly. Instead of saying that harming an animal is wrong because of the harm done to the *animal*, Kant says it is wrong because of the harm done to *ourselves*.

Second, we can note that babies also aren't rational or autonomous (yet) and neither are some people with severe mental disabilities. Can we treat them as means to an end, or do we have moral duties towards them? We may argue that we do, because babies have the potential to become rational wills, and will do so if cared for. But this argument doesn't work for people with severe mental disabilities – they will never develop a rational will. If we have duties to them, and yet allow these human beings do not have different psychological capacities from certain animals, then to deny those animals similar moral consideration would be speciesist, it seems. Whatever is the basis of our duty of care towards people with severe mental disabilities, we may argue, should equally give us a duty of care towards animals.

Is Kantian deontology right about how we may treat animals?

ARISTOTLE, DIAMOND AND VIRTUE ETHICS

Aristotle's theory suffers a similar flaw to Kant's. Animals have no share in eudaimonia, he argues, because they are incapable of either practical or theoretical reason. Our primary concern with eudaimonia has little place, therefore, for the consideration of animals.

However, more recent virtue theorists have argued that this is mistaken. A different understanding of the relationship between human beings and animals provides arguments for greater concern. There may well be ways of treating animals that are not virtuous. Although she doesn't phrase it in terms of virtue, one philosopher whose approach has much in common with virtue ethics is Cora Diamond.

DIAMOND, 'EATING MEAT AND EATING PEOPLE'

Diamond argues that eating meat is often wrong, but that arguments about speciesism fundamentally misunderstand ethics. If we start from the idea that we must consider the suffering or happiness of animals and human beings equally, we misunderstand what is important in our relationships with both animals and with other human beings. We can see this by looking at some examples.

First, we don't eat our dead. This isn't because we think it will cause them suffering (they're dead!) or because killing them for food would violate their rights (although it would). It is because *a person is not something to eat*. That is not true of animals – many animals are 'things to eat'. It is notable that Singer doesn't dispute this, but doesn't notice its significance. He thinks there is nothing wrong with a vegetarian eating a cow that is accidentally killed by lightning. Second, on the thinking of speciesism (equal concern for happiness of human beings and animals), there is no moral difference between having sex with a person of a different race and having sex with a (consenting) gorilla. Yet that is obviously not how we think about people and animals. An animal is not something to have sex with. The capacities of human beings and animals don't explain why we treat human beings and animals differently. Speciesist arguments are unconvincing because they don't recognise why we do treat people and animals differently.

We don't raise people for meat. We don't number children, but give them names. We celebrate babies being born and people getting married and we give people funerals. We don't do any of this for animals. This isn't because all these practices are in the interests of human beings, but because these practices form part of what it is to recognise a human being as the *kind* of being to be treated with moral concern. Our relations to other people in marking birth, sex and death as serious and important inform the concept of 'human being'. And so does the idea that we owe them moral duties. Moral duties aren't *the result* of the interests of a particular species of animal, *Homo sapiens*. Moral duties partly *constitute* recognising that animal as a human being. It is this recognition, not the thought that we shouldn't make some being suffer, that is the source of moral life as such. If we are to show that eating animals is wrong, we cannot do so by trying to eradicate the difference between human beings and animals that define those very concepts.

So what reason is there to be vegetarian? We must first recognise that there are many different practices in eating animals, and some may be wrong while others are not. For example, rearing your own pigs, looking after them well and killing them humanely for yourself is very different from picking up sliced pork in the supermarket. To state the obvious, the meat industry is an *industry*, with animals reared, slaughtered and shipped around the world on an *industrial* scale, and many of the things that are done to animals in the process are done not because they benefit the animals, but to make the process more efficient.

There are many ways we feel towards animals, and teach children to feel towards animals, that are in conflict with how we treat them in the meat industry. For example, animals feature heavily in nursery rhymes and other stories; we feed birds and squirrels; we stop children from harming pets and respond with horror if they are cruel to them. These emotional responses and behaviours towards animals reflect the idea that we and they are 'fellow creatures', not in the sense that we are biologically similar, but in the sense that we are all 'in the same boat' as living creatures. Like human beings, animals can die, they lead their lives without our knowledge of what they do, they can provide company for us. These thoughts recognise and respect the independent lives that animals have.

Explain what Diamond means by thinking of animals as 'fellow creatures'.

While it is a normal part of thinking of animals as fellow creatures that we eat them, it nevertheless also enjoins us to rear them well or hunt them fairly. But it conflicts strongly with thinking of them as simply part of the production of meat. That way of thinking strips them of respect. We might compare it to thinking of

Figure 3.14 We relate to animals in conflicting ways

human beings as slaves. In both cases, our capacity to treat the other as independent and to respond with pity and fellow-feeling to how their lives are going is diminished. Animals appeal to our sense of morality not by an assertion of equal interest but by appeal to our pity, to not be callous in how we treat our fellow creatures. This appeal does not try to obliterate the difference between people and animals, but recognises how people may respond to animals.

We can see the basis of Diamond's approach in virtue ethics in these last points about pity. Just as ethics is grounded in the 'good life' for human beings, we recognise – through our emotional responses to other animals – that they share with us the capacity for lives that go better or worse. Not to be emotionally responsive to this is to display the vice of callousness; to treat animals purely as a means to our own ends displays selfishness. As Diamond's examples of rearing one's own pigs or hunting them fairly show, killing animals for food may be morally permissible, if it is done for the right reason and in the right way, i.e. with the appropriate feelings. Because that is so often not the case, eating animals is often morally wrong.

> Does virtue ethics provide guidance on whether we should eat animals?

Simulated killing

> This section is informed by the discussion in Garry Young, *Ethics in the Virtual World*.

Simulated killing is the dramatisation of killing within a fictional context, e.g. in video games, films and plays. It is not merely the description of a killing, as in a novel, but a fictional enactment of killing that the audience or gamer can see and hear. There is a difference – possibly a morally significant difference – between witnessing such a killing and playing the role of the killer. So we will first discuss simulated killing in the context of playing the killer in video games and in acting, and then discuss simulated killing in the context of watching films and plays.

We might wonder whether simulated killing should even be a moral concern. No one is actually killed; no act has been done that violates one's moral duty. For example, in a video game, all that actually happens is that pixels change. It's 'just' a game.

There are two responses to this line of thought. Obviously, if simulated killing is wrong, it is not wrong for exactly the same reasons that killing is usually wrong. But, first, we need not be concerned just with what is actually done (the simulation). Morality may take a concern with what is being represented (the killing). Is it morally acceptable to create or participate in any representation? While it has become widely socially acceptable to play violent video games, video games involving rape and paedophilia are banned in the UK. And yet we can say, just as truly, that such games are 'just' games, and no one is actually raped or molested. Our discomfort with saying this shows that simulations are not necessarily morally neutral just because they are simulations. Second, we can be concerned about the *effects* of simulated killing both on the people involved and on how they then treat other people in real life.

PLAYING THE KILLER

Utilitarianism

In playing a video game, no one is actually harmed in simulated killings, so as long as the gamer is enjoying themselves, there is a gain of happiness. However, could engaging in simulated killing increase the risk of harmful behaviour in the real world? Could it lead to an increased risk of

1. killing
2. aggressive behaviour more generally
3. other forms of antisocial behaviour, e.g. gamers being less responsive to others' distress, or
4. changes in gamers' attitudes towards violence in general?

(This last effect, unless such changed attitudes are themselves accompanied by decreased happiness, won't figure in a utilitarian calculus. However, it is something that virtue theorists will be concerned with – see below.)

Some people think, intuitively, that playing violent games *must* involve an increased risk of this kind. But the claim is an empirical one, and our expectations are sometimes contradicted by psychological research. Garry Young argues that the evidence is not clear.

Ethics in the Virtual World, pp. 57–9

Some studies on the *short-term* effects of simulated killing (effects for up to 75 minutes after playing) have indicated that there is an increased risk of aggressive thoughts, emotions and behaviour. However, others found that this increased risk only occurred in people with more violent personalities, while others found that it only occurred in boys, not girls.

There have been very few studies looking at the *long-term* effects of simulated killing. Some reviews of the evidence have concluded that there is an increased risk of aggressive thoughts, emotions and behaviour and a decrease in empathy, but a number of the studies have been challenged as invalid or they found an effect so weak as to be insignificant. There is some evidence that journals are also more likely to publish studies that find a link than studies that don't, so there is a bias in the published evidence. Therefore, the evidence that simulated killing leads to more aggressive behaviour, etc., is unclear, though perhaps we can say that there is an increased risk for *some* people.

As we saw in PROBLEMS WITH CALCULATION (p. 225), act utilitarians don't just consider the actual consequences of an action. They consider the 'tendency' or probability of the action having certain consequences. Rule utilitarians consider the consequences of the rule, in this case allowing simulated killings. The evidence so far is that we cannot say that simulated killing will probably increase actual immoral behaviour.

However, even if simulated killing increased aggressive behaviour, utilitarians would weigh the decrease in happiness that results from such behaviour in the real world against the pleasure derived from playing the game. Simulated killing would only be wrong if, taking both the happiness and unhappiness caused into account, it leads to less happiness on balance than not engaging in simulated killing.

Are we mistaken in trying to apply the utilitarian calculus to the act of simulated killing directly? Mill's alternative is to consider the 'secondary principles' of common morality (p. 226). But common morality doesn't provide an obvious guide here, given that video games of this sort have not been around very long. If we look to other games, such as children's play (cops and robbers, aliens, monsters), simulated killing is widely permitted and considered part of normal development (at least for boys).

Explain the implications of utilitarianism for the morality of simulated killing.

Some people, therefore, might condemn playing violent video games as 'childish' behaviour that adults would be expected to outgrow. But the utilitarian force of such an objection is unclear. Does engaging in childish play decrease happiness? Perhaps an appeal to Mill's distinction between HIGHER AND LOWER PLEASURES (p. 212) adds some weight. Childish pleasures, such as those involved in simulated killing, will not count as higher pleasures for adults. Hence we may think worse of such a person who engages in such activity, but we would not condemn the activity itself.

Kantian deontology

Kantian concerns with simulated killing appeal to the same considerations as Kantian discussions of animals. Playing a game per se is no violation of one's moral duty. But if doing so damages one's rational will or leads to neglecting or violating one's duty to other people, then we can object. We could argue that just as treating animals with cruelty may lead to treating people with cruelty, so cultivating cruelty and an indifference to virtual suffering through simulated killing could undermine our willingness and ability to treat others as ends in themselves in real life. Kant notes that, at the time he was writing, butchers and doctors were not allowed to serve on English juries because they were hardened to suffering and death.

Compare Kantian and utilitarian concerns with the morality of simulated killing.

However, having reviewed the empirical evidence, it seems that there is not enough evidence to say that there is a link between simulated killing and neglecting one's duties to others.

Even if we don't fail in our duties to others, perhaps we somehow fail in our duty to ourselves. We could argue that repeatedly engaging in simulated killing erodes our sense of identity as rational, moral beings. But again, it is unclear whether this is true. *If* it does, then this would be a reason for thinking that it is wrong.

Virtue ethics

A similar concern is central to Aristotelian virtue ethics. As discussed in The role of education in the development of a moral character (p. 285), we become just by doing just acts. Likewise, we become unjust by doing unjust acts. Killing is often an unjust act. So the cumulative effect of playing games which involve simulated killing may lead to the development of character traits that are not virtuous, such as injustice and unkindness, or at least inhibit the development of character traits that are virtuous, such as justice and kindness. Simulated killing is wrong if it prevents the development of virtue, and so prevents the gamer from achieving eudaimonia.

Aristotle may be right that doing unjust acts develops the vice of injustice. But *simulated* killing is not an unjust act – no one is killed. So why think that *simulating* unjust acts will develop injustice? Once again, we can argue that the evidence doesn't support this claim.

Rather than focus on the development of character, we can ask whether a virtuous person would engage in playing video games that involve simulated killing. If so, then they will do so in the right way, with the right motive, and at the right times. What might that involve? For example, why would someone *want* to simulate killing someone else? Is taking pleasure in this activity virtuous?

Clearly, there is pleasure to be gained from violent video games – otherwise, they would not be so popular. But there may be more than one kind of pleasure one can take, and more than one motive for killing someone within the game. The virtuous person enjoys such pleasures appropriately, if there is an appropriate way to enjoy them. There may be morally better and worse ways of relating to simulated killing within the game. Is the point of the game just to kill people, or within the narrative is killing a necessary means to some further goal? Does the gamer enjoy simulated killing as part of doing well in the game (so the motive is competitiveness) or just enjoy simulated killing for its own sake? And so on.

There may also be morally better and worse ways of understanding the relationship between the game and reality. It can be wrong for someone who confuses the two to play the game, but okay for someone who doesn't. As discussed in GUIDANCE ON HOW TO ACT (p. 310), virtue ethics recognises that the right thing to do is not the same for everyone. The 'mean' is relative to each person and relates to each person's stage of moral development. If someone is at all likely to think of the game world as a model for the real world, playing such games is not virtuous for that person. Someone else could experience the rush of adrenalin as a helpful and safe expression of natural human aggression (good), while someone else again may indulge in fantasies of actual killing during play (bad). And so on.

Relating this back to the empirical evidence: someone who draws a clear conceptual *and emotional* distinction between simulated killing and real life may be at no risk of being more aggressive after playing or developing bad character traits. Someone who cannot draw such a distinction may be at risk, and so should not play.

However, these remarks don't settle the question of whether the virtuous person would *want* to play such a game.

Acting the killer

We can develop the points just made in relation to the actors in a film or play. Acting takes place within a context which is governed by a whole set of conventions about what particular actions mean. Arguably, actors don't *imitate* real-life killings, and even in films, which may be more lifelike with special effects, etc., violence is typically unrealistic. Instead, actors pretend to kill (and to die) on the understanding that certain actions are to be understood

1) How can Aristotle's doctrine of the mean be applied to simulated killing? 2) Is it morally acceptable to play the killer in video games?

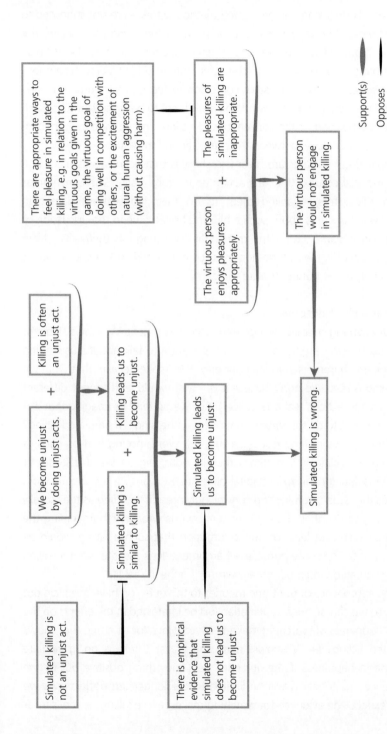

Map 3.13 Simulated killing and virtue

There are appropriate ways to feel pleasure in simulated killing, e.g. in relation to the virtuous goals given in the game, the virtuous goal of doing well in competition with others, or the excitement of natural human aggression (without causing harm).

The pleasures of simulated killing are inappropriate.

The virtuous person enjoys pleasures appropriately.

The virtuous person would not engage in simulated killing.

Killing is often an unjust act.

We become unjust by doing unjust acts.

Killing leads us to become unjust.

Simulated killing is similar to killing.

Simulated killing leads us to become unjust.

Simulated killing is wrong.

Simulated killing is not an unjust act.

There is empirical evidence that simulated killing does not lead us to become unjust.

Support(s)

Opposes

as killings. Furthermore, actors – even method actors – are not supposed to feel *genuine* lethal rage towards their fellow actors during the scene, nor genuine bloodlust and excitement. (Method actors may feel the fictional counterparts of such emotions 'in character', but would not feel such emotions as themselves.) Suppose an actor confessed to feeling real murderous rage after the play or filming. This would be disturbing, to both them and us. Such feelings are not part of the conventions of acting, and indicate a blurring, in the actor's psychology, between the character and the actor.

What these remarks are meant to show is that acting takes place in a complex social context that sets acting apart from reality. The conventions protect the actors, enabling them to do their job without damaging themselves. Concerns about such a blurring are at issue in the discussion of playing video games: does the gamer fail to distinguish themselves from their character? Is their moral goodness compromised by the immorality of their avatar, either during or after the game?

AN AUDIENCE'S PERSPECTIVE

Is there anything morally wrong with watching violent TV shows, films or plays? Such works are fictions, and it is common to talk about 'suspending disbelief' when immersed in a film or play. We 'make-believe' that what we are seeing is real. We don't believe it is – that would lead to very different emotions and actions (call the police!). But we pretend or imagine that it is real. Is it wrong to do this when what one is witnessing is a simulated killing?

Although we haven't discussed this, it is worth noting that on each of our theories, killing is sometimes morally right, e.g. in war (Aristotle) or euthanasia (utilitarianism) or capital punishment (Kant). If a dramatic work explores this issue carefully, and convincingly presents a killing as the morally right thing to do, then it is hard to see what is wrong with imagining the simulated killing (at least on the assumption that such a killing *would* be morally right). So for the purposes of argument, let's assume that the killing that is simulated would be morally wrong if done in real life.

The approaches of our three theories to this question have been laid out above, so we can be brief. A utilitarian will be interested in the effects on the overall happiness of watching make-believe killings (or of a rule that allows simulated killings in TV shows, films and plays). There is no immediate decrease in happiness if the audience gets something positive out of the experience. So concerns will be limited to the longer-term effects. As we might expect, the evidence for watching make-believe killings is very similar to the evidence connecting playing violent video games to aggression in real life. There is some evidence that the link is stronger in some groups of people than others, but overall, we don't have enough evidence to conclude that, in general, watching violence on screen or on the stage is likely to make one a less moral person. Even if there were a link, the risk of diminishing happiness needs to be weighed against the enjoyment gained by watching such works.

Let us take deontological and virtue ethical concerns together. Irrespective of consequences for how one acts, does watching simulated killing damage one's character or good will intrinsically? Immoral simulated killings can take place within two fictional contexts. In one, the killing is represented *as* immoral, the killer as morally or emotionally wretched. The work can be understood as a morality tale – this is how not to be. But the killing can also be represented as moral – the morality *of the work* is different. This is the most problematic case. Is it wrong to imagine that something that is immoral is actually moral?

Kant would argue that it is certainly irrational. What is immoral *cannot* be moral. We can coherently imagine that contingent truths are different. But moral truths are established by a test of what is possible – so they are not contingent, but necessary. But is there anything morally wrong with imagining something impossible?

Again, understanding the relation between the work and moral reality is important. For example, do we think that the author intends the (immoral) values to be moral values only *within* the fiction? Or is the message that we should live according to the values portrayed? On the one hand, there may be something not virtuous about joining with the immoral imagination of the author. On the other hand, one may argue that it can help one understand morality more deeply. But this will only occur if one can keep one's distance from the 'morality' of the dramatisation. A virtuous person will be alive to the moral implications of the story being told, not simply in terms of its effects but in terms of its representation of what a good life is and the place of killing within it. Their make-believe will be coloured by this awareness.

> Explain the different relations between simulated killing and morality within a fictional work.

> What, if anything, is wrong with watching simulated immoral killing?

Telling lies

UTILITARIANISM

A simple act-utilitarian approach to lying would consider whether telling a lie creates greater happiness than telling the truth (or keeping silent). If it does, then it is morally right. If it doesn't, then it is morally wrong.

Mill's brief discussion of lying in *Utilitarianism*, Ch. 2, demonstrates that his version of utilitarianism does not evaluate actions just in terms of immediate or obvious consequences, but places them within a bigger picture. A person's being truthful is of great benefit to people's happiness generally, and our being able to trust what others say is not only the basis of social well-being but also a foundation of civilisation and virtue more generally. Weakening either our tendency to be truthful or other people's trust is, therefore, severely damaging to happiness. To tell a lie just for the sake of convenience is therefore morally wrong.

Explain Mill's position on the morality of lying.

That said, Mill allows that lying is sometimes permissible, e.g. when it is the only way we can withhold information from someone who intends to do harm. We need to carefully consider which situations permit lying by weighing up the conflicting utilities involved. Mill discusses Kant's example of the would-be murderer who asks you where his victim is (p. 260). In this case, the harm done by lying is outweighed by the good done by saving a life, and lying is permissible.

Rule utilitarianism may argue that the rule 'don't lie' will, if everyone followed it, create more happiness than a rule that permitted lying. However, we can object, with Mill, that *never* lying will lead to harm in certain situations. We need a rule that allows for exceptions. It may be very difficult to put such a rule into words, since the situations in which telling the truth will lead to more harm than good are quite varied. We might lie to prevent someone from doing harm to others, or from doing harm to themselves, or because the truth would hurt (e.g. in cases of terminal illness or sexual infidelity), or because the truth would be damaging to some long-term good (e.g. in politics), or … It is hard to know what the right 'rule' for lying should be.

KANTIAN DEONTOLOGY

In THE CATEGORICAL IMPERATIVE (p. 253), we saw that Kant rules out making a false promise as immoral because it involves a contradiction in conception. The same applies to lying in general. If we lie, we are usually following the maxim 'to tell a lie to get what I want'. If everyone told lies when they wanted to, people would stop believing each other. But you can deceive someone with a lie only if they believe you. So the maxim cannot be universalised, and lying is wrong.

Briefly explain why Kant claims that lying is wrong.

We can object, however, that one's maxim may be more specific than lying whenever one wants. For instance, you may adopt the maxim 'to lie when it is necessary to save a life'. Arguably, this can be universalised.

Because in most situations, no lives are at stake, if everyone acted on this maxim, people would still believe each other most of the time. This would mean that in Kant's example of the would-be murderer who asks you where his victim is (p. 260), it would be permissible to lie.

There is a question why Kant didn't simply take this approach when discussing the example. Why does he argue that even in this case, lying to the would-be murderer is morally wrong? Perhaps Kant might reply that if everyone lies when it is necessary to save a life, then the would-be murderer knows this. So they won't believe us when we answer their question about where their victim is hiding. So we can't deceive them. The maxim 'to lie when it is necessary to save a life' isn't universalisable after all.

In fact, in his essay on lying, Kant adds a further argument against lying. We don't know what consequences will follow from our lying. Suppose we lie about the person hiding in our house, saying they ran down the street. Suppose that, unknown to us, they did exactly that. They left their hiding place and ran off. And so our lie sends the murderer straight to where the person is. We would be responsible, Kant claims, for this consequence. If we are tempted to lie because we think the consequences will be better than if we told the truth, it is possible that we are mistaken. We will have failed to do our duty, achieved nothing, and be responsible for the results. It is better to do our duty.

But, we can object, why aren't we similarly responsible if we tell the truth: if we say where the person is hiding, and the murderer finds them there?

What if we turn to THE SECOND FORMULATION OF THE CATEGORICAL IMPERATIVE (p. 257)? To lie to someone is to treat them as a means to our own ends. They are not able to make an informed choice about what to do, but are manipulated in a way that they are unaware of. They can't share in our ends, because we have not been honest about what our ends are. We should not lie even when the other person's ends are immoral, and we are trying to prevent those ends being realised. We should not deceive the other person about our intention to thwart their ends. We must give them the chance to share *our* end of persuading them not to act on *their* immoral ends.

Explain why lying involves treating the other person as a means, not an end in themselves.

What seems to follow from Kant's deontology is that *if everyone were morally good*, then lying would always be wrong. But sometimes we need to protect ourselves (and others) from the wrong actions of others, and lying may be the only means of doing so. If the action someone intends to do would treat me as a means to an end, then we can, by lying, prevent this result. Kant himself recognises this in his *Lectures on Ethics*: 'if I cannot save myself by maintaining silence, then my lie is a weapon of defence'.

Is Kant right that lying is always wrong?

ARISTOTELIAN VIRTUE ETHICS

When Aristotle discusses truthfulness, he opposes being truthful to boasting and mock-modesty (Bk 4.7). So his primary focus is on being truthful about oneself. But he also comments that 'falsehood is *in itself* mean and culpable, and truth noble and worthy of praise'. One way of understanding this is to say that lying is an act, like adultery and murder (Bk 2.6), that has no mean. Lying is already an excess or deficiency in some way, and cannot be virtuous. An alternative interpretation is to say that truth is a final end, something that we should seek not for some further purpose, but for its own sake. This doesn't entail that lying is always wrong. Pleasure is a final end, but we should not always pursue it – there are appropriate and inappropriate ways of doing so. Perhaps the same can be said of truthfulness.

Aristotle is not particularly critical of boastfulness – to lie about what you have or can do, just because you enjoy lying, is contemptible but 'futile rather than bad'. To lie in order to gain or protect one's reputation is not particularly blameworthy, since having a good reputation, in Aristotle's eyes, is good. Someone who lies to gain money, on the other hand, 'is an uglier character'. These remarks indicate that there are better and worse motives for lying.

But they also suggest that lying is never virtuous. We might object, however, that as discussed above, there are occasions and motives that justify lying. Here we can appeal to our discussion of CONFLICTS BETWEEN VIRTUES (p. 313) and Aristotle's theory of practical wisdom. If there are few rules in ethics, it is unlikely that lying is *always* wrong. Instead, we will need practical wisdom to judge when it is justified and when it isn't. If we seek to deceive someone, to do so virtuously, we would need to do so at the right time, with the right motive, about the right truths, and in the right way.

This last point returns us to the point that there are ways of not sharing the truth other than lying. Perhaps the virtuous person will exhaust all the alternatives first before resorting to a lie.

> **?**
> How would a virtue ethicist attempt to justify a lie?

Key points: applied ethics

- To steal is to take someone else's property with no intention of returning it and without their permission.

- Simple act utilitarianism says that it is right to steal on some occasion if stealing will maximise happiness on that occasion. Examples could be stealing to save a life or Robin Hood's stealing from the rich to give to the poor.
- We can object that a society that allowed this would be unhappier than one that prohibited stealing, as people would cease to trust one another.
- Stealing presupposes property. Whether a society without property (where stealing would be impossible) would be happier than one in which there is property (and so stealing is possible) is irrelevant to whether it is morally right to steal, unless stealing is a good way of bringing about a society without property.
- Some rule utilitarians argue that the rule 'Do not steal' will lead to more happiness than a complicated rule that allowed exceptions, as people may apply the exceptions mistakenly. However, the general rule to prevent immediate and significant suffering, even if that breaks a moral rule, could be used to allow stealing in special cases.
- Kant argues that stealing is morally wrong as it leads to a contradiction in conception. We can question whether this depends on the exact maxim, e.g. whether 'To steal in order to save a life' would lead to a contradiction in conception. However, even in these cases, stealing involves treating someone as a means to an end.
- Aristotle claimed that stealing is never 'in the mean' and so it is always wrong. We can use ideas from Aristotle's ethics to argue that this is too strict. For example, if a situation is unjust because it was brought about by people deliberately acting unjustly, then stealing in order to rectify that injustice would not itself be unjust.
- Utilitarians argue that what matters is pain and pleasure, and so who is suffering is irrelevant. To think otherwise is speciesism.
- Utilitarianism claims that whether eating meat is wrong depends on whether it produces more suffering than alternatives. If you bring another animal into existence, killing an animal painlessly won't reduce happiness, so it is permissible.
- Kant argues that animals can be treated as means, as they don't have a rational will. However, we must not treat animals in ways that would lead us to become unvirtuous, and fail in our duties to other people.
- We can object that the harm done to the animal, not ourselves or other people, is what is wrong about harming an animal. We can also object

that some human beings do not have rational wills, and we should treat animals with the same consideration as we treat them.

- While Aristotle does not recognise moral duties to animals, contemporary virtue ethicists argue that how we should treat animals depends on our relationship to them, not just their capacities.
- Diamond argues that our practices – that we get married, name children, give people funerals, and don't eat people – recognise human beings as a kind of being to be treated with moral concern. Speciesist arguments fail to recognise this important difference between human beings and animals.
- Diamond also argues that we recognise animals as 'fellow creatures', beings with independent lives which deserve respect and pity. While our relationship to them as fellow creatures allows that we may eat them, it conflicts with how animals are treated as part of the meat industry.
- Utilitarianism argues that playing the killer in video games, or watching simulated killings in dramatisations, is wrong if it leads to greater unhappiness than happiness, e.g. through effects on behaviour in the real world. Kantian deontology is likewise concerned by the effects of such activities on our doing our duty, and Aristotelian virtue ethics is concerned by the effects on our character traits.
- However, the evidence that there are such adverse effects from either playing such games or watching violent dramatisations is not clear. But some people may be susceptible to them.
- We can distinguish between different types of pleasure and different motives for playing video games involving simulated killing. A virtuous person would only gain pleasure from playing the killer if such pleasure is appropriate and they would only play such games at the right times, in the right way, with the right motive, and for the right reasons, and would correctly understand the relationship between the game and reality.
- A simulated killing may be presented as either moral or immoral within a dramatisation. We may raise concerns about imagining what is immoral as being moral, especially if the fiction indicates that we should adopt its values in the real world.
- Mill argues that lying is rarely justified because trust is so significant for our happiness. However, it can be justified in situations in which it will prevent significant harm.

- Rule utilitarianism is faced with the challenge of specifying exactly which rule concerning lying will maximise happiness.
- Kant argued that the maxim to lie when you want cannot be universalised, and so lying is always wrong. We may object that a more specific maxim may be universalisable, which would allow lying in certain circumstances, e.g. to save a life.
- Kant also argues that we should not lie because we believe it will lead to good consequences. It may not, and then we will have failed in our duty and be responsible for the bad consequences.
- To lie is to treat someone as a means to an end. However, we can argue that it is justifiable if we lie in order to prevent ourselves being treated as a means to an end.
- Remarks by Aristotle indicate that he thinks truth is a final end, and that lying always fails to be virtuous. But we may develop his theory to argue that there are few rules in ethics, and that practical wisdom may judge lying to be appropriate on certain occasions.

Summary: applied ethics

In this section on applied ethics, we have considered the application of three normative ethical theories – utilitarianism, Kantian deontology and Aristotelian virtue ethics – to four practical issues, stealing, eating animals, simulated killing, and telling lies. We have seen how each theory can be used to defend claims about what is right or wrong in particular cases. But we have also seen how the practical implications of each theory can be used as an objection to the theory if its claims about what is right or wrong are counter-intuitive. We have also seen that applying a theory to practical cases is not always straightforward, but can require hard thought and careful judgement.

III. Metaethics

What is metaethics?

NORMATIVE ETHICAL THEORIES (p. 205) provide an account of which actions, motives and character traits are right or good. They are intended to provide guidance on how to live. Metaethics, by contrast, does not do this. It asks about what morality is, philosophically speaking. It asks questions in philosophy of language, philosophy of mind, metaphysics and epistemology.

1. Philosophy of language: what do statements like 'Murder is wrong' or 'Courage is good' mean? Are these statements of fact? Can ethical claims be true or false? Or are they something else, such as expressions of our approval or disapproval of certain actions or character traits?
2. Philosophy of mind: what is it to hold a particular moral view, e.g. that murder is wrong? If 'murder is wrong' states a truth, then moral views are factual beliefs. On the other hand, if 'murder is wrong' expresses a feeling, then moral views are attitudes of approval or disapproval (or something similar). Which theory is correct? One relevant issue is whether holding a moral view is a matter of being motivated to act in certain ways, e.g. not to murder. If it is, what does this imply about the nature of morality?
3. Metaphysics: suppose we think that ethical language states truths. Are these truths objective? Are there moral properties, like being right or wrong, that are part of reality?
4. Epistemology: if there are ethical truths, how do we discover what these truths are? On the other hand, suppose we deny that ethical statements are true or false, arguing that they are expressions of subjective feeling. In that case, is there such a thing as moral reasoning? Can we provide reasons that justify our actions?

?

What is metaethics?

THE ORIGINS OF MORAL PRINCIPLES: REASON, EMOTION/ATTITUDES, OR SOCIETY
One way to begin thinking about these questions is to ask where our views about what is right and wrong, good and bad, come from. Now, of course, in one straightforward sense, our moral principles come from the people we knew when we were children, our parents, teachers and so on. The same is true of a great many of our beliefs and preferences. The origin of my belief that the sun is 93 million miles away from the Earth is my physics teacher at school. The origin of my taste in music is the group of friends I had as a teenager. The origin of my moral principles is my parents. And so on. But this kind of answer only says what the *cause* of my belief is. It is particular, not general, because it only explains my belief. And it is contingent, because something else could have caused my belief. Perhaps my taste in music could have come from my physics teachers and my belief about the distance of the sun from my teenage friends!

Suppose we could generalise from just my beliefs and tastes to where people's beliefs and tastes in general come from. Still, in asking about the origin of our moral principles, we aren't looking for a purely causal, particular or contingent answer – an answer that psychology or sociology might provide. We are interested in the *ultimate* origin of *anyone's* moral principles, and we want a philosophical answer that tells us something about the nature of morality. Just talking about how someone, or even most people, acquire their moral principles doesn't help for two reasons.

First, if I got my belief about the distance of the sun from my physics teacher, where did he get his belief from? If he got it, in turn, from his teacher, we can ask the question again – where did his teacher get his belief from? And so on. This is a regress and uninteresting. Much more interesting, philosophically, is what's the ultimate origin of the belief? How do people arrive at beliefs of this kind in the first place? In this case, it is a set of experiments and calculations conducted by scientists (in ancient Greece, Aristarchus; in modern times, Christiaan Huygens and Giovanni Cassini). We could, if we wanted, repeat these experiments and calculations for ourselves. This tells us that the origin of the belief is in scientific investigation – a much more informative answer than 'my teacher', and one that offers a *justification* of the belief, not only a causal story.

Second, our beliefs about the distance of the sun are objectively true or false, but our tastes in music aren't about truth at all – yet (let's suppose) we acquire both from people we knew in childhood. And while our beliefs about the distance of the sun originate in scientific investigation, the same is not true of our tastes in music! Saying that we also acquired our moral principles from people we knew in childhood is uninformative, because it doesn't distinguish between *different kinds of psychological state*. For instance, it doesn't say whether moral principles are more like beliefs about the distance of the sun or musical tastes or something else again.

In our discussions of metaethics, we will look at theories that defend one of three claims about the origin of moral principles.

Different forms of MORAL REALISM (p. 351) argue that there are moral truths, and we can discover these truths by using *reason*. On some versions, the reasoning is largely empirical, so the origin of moral principles is somewhat similar to the origin of scientific beliefs in rational investigation of the natural world. On other versions of moral realism, we must use rational intuition, so the origin of moral principles is somewhat similar to the origin of mathematical beliefs in a priori reasoning.

The claim that our principles have their origins in *emotions or attitudes* is defended by versions of 'non-cognitivism' (see below), including Emotivism (p. 383) and Prescriptivism (p. 386). On these views, we don't discover moral truths using reason. Our moral principles aren't about truth at all; they are expressions of how we feel and how we want ourselves and other people to act. Our moral principles originate in our emotions and attitudes (even if these emotions and attitudes are influenced by other people's emotions and attitudes).

Moral relativism claims that the origin of moral principles is society (see Mackie's argument from relativity, p. 371). We will discuss this theory only in passing, but it is important to be aware of it. Moral relativism argues that morality originates in how a society regulates the relationships between people. Moral principles are not expressions of how *individuals* feel, because they are essentially social, shared. But neither are they discovered by reason, because there are no truths about which moral principles societies *should* have. There are just the moral principles that societies in fact have. Within any society, moral principles record how that society says people should behave. They are essentially social, arising and evolving in a social context through interaction with how the society itself changes over time.

Briefly explain what it means to say that moral principles originate in reason, in emotion/attitudes, or in society.

THE DISTINCTION BETWEEN COGNITIVISM AND NON-COGNITIVISM

Theories in metaethics fall into two broad families – cognitivism and non-cognitivism. The distinction is now understood by philosophers to depend on whether one thinks that moral judgements express beliefs or not.

Cognitivism claims that ethical language expresses beliefs. Beliefs can be true or false, so ethical claims can be true or false. To believe that murder is wrong is to believe that the sentence 'Murder is wrong' is true. Because (usually) a claim is true because it correctly describes how the world is, cognitivists (usually) also claim that ethical language aims to describe the world.

Non-cognitivism claims that ethical language does not express beliefs, but some other, non-cognitive mental state. And so ethical claims do not try to describe the world and cannot be true or false. Different non-cognitivist theories disagree on exactly what kind of mental state is expressed by moral judgements, but it is usually an attitude or feeling. So 'Murder is wrong' is neither true nor false, but an expression of, say, the speaker's disapproval of murder.

Outline three differences between cognitivism and non-cognitivism.

Mental states and 'direction of fit'

We can understand the difference between a cognitive mental state and a non-cognitive mental state in terms of the idea of 'direction of fit'. A man goes shopping, taking his shopping list with him. When shopping, he uses his list to guide what he puts in his basket. At the end of the shop, what is in his basket should 'fit' his list. If it doesn't, the mistake is with the basket, and the basket should be changed to fit the list. Now suppose that the man is being followed by a store detective. She makes a list of each thing that the man puts in his basket. At the end of the shop, her list should 'fit' his basket. If it doesn't, the mistake is with her list, and the list should be changed to fit the basket.

> Elizabeth Anscombe,
> *Intention*

The shopper's list is a list of what he wants. Desires have a 'world-to-mind' direction of fit. We seek to change the world to fit our desires and thereby satisfy them. They are not true or false, but represent how the world should be. By contrast, the detective's list is a list of what she believes is in the shopper's basket. Beliefs have a 'mind-to-world' direction of fit. We change our beliefs to fit the world, and thereby have true beliefs. They represent how the world is, not how we want it to be.

> Explain the difference between cognitive and non-cognitive mental states in terms of their direction of fit.

So which direction of fit do moral views have? Is the thought 'murder is wrong' a belief about how the world is, or is it like a desire to make the world a place in which there is no murder? Both answers are plausible and both answers face challenges.

Issues

Non-cognitivists argue that moral judgements are, like desires, motivating. Holding the view that murder is wrong involves being motivated not to murder. But, they continue, factual beliefs are not motivating. The sun is 93 million miles from the Earth – so what? Believing that fact inclines me to do nothing in particular at all. Because moral views are motivating, they are not beliefs, but non-cognitive attitudes.

Cognitivists can respond that some beliefs, including moral beliefs, are motivating. Or they can argue that moral beliefs aren't motivating. Instead, caring about what is morally good or right is motivating. It is possible, therefore (but perhaps psychologically very unusual), to believe that murder is wrong and not be motivated to refrain from murdering because one simply doesn't care about morality.

Cognitivism argues that what is right or wrong is something we can be mistaken about. It isn't just 'up to us' whether murder is wrong. People who

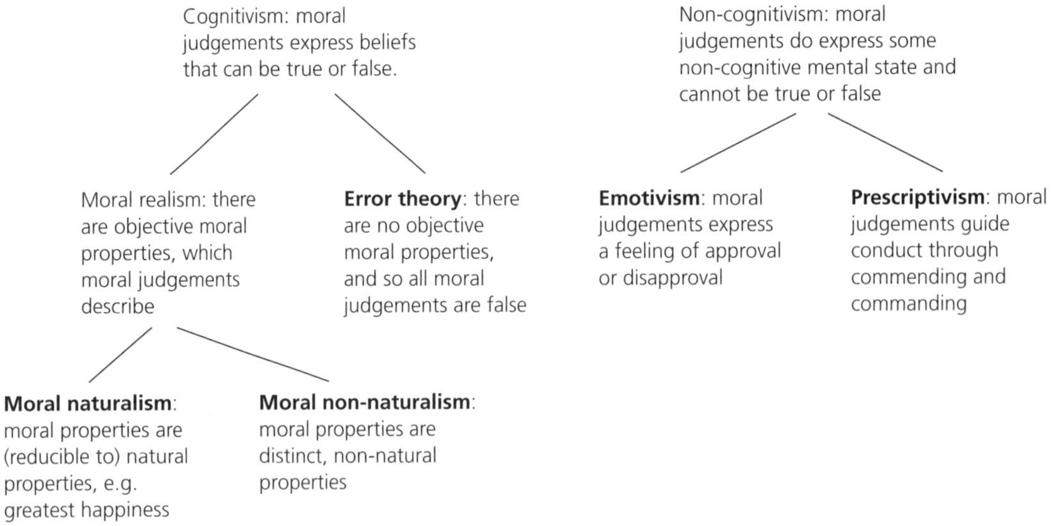

Cognitivism: moral judgements express beliefs that can be true or false.

Non-cognitivism: moral judgements do express some non-cognitive mental state and cannot be true or false

Moral realism: there are objective moral properties, which moral judgements describe

Error theory: there are no objective moral properties, and so all moral judgements are false

Emotivism: moral judgements express a feeling of approval or disapproval

Prescriptivism: moral judgements guide conduct through commending and commanding

Moral naturalism: moral properties are (reducible to) natural properties, e.g. greatest happiness

Moral non-naturalism: moral properties are distinct, non-natural properties

Figure 3.15 An (incomplete) map of metaethical theories

Explain one challenge facing cognitivism and one facing non-cognitivism, first in prose, then as two argument maps.

See RATIONALISM, EMPIRICISM AND INNATISM, p. 114.

think that murder is just fine are mistaken and vicious. Morality isn't simply a matter of taste. Non-cognitivism, therefore, faces the challenge of explaining why we make a distinction between morality and personal taste. Is non-cognitivism going to lead to nihilism about morality, the view that nothing is right and wrong?

Non-cognitivism can argue that it is a simpler theory. It has a simpler metaphysics and a simpler epistemology. Cognitivism needs to explain how moral claims *can* be objectively true or false. Are there moral properties 'in the world'? What kind of property could they be, and how can we find out about them? Issues of rationalism and empiricism arise here.

We will discuss these issues and more, in detail, in the rest of this chapter. We will look at how five different theories handle them (there are many other metaethical theories we won't discuss).

Key points: the distinction between cognitivism and non-cognitivism

- Metaethics studies what morality is. It asks questions about the meaning of ethical language, the nature of moral views, the metaphysics of moral values, and the epistemology of moral judgements.

- In asking about the origins of moral principles, we are seeking an answer that explains the nature of morality and may offer a justification – not just a cause – of our moral beliefs.
- Moral realism holds that our moral principles originate in reason – either in rational intuition or empirical investigation of the world. Emotivism and prescriptivism hold that they originate in emotions and other non-cognitive attitudes. Moral relativism holds that they originate in society.
- Cognitivism claims that moral judgements express beliefs, are true or false, and aim to describe the world. Non-cognitivism claims that moral judgements express non-cognitive attitudes, are not true or false, and do not describe the world.
- Beliefs (and other cognitive states) have mind-to-world direction of fit; we change our beliefs to fit the world. Desires (and other non-cognitive states) have world-to-mind direction of fit; we change the world to satisfy our desires.
- Cognitivists face challenges from explaining moral motivation and the metaphysics and epistemology of objective moral truths. Non-cognitivists face the challenge of avoiding moral nihilism.

A. Moral realism

From cognitivism to moral realism

As we said, cognitivism is the view that ethical language expresses ethical beliefs about how the world is. Cognitivists argue that moral judgements can be true or false, and so aim to describe the world. Furthermore, we can be mistaken about whether a moral judgement is true or false. Our thinking it is true does not make it true.

Here are three quick arguments in favour of cognitivism:

1. We think we can make mistakes about morality. Children frequently do, and have to be taught what is right and wrong. If there were no facts about moral right and wrong, it wouldn't be possible to make mistakes.
2. Morality feels like a demand from 'outside' us. We feel answerable to a standard of behaviour which is independent of what we want or feel. Morality isn't determined by what we think about it.

Outline two reasons for thinking moral cognitivism is true, first in prose, then in an argument map.

A different answer is provided by Kant's account of morality. See THE CATEGORICAL IMPERATIVE, p. 253.

What is moral realism?

3. Many people believe in moral progress. But how is moral progress possible, unless some views about morality are better than others? And how is *that* possible unless there are facts about morality?

But if there are truths about morality, what kind of truths are they? Moral realism claims that good and bad are properties of situations and people, right and wrong are properties of actions. Just as people can be 5 feet tall or run fast, they can be morally good or bad. Just as actions can be done in 10 minutes or done from greed, they can be right or wrong. These moral properties are a genuine part of the world. Whether moral judgements are true or false depends on how the world is, on what properties an action, person or situation actually has.

Moral realism in the last 150 years has focused on trying to clarify the precise nature of the relation between moral properties and natural properties. This has led to two positions: MORAL NATURALISM (p. 354) and MORAL NON-NATURALISM (p. 357). Moral naturalism claims that moral properties are natural properties; moral non-naturalism claims that they are a distinct, non-natural kind of property.

The debate is important because it has significant implications for our understanding of both philosophy and morality. Philosophy, first. Moral claims are not analytically true. That a particular action of killing someone, say, is morally wrong is not something that is true by definition of the concepts involved. So if moral claims are true at all, they must be synthetic propositions. Now, if we think that empiricism is correct, then we could only gain knowledge of moral judgements through empirical investigation, i.e. sense experience and scientific investigation. If that is possible, then moral properties must be natural properties. But is it possible? Could we really learn the difference between right and wrong through sense experience? Could science improve or correct our ethical views? Perhaps this sounds rather odd, and we don't learn about morality in these ways. Then if realism is true, we must gain moral knowledge in some other way, and that would mean that empiricism is false. It would also mean that moral properties are not natural properties, and so then there is more to the world than what can be investigated by science. So the debate between moral naturalism and moral non-naturalism has significant implications for the debate between rationalism and empiricism and for our view of what exists.

The implications for morality go back to the debate between COGNITIVISM AND NON-COGNITIVISM (p. 348). If we can show that moral naturalism is false and

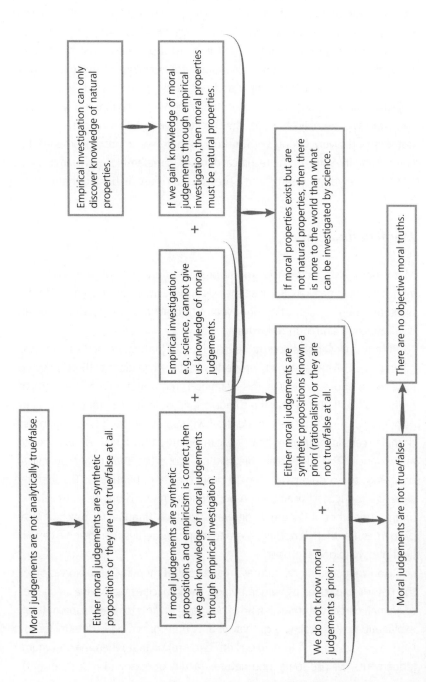

Moral judgements are not analytically true/false.

Either moral judgements are synthetic propositions or they are not true/false at all.

If moral judgements are synthetic propositions and empiricism is correct, then we gain knowledge of moral judgements through empirical investigation.

Empirical investigation, e.g. science, cannot give us knowledge of moral judgements.

Empirical investigation can only discover knowledge of natural properties.

If we gain knowledge of moral judgements through empirical investigation, then moral properties must be natural properties.

If moral properties exist but are not natural properties, then there is more to the world than what can be investigated by science.

Either moral judgements are synthetic propositions known a priori (rationalism) or they are not true/false at all.

We do not know moral judgements a priori.

Moral judgements are not true/false.

There are no objective moral truths.

Map 3.14 A line of thought about epistemology in ethics

that moral non-naturalism is false, then we have shown that moral realism is false. That means that we face the question of whether there are *any objective moral truths*. If morality isn't objective, we may think that has serious implications for how we live our lives. For instance, why bring up children not to steal and not to lie if it is just a subjective matter whether these things are wrong or not? We don't force children to play particular sports – which sports they enjoy and pursue is up to them. If there is no objective morality, shouldn't we do the same with stealing and lying? We can draw similar implications for the criminal law and punishment. If there is nothing objectively wrong with murder, should we imprison someone for committing it? Some of the technical debates in metaethics can seem distant from our everyday concerns, but issues such as these lie behind them.

Moral naturalism

Moral naturalism claims that moral properties are natural properties. But what counts as natural? Because there is disagreement on the answer to the question, there is more than one type of 'moral naturalism', which we can call 'reductive' and 'non-reductive'.

Many philosophers accept the definition of 'natural properties' that was given by G. E. Moore, namely properties that we can identify through sense experience and science. On this definition, moral naturalism is a form of reductionism. It claims that the things in one domain – moral properties of goodness and rightness – are *identical* with some of the things in another domain, certain properties that we can identify through sense experience and science. The most plausible natural properties that might be moral properties are certain psychological properties, e.g. happiness. The identity claim is a reduction because we have 'reduced' moral properties – which we might have thought were a different kind of thing – to psychological properties. I.e. there is *nothing more* to moral properties than being a certain kind of psychological property.

Non-reductive moral naturalism argues that morality is an expression of the natural capacities of human beings, the capacities we have as a species of animal, part of nature. This kind of naturalism wants to reject 'supernatural' explanations of morality, e.g. that what is right or wrong is determined by God (as some theories in religious ethics claim) or that when making moral judgements, we use some 'non-natural' faculty of reason (as Kant thought).

There is a parallel between the metaphysics of reductive moral naturalism and MIND–BRAIN TYPE IDENTITY THEORY (p. 214) in the Metaphysics of Mind.

Moral properties are a kind of natural property, but they can't be reduced to some other kind of property, such as the properties that science investigates.

The difference between reductive and non-reductive moral naturalism may become clearer as we look at examples of each.

UTILITARIANISM AS NATURALISM

UTILITARIANISM (p. 205) claims that the only good is happiness. This can be interpreted as a form of reductive claim. We can interpret this to mean not simply that happiness is the only thing that is good, but that happiness is what goodness is. They are the same property. Happiness is a natural (psychological) property, and therefore, so is goodness. Because happiness is a natural property, so is maximising happiness. Whether an act maximises happiness is a (complex) natural property. According to utilitarianism, an act is right if it maximises happiness. Therefore, rightness is also a natural property. On this interpretation, utilitarianism is a form of reductive moral naturalism.

Bentham appears to understand utilitarianism in these ways. For example, he opens Ch. 1 of *An Introduction to the Principles of Morals and Legislation* by saying that pleasure and pain not only determine what we *ought* to do, they determine what we *shall* do. This is a psychological claim: we are only ever motivated by pleasure and pain. Utilitarianism starts from recognising this natural fact, and builds on it. This is how Moore interprets Bentham as well as MILL'S 'PROOF' OF UTILITARIANISM (p. 220). A brief reminder: Mill argues that happiness is desired. From this, he infers that happiness is good. This only works, says Moore, if Mill thinks that what is good is the same as what is desirable, and that what is desirable is the same as what is desired. So Mill must be thinking that goodness is the natural property of what is desired.

Principia Ethica, §§36–41

In the previous discussion of Mill's proof, we argued that Moore has misinterpreted Mill. Mill takes what people desire (which is a natural property) as *evidence* for what is desirable (good). He does not say that goodness is the same property as being desired. And when he claims that what is good is what is desirable, nothing he says implies that he thinks that 'being desirable' (as opposed to being desired) is a natural psychological property. So we simply can't say whether Mill is a reductive naturalist or not.

However, there is some evidence of reductive naturalism in Mill's claim, at the end of the proof, that 'to think of an object as desirable … and to think of it as pleasant are one and the same thing'. So for something to be good is for it to be desirable, which is the same as being pleasant, which is for it to contribute to happiness. This sounds very much like what Bentham says as well – to say that something is good and to say that something produces happiness is to say the same thing. If the words 'good' and 'happiness' have the same meaning, goodness and happiness are the same property (just like 'bachelor' and 'unmarried man' mean the same and being a bachelor is the same property as being an unmarried man).

Whether or not Bentham and Mill are reductive naturalists, a reductive naturalist interpretation of utilitarianism can argue that it solves some of the issues facing cognitivism. If goodness is just happiness, then there is no puzzle about what kind of thing goodness is. Furthermore, we can discover what creates happiness empirically. So we have an answer to the question about how we find out what is morally right and wrong: through experience. We can explain how morality can be objective in terms of what, objectively, contributes to people's happiness.

It is true that *if* reductive moral naturalism is true, we can discover moral properties through experience. But this fact won't help show that reductive moral naturalism *is* true. Given the different normative ethical theories that exist, claiming that goodness *is* happiness (or any other natural property) is obviously contentious. Such a claim isn't something that we can demonstrate by empirical reasoning – no scientific experiments will show that goodness is, after all, just happiness. So from the psychological facts *alone*, we cannot deduce any moral knowledge. We have to defend the identity claim philosophically.

Explain utilitarianism as a form of reductive moral naturalism.

Thinking harder: naturalism in virtue ethics

Some philosophers have read Aristotle's FUNCTION ARGUMENT (p. 274) as presenting a reduction of the good to the natural, understood in terms of 'function'. The facts about human nature, in particular psychological facts about our desires, our needs and our ability to reason, are the basis for moral truths. There are facts about what our characteristic activity is, there are facts about what traits enable us to perform our characteristic activity well. And so it turns out to be a psychological fact whether a character trait, such as courage or being short-tempered, is good or bad.

Annas rejects this and argues that Aristotelian virtue ethics is a form of non-reductive moral naturalism. Morality is *based on* natural facts about human nature. The sciences of biology, ethology and psychology can help us to identify the patterns of flourishing for each species, and so help us understand what eudaimonia involves for us. Furthermore, it is a *natural* fact about human beings that we are rational animals. Rationality is a natural capacity of human beings, it characterises us as the species of animal that we are. However, virtue ethics can't be *reduced* to claims about natural facts. The rationality involved in practical wisdom is not just a matter of knowing and applying facts that we can discover through sense experience and science. As rational animals, we create and evaluate ways of living, rather than simply live according to a set pattern. We look at the *reasons* for living a particular way. The person who has practical wisdom is not simply able to grasp some psychological fact about a situation that someone without practical wisdom cannot grasp. Instead, they understand the *reasons* for feeling, choosing or acting a certain way in a certain situation. This is why virtue is in accordance with 'right reason'.

For Aristotelian virtue ethics to be a form of reductive moral naturalism, we would have to claim that whether some consideration is a reason or not is itself a natural property.

We discuss reasons and non-reductive naturalism in extension material.

Explain the difference between reductive moral naturalism and non-reductive Aristotelian naturalism.

Moral non-naturalism: Moore's intuitionism

Moral non-naturalism claims that moral properties are not natural properties. We saw above that there are two different understandings of 'natural property'. There are, therefore, different kinds of moral non-naturalism. We will look at just one, Moore's intuitionism. We noted above that Moore understands 'natural property' to mean a property that we can discover through sense experience and the sciences, including psychology. So Moore's theory attacks and rejects *reductive* moral naturalism.

MOORE, *PRINCIPIA ETHICA*, §§6–14

The naturalistic fallacy

Reductive moral naturalism claims that moral properties are identical to natural properties (of the kind that can be discovered by sense experience and science). In *Principia Ethica*, G. E. Moore argued that moral properties are not natural properties. Moral properties may be *correlated* with certain natural properties, but they are not identical. Correlation is not identity. For example, having a heart is correlated with having kidneys – every animal that has a heart has kidneys and vice versa. But hearts and kidneys are not the same thing! Or again, having a size and having a shape are correlated – everything that has a size has a shape and vice versa. But size and shape are distinct properties. So even if goodness is correlated with happiness or pleasure, say, that does not show that they are the same property.

Explain the difference between correlation and identity.

Moore called the attempt to identify goodness with any natural property the *naturalistic fallacy*. To see this, we need to think more about goodness. Goodness, Moore argued, is a simple and unanalysable property. It cannot be defined in terms of anything else (§6). Of course, we can say how people use the term 'good', what they apply it to or again, what has the property of goodness (§8). For instance, it makes perfect sense to say that pleasure is good in this sense (§9). But this is to accept that there are two things here, not one. There is the pleasure, and pleasure has this additional property, goodness. Compare: when we say 'You weigh 60 kilos', we attribute you with the property of weighing 60 kilos. We don't think that you are the *same thing* as that weight – you are a person, not a weight! Likewise, we can meaningfully say that pleasure is good if we distinguish between pleasure and goodness (§12). But we can't give a definition that defines goodness in terms of its parts that together 'make up' goodness (§10).

Colours are similar. We can say what things are yellow, e.g. the sun, ripe lemons, etc., but these things don't define the colour yellow. Yellow is a simple property, and no one can explain what yellow is to someone who doesn't know. You have to see it for yourself to understand what it is (§7). (For instance, we can't define yellow – which is part of our visual experience of the world – in terms of wavelengths of light (§10). It might be correlated with these, such that seeing yellow is always caused by certain wavelengths of light. But it is a mistake to think that they are one and the same thing. Unlike wavelengths of light, colours are conceptually related to vision.)

See LOCKE'S DISTINCTION BETWEEN PRIMARY AND SECONDARY QUALITIES, p. 80.

Unlike colours, goodness is not a natural property (§25). It cannot be investigated by empirical means. It is real, but it is not part of the natural world, the world of science. So, because goodness cannot be analysed in terms of *any* other property, it is a mistake to think that the property of goodness is identical with any *natural* property.

What, according to Moore, is the 'naturalistic fallacy'?

The 'open question' argument

Moore supports his view that a definition of goodness is impossible by the 'open question' argument (§13). An open question is a question to which the answer could be more than one thing, for instance, it could be 'yes' or 'no'. If goodness just is pleasure, say, then it wouldn't make sense to ask 'Is pleasure good?' This would be like asking 'Is pleasure pleasure?' This second question isn't an open question, because the answer *has* to be 'yes'. It cannot, logically, be 'no'. Put another way, we can say that asking 'It is pleasurable, but is it pleasurable?' is a closed question, rather like 'He is a bachelor, but is he an unmarried man?' Now, if goodness is the same thing as pleasure, then 'It is pleasurable, but is it good?' is also a closed question. But, says Moore, this *isn't* a closed question – the answer can logically be 'yes' or 'no'. The same is true of 'Is pleasure good?' And so goodness cannot be pleasure, or any other property. 'Is *x* good?' is always an open question while 'Is *x x*?' is not. And so goodness cannot be defined as any other property.

Explain Moore's open question argument.

Thinking harder: is the 'naturalistic fallacy' a real fallacy?

Moore's open question argument doesn't work. Here is a similar argument. 'The property of being water cannot be any other property in the world, such as the property of being H_2O. If it was then the question "Is water H_2O?" would not make sense – it would be like asking "Is H_2O H_2O?" So water is a simple, unanalysable property'. This is not right, as water *just is* H_2O.

The reason the argument doesn't work is because it confuses concepts and properties. Two different concepts – 'water' and 'H_2O' – can pick out the same property in the world. Before the discovery of hydrogen and oxygen, people knew about water. They had the concept of water, but not the concept of H_2O. So they didn't know that water is H_2O. 'Water is H_2O' is not *analytically* true. However, water and H_2O are one and the same *thing* – the two concepts refer to just one thing in the world. Water is identical to H_2O.

Likewise, the concept 'goodness' is a different concept from 'happiness'. 'Happiness is good' is not an analytic truth. We can accept that Moore has demonstrated this. But perhaps the two concepts refer to exactly the same property in the world, so that goodness is happiness. Moore's open question argument does not show that they are different properties.

Explain the claim that 'goodness' and 'happiness' are two concepts that refer to the same thing.

INTUITIONISM

If moral properties are not natural properties, then how do we discover them? How do we know what is good? In Mill's 'proof' of utilitarianism (p. 220), Mill claims that we cannot prove what is good or not. To prove a claim is to deduce it from some other claim that we have already established. Moore agrees. But unlike Mill, he does not think that we can argue inductively from evidence either. All we can do is consider the truth of the claim, such as 'pleasure is good', itself. Moore calls such claims 'intuitions'.

What does this mean? The claim that some truths can be known by rational 'intuition' is made by rationalism. But what is a moral intuition, and how can we tell if it is true? Moore leaves these questions open: 'when I call such propositions Intuitions, I mean *merely* to assert that they are incapable of proof; I imply nothing whatever as to the manner or origin of our

See Deductive argument, p. 7.

See The intuition and deduction thesis, p. 150.

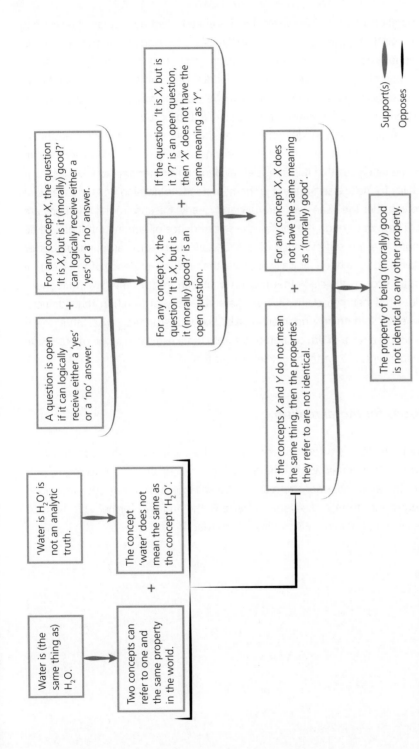

Map 3.15 Moore's open question argument

Water is (the same thing as) H₂O.

'Water is H₂O' is not an analytic truth.

Two concepts can refer to one and the same property in the world.

The concept 'water' does not mean the same as the concept 'H₂O'.

+

A question is open if it can logically receive either a 'yes' or a 'no' answer.

For any concept X, the question 'It is X, but is it (morally) good?' can logically receive either a 'yes' or a 'no' answer.

+

For any concept X, the question 'It is X, but is it (morally) good?' is an open question.

If the question 'It is X, but is it Y?' is an open question, then 'X' does not have the same meaning as 'Y'.

+

For any concept X, X does not have the same meaning as '(morally) good'.

If the concepts X and Y do not mean the same thing, then the properties they refer to are not identical.

+

The property of being (morally) good is not identical to any other property.

Support(s)

Opposes

Principia Ethica,
Preface

cognition of them'. However, he has already said more than this. He has argued that these claims are not analytically true. And he has argued that we cannot know them through empirical investigation. So they must be some variety of synthetic a priori knowledge. He claims that we can know propositions about what is good to be true (or false) by considering the proposition itself. Intuitions are 'self-evident' propositions.

A self-evident judgement rests on the 'evidence' of its own plausibility, which is grasped directly. This doesn't necessarily mean that everyone can immediately see that it is true. 'Self-evident' is not the same as 'obvious'. Our ability to make a self-evident judgement needs to develop first, and we need to consider the issue very carefully and clearly. Because moral intuitions are not known through the senses, the self-evidence of a moral intuition will be more like the self-evidence of a necessary truth, such as mathematics or claims about what is logically possible, than the self-evidence of a perceptual truth, such as the claim that there is a table in front of me. So, intuitionism does not need to claim that we have a faculty of intuition that 'detects' whether something is good or not, a bit like a supernatural sense. Intuitionism is simply a form of ethical non-naturalism that claims that some of our moral judgements are synthetic yet self-evident.

See NECESSARY/
CONTINGENT TRUTH,
p. 116.

We discuss moral intuitions further in extension material.

What is intuitionism?

Issues for moral realism

Moral realism is a form of cognitivism. If we can show that cognitivism is wrong, then it follows that moral realism is wrong. Objections to cognitivism are therefore objections to realism. We will look at four objections to moral cognitivism from A. J. Ayer and David Hume and two further objections to realism (but not cognitivism) from John Mackie.

A. J. AYER'S VERIFICATION PRINCIPLE

AYER, *LANGUAGE, TRUTH AND LOGIC*, CHS 1, 6; *THE CENTRAL QUESTIONS OF PHILOSOPHY*, PP. 22–7

In the 1930s, a school of philosophy arose called logical positivism, concerned with the foundations of knowledge. It developed a criterion for when a statement is meaningful, called the principle of verifiability, also known as the verification principle. On A. J. Ayer's version, the verification principle says that a statement only has meaning if it is either analytic or empirically verifiable. He explains and defends the principle in *Language, Truth and Logic*, Ch. 1, and discusses it further in *The Central Questions of Philosophy*, pp. 22–7.

A statement is analytic if it is true or false in virtue of the meanings of the words. For example, 'Bachelors are unmarried' is analytic and true; 'Squares have three sides' is analytic and false. A statement is empirically verifiable if empirical evidence would go towards establishing that the statement is true or false. For example, if I say 'The moon is made of green cheese', we can check this by scientific investigation. If I say 'The universe has 600 trillion planets', we can't check this by scientific investigation in practice, but we can do so *in principle*. We know how to show whether it is true or false, so it is 'verifiable' even though we can't actually verify it. Furthermore, we don't need to be able to *prove* that an empirical claim is true or false. For empirical verification, it is enough for empirical evidence to raise or reduce the probability that a statement is true.

The principle can be understood as a development of HUME'S FORK (p. 152). However, while Hume's 'fork' provides an account of what we can *know*, the verification principle is an account of what statements have *meaning*. But the verification principle defines meaning in terms of *how we can know* whether a statement is true or false. Unless there is some way of showing, at least in principle, that a statement is true or false, then it doesn't really say anything, it doesn't make a meaningful claim. The verification principle claims that the only alternative to knowing something analytically is to use empirical experience. So like Hume's fork, it defends a form of empiricism.

See ANALYTIC/SYNTHETIC PROPOSITIONS, p. 115.

What is the verification principle?

In Ch. 6, Ayer applies the principle to ethical language. Moral judgements, such 'murder is wrong' or 'pleasure is good', are not analytically true. This seems clear. But, he argues, empirical investigation can't show them to be true (or false) either. He agrees with Moore that 'X is wrong' cannot mean 'X would cause unhappiness' (or any other proposition substituting a natural property for 'wrong'). The open question argument shows that it is never a contradiction to say 'X would cause unhappiness, but it is right to do it nonetheless.' So Ayer agrees that ethical naturalism is wrong. We can show that murder causes grief and pain, or that it is often done out of anger. But we cannot demonstrate, in the same way, that it is wrong. We can show that people pursue pleasure, but we can't show that it is good. And so we can't use empirical experience to discover what is right or wrong.

As a non-naturalist, of course, Moore believed that moral judgements are about non-natural properties. While they are neither analytic nor empirically verifiable, they are nevertheless true or false. Ayer rejects this, and argues that Moore's intuitionism is unsatisfactory. We can't establish the truth or falsity of a moral claim by appealing to intuition unless we are able to provide some criterion for deciding between conflicting intuitions. Given the verification principle, only an empirical criterion will do. But there is no empirical test that will establish which intuition is correct and which is incorrect. (If there were, then moral properties would be natural properties again.) And so, Ayer concludes, moral judgements don't state truths or falsehoods at all and are therefore not genuinely meaningful.

Explain Ayer's rejection of both moral naturalism and non-naturalism, first in prose then as an argument map.

We look at Ayer's non-cognitivist theory of how moral language functions in Emotivism, p. 383.

Discussion

As the last sentence shows, Ayer's objection is to cognitivism. Moral realism fails because it assumes that cognitivism is true. The objection depends on the verification principle. But the principle faces a famous objection. According to the verification principle, the principle itself is meaningless. The claim that 'a statement only has meaning if it is analytic or can be verified empirically' is not analytic and cannot be verified empirically. But if the principle of verification is meaningless, then what it claims cannot be true.

So if the principle is true, it is meaningless, and so not true. Obviously, if it is false, it is false. Either way it is not true. Therefore, it does not give us any reason to believe that ethical language is meaningless.

Ayer claims that the principle is intended as *a definition*, not an empirical hypothesis about meaning. In other words, it is intended to reflect and clarify our understanding of 'meaningful' uses of words. Ayer accepts that the principle isn't obviously an accurate criterion of 'literal meaning', but that is why he provides arguments in specific cases, such as ethical language, which support it.

But in that case, the verification principle is only as convincing as the arguments that are intended to show that it is the right definition of 'meaningful'. If we do not find the arguments convincing, the principle provides no independent support. Ayer accepts Moore's rejection of naturalism. This still leaves Ayer's challenge to Moore's intuitionism hanging: can intuitionism provide an account of how we can decide between conflicting intuitions?

Explain the objection that the verification principle cannot be the right account of meaning because it is self-defeating.

THE ARGUMENT FROM HUME'S FORK

Hume presents three objections to cognitivism, and so to moral realism. All three objections appear in the first section of the first part of the third book of his *Treatise of Human Nature*. The first argument we will look at is based on HUME'S FORK (p. 152).

We discuss a further argument from Hume against moral realism in extension material.

HUME, *TREATISE OF HUMAN NATURE*, BK 3, PT 1, §1

A brief reminder: Hume's fork is the claim that we can have knowledge of just two sorts of claim: relations of ideas or matters of fact. Relations of ideas can be discovered just by thinking, by recognising the truth of an analytic proposition or by deductive reasoning. To deny a relation of ideas is to contradict oneself. Matters of fact are claims about what exists, and they are established by sense experience and causal inference.

We should add that Hume understands the faculty of knowledge as 'reason'. So because there are just two types of knowledge, reason makes just two types of judgement – judgements about relations of ideas and judgements about matters of fact. With this in place, Hume presents the following argument:

P1. There are only two types of judgements of reason, relations of ideas and matters of fact.

P2. Moral judgements are not relations of ideas.

P3. Moral judgements are not matters of fact.

C1. Therefore, moral judgements are not judgements of reason.

This raises an issue for cognitivism. If moral judgements are not judgements of reason, then according to Hume's fork, we cannot have any knowledge of them. This is because, Hume goes on to argue, moral judgements are neither true nor false, but function in some other way (non-cognitivism).

Should we accept the argument? The arguments for, and against, (P1) were discussed at length at in the debate over THE INTUITION AND DEDUCTION THESIS (p. 150). If the claim is true, then empiricism about knowledge is true.

What of (P2)? Hume presents two arguments for this. First, relations of ideas are supposed to be certain – to deny them is a self-contradiction. But moral claims aren't conceptual truths, like 'black is the opposite of white', or truths of logic or mathematics, like 3 × 5 = 30/2. So what relations of ideas are moral claims supposed to be? Second, there is no relation of ideas that applies just to morality. Any relation that describes moral or immoral actions also applies to physical objects, but these aren't moral or immoral. Take murder, for example, which involves one thing killing another. A plant can kill another plant. There is nothing in the idea of 'killing' that gives us moral wrongness.

We can object that murder is not simply killing. It is wilful, premeditated killing. But, Hume responds, this just means that the action has a different *cause*. But the relation between cause and effect, that one thing brings about the death of another, which we describe as 'killing' remains the same. That some event has a particular cause is a matter of fact, not a relation of ideas. It is up to the person who wants to claim that moral judgements are relations of ideas to show what relations of ideas they are, and how they are unique to morality.

How about (P3)? If we claim that moral judgements are a matter of fact, we must identify *which* fact. But, Hume says,

> Take any action that is agreed to be vicious—willful murder, for instance. Examine it in all lights, and see if you can find the matter of fact ... that you call 'vice'. However you look at it, all you'll find are certain passions, motives, volitions, and thoughts; those are the only matters of fact in the case. The vice entirely escapes you as long as you focus on the object ...

Let's allow that the death was caused by an act of will. How is that the fact that it is wrong? We cannot, through empirical investigation, find the property of 'moral wrongness'. The judgement that murder is wrong doesn't state an empirical fact.

The conclusion of Hume's argument follows from his premises, i.e. the argument is valid. So if Hume successfully defends each premise, (P1), (P2) and (P3), then he has shown that moral judgements are not judgements of reason, i.e. they are neither true nor false and so cognitivism – and therefore moral realism – is false.

Explain the objection to moral cognitivism based on Hume's fork.

Discussion

To answer the objection, the moral realist needs to either deny Hume's fork or meet Hume's challenge of identifying some relation of ideas or some matter of fact that constitutes moral judgement. Moore, of course, will deny Hume's fork. Moral intuitions are not relations of ideas in Hume's sense because they are not analytic truths. They are synthetic propositions that are self-evident and so aren't established the way that other, empirical matters of fact are. But as with the objection from Ayer's verification principle, Hume's objection puts pressure on intuitionists to say more about how this is possible.

Reductive naturalists will argue that moral judgements are matters of fact. However, it will take philosophical reasoning to show *which* matters of fact they are. We can understand MILL'S 'PROOF' OF UTILITARIANISM (p. 220) in this way – he gives us reasons to accept the empirical evidence of what people want as evidence for what is good.

Although it is not directly relevant to moral realism, we can also find an account of moral judgements as a relation of ideas in Kant's moral theory.

Explain one theory that claims that moral judgements are judgements of reason as a response to the challenge from Hume's fork to moral realism.

We could argue that whether a maxim is universalisable or not is a relation of ideas, established by the test of contradiction. This was not a relation that Hume considered.

HUME'S ARGUMENT FROM MOTIVATION

HUME, *TREATISE OF HUMAN NATURE*, BK 3, PT 1, §1

A second argument that Hume presents against cognitivism, and therefore moral realism, is this:

P1. Moral judgements can motivate actions.
P2. Reason cannot motivate action.
C1. Therefore, moral judgements are not judgements of reason.

Again, cognitivism claims that moral judgements express beliefs, which can be true or false. And the faculty of judging what is true or false is reason. Hence, Hume's conclusion is a rejection of cognitivism.

Hume assumes (P1) to be true. His argument for (P2) depends on his fork. Neither relations of ideas nor matters of fact are motivating. Hume argues earlier in the *Treatise* that we are always motivated by our emotions and desires. But, he claims, emotions and desires are not psychological states that can be true or false. As we can say now, they have a world-to-mind 'direction of fit'. They don't show us how the world is, they motivate us to act on it, to change it. By contrast, judgements of relations of ideas and matters of fact have a mind-to-world direction of fit. A psychological state that simply presents a truth can't motivate us to act, because there is no pressure to change the world to fit the mind. Simply understanding that some relation holds between two ideas doesn't entail that we should act one way rather than another. Knowing that 3 × 5 = 30/2 doesn't motivate us one way or another. And knowing facts about the world might well tell us what exists, and how to achieve what we want. Knowing such things might *direct* our existing desires in one way or another. But how could it

Treatise of Human Nature, Bk 2, Pt 3, §3

See MENTAL STATES AND 'DIRECTION OF FIT', p. 349.

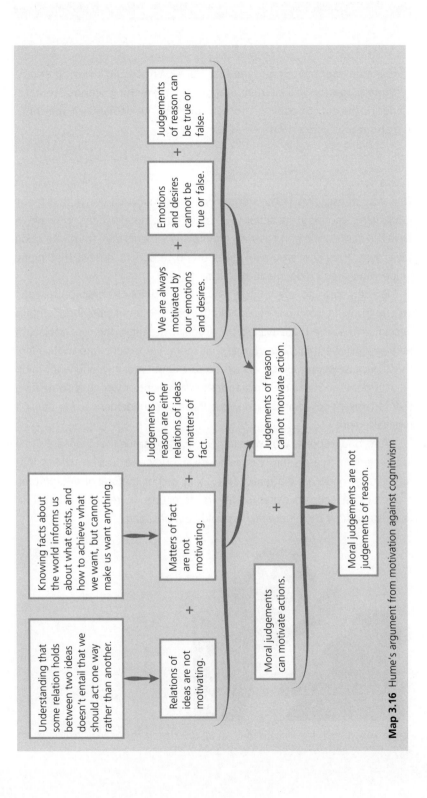

Map 3.16 Hume's argument from motivation against cognitivism

Understanding that some relation holds between two ideas doesn't entail that we should act one way rather than another.

Knowing facts about the world informs us about what exists, and how to achieve what we want, but cannot make us want anything.

Relations of ideas are not motivating.

Matters of fact are not motivating.

+

Judgements of reason are either relations of ideas or matters of fact.

We are always motivated by our emotions and desires.

+

Emotions and desires cannot be true or false.

+

Judgements of reason can be true or false.

Judgements of reason cannot motivate action.

Moral judgements can motivate actions.

+

Moral judgements are not judgements of reason.

Explain Hume's argument from motivation against cognitivism.

make us want anything in the first place? What could knowing that there is food in the kitchen lead me to do anything without some desire (to eat, to cook …) to act upon? So judgements of reason cannot motivate action.

Discussion

One way of escaping Hume's argument is to claim that (P1) – that moral judgements can motivate actions – is false. To do good actions, we have to have the *desire* to be good as well. If moral judgements *don't* motivate us on their own, then this argument gives us no reason to believe that moral judgements aren't judgements of reason.

On this view, to say 'Murder is wrong' is simply to describe murder. Strictly speaking, someone could hold this belief, but not care about what is wrong, and so be quite willing to murder if it suited them (a sociopath perhaps?). If we think, like Hume, that moral judgements are motivating, this is because people almost always *do* care about morality, and want to do what is right. So making claims about what is right or wrong is something that is relevant to what they do. But the moral judgement alone doesn't motivate them.

Can a moral realist defend the view that moral judgements are motivating?

A second response would be to deny (P2) and argue that there are some judgements of reason that can motivate us. However, realism claims that moral judgements are matters of fact – they ascribe (natural or non-natural) properties to actions, states of affairs or people. It remains difficult to understand how such judgements could be motivating.

Figure 3.16 Is simply knowing that they are about to hurt someone enough on its own to motivate anyone, at least a little, not to do it?

HUME'S IS–OUGHT GAP

HUME, *TREATISE OF HUMAN NATURE*, BK 3, PT 1, §1

Hume concludes §1 by drawing a famous distinction between sentences that talk about what *is* the case (judgements of reason) and moral judgements, which talk about what *ought* to be the case. What is the relation between what is and what ought to be? How, for instance, do we get from the fact that some action will cause pain to the claim that we ought not to do it? What's the connection? '[T]his "ought" (or "ought not") expresses some *new* relation or affirmation, it needs to be pointed out and explained; and a reason should be given for how this new relation can be—inconceivably!—a deduction from others that are entirely different from it'.

How is this an objection to cognitivism? Hume is commenting on how moral arguments work. Suppose I say 'Eating meat causes animal suffering. Therefore, you shouldn't eat meat'. According to cognitivism, the conclusion states a truth, and this truth is inferred from the premise. But how is this a rational inference, Hume asks? The premise tells me how the world is; the conclusion tells me how the world ought to be. But I can't infer one from the other. There is a 'gap' between what is and what ought to be, so that we can't reason from one to the other. If moral judgements were true or false, we *would* be able to infer them from other truth claims, such as matters of fact. But we can't. This is a reason to think that moral judgements don't make truth claims, and so cognitivism is false.

Explain Hume's claim that there is a 'gap' between ought and is.

We discuss further responses to Hume's objections from non-reductive naturalism in extension material.

MACKIE'S ARGUMENT FROM RELATIVITY

(We are concerned here only with the argument from relativity as an objection to moral realism. We discuss moral relativism, the distinct metaethical theory, in extension material.)

So far, we have looked at arguments that attack realism by attacking cognitivism. John Mackie presents two arguments that attack realism but without arguing that moral judgements are non-cognitive. What Mackie aims to show is that there cannot be any objective moral truths or objective moral properties. Realism, of course, claims that there are. And so Mackie's arguments lead to a rejection of moral realism. His first argument is from relativity.

MACKIE, *ETHICS: INVENTING RIGHT AND WRONG,* CH. 1, §8

Mackie starts from the common observation that, as a matter of fact, moral codes differ from one society to the next; i.e. there is relativity of morality to societies. According to one society, slavery is permissible under certain conditions, while according to another, it is never permissible; or again, female circumcision is right v. it is wrong; or all people should be treated as equals v. people should be treated according to their caste. This claim, which we may call 'descriptive relativism', is a factual one, and one that certainly seems correct.

We can use this fact, Mackie argues, to show that there are no *objective* moral truths, but the argument is indirect. The mere fact that there is moral disagreement between societies doesn't by itself show that moral realism is wrong. Societies have also disagreed on empirical matters of fact; e.g. some have thought that the Earth is flat, others that it is round, or again, that some people can magically move objects by thought v. there is no magic, and so on. Even scientific theories have disagreed, e.g. Newtonian ideas of space, time and motion v. Einstein's theory of relativity. But in all these cases, we should be happy to say that there are objective truths, and some people just made mistakes. So disagreement over a claim doesn't show that there is no objective truth. So the mere fact that societies have disagreed over morality still leaves open the possibility that there are objective moral truths but some societies have held mistaken beliefs about what is morally good and right.

The argument against moral realism comes when we consider how we should understand and explain the moral disagreements between societies. The realist must argue that different societies, with their different ethical values and practices are all trying to get at the truth about ethics. The relativist argues that this is implausible, and we should understand the morality of a society as a reflection of its way of life.

With scientific disagreements, the best explanation is that different societies don't have sufficient evidence to discover the truth. It is perfectly plausible to think that there is just one way the

Explain why moral disagreement on its own doesn't disprove moral realism.

world is, empirically speaking, but it is not always easy to discover how that is. Our empirical beliefs are caused by, and change in response to, discoveries of what is true about the world. In contrast, says Mackie, the idea that two societies which disagree are both trying to find 'the truth' about ethics doesn't sit well with an understanding of the history of societies and how ethical practices develop. It is far more plausible to say that different ways of life have given rise to different moral beliefs than to argue that societies' different moral beliefs result from very inadequate or badly distorted perceptions of the one moral reality. There are different ways that human beings live, and they have developed different conventions about how to live, and these conventions are reflected in their moral judgements.

Mackie goes on to note that the realist can respond that there are *general ethical principles* that different societies share. For example, most societies have prohibitions on killing, lying and theft, and encourage care of the weak. If disagreement supports the view that there is no objective moral truth, then agreement supports the view that there is. Different ethical practices reflect the different particular conditions in which different societies are situated, but not different ethical principles. This explains why societies disagree and recognises how and why different ethical practices develop without giving up on moral realism.

Mackie argues that this response to the argument from relativity is weak. At best, it shows only that the fundamental principles of morality are objective. Other moral judgements are relative to particular circumstances, so a judgement that, say, 'stealing is wrong' is true in some societies but could be false in others. Although this is the kind of thing that utilitarianism might defend, it does not reflect how most people understand morality. People hold their moral judgements not on the basis of general principles, but because something about the act arouses their disapproval. They have an 'intuition' that it is wrong. *Which* acts arouse people's disapproval differs from one society to another, so we cannot argue that these moral judgements are objective.

Explain the objection to moral realism from moral relativity, first in prose, then as an argument map.

Discussion

There are several responses that the moral realist can make to Mackie's last argument, that the response from realism to the argument from relativity is weak.

One response is to say that moral realism isn't trying to describe how most people think about morality, it is trying to give the correct metaethical theory. For example, if utilitarianism is the correct normative ethical theory, then perhaps it is simply true that the only objective moral fact is given by the principle of utility, because there are just two moral properties: good, which is happiness, and right, which is maximising happiness. Nothing that Mackie has said shows otherwise.

On this point, we should note that Moore would say exactly this. When Moore talks about moral intuitions (p. 360), he doesn't mean people's gut reactions, as Mackie seems to think. He means rational, self-evident propositions. Although we didn't discuss it, Moore went on to argue that we can only have intuitions in this sense about fundamental moral principles, and that our intuitions support utilitarianism! If Mackie is trying to attack intuitionism, he completely misunderstands it here.

A second response is to object to Mackie's claim that any moral judgements that are relative to the circumstances of a society are not objective. This misunderstands the nature of moral reality, we could say – as well as the nature of truth. For example, some plants grow in hot countries but not in cold countries. So 'Chilli plants will grow well' is a relative truth – it is true in one country but not another. But this doesn't make it any less *objective*. Whether a chilli plant will grow well in the country you are in is a mind-independent fact. We can even turn the relative truth into a universal truth by stating the conditions that apply, e.g. 'Chilli plants will grow well in hot countries'. Moral realists can say the same about moral judgements. Some ethical practices will be permissible in some circumstances but not in others. Whether a moral judgement is true will depend on whether the practice is actually morally right or wrong in those circumstances. If someone's 'intuition' is that 'stealing is wrong' and they live in conditions in which stealing is wrong, then their intuition is objectively true. One person can think 'Chilli plants grow well' and another, living in different conditions, can think 'Chilli plants don't grow well', and they can both be objectively correct, given the conditions they live in. So two people, living in different conditions, can have conflicting intuitions about stealing and both be objectively correct, given the conditions they live under. They only make a mistake if they think 'stealing is always wrong, in every society' (and this is not true). And 'Stealing is wrong under conditions *C*' (if we can spell out the conditions) is not a relative truth at all, but a universal one.

MACKIE'S ARGUMENTS FROM QUEERNESS

Mackie presents a second argument against moral realism, which he calls an argument from 'queerness'. The oddity of moral properties and how we would know about them if they exist makes it implausible to think that there are any moral properties. The argument has two aspects, metaphysical and epistemological.

Does Mackie's argument from relativity show that moral realism is false?

MACKIE, *ETHICS: INVENTING RIGHT AND WRONG*, CH. 1, §9

Metaphysical queerness

If there were moral properties, Mackie argues, they would have to be very different from anything else in the universe. His argument for this claim rests on the connection between morality and motivation. Moral judgements motivate us – we avoid actions we believe are wrong and try to do actions that are right. But that means, if there were moral properties, simply *knowing* what is good or bad, right or wrong, would be enough to motivate us to act in certain ways. For this to be true, 'goodness', say, would have to have 'to-be-pursuedness' built into it.

If this is a confusing idea, that's Mackie's point. How could an objective property motivate us in this way? How could there be some direct, immediate relation between some fact of the world and our desires? Just to know something true about the way the world is doesn't entail being motivated to do anything about it. As we might say, the direction of fit is wrong.

We may add that, clearly, moral properties cannot be natural properties discovered by sense experience and science. None of the properties we discover this way are intrinsically motivating. So if there are moral properties, they must be non-natural properties. What Mackie's argument is supposed to show is how peculiar such non-natural properties would have to be.

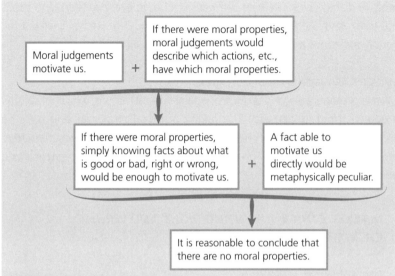

Explain Mackie's argument from metaphysical queerness.

Map 3.17 Mackie's argument from metaphysical queerness

Epistemological queerness

Suppose there were moral properties. If some actions, such as an act of courage, have the property of being objectively right; or again, if some states of affairs, such as being in pain or cowardice, have the property of being objectively bad – how could we know? Intuitionism, Mackie claims, says no more than that we have some special faculty – but this is a terrible answer that doesn't explain how we have this knowledge at all. If we think of our usual ways of knowing about the world – sense perception, introspection, hypothetical reasoning, even conceptual analysis – none of these can explain knowledge of morality. To say that we know moral judgements to be true or false 'by intuition' is only to say that we don't know them in any of the usual ways. The theory doesn't give us any real answer as to *how* we know truths by intuition.

The non-naturalist might well reply that it is not only knowledge of morality that faces this objection. We can't explain our knowledge of mathematics, necessary truths, the existence and nature of substance, space or causation in any of these ways either. Here, the non-naturalist is appealing to rationalist arguments about the scope of a priori knowledge. Is our knowledge of moral properties any more puzzling than our knowledge of these other things?

Mackie accepts the point: either empiricism can account for knowledge in these areas, or they all face the objection that they appeal to something 'non-natural'. To a significant extent, then, Mackie's argument depends on empiricism, rather than rationalism, being the correct account of our knowledge.

But Mackie presses the argument from epistemological queerness by asking what the connection between natural properties and moral properties is. For instance, we commonly say things like 'that's wrong because it is cruel'. If we take cruel to mean 'causing pain for fun', then cruelty is a natural property. It is a psychological fact that something causes pain, and another psychological fact that someone's motive is taking pleasure in doing this. But what is the relation between these facts and the 'fact' that acting in this way is wrong? How can we establish whether it is wrong or not? It isn't an analytic truth, and we can't deduce it. Intuitionism fails to tell us how morality is related to anything else, how natural facts contribute to moral thinking. This makes it even more puzzling how we could come to know about moral properties.

See also HUME'S IS–OUGHT GAP, p. 371.

Explain Mackie's argument from epistemological queerness.

Discussion

Mackie's argument from queerness depends on his understanding of what moral realism claims. In particular, he takes moral realism to be committed to the idea that moral properties are mind-independent and part of reality. Both these ideas need careful thought.

'Reality' here can't mean simply the world as physics describes it – space, time, matter and perhaps causal relations between them. Obviously, physics won't tell us right from wrong. But why should we think that all reality is like physical reality? Moral properties, if they exist, aren't going to be like physical properties. Even reductive naturalists think the most likely natural properties to be moral properties are psychological properties.

Are psychological states 'part of reality'? They certainly exist – whether one is happy or not is a psychological fact. In one sense, it is not a mind-independent fact, because it is a fact about a mind. In another sense, we can argue that it is a mind-independent fact, because whether you are happy or not is true or false independent of what anyone thinks. Anyone can make a mistake about whether or not you are happy, even you (you might think you are happy when, really, if you were completely honest with yourself, you'd realise you are not)! Perhaps this is controversial. So let's talk about EUDAIMONIA (p. 271) instead. Whether someone is eudaimon is, according to Aristotle, objectively true or false, but it is a fact about someone's life, including their mind. There are lots of facts that are about human beings and their activities, e.g. not just psychological facts, such as whether someone is in love, but also cultural facts, such as facts about whether a piece of music is baroque or classical. But they are still facts, because they are independent of our judgements and made true by the way the world is, in this case, the human world.

Moral realism claims that moral judgements are mind-independent in the sense that whether a moral claim is true does not depend on whether we think that it is true. It doesn't have to claim that moral judgements are not about minds. If moral facts are facts about our minds, perhaps they are not all that 'queer' after all.

Reductive naturalism argues that we can make the case even more strongly. Consider utilitarianism as an example. Mill argues that our experience *does* give us evidence of what is good. What is good is what is desirable, and the best evidence for what is desirable is what people generally desire. Once we recognise this, there is no particular epistemological difficulty in discovering moral properties. Furthermore, if we say that goodness *is* happiness, then there is no metaphysical queerness about goodness either. It is simply a natural psychological property. And yet it is a motivating one. We desire happiness and are motivated to pursue it. Saying that something is good is to say that it produces happiness, so it is no puzzle how moral properties and moral judgements motivate us.

Does Mackie show that moral properties don't exist?

These responses are driven by (reductive or non-reductive) moral naturalism. We can show how moral properties are not queer by seeing how they fit with our understanding of human life. But Mackie's arguments from queerness originally targeted non-naturalism. It is harder to see how non-naturalist theories such as Moore's intuitionism can respond.

Key points: moral realism

- Cognitivism appeals to our experience of morality: we feel we can make mistakes, that moral demands are independent of us, that moral progress is possible.
- Moral realism claims that moral judgements are made true or false by objective moral properties.
- Reductive moral naturalism claims that moral properties are identical with some properties that can be identified through sense experience and science, e.g. utilitarianism can be interpreted as claiming that the moral property 'goodness' is the natural property 'happiness'.
- If reductive naturalism is true, we can discover moral properties through empirical investigation. But we cannot show that reductive naturalism is true by empirical investigation.
- Non-reductive moral naturalism claims that morality is based on the natural capacities of human beings as rational animals. Annas argues that Aristotelian virtue ethics can be interpreted in this way. While eudaimonia is based on human nature and rationality is a natural human capacity, moral reasoning involves more than knowing and applying facts discovered by sense experience and science, but considers moral reasons.
- Moral non-naturalism claims that moral properties are not natural properties in the sense understood by reductive naturalism.
- Moore argued for the claim that goodness cannot be defined. To identify goodness with any type of natural property is a 'naturalistic fallacy'. This is shown by the open question argument.
- However, we can object that Moore shows only that moral concepts are distinct from natural concepts. He doesn't show that moral properties are not natural properties.
- Intuitionism claims that some moral judgements are self-evident judgements that rest on being grasped directly. Intuitions are a type of synthetic a priori knowledge.
- Ayer argued that a statement only has meaning if it is either analytic or empirically verifiable. Moral statements are neither, so they are meaningless. So cognitivism (and so moral realism) is false.
- However, the principle of verification, according to itself, is not meaningful, because it is neither analytic nor empirically verifiable. So it doesn't give us a reason to reject moral realism.

- Hume gives three arguments for the claim that moral judgements are not judgements of reason, and so cognitivism is false. First, judgements of reason are either about relations of ideas or matters of fact, but moral judgements are about neither of these. Second, moral judgements motivate, but judgements of reason do not. Third, we cannot deduce statements about 'ought' from statements about what 'is', which shows that statements about 'ought' do not state truths.

- Moral realists can object that Hume is wrong that there are only two types of judgement of reason. Alternatively, reductive naturalists will argue that moral judgements are about matters of fact. Moral realists can also argue that, like judgements of reason, moral judgements do not motivate.

- Mackie notes that different societies disagree in their views about morality. We can explain these differences as resulting from different ways of living, but not in terms of societies making mistakes about objective moral truth. So moral relativity is evidence that there are no objective moral truths.

- While moral realists can respond that there are universal fundamental moral principles that are objective, Mackie claims that this fails to understand ordinary morality and still means that most moral judgements are not objective. But the realist can reject both inferences.

- Mackie argues that if there were objective moral properties, they would be metaphysically mysterious, since it is completely unclear how objective properties could motivate us as morality does. It would also be a complete mystery how we could come to know them or how we could infer them from natural properties. So we should reject moral realism.

- Moral realists can point out that some psychological properties are mind-independent in being objectively true or false, while still being about minds. Moral properties could be like this, and so not strange at all. However, this response is only available to forms of naturalism, rather than non-naturalism.

B. Moral anti-realism

MORAL REALISM (p. 351) is the view that there are moral properties, such as being right or wrong or being good or bad, that states of affairs, actions and people have. They have these properties independent of whether people believe that they have these properties. In this sense, moral properties are 'mind-independent'. Moral anti-realism denies that mind-independent moral properties exist. There are no such properties.

Moral anti-realists can defend this claim for two completely different reasons. According to one set of arguments, we arrive at error theory. According to the other set of arguments, we arrive at various forms of non-cognitivism. We shall look at each in turn.

Error theory

As described in THE DISTINCTION BETWEEN COGNITIVISM AND NON-COGNITIVISM (p. 348), cognitivism (in ethics) is the view that moral judgements express beliefs that can be true or false. Moral realism is a form of cognitivism, as it claims that mind-independent moral properties make moral judgements true or false. Error theory accepts cognitivism, but rejects moral realism.

Error theory was developed and defended by Mackie. Mackie agrees with moral realists that we understand moral judgements to be cognitive. The way we use ethical language is to make objective claims about a moral reality. Moral judgements express beliefs about mind-independent moral properties, and these beliefs can be true or false. This is how moral language functions. But, in fact, there is no such moral reality. Mackie is an anti-realist. And so he argues that all moral judgements are false. 'Murder is wrong' is false, because the property of being wrong does not exist. 'Murder is right' is false, because the property of being right does not exist. There are no moral properties. This is the error we make. Ethical language rests on a mistake.

Some people really believe in fairies. They don't think that when we are talking about fairies, we are using language 'fictionally' (like when we talk about Sherlock Holmes). Imagine that everyone believed in fairies in this way. An 'error theory' of fairies would say that while talk of fairies is cognitivist, there are no fairies. It is not true that fairies have wings, because there are no fairies. It is not true that fairies don't have wings, because there are no fairies. All claims about fairies are false, because there are no fairies.

The way Mackie phrases his argument is to say that there are no 'objective' moral values. A claim is objective, according to Mackie, if:

1. It can be something we know.
2. It can be true or false.

3. Its truth is independent of what we want or choose.
4. It is about something mind-independent.
5. It is about something that is part of reality, part of the 'fabric of the world'.

? What is error theory?

His claim is that moral judgements cannot be objective in any of these senses, because there are no moral properties.

Discussion

We looked at Mackie's defence of the claim that there are no objective moral properties in MACKIE'S ARGUMENT FROM RELATIVITY (p. 371) and MACKIE'S ARGUMENTS FROM QUEERNESS (p. 375), when we also looked at responses from moral realism. We won't repeat those discussions here.

However, it is worth briefly revisiting one of them. Moral realists agree with much of Mackie's idea of objectivity. Moral realism wants to defend the claims that moral judgements can be true, and whether they are true does not depend on whether we want them to be so. It says that we can know some true moral judgements and that moral properties are real, so they are part of reality. However, in the DISCUSSION (p. 377) of Mackie's arguments from queerness, we saw that the claim that moral judgements are mind-independent was ambiguous. Moral realists claim that moral judgements are mind-independent in the sense that they are true or false whether or not we *think* they are true or false. But they may not be mind-independent in the sense of being about something other than minds. It may be that moral judgements are about psychological properties, such as happiness. One response to Mackie's error theory, then, is to say that he has misunderstood what it is for a moral property to be objective.

? Is Mackie's error theory true?

However, error theory does not only reject moral realism. It also defends cognitivism. But is this right? Is it true that moral judgements express beliefs that can be true or false? A different form of moral anti-realism is given by non-cognitivism.

Non-cognitivism and moral anti-realism

As we saw in THE DISTINCTION BETWEEN COGNITIVISM AND NON-COGNITIVISM (p. 348), non-cognitivist theories of ethics claim that ethical language does not try to describe the world and cannot be true or false. Moral judgements do not express beliefs, but some other, non-cognitive mental state. Different non-cognitivist theories disagree on exactly what moral judgements express, but they agree that moral language does not function to state facts. We will look at two theories, one that claims that moral judgements express emotions and the other that they express prescriptions for how to act.

Non-cognitivist theories are anti-realist. Since moral judgements do not describe the world and are neither true nor false, then there are no mind-independent moral properties that would make moral judgements true or false. For example, to say 'racism is wrong' is not to claim that racism has any kind of property. It is, instead, to express disapproval of racism (on one theory) or to recommend that we do not act in racist ways (on another).

> Explain why non-cognitivist metaethical theories are anti-realist.

Emotivism

Emotivism claims that moral judgements *express* the feeling or attitude of approval or disapproval. To say that 'Murder is wrong' is to express one's disapproval of murder. Ethical language is 'emotive'.

In one sense, emotivism claims that morality is 'subjective'. However, there is an important distinction between emotivism and the theory that is called 'subjectivism'. Subjectivism claims that moral judgements *assert* or *report* approval or disapproval, and there is a difference between expressing disapproval and asserting it. We can understand this better by looking at what subjectivism claims, and then contrasting it with emotivism.

EMOTIVISM AND SUBJECTIVISM

One form of subjectivism claims that to say '*X* is wrong' is simply to say that '*X* is generally disapproved of'. But this can't be right, because it is not a contradiction to say 'Most people approve of *X*, but *X* is wrong nonetheless'. For example, racism has been very common historically. We may argue that 'racism is wrong' even while acknowledging that most people approved of it.

A second form of subjectivism, 'speaker subjectivism', claims that the meaning of '*X* is wrong' is something like 'I disapprove of *X*' or again 'I think *X* is wrong'. This is a (psychological) fact about oneself, so the statement can be true or false. Speaker subjectivism, therefore, is an unusual form of reductive moral naturalism: the facts that make moral judgements true are facts about the individual speaker's mind.

Figure 3.17 Emotivism claims these people are expressing their disapproval of racism, not trying to state a fact of any kind

Explain speaker subjectivism and one objection to it.

Speaker subjectivism entails that we cannot make mistakes about what is right or wrong. If I say 'Murder is right', I am simply stating 'I approve of murder'. If I am sincere, then I do approve of murder, and so murder is, indeed, right ('for me', we might say). But, we can object, we naturally think that people *can* make mistakes about morality. Speaker subjectivism makes no sense of deliberation, trying to *figure out* what is right or wrong. Why should I bother to deliberate? *Whatever* I come to feel will be right!

By contrast, emotivism claims that moral judgements do not express *any* kind of truth or falsehood, because they are not cognitive. Where subjectivism is a form of cognitivism, emotivism is a form of non-cognitivism.

What is the difference between subjectivism and emotivism?

This enables emotivism to explain, and respond to, the objections to subjectivism above. To say that 'most people approve of racism' does not contradict 'racism is wrong', because 'racism is wrong' doesn't state something true or false. It doesn't *state* anything at all. Instead, it expresses the speaker's disapproval of racism. And we cannot be infallible in the sense of getting the answer right; there are no moral truths.

AYER'S DEFENCE

AYER, *LANGUAGE, TRUTH AND LOGIC*, CH. 6

We saw in A. J. AYER's VERIFICATION PRINCIPLE (p. 363) that Ayer uses the verification principle to reject cognitivism. Moral judgements do not make claims that are true or false as they are neither analytic nor can they be verified empirically. Ayer goes on to develop and defend emotivism. Moral judgements express feelings: 'If I say to someone, "You acted wrongly in stealing that money" … I am simply evincing my moral disapproval of it. It is as if I had said, "You stole that money," in a peculiar tone of horror'. Through expressing our feelings, we also aim to arouse feelings in others, and so get them to act in certain ways.

What is emotivism?

EMOTIVISM AFTER AYER

Ayer's defence of emotivism depends on the verification principle. However, defending the central claim that moral judgements express emotions, rather than state facts, does not depend on the principle of verification. For example, Charles Stevenson argues that moral words have emotive meanings, which are not descriptive. The central ethical terms – 'right', 'wrong', 'good' and 'bad' – only have emotive meanings, of expressing approval or disapproval. But many moral terms ('steal', 'honesty', 'respect') have both descriptive and emotive meanings. To be told that someone is 'honest' is to learn something about them. For instance, they can't be honest while lying frequently! And whether someone lies frequently is a matter of fact. But the term 'honest' isn't just a description; it also has an emotive meaning of approval.

Facts and Values

The emotive meaning of moral judgements is related to their use. The purpose of moral judgements is not to state facts, but to influence how we behave through expressions of approval and disapproval. 'X is good', and other moral judgements, are used both to express the speaker's attitudes and to influence the attitudes of other people. Moral terms are 'dynamic', and the main purpose of making moral judgements is to influence other people's emotions and behaviour.

One advantage of emotivism is that it easily explains how and why it is that moral judgements motivate us. If moral language were just descriptive, stating how things are, why would that get us to act in certain ways? We need to care. And what we care about is captured in our attitudes to the world. Emotivism connects caring, approving, disapproving, with the very meaning of ethical words.

Explain two arguments supporting emotivism, first in prose, then in argument maps.

Prescriptivism

R. M. Hare argued that moral words are not descriptive and *emotive* in meaning, as Stevenson argued. Instead, they are descriptive and *prescriptive*. 'The function of moral principles is to guide conduct.'

PRESCRIPTIVE MEANING

What is the difference between prescribing and persuading?

See also HYPOTHETICAL AND CATEGORICAL IMPERATIVES, p. 253.

What, according to Hare, are the two types of prescriptive meaning?

HARE, *THE LANGUAGE OF MORALS*, CH. 1

Hare criticises emotivism for mistaking the 'force' of moral statements. When I express a moral judgement, I am not trying to influence or persuade you, nor am I expressing my feelings. I am prescribing what you ought to do. Whether, *as a result*, you act as I prescribe is a different matter. Simply saying you should do x isn't an attempt to persuade you – that may require a lot of argument.

So what is it to 'prescribe' something? There are two types of prescriptive meaning, Hare claims. First, there are imperatives that tell someone to do something. Imperatives explicitly state what to do, e.g. 'Shut the door'. Hare argues that some moral judgements work in a similar way. For example, 'Eating meat is wrong' entails the imperative 'Do not eat meat'. How so? To accept the imperative, 'Shut the door', is to shut the door. To accept that eating meat is wrong is to not eat meat. So if you ask 'should I eat meat?', and I answer 'eating meat is wrong', then I have answered your question.

Second, there are value judgements. The most general value terms are 'good' and 'bad'. We use the word 'good', says Hare, when we want to *commend* something to someone. Although not explicit about what to do in the way imperatives are, this commendation provides guidance for our choices. How so?

GOOD

HARE, *THE LANGUAGE OF MORALS*, CHS 5, 7

We can talk about good chocolate, good teachers and good people. In each case, we are saying the chocolate, teacher or person is praiseworthy in some way. This use of language is quite distinct from *describing* something. Suppose I say 'That's a good strawberry, because it is sweet and juicy'. If we think 'good' as applied to strawberries just means 'sweet and juicy', then all I have said is 'That's a sweet and juicy strawberry because it is sweet and juicy'. But this isn't what I said. I commended the strawberry, I didn't merely describe it.

This, Hare argues, is what is correct about Moore's attack on THE NATURALISTIC FALLACY (p. 358) and HUME'S IS–OUGHT GAP (p. 371). Because there is a distinction between describing and commending, nothing about being honest (i.e. telling the truth: descriptive meaning) can make me commend honesty (telling the truth is how to behave: prescriptive). More generally, nothing about the facts can *entail* a moral judgement.

Explain the distinction between commending and describing.

However, 'good' is not purely a term of praise. Whenever we call something good, in each case there is a *set of standards* that we are implicitly relying on. Good chocolate is rich in the taste of cocoa. Good teachers can explain new ideas clearly and create enthusiasm in their students. A good person – well, a good person is someone who is the way we should try to be as people. When we use 'good' to mean 'morally good', we are appealing to a set of standards that apply to someone as a person. However, because nothing about the facts entails a moral judgement, there are no facts that establish one set of moral standards as objectively correct. We have to *adopt* the standards; they are not part of the world, waiting for us to discover them.

Explain what Hare means by 'morally good'.

The descriptive meaning of 'good' in any context comes from the set of standards that is being assumed. Its descriptive meaning picks up on the qualities that the something must have to be (a) good ... (chocolate, teacher, person, whatever). Because 'good' is always used relative to a set of standards, it always has a descriptive meaning. If you know what the standard for a good teacher is, then you learn something factual about a teacher when I say 'she's a good teacher'.

This has an important implication: if we have two identical things, we cannot call one of them good and the other not good. Whenever we apply a standard in making a prescription, we are committed to making the same judgement of two things that match the standard in the same way. If I say this chocolate is good but that chocolate is not, I must think that there is some *relevant difference* between the two.

'Good' is used *primarily* to commend. For each type of thing that we describe as good, the standard is different, but in each case, we are commending it. However, we don't always use 'good' to commend. In fact, any word that both commends and describes can be used just to describe and not commend. For example, we often use the word 'honest' to commend someone. But I can say 'If you weren't so honest, we could have got away with that!' This is an expression of annoyance, not praise. Likewise, I can agree that a 'good person' is one who is honest, kind, just, etc. But I can still think that good people are not to be commended, because, as Woody Allen said, 'Good people sleep better than bad people, but bad people enjoy the waking hours more'.

So, according to Hare, the main features of 'good' are these:

1. It is used to commend, to provide guidance for choosing what to do.
2. It assumes a set of standards, features in virtue of which something counts as 'good' or not.
3. Two identical things must both be good or not. To think otherwise is logically contradictory.

Figure 3.18 1950s advertising promoted a particular set of standards for the 'good wife', standards which we may question

Compare prescriptivism and emotivism on the meaning of 'good'.

MORAL LANGUAGE

HARE, *THE LANGUAGE OF MORALS*, CH. 10, §2

In moral language, 'good' refers, directly or indirectly, to being a good person. A good action, then, will be one that a good person does. Calling something or someone 'morally good' is intended to guide people's choices. The standards for who counts as a 'good person' are moral standards. However, moral standards are adopted, rather than being true or false.

The same three features that apply to 'good', Hare argues, also apply to 'ought' and 'right'.

1. We say 'you ought to pay back the money' (in a particular situation) or again 'stealing is wrong' (in general) to guide people's choices and actions.
2. The standards that we are assuming in making these judgements relate to being a good person.
3. Two actions, in similar situations, must either both be right or not. If I think that it is wrong for you to steal from me, because it infringes my rights of ownership, then I must think that it is wrong for me to steal from you, because it infringes your rights of ownership – unless I can say that there is some relevant difference between the two cases. We must be willing to 'universalise' our moral judgements. Not to do so is logically contradictory.

Explain what Hare means by 'universalising' our moral judgements.

Issues for moral anti-realism

CAN MORAL ANTI-REALISM ACCOUNT FOR HOW WE USE MORAL LANGUAGE?
Emotivism and prescriptivism both face objections regarding their analysis of moral language. Let's take emotivism first.

Emotivism and moral language
We can object, first, that being emotive and influencing people's attitudes is something that lots of non-moral language does as well, e.g. advertising. So we will need to say more to distinguish morality from advertising.

Second, does moral language always function to influence others? We may express our moral attitudes to others who already agree with them or that we know to be indifferent to our views – so influencing their attitudes is not the purpose. But this doesn't show that we aren't expressing a moral judgement.

Third, moral language isn't always particularly or necessarily emotive. The key moral terms 'good', 'right', 'wrong' and 'bad' may arouse emotions in others or express ours, but again, this depends on context. We do not think that it is always good to arouse emotions in others on moral issues, especially by using emotive language. Moral discussion can be, and sometimes should be, dispassionate.

Explain two objections to emotivism, first in prose, then in an argument map.

Is the purpose of moral language to express our emotions and influence others?

But how strong are these objections? The *purpose* of moral language, says emotivism, is to influence what people do. Without this, we would have no moral language or judgements at all. However, that doesn't mean that it *always* has to be used for this purpose. This is normal – many types of language can be used in 'non-standard' ways in different situations. For example, it is possible to use fact-stating language to insult someone, e.g. 'You have a big nose'. That it is an emotive statement on this occasion doesn't make the *meaning* of the sentence 'emotive' – it states a factual claim. Likewise, language which is standardly emotive can be deployed without the intention to arouse emotion or influence action. The objections don't show that moral language isn't 'essentially' emotive, only that it isn't always emotive.

Prescriptivism and moral language

How does prescriptivism fare? We may object that moral language does not only prescribe, but has many other functions. Hare has in mind the situation in which someone asks what to do. But there are lots of other situations in which we use moral language – we can exhort or implore someone, we can confess, we can complain, and so on.

However, Hare can reply in the same way as the emotivist above. Prescriptivism says that it is essential to morality that it guides choices and actions. This isn't to say that, on every occasion, a moral judgement is being made to offer such guidance to the listener. The important point is that in holding a particular moral judgement, e.g. 'stealing is wrong', I am committed to acting on it.

We should accept this point. But it doesn't necessarily support prescriptivism. It is not only commending and commanding that make a link between language and action. Language that expresses desires and attitudes *also* makes such links. Suppose I say 'I like apples', but I never eat apples, refuse anything made from apples, etc. There is something inconsistent here. Likewise, I can say 'I disapprove of stealing', but steal myself and never comment on others' thefts. Just by connecting ethical language to action, Hare hasn't shown that ethical language must be prescriptive. It could just as well express what we want or our attitudes.

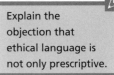

Explain the objection that ethical language is not only prescriptive.

Thinking harder: non-cognitivism and moral language

The objections to emotivism and prescriptivism above both rest on the claim that there isn't just one thing that moral language does. It can be used in many ways, and express many different psychological states. This is a problem for non-cognitivist theories generally. They have to argue that one use of moral language is essential or privileged to get around counterexamples to their theory.

Cognitivist theories, including error theory, don't face this objection in the same way. According to cognitivist theories, moral judgements are statements of fact. The meaning of moral judgements is given by what would make them true. So we can understand what 'murder is wrong' means by understanding what it is for murder to be wrong. Now, we can use the claim 'murder is wrong' to do other things, such as influence people's behaviour or complain or express anger or … But these effects don't give us the meaning of moral judgements. The many uses of moral language don't threaten cognitivist theories the way that they threaten non-cognitivist theories.

Although error theory is a form of moral anti-realism, because it is a cognitivist theory it doesn't face the objection that it can't account for how we use moral language.

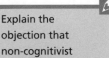

Explain the objection that non-cognitivist theories cannot explain the many uses of moral language.

Thinking harder: disagreement and moral argument

There is one particular use of moral language that provides a strong objection to non-cognitivist theories, including emotivism and prescriptivism, and that is how we argue about morality. We start with the objection as it applies to emotivism.

Emotivism on moral reasoning

If I say 'abortion is wrong' and you say 'abortion is right', according to emotivism, it seems that I am just expressing my disapproval of it and you are expressing your approval. I'm just saying 'Boo! to abortion' and you're saying 'Hurrah! for abortion'. I am also trying to influence your attitudes, and you are trying to influence mine. But we are not doing so *rationally*, or by appealing to facts about what is good or bad. Trying to influence people without reasoning is just a form of manipulation. Emotivism reduces moral argument to propaganda. While *sometimes* moral argument might take this form, we do usually take ourselves to be *reasoning* about what is right, not simply mouthing off.

We can put the point another way. If, as emotivism claims, moral judgements and arguments are about influencing people's attitudes, then a good moral argument will be one that is *effective*. That is all. There is no other, e.g. rational, criterion by which we might judge that it is a good or bad argument. Whatever I appeal to, to make you change your mind, no matter how irrelevant or far-fetched, if it makes you change your mind, it is a good argument. This is highly unsatisfactory.

Ayer responds that moral arguments are not arguments over moral judgements, but over facts: 'we do not attempt to show by our arguments that [the other person] has the "wrong" ethical feeling towards a situation whose nature he has correctly apprehended. What we attempt to show is that he is mistaken about the facts of the case'. When arguing over animal rights, say, we are constantly drawing facts to each other's attention. I point out how much animals suffer in factory farms. You point out how much more sophisticated human beings are than animals. I point out that it is unkind to kill animals for food. You respond that people are not motivated by unkindness, and indeed, farmers can be very kind to the animals when alive. And so on. But if we both agree on the facts, but still disagree morally, there is nothing left to discuss, says Ayer, no further argument can take place. Moral judgements always *presuppose* a system of values; but no arguments for these values can be given.

But there are two objections to this response from Ayer. First, if you and I disagree about a moral judgement, and moral judgements have no truth value, are we right to say that there is a 'disagreement' here at all? Isn't a disagreement when you think some claim is true and I think it is false? If so, then moral disagreement is only possible if cognitivism is true, since only cognitivism says that moral claims can be true or false.

Second, emotivism does not give us an adequate account of deliberation. If you are unsure about whether something, lying say, is right or wrong, we can understand that you are trying to work out what your attitude towards lying *should* be. But why can't you settle the question of whether lying is right or wrong by simply noting whatever attitude you *already have* towards it? If emotivism is right, it seems that thinking hard about the question is irrational.

We can put the point another way: emotivism doesn't explain how someone can *rationally* change their mind on a moral issue. First, they have one attitude, then they have another. But what *reason* do they have to change their mind?

> Is moral argument always only about the facts?

> Can emotivism explain moral deliberation?

Figure 3.19 Why worry about whether you are doing the right thing, if the right thing is whatever you think it is?

Prescriptivism on moral reasoning

Prescriptivism argues that it can do better than emotivism at explaining moral reasoning. First, we can ask about someone's reasons for prescribing what they do. Second, morality involves consistency – moral judgements must be universalised. For example, Singer claims there is *no relevant difference* between the suffering of people and the suffering of animals. If we are going to say that causing the suffering of people is wrong, we are committed to saying the suffering of animals is wrong – unless we can find a relevant difference. Moral disagreements can be about the consistency in applying certain standards, and reason can help resolve this.

See WHICH BEINGS' HAPPINESS SHOULD WE INCLUDE?, p. 227.

Third, we can infer prescriptions from other prescriptions. A famous argument against abortion says 'Taking an innocent human life is wrong. Abortion is the taking of an innocent human life. Therefore abortion is wrong'. This has the same logical force, Hare claims, if we rephrase it as imperatives: 'Do not take innocent human life. Abortion is the taking of an innocent human life. Therefore, do not commit abortion'. To reject or refuse the conclusion, we must reject or refuse at least one premise. And so our prescriptions are logically related to one another. So we can use reason to discuss these relations. Moral arguments are not only about the facts, but about moral judgements as well.

We can object that the only kind of rationality prescriptivism can recognise in moral arguments is consistency. In requiring us to universalise moral judgements, Hare's theory is similar to KANTIAN DEONTOLOGICAL ETHICS (p. 248). However, Kant argues that the standards for a good person (the good will) are themselves set by reason, and are therefore objective. Hare rejects this. Neither the empirical facts nor reason entails that we must have certain standards rather than others. If I argue that racism is morally right, and equality is morally wrong, *as long as I am prepared to universalise this claim*, there is no objective ground on which to disagree with me. Suppose you say 'But what if you were of a different race. Would you say you should be treated as inferior?' I can reply 'Yes'. Now what?

Compare emotivism and prescriptivism on moral reasoning.

Hare responds that to prescribe that one's own interests be frustrated like this is irrational. And so his moral system will give us the Golden Rule of 'Do unto others as you would have them do unto you' – anything else would be inconsistent.

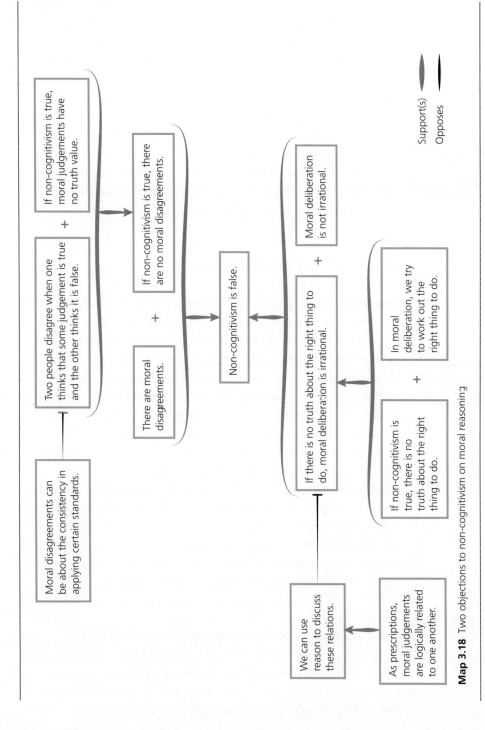

Map 3.18 Two objections to non-cognitivism on moral reasoning

Text within the figure:

If non-cognitivism is true, moral judgements have no truth value.

Two people disagree when one thinks that some judgement is true and the other thinks it is false.

Moral disagreements can be about the consistency in applying certain standards.

If non-cognitivism is true, there are no moral disagreements.

There are moral disagreements.

Non-cognitivism is false.

Moral deliberation is not irrational.

If there is no truth about the right thing to do, moral deliberation is irrational.

In moral deliberation, we try to work out the right thing to do.

If non-cognitivism is true, there is no truth about the right thing to do.

We can use reason to discuss these relations.

As prescriptions, moral judgements are logically related to one another.

Support(s)

Opposes

Can either
emotivism or
prescriptivism
successfully explain
moral reasoning?

But we can press the objection in a different form. Suppose you say that we shouldn't steal because stealing would make life very difficult. This is *your reason* for prescribing that we shouldn't steal, implicitly appealing to the standard that the good person does not make life difficult. But Hare says that moral standards are not objectively correct. Suppose I do not adopt your standard – I have a different standard for 'good'. Then not only do I reject your moral judgement that stealing is wrong, I also don't accept your reason for this judgement as a moral reason. So, on Hare's view, there are no reasons to do a particular action *independent* of what standards we adopt. And so moral rationality is no more than consistency. But this does not rule out very objectionable values.

Error theory and moral reasoning

See Philosophical
argument, p. 6.

The arguments above don't cause difficulties for cognitivist theories, including error theory. According to cognitivism, moral judgements can be true or false. We can therefore use them normally in reasoning, the same way we use any statements that can be true or false, such as in science or history. Just as with any argument, in moral arguments a good argument uses good or plausible premises to raise the probability that the conclusion is true. For example, 'Lying treats other people with disrespect, so it is wrong to lie'.

Moral realism claims that sometimes the conclusion – a moral judgement – is true. Error theory, of course, claims that moral judgements are always false. But this doesn't show that there is anything wrong with moral arguments, except that they make a false assumption – that there are objective moral facts. No set of premises, therefore, can show that a moral judgement is true. This does suggest that moral argument is pointless (rather like arguing about the 'real' properties of fairies). But any objection here is really to the central claim of error theory – that there are no moral properties – not to its account of moral reasoning.

WHETHER MORAL ANTI-REALISM BECOMES MORAL NIHILISM
We saw that our first objection to moral anti-realism, concerning moral language in general, and moral reasoning in particular, targeted non-cognitivist theories more than error theory. Our next two objections pose challenges to all three of the anti-realist theories we've discussed.

Moral nihilism is the rejection of all moral values and principles. It is the view that nothing is of moral value, that we have no moral duties. Moral anti-realism claims that there are no mind-independent moral properties, no objective moral truths, and non-cognitivist forms of anti-realism claim that morality is an expression of our emotions or attitudes. We may object that if this is so, then *really* there are no moral values – we invent them. *Really*, we have no obligation to be moral, because we have no obligation to have certain emotions or adopt certain standards of value. If moral properties are not objective, if moral judgements are not objectively true, then why accept morality at all?

Moral anti-realists can argue that this is either an unfair simplification of their theories or a straightforward misunderstanding. Error theory allows that we can have *subjective* moral values, and all three theories will argue that living without moral values is itself a choice or expression of feeling, and one that moral people will disapprove of morally. The theory that moral values are a reflection of our feelings does not imply that we should stop having moral feelings. The emotivist may still show disapproval of anyone who advocates that morality doesn't matter or is just a matter of taste. Similarly, the fact that we must adopt standards of value doesn't show that we should stop making prescriptions, and we may prescribe that people live according to particular standards.

The moral nihilist can respond that this is unjustifiable. Can we really justify interfering with how other people behave – when they behave 'immorally' – just because their actions don't accord with our feelings or choices? This seems very petty. But this isn't the reason we are interfering, claims the anti-realist. It is not because it offends us, but because they are being racist or cruel or cowardly or whatever.

But as we saw in Disagreement and moral argument (p. 392), the difficulty here is that my taking racist discrimination as a good reason to prevent an action is *itself* an expression of my feelings or the standards on which I make prescriptions. For the anti-realist, moral disagreement is always eventually a stand-off between subjective points of view. For the moral realist, by contrast, that racist discrimination is a good reason to interfere with someone's action is a moral fact, based on the moral properties of racism. The cognitivist claims to have the backing of reality.

Does moral anti-realism lead to moral nihilism?

MORAL PROGRESS

If there is no moral reality, we can argue, then our moral views cannot become better or worse. Obviously, they have changed – people used to

Figure 3.20 Did the US civil rights movement constitute 'moral progress'?

believe that slavery was morally acceptable and now they do not. But how can we say that this is *progress* if there is no objective moral truth? There are two responses moral anti-realists can give.

First, they can claim that there can be very real improvements in people's moral views if they become more rational. This can happen in several different ways.

1. People may come to know certain facts that they didn't know before. In the case of slavery, people believed many things about slaves that were not true (one popular false belief was that they were stupid). Moral progress here means basing one's morality on the facts, not false beliefs (Ayer).
2. People can become more consistent, more willing to universalise their principles (Hare). For example, Singer argues that if we were consistent in our feelings about preventing suffering, we would not eat meat. If he is right, then vegetarianism would be moral progress.
3. People can become more coherent in their moral judgements. Many of us have moral feelings that come into conflict with each other, e.g. over lying. Moral progress here would be a matter of working out the implications of our views, and changing what needs changing to make them coherent with each other.

Explain how moral anti-realism can account for moral progress.

Because people are ignorant, do not always think logically, and have not resolved the conflicts between their different feelings and conventions, there is plenty of room for moral progress. But moral progress just means becoming more rational in our moral thinking, not becoming more 'correct' in our moral judgements.

The second response moral anti-realists can give is this: if we disapprove of past moral codes and approve of our own moral code, then we will say that we have made moral progress. Society has moved from moral principles that were bad (i.e. principles we disapprove of) to moral principles that are good (i.e. principles we approve of). That is what moral progress is.

This response means that moral progress is relative to a particular moral point of view. Non-cognitivists will say that talk of moral progress is itself non-cognitive, an expression of someone's moral attitudes rather than a claim that can be true or false. If two people disagree over whether we have made moral progress in the last 200 years, say, this disagreement should be understood in the same way that any moral disagreement is understood. There is no special problem about how to explain moral progress.

> 1) Can moral anti-realism adequately explain moral progress? 2) Can moral judgements be objectively true?

Key points: moral anti-realism

- Moral anti-realism claims that there are no objective, mind-independent moral properties.
- Mackie argues that moral judgements are cognitive, but false. They refer to objective moral properties, but no such properties exist. This is error theory.
- In addition to challenging Mackie's arguments against objective moral properties from relativity and queerness, moral realists can argue that Mackie misunderstands objectivity. Moral judgements can be mind-independent by being objectively true or false while still being about properties that depend on minds to exist.
- Non-cognitivism claims that moral judgements express a non-cognitive mental state. Therefore, they do not aim to describe the world and cannot be true or false. Therefore, there are no mind-independent moral properties that would make moral judgements true or false, and non-cognitivist theories are anti-realist.
- Emotivism claims that moral judgements express approval or disapproval and aim to influence the feelings and actions of others.
- Emotivism is not subjectivism. Speaker subjectivism claims that 'X is wrong' means 'I disapprove of X', and so moral judgements can be true or false. While subjectivism is a form of cognitivism, emotivism is a form of non-cognitivism. Expressing a feeling is not stating a truth.

- Without appealing to the verification principle, Stevenson argued that the uses of moral judgements show that they have emotive meaning. They express emotions, and are intended to influence the emotions and actions of other people.
- Hare's prescriptivism argues that ethical language is not emotive in meaning, but prescriptive. Prescriptive language either provides an explicit imperative or commends according to a set of standards.
- Description and prescription are logically distinct, which is why you cannot infer a moral judgement from natural facts.
- Moral standards must be adopted. They are not themselves objectively true or false.
- Standards apply universally, so to be consistent, speakers must be willing to universalise their moral judgements. If not, they must point to a relevant difference between cases.
- We can object that many types of language are emotive, so emotivism hasn't identified what is distinctive about ethical language.
- We can also object that ethical language doesn't always function to influence others or to express our emotions, or again that it isn't always prescriptive. While it is linked to action, the expression of many psychological states is linked to action.
- Emotivists and prescriptivists can both reply that the primary or essential function of ethical language is as they claim, and other uses are 'secondary'.
- We may object that emotivism doesn't allow for moral reasoning. If moral judgements are attempts to influence others' feelings without appealing to reason, this is just manipulation.
- Ayer argued that all moral discussion is disagreeing over the facts.
- We can object that emotivism cannot explain how someone would rationally change their mind.
- Hare argues that the requirement to universalise our prescriptions and the logical relations between prescriptions enables prescriptivism to recognise and explain moral reasoning.
- We can object that prescriptivism reduces rationality in morality to consistency. There are no rational limits on what someone can prescribe, nor on their reasons, as long as they are consistent.
- Moral anti-realism faces the objection that it becomes moral nihilism, the rejection of all moral values. It can respond that moral nihilism is a morally bad view, and we can morally disapprove of nihilism just as we disapprove of other morally bad things.

- We may object that if there is no moral truth, as moral anti-realism argues, we cannot talk of moral progress, because changes in moral views are neither right nor wrong.
- Moral anti-realists can reply that moral beliefs can improve by becoming more rational, i.e. changing in the light of previously unknown facts or becoming more consistent or coherent. Furthermore, we can say that the change from previous views to current views is morally good (i.e. we prescribe or approve of the change).

Metaethics and applied ethics

In our previous discussion of APPLIED ETHICS (p. 321), we looked at how the three normative ethical theories discussed – utilitarianism, Kantian deontological ethics, and Aristotelian virtue ethics – could be applied to four issues, stealing, eating animals, simulated killing, and lying. What do different metaethical theories mean for how we think about issues in applied ethics?

MORAL REALISM

MORAL REALISM (p. 351) claims that there are moral properties (of right, wrong, good, bad, etc.), and some actions have moral properties. Thus there is a true answer to any question in applied ethics. Whether stealing is wrong depends on whether stealing has the property of being wrong – or if stealing in general is not always wrong, then we can ask whether this or that particular act of stealing is right or wrong. And the same applies to the other issues we discussed.

However, moral realism doesn't tell us *what* property wrongness is, e.g. whether it is failing to bring about the greatest happiness or acting on a maxim you can't universalise or something else. So in this sense, moral realism doesn't make any difference to applied ethics. It simply supports the thought that what we are doing when we do applied ethics is trying to discover the truth in answer to the question.

The same is true if we look at MORAL NON-NATURALISM (p. 357). You can be a moral non-naturalist and be a utilitarian or a Kantian deontologist or an Aristotelian virtue theorist! A non-naturalist utilitarian holds that actions that maximise happiness have the non-natural property of being right; a non-naturalist Aristotelian holds that certain character traits have the non-natural property of being good; a non-naturalist Kantian holds that actions whose maxims can be universalised have the non-natural property of being right.

MORAL NATURALISM (p. 354) has more complicated implications for applied ethics, as it conflicts with Kantian deontological ethics. According to moral naturalism, moral properties are natural properties, i.e. they can be discovered empirically through the senses and scientific investigation. But according to Kantian deontological ethics, whether an act is right or wrong depends on whether the maxim can be universalised. And whether a maxim can be universalised is a question answered by a priori reason, not something that we can discover empirically. So if moral naturalism is correct, then Kantian deontological ethics is incorrect. Moral naturalism doesn't tell us whether, say, lying is right or wrong, because it doesn't tell us *which* natural properties are moral properties (you can still believe in utilitarianism or Aristotelian virtue ethics, for instance). But it does tell us that we won't discover the answer by a priori reasoning, e.g. by investigating whether the maxim 'to tell a lie' can be universalised.

Explain why moral realist theories make little difference to answers in applied ethics.

NON-COGNITIVISM

Non-cognitivist theories say that moral judgements, such as 'Stealing is wrong', are neither true nor false. It is tempting, therefore, to say that if non-cognitivism is correct, then there is no 'right answer' to questions in applied ethics. But this is a mistake (unless expressed very carefully).

Non-cognitivists do *not* claim that whether stealing is wrong is subjective in the sense of 'up to the individual choice'. Nor do they say that stealing is wrong 'for' some people and not for others (see EMOTIVISM AND SUBJECTIVISM, p. 383). If, when asked 'Is stealing wrong?', you say 'Some people think it is and other people think it isn't, and that is all that can be said', you haven't answered the question (even if what you say is true!). Instead, according to the non-cognitivist, if you are asked 'is stealing wrong?', you are being asked to express your emotion about stealing or to lay down a prescription. As Hare says, if you respond 'Do not steal', you have answered the question.

Thus, according to non-cognitivism, just because there is no truth in ethics, this doesn't mean that all we can say in applied ethics is that 'people have different views' or 'it is subjective'. The view that 'morality is subjective because there aren't any moral values' is nihilism, and non-cognitivism argues that it is not nihilism (see WHETHER MORAL ANTI-REALISM BECOMES MORAL NIHILISM, p. 396). So, forget about what other people think – you can't answer the question by thinking about them. Do *you* think that stealing is wrong?

Why or why not? Both emotivism and prescriptivism claim that we can still give reasons that support our moral views (see DISAGREEMENT AND MORAL ARGUMENT, p. 392), even if our views aren't true or false, but expressions of how we want people to behave.

ERROR THEORY

By contrast to the metaethical theories above, which make little or no difference to how we answer questions in applied ethics, error theory completely undermines applied ethics. It claims that all direct answers to questions in applied ethics are false – it is false to say that stealing is wrong, and it is false to say that stealing is right. This does not mean that whether stealing is wrong is 'subjective' (for instance, error theory doesn't say that 'stealing is wrong' is true for some people but false for others – it's always false). Subjectivism misunderstands the logic of our moral language, which aims to state objective truths.

In order to discuss applied ethics meaningfully, we first need to develop moral language so that it has new meaning. As long as moral language remains objective, we will only state falsehoods. If, however, we can accept that morality is not objective and learn to use moral language in some other way – subjectively or non-cognitively – then we can start doing applied ethics meaningfully. But error theory, on its own, doesn't tell us what the new meaning of moral language should be.

> Explain how a non-cognitivist would answer questions in applied ethics.

Summary: metaethics

In this section on metaethics, we have considered two families of theories:

1. Cognitivism: the view that moral judgements express beliefs and can be true or false. This is because they describe how the world is.
2. Non-cognitivism: the view that moral judgements express a non-cognitive mental state, are neither true nor false, and do not aim to describe reality.

We looked at three cognitivist theories, the first two being forms of moral realism, and the third a form of moral anti-realism:

1. Moral naturalism: the view that moral properties are natural properties. Naturalism can be reductive – moral properties are properties that can

be identified by sense experience and science; or non-reductive – morality is an expression of the natural capacities of human beings as a species of animal.
2. Moral non-naturalism: the view that moral properties are non-natural properties. We considered Moore's intuitionism and its attack on reductive naturalism.
3. Error theory: the view that moral judgements are all false, because there are no moral properties.

We looked at two non-cognitivist theories, which are both types of moral anti-realism:

1. Emotivism: the view that moral judgements express approval or disapproval and aim to influence the feelings and actions of others.
2. Prescriptivism: the view that moral judgements are prescriptive, guiding our actions.

In our discussion and evaluation of these theories, we looked at the following issues:

1. What is metaethics?
2. What is the origin of our moral principles?
3. What is the difference between cognitivism and non-cognitivism in metaethics?
4. Is it a fallacy to think that moral properties can be reduced to natural properties that can be discovered by sense experience and science?
5. What is a moral 'intuition'?
6. If there are objective moral properties, how could we know about them?
7. Do moral judgements motivate us? If so, does this show that moral realism is false?
8. Do the different moral views of different societies support the claim that there are no objective moral judgements?
9. Does moral language state facts, express emotions, or prescribe how to act?
10. What is the best explanation of moral disagreement and reasoning?
11. If there are no objective moral truths, should we reject all moral values?
12. Is moral progress possible if morality is not objective?

Preparing for the AS exam

This chapter is about preparing for the AS level exam. If you are preparing for the A level exam, please see Chapter 4 of the second textbook, *Philosophy for A Level: Metaphysics of God and Metaphysics of Mind*.

To get good exam results, you need to have a good sense of what the exam will be like and what the examiners are looking for, and to revise in a way that will help you prepare to answer the questions well. This probably sounds obvious, but in fact, many students do not think about the exam itself, only about what questions might come up. There is a big difference. This chapter will provide you with some guidance on how to approach your exams in a way that will help get you the best results you can.

It is divided into four sections: the examination, understanding the question, revision, and exam technique. In the last two sections, I highlight revision points and exam tips. These are collected together at the end of the chapter.

The examination

The structure of the exam

There is one exam, lasting three hours and covering the whole AS. It has two sections: Section A Epistemology and Section B Moral Philosophy. All the questions are compulsory – there is no choice in what you can answer.

Each section has three types of question. First, there are questions that ask you to define a concept or explain a single philosophical idea or argument. These take the form of one 2-mark and one 5-mark question. Second, there are two 9-mark questions that ask you to explain more complex material. You could be asked to explain a theory or a complex argument, to compare two theories, or to explain a claim and an objection to it. Third, there is one 15-mark open-ended essay question that asks you to evaluate a philosophical claim.

Here are the questions from the specimen exam paper:

Section A Epistemology
1. What is an 'analytic truth'? (2 marks)
2. Explain what Plato is trying to show about knowledge in his 'slave boy' argument. (5 marks)
3. Explain how *one* of Gettier's original counterexamples attacks the tripartite view of knowledge. (9 marks)
4. Explain Descartes' third wave of doubt (the 'evil demon' argument). (9 marks)
5. How convincing is Berkeley's idealism? (15 marks)

Section B Moral Philosophy
1. According to Hare's prescriptivism, what does '*x* is morally right' mean? (2 marks)
2. Explain the criticism that utilitarianism could lead to the 'tyranny of the majority'. (5 marks)
3. Explain Moore's open question argument. (9 marks)
4. Explain what Aristotle meant by an 'involuntary action'. (9 marks)
5. Is it wrong to steal? (15 marks)

If you've been doing the questions in the margin of this textbook, these kinds of questions should be very familiar.

Assessment objectives

The examiners mark your answers according to two principles, known as 'Assessment Objectives' (AOs). They are:

AO1: Demonstrate knowledge and understanding of the core concepts and methods of philosophy, including through the use of philosophical analysis.

AO2: Analyse and evaluate philosophical argument to form reasoned judgements.

AO1 requires you to understand how philosophers have argued, and AO2 requires you to be able to argue – to construct and evaluate arguments – yourself. Except for the 15-mark questions, all the marks available are for AO1. For the 15-mark questions, 7 marks are for AO1 and 8 marks are for AO2. How well you write also makes a contribution, so it is important to write clearly and grammatically, so that the examiner can understand what you mean. Don't try to impress using big words or long sentences – it just gets in the way of clarity and precision.

Understanding the question: giving the examiners what they are looking for

The key to doing well in an exam is understanding the question. I don't just mean understanding the *topic* of the question, like 'idealism' or 'utilitarianism'. Of course, this is very important. But you also need to understand what the question is asking you to *do*. Each type of question tests different kinds of philosophical knowledge and skill.

> More information on this is available in the Mark Schemes that the AQA publish online.

Short-answer questions

The first questions of each section test the *accuracy* and *precision* of your understanding.

Two-mark questions ask you to define a concept. The examiners want you to be *concise*. State the definition as clearly and precisely as you can and then move on. Don't waffle or talk around the concept. So my answer to 'According to Hare's prescriptivism, what does "*x* is morally right" mean' is this:

> Taken from
> PRESCRIPTIVE MEANING,
> p. 386.

According to Hare, '*x* is morally right' is an imperative to 'do *x*' to meet the standards for being a good person.

Five-mark questions ask you to explain an important philosophical concept, claim or argument. Explaining involves not just describing the idea, but giving a sense of the reasoning or thought behind it. It is important not only to state the essential points but to *order* them and *link* them logically. Say enough to give a full explanation, but again, stay concise and don't waffle. If you are explaining an argument, it's fine to use numbered premises and conclusion.

My answer to 'Explain what Plato is trying to show about knowledge in his "slave boy" argument' is this:

> In his slave boy argument, Plato tries to show that there is innate knowledge. He starts from 'Meno's paradox', which claims that it is impossible to learn anything. This is because, for anything you might learn, either you already know about it, and so learning is unnecessary; or you don't know about it, so you won't know how to go about learning it. Plato's solution to this puzzle is to say that learning is a form of remembering knowledge that is innate. To show this, Socrates gets a slave boy, who doesn't know any geometry, to solve a problem in geometry simply by asking him questions. Because the slave boy didn't gain the knowledge from experience, he must have recovered the answers from within his mind, i.e. the knowledge must be innate. Plato's example is supposed to show that all we need to recover our innate knowledge is the right 'prompts' from experience (in this case, Socrates' questions).

Taken from PLATO'S SLAVE BOY ARGUMENT, p. 121.

Nine-mark questions

On the difference between understanding and evaluation, see UNDERSTANDING ARGUMENTS AND ARGUMENT MAPS, p. 10, EVALUATING ARGUMENTS, p. 13, and EVALUATING CLAIMS, p. 14.

Nine-mark questions generally ask you to explain a more complex argument or a set of arguments, a theory or a comparison between theories, or some other material. The marks are still all for AO1, your understanding of the argument or theory, so you should not *evaluate* it. This is very important, because any time spent on evaluation is simply wasted – no marks are available, and what you have written is redundant. So if you are asked to explain a theory, you should not discuss whether it is convincing or true. If you are asked to explain an argument, you should not discuss whether it is a *good* argument.

As with the 5-mark questions, the examiners are looking for clarity, precision and an *explanation* that sets out the central claims in a way that demonstrates the logical links between them. The answer needs to work as a single 'whole', rather than a number of disconnected 'bits'. In addition, you will need to stay focused and relevant and use technical philosophical language appropriately (i.e. with clarity, precision and only when it is needed).

My answer to 'Explain what Aristotle meant by an "involuntary action"' is this:

> Aristotle divides actions into three types: voluntary, non-voluntary and involuntary. Voluntary action is action that you bring about in the knowledge of what you are doing. Actions can be involuntary as a result of either force or ignorance – either you aren't choosing to bring about the action, or you do not know what you are doing. When we act involuntarily, we do so with pain and regret.
>
> *Force*: We can be forced to do things involuntarily by physical forces, e.g. losing one's balance on a moving train, and by negative psychological pressure, e.g. threat of pain. Where no one could withstand such pressure, we don't blame someone for what they do. This shows that what they do is involuntary.
>
> *Ignorance*: The kind of ignorance that makes an act involuntary relates to the particular circumstances of the action, e.g. what you are actually doing, what its consequences will be, what tools you are using to act with, or how (in what manner) you are acting. Some actions done as a result of ignorance are involuntary, some are simply 'not voluntary'. The difference lies in whether the action is one that causes us pain or regret. If you accidentally step on someone's foot, and you regret this, then stepping on their foot is involuntary. But if you don't care, then it is simply non-voluntary.

Taken from
VOLUNTARY AND
INVOLUNTARY ACTIONS,
p. 301.

Fifteen-mark questions

When you are answering a short-answer question or 9-mark question, what you need to do is straightforward. You don't need to make any choices about *what* concepts or arguments to talk about, since that is specified by the question. By contrast, 15-mark questions are much more open-ended. You are asked to evaluate a claim. To do this, you will need to construct and evaluate arguments for and against the claim. Because there are marks

See EVALUATING
ARGUMENTS and
EVALUATING CLAIMS,
pp. 13–14.

available for AO2, if you do not evaluate the philosophical claims, theories
and arguments that you discuss, then you cannot get a good mark for the
question, no matter how clear and accurate you are in explaining them.

In addition to evaluating individual claims and arguments, your answer
as a whole needs to work as one long argument. Arguments have a clear
conclusion – you need to decide from the very beginning what your
conclusion will be. For 'How convincing is Berkeley's idealism?', your
conclusion could be:

1. 'very convincing', i.e. you defend BERKELEY'S IDEALISM (p. 96);
2. 'not at all convincing', i.e. you attack his idealism – for this conclusion,
    you don't need to show that any *other* theory of perception is convincing
    (perhaps none of them are!);
3. something conditional, 'Berkeley's idealism would be convincing if …',
    e.g. you might argue that if we had independent reasons to believe that
    God exists, his arguments would be more persuasive;
4. something comparative, e.g. 'Berkeley's idealism is less convincing
    than …' – for this conclusion, you'll need to make sure that you focus
    mainly on Berkeley's theory and bring in the other theory, e.g. indirect
    realism, *only* for the sake of comparison.

With your conclusion in mind, you need to select which arguments and
theories you will discuss. You want to discuss the arguments that you think
are the most critical ones – the ones that either provide the strongest reasons
for the claim or the strongest objections to it. You need to evaluate the
points and arguments/objections you discuss. Are there false or unknown
premises? Is the argument valid – or if it is inductive, is it cogent? Your
evaluation should never be simply 'there are points against and points in
favour'. If there are points against and points in favour, provide an argument
that the points on one side are stronger (more cogent) than the points on
the other side. Distinguish the arguments that are crucial for your conclusion
from ones that are not.

The examiners are more interested in the *quality* of what you write than
the quantity. You have demonstrated what you *know* in the other exam
questions. Now you need to show that you can *argue*. Three points are
relevant here:

1. Don't aim for a comprehensive discussion of the question, covering all the angles. Perhaps just discuss two arguments – ones that you think are really strong or important – but discuss them with depth and rigour (i.e. consider objections and replies to each argument). One good discussion is worth more than many weak or superficial points.
2. The examiners don't expect you to try to provide a 'balanced' account in the sense of trying to find points for and against a particular claim. They are testing your skill at arguing. So your answer can take the form of a very strong argument in favour of your conclusion and then strong replies to objections that can be raised.
3. To make your answer coherent, what you argue at each point in the answer should make some contribution to your conclusion. It fits into a logical structure.

There is no single right way to do all this (which is one reason I don't give a sample answer here). So you will need to plan your approach and answer to the question carefully. How to do this, and much more on answering essay questions, was discussed in WRITING PHILOSOPHY (p. 19). Once again, it's fine to use numbered arguments. It's also fine to use bullet points, particularly if you are running out of time.

Revision: it's more than memory

There are lots of memory tricks for learning information for exams. This section isn't about those. Revision isn't just about learning information, but also about learning how to use that information well in the exam. If you've been answering the questions throughout this book, then you have been putting into practice the advice I give below.

In revising for the exam, you need to bear in mind the structure of the exam and the AOs. First, the five questions in each section are all compulsory and cover different areas of the syllabus, so you'll need to revise the whole syllabus. Second, thinking about the 15-mark questions, structure your revision around the central questions or topics that the syllabus covers. In Epistemology, these are knowledge, perception, innate knowledge, rational intuition and deduction, and scepticism. In Moral Philosophy, they are the three normative theories (utilitarianism, Kantian deontology, Aristotelian virtue theory), the four applied issues (stealing, eating animals, simulated

See THE EXAMINATION, p. 405.

killing, lying), and the debates in metaethics between cognitivist and non-cognitivist theories (covering naturalism, intuitionism, error theory, emotivism, prescriptivism).

AO1 tests your understanding of central concepts and claims in these areas and how arguments are constructed for or against claims. We can break this down further. For the short-answer questions,

R1. Learn the concepts and definitions that are central to the philosophical theories studied.

The Glossary (p. 421) can help with this.

For the 5- and 9-mark questions,

R2. Learn who said what. What are the most important claims they made? What arguments did they use to defend their claims?

However, AO1 tests your *understanding*, not just your knowledge, of these claims and arguments. So you will need to show how the arguments are supposed to work. What are the premises and conclusion, and how is the conclusion supposed to follow from the premises?

R3. Spend time identifying the main claims and arguments involved in each issue you have studied, putting arguments in your own words, stating clearly what the conclusion is and what the premises are, and constructing argument maps. Explain how the reasoning is supposed to work.

This is difficult, because philosophical ideas and arguments are abstract and complicated, so it can be hard to know just what they mean. But the examiners also want precision. So it is worth thinking further about whatever you find hardest to understand.

> R4. Revise those concepts, claims and arguments that are hard to understand. Try to identify the differences between different interpretations. Which interpretation is best and why?

The exam questions do not explicitly ask for examples, but examples can prove very helpful when explaining a claim, objection or theory. If you are going to use examples, you want them to be good – clear, relevant, and supportive of the point you want to make. You can either remember good examples you have read, or create your own. In either case, you should know precisely what point the example is making. An irrelevant example demonstrates that you don't really know what you are talking about.

> R5. Prepare examples beforehand, rather than try to invent them in the exam. They must be short and they must make the right point – so try them out on your friends and teachers first.

What about AO2? How do you revise evaluation? Fifteen-mark questions test you on how well you build an argument, deal with objections, and come to a supported conclusion. The best way to prepare for it is to spend time *thinking* about the arguments and issues. For example, you might know and even understand Hume's arguments against rationalism, but you may never have stopped to really work out whether you think they are any good. Get involved!

So think about the different kinds of objection that can be raised to claims and arguments. Relate a particular argument to other arguments and viewpoints on the issue, and reflect on whether the objections to an argument undermine it. Work through the arguments so that you understand for yourself the pros and cons of each viewpoint.

See EVALUATING ARGUMENTS and EVALUATING CLAIMS, pp. 13–14.

> R6. Think reflectively about the arguments and issues. Practise arguing for and against a particular view. Think about the place and importance of the arguments for the issue as a whole.

Your answer needs to work as an argument itself, a coherent piece of reasoning. This means that what you write should also take the form of premises and conclusion. The premises will be your judgements as you go along, in response to this view or that objection. These judgements need to add up to a conclusion. You shouldn't end your essay with a totally different point of view than your evaluations in the essay support. In other words, do the judgements you reach reflect the arguments you have presented?

> R7. Think about how your judgements on the various arguments you have studied add up. Do they lead to one conclusion, one point of view being right? Or do you think arguments for and against one position are closely balanced?

These first seven revision points relate to taking in and understanding information. There are two more points that will help you organise the information, learn it better, and prepare you for answering exam questions. This is especially important in relation to the 15-mark questions.

Fifteen-mark questions are open-ended, and so you will need to choose to discuss what is *relevant* to the question being asked. Knowing what is relevant is a special kind of knowledge, which involves thinking carefully about what you know about the theories in relation to the question asked. A good way of organising your information is to create answer outlines or web-diagrams for particular issues.

For example, you could create an outline or web-diagram for innate knowledge. Think about the essential points, and organise them, perhaps like this:

1. What is innate knowledge? Is there more than one interpretation?
2. Who argued against innate knowledge? What are the main arguments?
3. Who argued for innate knowledge? What knowledge did they say was innate? What arguments did they use?
4. What is your conclusion on the issue, and why?

With an outline structured like this, you should be able to answer any question that comes up on innate knowledge.

> R8. Create structured outlines or web-diagrams for particular issues. Try to cover all the main points.

Finally, once you've organised your notes into an outline or web-diagram, time yourself writing exam answers. Start by using your outline, relying on your memory to fill in the details. Then practise by memorising the outline as well, and doing it as though it were an actual exam. You might be surprised at how quickly the time goes by. You'll find that you need to be very focused – but this is what the examiners are looking for, answers that are thoughtful but to the point.

> R9. Practise writing timed answers. Use your notes at first, but then practise without them.

Exam technique: getting the best result you can

If you've understood the exam structure, and know what to expect, the exam will seem less daunting. You'll have a good idea about how to proceed, and a sense of how the questions are testing different aspects of your knowledge. This section gives you some tips on how to approach the questions when you are actually in the exam.

Exams are very exciting, whether in a good way or a bad way! It can be helpful, therefore, to take your time at the beginning, not to rush into your answers, but to plan your way. The tips I give below are roughly in the order that you might apply them when taking the exam.

First, how long should you spend on each part? The marks give a rough guide. There are 80 marks available, 40 for Section A and 40 for Section B. You have 3 hours or 180 minutes. That's a little over 2 minutes for each mark. However, this isn't exact – the answer for each 2-mark question will probably take less than 4 minutes, while you should probably leave more than 30 minutes for each 15 mark question, especially because these answers require more planning. And because the exam covers five topics, you'll probably find that you know the answer to some of the questions better than others. Give yourself a little extra time for the questions you find difficult. You don't need to answer the questions in the order in which they are set. You might want to answer the ones you are confident about first, to get the best marks you can, and come back to the others later on. Don't lose marks on the questions that you can do, by not giving yourself enough time to answer them well.

E1. The number of marks available for each part is a rough guide to how long you spend on it. But allow a little extra time for the 15-mark questions and parts you find difficult. Choose what order to answer the questions in.

Before you start to write your answer to any part, read the question again very closely. There are two things to look out for. First, notice what the question is asking you to do. Remember that you need to display your *understanding*, not just your knowledge, of the philosophical issues. So you'll need to explain claims and arguments, not just state them. Second, notice the *precise* phrasing of the question. For example, in answering the sample question 'Explain Descartes' third wave of doubt (the "evil demon" argument)', it would be a mistake to talk about Descartes' first or second waves. Many students have a tendency to notice only what the question is about, e.g. doubt or utilitarianism. They don't notice the rest of the words in the question. But the question is never 'So tell me everything you know about *x*'! Make sure you answer the actual question set, and don't discuss anything that doesn't help answer that question.

See Understanding the question, p. 407.

E2. Before starting your answer, read the question again very closely. Take note of every word to make sure you answer the actual question set. Remember to explain, and not just state, claims and arguments.

With 15-mark questions, and for many 9-mark questions as well, before you start writing, it is worth organising your thoughts first. What are you going to say, in what order? Whether you are explaining or evaluating arguments, you need to present ideas in a logical order. Especially for 15-mark answers, if you've memorised an outline or a web-diagram, quickly write it out at the beginning so that you note down all the points. It is very easy to forget something or go off on a tangent once you are stuck into the arguments. Having an outline or web-diagram to work from will help you keep your answer relevant and structured. However, you might discover, as you develop your answer, that parts of the outline or diagram are irrelevant or just don't fit. Don't worry – the outline is only there as a guide. It will also remind you how much you still want to cover, so it can help you pace yourself better. If you do run out of time, you can indicate to the examiners that they should look at your plan – they will give marks for it.

E3. For longer answers, before you start writing, it can be worth writing out your outline or web-diagram first. This can help remind you of the key points you want to make, and the order in which you want to make them.

Because philosophy is about the logical relationship of ideas, there are a number of rules of thumb about presentation. Here are four important ones.

E4. Four rules of thumb:

a. Use philosophical terms to be precise and concise, not simply to sound 'impressive', and make sure it is clear from the context that you know what they mean.
b. Keep related ideas together. If you have a thought later on, add a footnote indicating where in the answer you want it to be read.
c. In 15-mark questions, explain a theory before evaluating it.
d. In 15-mark questions, apart from the conclusion for the essay as a whole, don't state the conclusion to an argument before you've discussed the argument, especially if you are going to present objections to that conclusion. You can state what the argument hopes to show, but don't state it *as* a conclusion.

If you use examples, you need to keep them short and relevant, and explain why they support your argument. An example is an illustration, not an argument in itself.

E5. Keep your examples short and make sure they support the point you want to make. Always explain how they support your point.

For 15-mark questions, it is worth noting that evaluation is more than just presenting objections and responses side-by-side. Get the objections and the theory to 'talk' to each other, and come to some conclusion about which side is stronger.

E6. For 15-mark questions, make sure your discussion is not just reporting a sequence of points of view, but presents objections and replies, evaluates the arguments, and reaches a particular conclusion.

Finally, it is very easy to forget something, or say it in an unclear way. For all the questions except the 15-mark questions, you may have time to write a rough draft and then once you are happy with it, write it out as neat into the answer booklet. The exam should test your ability to think, not your ability to write fast! Accuracy, clarity, concision and logical links can all improve in a second draft. For the 15-mark questions, leave time to check your answer at the end. You might find you can add a sentence here or there to connect two ideas together more clearly, or that some phrase is imprecise. These little things can make a big difference to the mark.

E7. For questions other than 15-mark questions, you may have time to write two drafts – rough and final. For 15-mark questions, leave time to check your answer at the end. Don't be afraid to add to or correct what you have written.

Revision tips

R1. Learn the concepts and definitions that are central to the philosophical theories studied.

R2. Learn who said what. What are the most important claims they made? What arguments did they use to defend their claims?

R3. Spend time identifying the main claims and arguments involved in each issue you have studied, putting arguments in your own words, stating clearly what the conclusion is and what the premises are, and constructing argument maps. Explain how the reasoning is supposed to work.

R4. Revise those concepts, claims and arguments that are hard to understand. Try to identify the differences between different interpretations. Which interpretation is best and why?

R5. Prepare examples beforehand, rather than try to invent them in the exam. They must be short and they must make the right point – so try them out on your friends and teachers first.

R6. Think reflectively about the arguments and issues. Practise arguing for and against a particular view. Think about the place and importance of the arguments for the issue as a whole.

R7. Think about how your judgements on the various arguments you have studied add up. Do they lead to one conclusion, one point of view being right? Or do you think arguments for and against one position are closely balanced?

R8. Create structured outlines or web-diagrams for particular issues. Try to cover all the main points.

R9. Practise writing timed answers. Use your notes at first, but then practise without them.

Exam tips

E1. The number of marks available for each part is a rough guide to how long you spend on it. But allow a little extra time for the 15-mark questions and parts you find difficult. Choose what order to answer the questions in.

E2. Before starting your answer, read the question again very closely. Take note of every word to make sure you answer the actual question set. Remember to explain, and not just state, claims and arguments.

E3. For longer answers, before you start writing, it can be worth writing out your outline or web-diagram first. This can help remind you of the key points you want to make, and the order in which you want to make them.

E4. Four rules of thumb:

    a.   Use philosophical terms to be precise and concise, not simply to sound 'impressive', and make sure it is clear from the context that you know what they mean.

    b.   Keep related ideas together. If you have a thought later on, add a footnote indicating where in the answer you want it to be read.

    c.   In 15-mark questions, explain a theory before evaluating it.

    d.   In 15-mark questions, apart from the conclusion for the essay as a whole, don't state the conclusion to an argument before you've discussed the argument, especially if you are going to present objections to that conclusion. You can state what the argument hopes to show, but don't state it *as* a conclusion.

E5. Keep your examples short and make sure they support the point you want to make. Always explain how they support your point.

E6. For 15-mark questions, make sure your discussion is not just reporting a sequence of points of view, but presents objections and replies, evaluates the arguments, and reaches a particular conclusion.

E7. For questions other than 15-mark questions, you may have time to write two drafts – rough and final. For 15-mark questions, leave time to check your answer at the end. Don't be afraid to add to or correct what you have written.

Good luck!

Glossary

(with Joanne Lovesey)

a posteriori: Knowledge of propositions that can only be known to be true or false through sense experience.

a priori: Knowledge of propositions that do not require (sense) experience to be known to be true or false.

ability knowledge: Knowing 'how' to do something, e.g. 'I know how to ride a bike'.

abstract: Theoretical (rather than applied or practical) and removed from any concrete objects or instances.

acquaintance knowledge: Knowing 'of' someone or some place. For example, 'I know the manager of the restaurant', or 'I know Oxford well'.

ad hoc: A statement or a move in an argument that suits the purpose at hand but has no independent support.

analogy: Similarity in several respects between different things.

analysis: Process of breaking up a complex concept, expression or argument in order to reveal its simpler constituents, thereby elucidating its meaning or logical structure.

analytic: A proposition that is true (or false) in virtue of the meanings of the words. For instance, 'a bachelor is an unmarried man' is analytically true, while 'a square has three sides' is analytically false.

antecedent: The proposition that forms the first part of a conditional statement, usually the part of the sentence that comes after 'if'. E.g. in both 'If it rains then I will get wet' and 'I will get wet if it rains', the antecedent is 'it rains'.

anti-realism, moral: The theory that claims that there are no moral properties. Error theory and moral non-cognitivism are both anti-realist.

applied ethics: The branch of ethics concerned with the application of normative ethical theories to particular issues, such as lying or stealing.

arête: An 'excellence', or more specifically, a 'virtue' – a quality that aids the fulfilment of a thing's *ergon* (Aristotle).

argument: A reasoned inference from one set of claims – the premises – to another claim, the conclusion.

argument map: Visual diagram of the logical structure of an argument, i.e. how the premises logically relate to one another and to the conclusion.

assertion: The claim that a proposition is true.

assumption: A proposition accepted without proof or evidence as the basis for an inference or argument.

attitude: A mental state regarding how the world is or should be. A cognitive attitude, e.g. belief, has a mind-to-world direction of fit. A non-cognitive attitude, e.g. desire, has a world-to-mind direction of fit.

begging the question: The informal fallacy of (explicitly or implicitly) assuming the truth of the conclusion of an argument as one of the premises employed in an effort to demonstrate its truth.

belief: Affirmation of, or conviction regarding, the truth of a proposition. E.g. 'I believe that the grass is green'.

Cartesian circle: Refers to the circular reasoning Descartes seems to employ regarding clear and distinct ideas and God: Descartes cannot rely on clear and distinct ideas before proving God exists, but he cannot prove that God exists without relying on clear and distinct ideas.

Categorical Imperative: 'Act only on that maxim through which you can at the same time will that it should become a universal law' (Kant).

character: A person's habitual dispositions regarding what they feel, how they think, how they react, the choices they make, and the actions they perform, under different circumstances.

character trait: An attribute that is exhibited by an individual as a matter of habit, e.g. honesty or being bad-tempered.

choice: What we decide upon as a result of deliberation, typically giving rise to voluntary action. Deliberate desire regarding something that is in one's power (Aristotle).

circular: An argument is circular if it employs its own conclusion as a premise.

claim: A proposition that is asserted or affirmed to be true.

clear and distinct ideas: A clear idea is 'present and accessible to the attentive mind'; a distinct idea is clear and also sharply separated from other ideas so that every part of it is clear (Descartes).

cogent: An inductive argument in which the truth of the premises (significantly) raises the probability that the conclusion is true.

cogito, **the:** 'I think', Descartes' first certain knowledge.

cognitivism: A cognitivist account of ethical language argues that moral judgements express beliefs, can be true or false, and aim to describe the world. So 'lying is wrong' expresses the belief that lying is wrong, and is either true or false.

coherent: A set of statements are coherent if they are consistent and increase each other's probability.

common sense: The basic perceptions or understandings that are shared by many (most) people.

compatible: Two claims are compatible if they are consistent. Two properties are compatible if it is possible for something to have both of them at once.

composition, fallacy of: The informal fallacy of attributing some feature of the members of a collection to the collection itself, or reasoning from part to whole. E.g. 'sodium and chloride are both dangerous to humans, therefore sodium-chloride (salt) is dangerous to humans'.

concept: Any abstract notion or idea by virtue of which we apply general terms to things.

conclusion: A proposition whose truth has been inferred from premises.

conditional: A proposition that takes the form of 'if …, then …'. The conditional asserts that if the first statement (the antecedent) is true, then the second statement (the consequent) is also true. E.g. 'If it is raining then the ground is wet' asserts that if it is true that it is raining, it is true that the ground is wet.

conscience: An inner awareness, faculty, intuition or judgement that assists in distinguishing right from wrong.

consequent: The proposition that forms the second part of a conditional statement, usually the part of the sentence that occurs after 'then'. E.g. In both 'If it will rain then I will get wet and 'I will get wet if it will rain', the consequent is 'I will get wet'.

consequentialism, act: The theory that actions are morally right or wrong depending on their consequences and nothing else. An act is right if it maximises what is good.

consistent: Two or more claims are consistent if they can both be true at the same time.

contingent: A proposition that could be either true or false, a state of affairs that may or may not hold, depending on how the world actually is.

contradiction: Two claims that cannot both be true, and cannot both be false. Or one claim that both asserts and denies something. E.g. 'It is raining and it is not raining'.

contradiction in conception: In Kantian ethics, the test for whether we can will a maxim to become universal law can be failed if it would somehow be self-contradictory for everyone to act on that maxim.

contradiction in will: In Kantian ethics, the test for whether we can will a maxim to become universal law can be failed if, although the maxim is not self-contradictory, we cannot rationally will it.

copy principle, Humean: All simple ideas are copies of impressions.

counter-argument: An argument that attempts to establish a conclusion that undermines another argument, or the conclusion of another argument.

counterexamples, method of finding: If a theory makes a general claim, such as 'all propositional knowledge is justified true belief', we only need to find a single instance in which this is false (a counterexample) to show that the general claim is false and so something is wrong with the theory.

counter-intuitive: Something that doesn't fit with our intuition.

deduction: An argument whose conclusion is logically entailed by its premises, i.e. if the premises are true, the conclusion cannot be false.

definition: An explanation of the meaning of a word. Philosophical definitions often attempt to give necessary and sufficient conditions for the application of the term being defined.

deontology: The study of what one must do (*deon* (Greek) means 'one must'). Deontology claims that actions are right or wrong in themselves, not depending on their consequences. We have moral duties to do things which it is right to do and moral duties not to do things which it is wrong to do.

desirable: 1) Worthy of being desired. 2) Capable of being desired.

desire: A state of mind that motivates a person to act in such a way as to satisfy the desire, e.g. if a person desires a cup of tea, they are motivated to make and drink a cup of tea.

dilemma: Two mutually exclusive and exhaustive options (horns), both of which face significant objections.

direct realism: Physical objects exist independently of our minds and of our perceptions of them, and the immediate objects of perception are mind-independent objects and their properties.

direction of fit: The direction of the relation between mind and world. In one direction, the mind 'fits' the world, as in belief. We change our beliefs to fit the facts. In the other direction, the world 'fits' the mind, as in desire. We act on our desires to change the world to satisfy our desires.

disanalogy: A point of dissimilarity between two things, something that two things don't have in common.

disjunction: An either/or claim. An example of a disjunction is: 'Either it will rain or it will be sunny'.

disjunctive theory of perception: If something looks a certain way, then one of two quite different things is going on: either I directly perceive a mind-independent physical object that is *F* or it appears to me just as if there is something that is *F*, but there is nothing that is *F*.

distinction: A difference or contrast between things.

doctrine of the mean: Aristotle's claim that virtue requires us to feel, choose and act in an 'intermediate' way, neither 'too much' nor 'too little', but 'to feel [passions] at the right times, with reference to the right objects, towards the right people, with the right motive, and in the right way'.

duties, general/specific: Duties are obligations we have towards someone or something. General duties are those we have towards anyone, e.g. do not murder, help people in need. Specific duties are those we have because of our particular personal or social relationships, e.g. to keep one's promises or to provide for one's children.

duties, perfect/imperfect: Perfect duties are those we must always fulfil and have no choice over when or how (e.g. do not kill). Imperfect duties are cases in which we have some choice in how we fulfil the obligation (e.g. giving to charity). No specific person can demand that we fulfil an imperfect duty towards them.

emotivism: The theory that claims that moral judgements express a feeling or non-cognitive attitude, typically approval or disapproval, and aim to influence the feelings and actions of others.

empirical: Relating to or deriving from experience, especially sense experience, but also including experimental scientific investigation.

empiricism: The theory that there can be no a priori knowledge of synthetic propositions about the world (outside my mind), i.e. all a priori knowledge is of analytic propositions, while all knowledge of synthetic propositions is gained through sense experience.

empiricism, classical: The theory that all knowledge is gained from experience: All concepts are gained from sense experience or experience of our own minds; and all knowledge of synthetic propositions about the world (outside my mind) is gained through sense experience.

end: What an action seeks to achieve or secure, its aim or purpose.

end, final: An end that we desire for its own sake, we can't give some further purpose for why we seek it.

enumerative induction: The method of reasoning that argues from many instances of something to a general statement about that thing. E.g. the sun has risen in the morning every day for *x* number of days, therefore the sun rises in the morning.

epistemology: The study (-*ology*) of knowledge (*episteme*) and related concepts, including belief, justification and certainty. It looks at the possibility and sources of knowledge.

equivocation, fallacy of: The use of an ambiguous word or phrase in different senses within a single argument. E.g. 'All banks are next to rivers, I deposit money in a bank, therefore I deposit money next to a river'.

ergon: 'Function' or 'characteristic activity' of something, e.g. the *ergon* of a knife is to cut, the *ergon* of an eye is to see.

error theory: The theory that moral judgements make claims about objective moral properties, but that no such properties exist. Thus moral judgements are cognitive, but are all false. Moral language, as we mean to use it, rests on a mistake.

ethics: The branch of philosophy concerned with the evaluation of human conduct, including theories about which actions are right or wrong (normative ethics) and the meaning of moral language (metaethics).

eudaimonia: Often translated as 'happiness', but better understood as 'living well and faring well'. According to Aristotle, eudaimonia is not subjective and is not a psychological state, but an objective quality of someone's life as a whole. It is the final end for human beings.

experience machine: Nozick's thought experiment concerning a virtual reality machine which someone plugs into for life. The machine will create the experience of a very happy life, but Nozick argues that we value being in touch with reality more, so we won't choose to plug in.

explanation: An intelligible account of why something happens. The thing to be explained (the explanandum) is usually accepted as a fact, and what is used to explain it (the explanans) is usually plausible but less certain.

external world: Everything that exists outside of our minds.

faculty: A mental capacity or ability, such as sight, the ability to feel fear, and reason.

fallacy/fallacious: An error in reasoning. More exactly, a fallacy is an argument in which the premises do not offer rational support to the conclusion. If the argument is deductive, then it is fallacious if it is not valid. If the argument is inductive, it is fallacious if the premises do not make the conclusion more likely to be true.

false: A proposition is false if things are not as it states. E.g. the proposition 'grass is always purple' is false, because there is grass that is not purple.

felicific calculus: In Bentham's ethics, the means of calculating pleasures and pains caused by an action and adding them up on a single scale. The total amount of happiness produced is the sum total of everyone's pleasures minus the sum total of everyone's pains.

first principles: Basic or foundational propositions in an area of knowledge or theory that are not deducible from other propositions.

Formula of Humanity: A version of the Categorical Imperative: 'Act in such a way that you always treat humanity, whether in your own person or in the person of any other, never simply as a means, but always at the same time as an end' (Kant).

function argument: Aristotle's argument that the human good (*eudaimonia*) will be achieved by performing our characteristic activity (*ergon*) well. Traits that enable us to fulfil our *ergon*, which is rational activity, are virtues (*arête*).

Gettier case: A situation in which we have justified true belief, but not knowledge, because the belief is only accidentally true, given the evidence that justifies it.

Golden Rule: The moral guideline that says 'do unto others as you would have them do unto you'.

good: In ethics, what is good provides a standard of evaluation and what we should aim at in our actions and lives.

hallucination: A non-veridical perceptual experience that is not coherently connected with the rest of our perceptual experience.

hallucination, argument from: Against direct realism: The possibility of hallucinatory experiences that are subjectively indistinguishable from a veridical perception means that we don't immediately perceive physical objects, but sense-data.

hedonic calculus: *See* felicific calculus.

hedonism: The claim that pleasure is happiness and the only good.

Hume's 'fork': We can have knowledge of just two sorts of claim: the relations between ideas and matters of fact.

hypothesis: A proposal that needs to be confirmed or rejected by reasoning or experience.

hypothetical reasoning: Working out the best hypothesis that would explain or account for some experience or fact.

idea: An object of perception, thought, or understanding. Locke uses the term to refer to a complete thought, taking the form of a proposition, e.g. 'bananas are yellow'; a sensation or sensory experience, e.g. a visual sensation of yellow; or a concept, e.g. YELLOW.

idea, complex: An idea that is derived from two or more simple ideas.

idea, simple: A single, uniform conception, with nothing distinguishable within it.

idealism, Berkeley's: All that exists are minds and ideas. What we think of as physical objects are, in fact, bundles of ideas. The immediate objects of perception (ordinary objects such as tables, chairs, etc.) are ideas, mind-dependent objects. *Esse est percipi (aut percipere)* – to be is to be perceived (or to perceive).

identical, numerically: One and the same thing. Everything is numerically identical to itself, and nothing else.

identical, qualitatively: Two or more things are qualitatively identical if they share their properties in common, for example, two separate copies of the same picture.

illusion: A distortion of the senses such that what we perceive is different from what exists.

illusion, argument from: Against direct realism: Illusions can be 'subjectively indistinguishable' from veridical perception (e.g. a crooked stick in water), so we see sense-data, and not physical objects, immediately.

imperative: A command or order. A hypothetical imperative is a statement about what you ought to do, on the assumption of some desire or goal, e.g. if you want to pass your exam, you ought to study hard. A categorical imperative is a statement about what you ought to do, without regard to what you want.

impression: What we are immediately and directly aware of, which can either be impressions of 'sensation' or impressions of 'reflection' (Locke, Hume). Impressions of sensation derive from our senses, impressions of reflection derive from our experience of our mind, including emotions.

inconceivable: Impossible to imagine, think or grasp.

inconsistent: Two claims are inconsistent if they can't both be true at the same time.

indirect realism: We perceive physical objects, which exist independently of the mind, indirectly via sense-data which are caused by and represent physical objects.

induction: An argument whose conclusion is supported by its premises, but is not logically entailed by them, i.e. if the premises are true, then this makes it (more) likely that the conclusion is true, but it is still possible that the conclusion is false.

infallibilism: To be knowledge, a belief must be certain. If we can doubt a belief, then it is not certain, and so it is not knowledge.

inference: Coming to accept a proposition as true on the basis of reasoning from other propositions taken to be true.

inference to the best explanation: An inductive argument form where the conclusion presents the 'best explanation' for why the premises are true.

infinite: Without any bounds or limits. E.g. the natural numbers form an infinite series, the numbers continue in both directions (positive and negative numbers) without any end point.

innate: Knowledge or ideas that are in some way built into the structure of the mind, rather than gained from sense experience.

innatism, concept: The claim that some of our concepts are innate, not derived from experience, but somehow part of the structure of the mind.

innatism, knowledge: The claim that there is at least some innate knowledge, not derived from experience, but somehow part of the structure of the mind.

integrity: Acting on and living by the values that you endorse.

intention: A mental state that expresses a person's choice. It specifies the action they choose and often their reason or end in acting.

intuition: Direct non-inferential awareness of abstract objects or truths.

intuition, rational: The capacity to discover the truth of a claim just by thinking about it using reason.

intuitionism: The theory that some moral judgements are self-evident, i.e. their truth can be known just by rational reflection upon the judgement itself. Moral intuitions are a type of synthetic a priori knowledge.

invalid: Not valid. A deductive argument is invalid if it is possible for the premises to be true while the conclusion is false.

involuntary: According to Aristotle, an act is involuntary if it is either forced or done from ignorance that is not culpable (especially if it is regretted once the ignorance is removed).

is–ought gap: Hume's claim that judgements about what ought to be the case are very different from judgements about what is the case, and cannot be deduced from them. The claim is made as an objection to moral cognitivism.

justice: The principle that each person receives their 'due'. Aristotle distinguishes between wide and narrow senses. In the wide sense, anything legal is just, and anything illegal is unjust. In the narrow sense, justice is fairness.

justice in distribution: Justice concerning who gets which goods and other resources.

justice in rectification: Justice concerning how to correct an injustice.

justification: What is offered as grounds for believing an assertion.

lemma: A claim made part way through an argument.

matters of fact: States of affairs, how the world is. According to Hume, they are known through experience and induction, especially causal inference.

maxim: A personal principle that guides our decisions, e.g. 'to get a good education' (Kant).

meaning, descriptive: The aspect of the meaning of a sentence that asserts something about the world and can be evaluated as true or false.

meaning, emotive: The aspect of the meaning of a sentence that expresses or evokes an emotion.

meaning, prescriptive: The aspect of the meaning of a sentence that acts either to command or commend. For example, the prescriptive meaning of 'lying is wrong' might be 'do not lie'.

meaningful: Having a linguistic (semantic) meaning.

means: What is done to achieve an end. Instrumental means are actions done to achieve some further, independent end, e.g. chopping vegetables in order to eat them. Constitutive means are those which are done as achieving the end, e.g. relaxing on the beach is a way of having a good holiday.

metaethics: The philosophical study of what morality is, enquiring into the meaning of moral language, the metaphysics of moral values, the epistemology of moral judgements, and the nature of moral attitudes.

metaphysics: The branch of philosophy that asks questions about the fundamental nature of reality. *Meta-* means above, beyond or after; physics enquires into the physical structure of reality.

mind-dependent: Depending on a mind for existence or definition, e.g. ideas are mind-dependent.

mind-independent: Not depending on a mind for existence or definition. According to realism in perception, physical objects are mind-independent; according to moral realism, moral properties are mind-independent (in some important way).

morality: The rules, ideals and expectations governing fundamental aspects of human conduct. It concerns right and wrong, good and bad, in human action and character.

motive: A mental state or consideration that inclines someone to act in a certain way. Someone's motive could be a reason for acting, an end, or a desire.

naturalism, moral: A form of moral realism that claims that moral properties are natural properties. According to reductive naturalism, moral properties are identical with certain properties that can be identified through sense experience and science, e.g. the claim that goodness is happiness understood as pleasure (a psychological property). According to non-reductive naturalism, moral properties are natural – related to human nature – but not a kind of property that science can investigate, e.g. the good life is eudaimonia (a complex psychological, rational and normative property).

naturalistic fallacy: According to Moore, the mistake of identifying moral good with any natural property.

necessary: A proposition that must be true (or if false, it must be false), a state of affairs that must hold.

necessary condition: One proposition is a necessary condition of another when the second cannot be true while the first is false. For example, being a man is a necessary condition of being a bachelor, as if you are not a man you cannot be a bachelor.

nihilism: The view that there are no moral values.

no false lemmas: The 'no false lemmas' condition is sometimes added to the tripartite theory of knowledge and says that for something to count as knowledge it must be the case that you did not infer it from anything false.

non-cognitivism: The theory that claims that moral judgements express non-cognitive attitudes. Moral judgements do not make claims about reality and are not true or false (they are not fact-stating).

non-naturalism, moral: A form of moral realism that claims that moral properties are not natural properties.

non-voluntary: According to Aristotle, an action is non-voluntary if it is done from ignorance and if the ignorance is lifted, the agent does not regret the action.

normative: Relating to 'norms', rules or reasons.

normative ethics: The branch of ethics concerned with developing theories concerning what (e.g. which actions, which character traits, which intentions) is right or wrong, good or bad.

objection: A claim or argument that is given as a reason against the truth of another claim or argument.

objective: Independent of what people think or feel. A claim is objectively true if its truth does not depend on people's beliefs.

Ockham's razor: The principle that states that we should not put forward a hypothesis that says many different things exist when a simpler explanation will do as well. 'Do not multiply entities beyond necessity'. A simpler explanation is a better explanation, as long as it is just as successful.

ontology: The study (-*ology*) of what exists or 'being' (*ont*).

open question argument: Moore's argument that identifying the property 'good' with any other property is never correct because whether that property is, in fact, good is an open question (logically, it can receive a yes or no answer), whereas whether some property is itself is not an open question.

paradox: A claim or set of claims that are contradictory but present a philosophical challenge, e.g. 'This sentence is false' (if the sentence is true, it is false; if the sentence is false, it is true).

partiality: Favouring some people, e.g. family and friends, over others.

passions: In Aristotle, bodily appetites (for food, drink, sex, etc.), emotions, desires, and any feelings accompanied by pleasure or pain.

perception: Awareness of apparently external objects through use of the senses.

perception, immediate objects of: What we are directly aware of in perception, which may be physical objects or sensations of these.

perceptual variation, argument from: Against direct realism: Different people perceive the same physical object differently. Therefore, what each person perceives is how the object appears to them. This appearance is mind-dependent sense-data. Physical objects are therefore not perceived directly.

permissible: An action that is neither morally forbidden nor required (obligatory).

physical object: Material objects, including things like tables, books, our own bodies, plants, mountains.

plausible: Fits with what else we already know.

pleasures, higher and lower: According to Mill, one pleasure is higher than another if almost everyone who is 'competently acquainted' with both prefers one over the other. Higher pleasures include thought, feeling and imagination, while lower pleasures involve the body and senses.

possible: Capable of happening/existing/being the case. If something is possible, it could be true.

practical ethics: *See* applied ethics.

practical reason: Reasons and reasoning concerned with what we can change, and with making good choices.

practical wisdom: (*phronesis*) An intellectual virtue of practical reason, 'a true and reasoned state or capacity to act with regard to the things that are good or bad for man' (Aristotle). It involves knowledge of what is good or bad in general and what is good in a particular situation, and the abilities to deliberate well and act on that deliberation.

predicate: The part of a sentence or clause containing a verb or adjective, and stating something about the subject. E.g. in 'Jane is happy' the predicate is 'is happy'.

premise: A proposition that, as part of an argument, provides or contributes to a reason to believe that the conclusion is true.

prescriptivism: The non-cognitive theory that moral judgements are prescriptive, that is, moral judgements provide commands and recommendations about how to act.

preservation of truth: Valid deductive arguments preserve truth, meaning that when the premises are true, anything that logically follows from them will also be true.

primary quality: Properties that are 'utterly inseparable' from a physical object, whatever changes it goes through, even if it is divided into smaller and smaller pieces. The object has these properties 'in and of itself'. Locke lists extension (he also talks of size), shape, motion, number and solidity as primary qualities.

proof: The demonstration of the truth of a proposition using a valid deductive argument from known or certain premises to that proposition as its conclusion.

property: An attribute or characteristic of an object. E.g. the property of being green, or being tall.

property, moral: An attribute or characteristic of an object that is ethically normative, e.g. goodness or being a virtue.

property, natural/non-natural: Natural properties are those that we can identify through sense experience and science. Non-natural properties cannot be analysed in terms of or reduced to natural properties.

property, relational: A characteristic that something has only in relation to another thing. E.g. 'Pete is taller than Bob', or 'Alice loves Jack'.

proposition: A declarative statement (or more accurately, what is claimed by a declarative statement), such as 'mice are mammals'. Propositions can go after 'that' in 'I believe that …' and 'I know that …'.

propositional knowledge: Knowing 'that' some claim – a proposition – is true or false, e.g. 'I know that Paris is the capital of France'.

prove: To demonstrate that a proposition is true by giving a valid deductive argument from known or certain premises to that proposition as the conclusion.

queerness, argument from: Mackie's argument that moral properties, understood as non-natural properties, are (metaphysically and epistemologically) puzzling and improbable, which is a reason to believe they do not exist.

rationalism: The theory that there can be a priori knowledge of synthetic propositions about the world (outside my mind) gained through rational insight and reasoning.

rationalism, classical: The theory that there can be a priori knowledge of synthetic propositions about the world (outside my mind) that is innate and then developed through rational insight and reasoning. The concepts involved in innate knowledge are also thereby innate.

realism, moral: The theory that claims moral judgements are made true or false by objective moral properties that exist and are mind-independent (in some sense).

reason: A statement presented in justification for a claim. A good reason in some way raises the probability that the claim is true.

reasoning: The process of thinking about something in a logical way, in particular, drawing inferences on the basis of reasons.

reductio ad absurdum: A form of argument that shows that some claim leads to a contradiction.

reflection: Locke: Our experience of 'the internal operations of our minds', gained through introspection or an awareness of what the mind is doing. More generally, thinking.

relations of ideas: Hume: Relations of ideas are established by pure thought or reflection and are 'intuitively and demonstratively certain'. The negation of a relation of ideas is a contradiction.

relativism: The theory that some area of discourse, e.g. concerning truth, knowledge or morality, is 'relative to' a society or person. According to relativism, a proposition may be true 'for' one person but not another; or an action may be morally right in one society but not another.

reliabilism: The theory that you know that p if p is true, you believe that p, and your belief is caused by a reliable cognitive process.

represent: A relation of one thing (e.g. sense-data) to another (e.g. physical objects) established by an accurate and systematic correlation of the first to the second.

resemblance: A relation of similarity (in properties or appearance) between two things, e.g. sense-data and physical objects.

responsibility, moral: Accountability for the actions one performs and the consequences they bring about, for which a moral agent can be justly praised or blamed. Moral responsibility is commonly held to require the agent's freedom to have done otherwise.

right reason: (*orthos logos*) In Aristotle, the standard for judging whether a character trait or an action conforms to the mean. Virtues and right actions are in accordance with 'right reason'.

rights: Justified moral demands regarding how other people may treat us, especially the freedoms (e.g. from harm) or benefits (e.g. education) they ought to provide. We are entitled to our rights in the sense that others have a moral obligation to respect them.

sceptical: Not easily convinced, or having doubts or reservations. (Not to be confused with scepticism.)

scepticism: The view that our usual justifications for claiming our beliefs amount to knowledge are inadequate, so we do not in fact have knowledge.

scepticism, global: Scepticism about all knowledge claims, especially concerning the existence and nature of anything outside the mind.

scepticism, local: Scepticism about some specific claim, or more commonly, about some area/branch of supposed knowledge.

scope: The extent or range over which something applies, e.g. the scope of this textbook is the AQA syllabus for epistemology and moral philosophy.

secondary principles: In Mill, moral 'rules of thumb' that, if followed, generally produce happiness, e.g. 'tell the truth'. Mill argues that we have learned secondary principles through human history, through trial and error.

secondary quality: Properties that physical objects have that are 'nothing but powers to produce various sensations in us'. Locke lists 'colours, sounds, tastes, and so on', later adding smells and temperature.

self-evident: A proposition that can be known just by rational reflection on that proposition.

sensation: Our experience of objects outside the mind, perceived through the senses.

sense experience: Experiences given to us by our senses.

sense-data (singular **sense-datum):** Mental images or representations of what is perceived, the 'content' of perceptual experience. If sense-data exist, they are the immediate objects of perception and are 'private', mind-dependent mental things.

senses: Capacities that give us experience of the external world. They include sight, hearing, smell, taste, touch and bodily awareness.

sensible quality: A property that can be detected by the senses.

sentience: The ability to feel, perceive or experience subjectively, in particular the capacity to experience pleasure and pain.

signposts: Sentences that indicate what the text is about, what has been, is being, or will be argued. E.g. 'I will now argue that …'.

simulated killing: The dramatisation of killing within a fictional context, e.g. in video games, films and plays. It is not merely the description of a killing, as in a novel, but a fictional enactment of killing that the audience or gamer can see and hear.

skill analogy: The analogy between virtues and practical skills. In Aristotle, virtues are said to be like practical skills because we learn both through practice (what we do), not (just) theory; and we gain an expertise that is sensitive to individual situations.

solipsism: The view that only oneself, one's mind, exists. There are no mind-independent physical objects and there are no other minds either.

sophism: The use of plausible arguments that are actually fallacious, especially when someone dishonestly presents such an argument as if it were legitimate reasoning.

soul: In Aristotle, that part of the person that relates to mind and life. According to Aristotle, the soul has three parts – a part relating to being alive, a part characterised by desires and emotions that are responsive to reason, and rational intellect.

sound: A deductive argument is sound if it is valid with true premises.

speciesism: Unfair discrimination on the basis of what species something belongs to.

stealing: Taking someone else's property with no intention of returning it and without their permission (or without the legal right to do so).

subjective: That which depends upon the personal or individual, especially where it is supposed to be an arbitrary expression of preference.

subjectivism: The theory that moral judgements assert or report approval or disapproval, e.g. 'Murder is wrong' means 'Most people disapprove of murder'.

subjectivism, speaker: The theory that moral judgements assert the approval or disapproval of the speaker, e.g. 'Murder is wrong' means 'I disapprove of X'. Therefore, whether a moral judgement is true or false depends on the attitudes of the speaker.

sufficient condition: One proposition is a sufficient condition for another when the first cannot be true while the second is false. For example, being a dog is sufficient for being an animal, because something can't be a dog without also being an animal.

synthetic: A proposition that is not analytic, but true or false depending on how the world is.

systematic correlation: A relationship between two things whereby a change in one is always accompanied by a change in the other.

tabula rasa: Latin for 'blank slate'. Locke claims that at birth our mind is a *tabula rasa*, meaning we have no innate knowledge or ideas.

tautology: A statement that repeats the subject in the predicate, that 'says the same thing twice'. E.g. 'Green things are green'.

theoretical reason: Reasons and reasoning concerned with what we can't change and what is true.

thought experiment: A philosophical method designed to test a hypothesis or philosophical claim through imagining a hypothetical situation and coming to a judgement.

time-lag argument: Against direct realism: Because it takes time for us to perceive physical objects, we don't see them directly. For example, as light takes 8 minutes to reach the earth from the sun, if you look at the sun you are actually seeing it as it was 8 minutes ago. Therefore, you are not perceiving the sun directly.

tripartite view of knowledge: Justified true belief is necessary and sufficient for propositional knowledge (*S* knows that *p* if and only if *S* is justified in believing that *p*, *p* is true, and *S* believes that *p*).

true: A proposition is true if things are as it states. E.g. the proposition 'the grass is green' is true if the grass is green, and otherwise it is false.

tyranny of the majority: The unjust exercise of power by a majority of people over a minority who have different values or desires, e.g. outlawing a minority religion because most people want it outlawed.

unanalysable: Not subject to analysis.

universal: A statement that applies to all/every member of a class or domain. E.g. 'All whales are mammals' and 'Every boy likes ice cream'.

universalise: To apply to everything/everyone.

unperceived objects: Objects that exist when not perceived by anyone.

unsound: A deductive argument is unsound if it is either invalid or has at least one false premise.

utilitarianism, act: The theory that only happiness is good, and the right act is that act that maximises happiness. Hedonist act utilitarianism understands happiness in terms of the balance of pleasure over pain.

utilitarianism, preference: The theory that we should maximise happiness, which is understood not in terms of pleasure and pain, but in terms of the satisfaction of people's preferences.

utilitarianism, rule: The theory that only happiness is good, and the right act is that act that complies with those rules which, if everybody followed them, would lead to the greatest happiness (compared to any other set of rules).

utility: The property of an object or action in virtue of which it tends to produce happiness.

utility, principle of: The defining principle of act utilitarianism: 'that principle which approves or disapproves of every action whatsoever, according to the tendency which it appears to have to augment or diminish the happiness of the party whose interest is in question' (Bentham).

valid: An argument in which, if the premises are true, then the conclusion must be true. In this case, we say that the conclusion is entailed by the premises. Only deductive arguments can be valid.

value judgement: A judgement regarding whether something is good or bad in some way.

value theory: Any theory about what is good, e.g. a utilitarian value theory claims that only happiness is good.

veridical: A proposition that is true or an experience that represents the world as it actually is.

verification principle: The principle that all meaningful claims are either analytic or empirically verifiable (Ayer). A statement is analytic if it is true or false just in virtue of the meanings of the words. A statement is empirically verifiable if empirical evidence would go towards establishing that the statement is true or false.

vice: A trait that is morally bad. Aristotle argues that vices are dispositions to feel or choose not in the mean, but either too much or too little.

virtue: Traits or states of a person that enable them to achieve some good purpose, especially living a morally good life. Aristotle argues that virtues are traits in accordance with reason, and distinguishes virtues of intellect and virtues of character.

virtue epistemology: *S* knows that *p* if and only if *p* is true, *S* believes that *p*, and *S*'s belief that *p* is the result of *S* exercising their epistemic/intellectual virtues; in Zagzebski's definition, *S* knows that *p* if *S* believes that *p* and *S*'s belief arises from an act of intellectual virtue.

virtue ethics: The normative theory that starts from the question of what it is to be a good person, then derives an account of morally right action as what a good person would do. Aristotle argues that a good person has the virtues, which enable them to achieve eudaimonia.

virtue, epistemic/intellectual: A skill, ability or trait of the mind or person that contributes to the good end of gaining knowledge and forming true beliefs.

voluntary: According to Aristotle, we act voluntarily when we act as we choose. We know what we are doing, and we bring it about ourselves.

waves of doubt: Descartes' three arguments supporting scepticism. The first, an argument from illusion, throws doubt on always believing what our senses tell us. The second, an argument from dreaming, throws doubt on all sense perception, and therefore on the nature of reality. The third, the possibility that an evil demon is deceiving us, throws doubt on all judgement, including the existence of a physical world and the truths of mathematics.

will, good: In Kant, the good will is the will that is motivated by duty, which Kant argues means that it chooses in accordance with reason. It is the only thing that is morally good without qualification.

will, the: Our ability to make choices and decisions. Our wills are rational; that is, we can make choices on the basis of reasons.

Index by syllabus content

Epistemology

Moral Philosophy

Index by subject